THE YEAR BOOK OF WORLD AFFAIRS 1980

VOLUME 34

Editors:

GEORGE W. KEETON

AND

GEORG SCHWARZENBERGER

Managing Editor:

C. G. BURNHAM

THE YEAR BOOK

OF

WORLD AFFAIRS

1980

Published under the auspices of
THE LONDON INSTITUTE OF WORLD AFFAIRS

WESTVIEW PRESS

Boulder, Colorado

All editorial communications should be addressed to the
Director, London Institute of World Affairs, Thorne
House, 4–8 Endsleigh Gardens, London, WC1H 0EH

Published in Great Britain in 1980 by
Stevens & Sons Limited of
11 New Fetter Lane, London
Computerset by
MFK Graphic Systems (Typesetting) Ltd., Saffron Walden, Essex
Printed in Great Britain by
Page Bros. (Norwich) Ltd.

Published in the United States of
America in 1980 by Westview Press,
Inc., 5500 Central Avenue, Boulder,
Colorado 80303

Frederick A. Praeger, President and Editorial Director

Library of Congress Catalog Card Number 47–29156

ISBN 0 89158–876–0

CONTENTS

THE RISKS OF A NO-RISK SOCIETY

By THE RT. HON. LORD ZUCKERMAN, O.M., K.C.B., F.R.S.,
*Professor Emeritus in the Universities of Birmingham
and East Anglia; Formerly Chief Scientific Adviser
to the United Kingdom Government*

THE SCOPE AND LIMITS OF DÉTENTE

By THE RT. HON. LORD HOME
*Formerly Prime Minister and Foreign Secretary,
United Kingdom*

THE STRATEGIC BALANCE

By FRANK BARNABY
Director, Stockholm International Peace Research Institute

VALÉRY GISCARD D'ESTAING

By B. J. CRIDDLE
*Lecturer, Department of Politics,
University of Aberdeen*

FOREIGN INTERVENTION IN AFRICA

By COLIN LEGUM
*Associate Editor, The Observer (London);
Editor, Africa Contemporary Record (London);
Editor, Middle East Contemporary Survey (New York)*

EEC-CMEA RELATIONS

By ROBERT W. CLAWSON
*Associate Professor of Political Science, Kent State University;
Director, Center for International and Comparative Programs*

EQUALITY AND DISCRIMINATION IN INTERNATIONAL ECONOMIC LAW (IX): *THE COUNCIL FOR MUTUAL ECONOMIC ASSISTANCE*

By B. G. RAMCHARAN
Research Associate, London Institute of World Affairs

CHINESE FOREIGN POLICY: *OPTIONS FOR THE 1980s*

By ROBERT BOARDMAN
*Associate Professor of Political Science,
Dalhousie University, Nova Scotia, Canada*

TRENDS AND EVENTS

THIS annual survey is intended to serve three purposes:

(1) With every additional volume of the *Year Book*, it becomes increasingly difficult for new readers to derive the fullest benefit from the material available in earlier volumes. This survey brings together references to themes examined in the past which have particular current relevance.

(2) The specific object of an annual publication is to make possible analyses in a wider perspective and on the basis of more mature reflection than may be possible in a quarterly or monthly journal. Thus, it is not the object of this *Year Book* to provide instant information on current issues of world affairs. Yet, international affairs have a stereotyped and, largely, repetitive character, so that, frequently, a "new" happening, or "modern" development has been anticipated in one or more of the earlier volumes of the *Year Book*. *Trends and Events* provides evidence of some such continuity as may be traced over a span of years.

(3) References to earlier contributions also offer readers an opportunity to judge for themselves the adequacy of the conceptual and systematic frameworks chosen or taken for granted in the papers selected:

(A) EAST-WEST DÉTENTE

Boardman, R.: *China's Rise as a Nuclear Power* (25 Y.B.W.A. 1971)

Burmeister, W.: *Brandt's Opening to the East* (27 ibid. 1973)

Burnham, C. G.: *Czechoslovakia: 30 Years After Munich* (23 ibid. 1969)

Erickson, J.: *The World Strategic Balance* (23 ibid. 1969)

Geusau, F. A. M. Alting von: *Détente After Helsinki* (32 ibid. 1978)

Ginsburgs, G.: *Socialist Internationalism and State Sovereignty* (25 ibid. 1971)

——: *The Constitutional Foundations of the "Socialist Commonwealth"* (27 ibid. 1973)

Martin, L.W.: *Ballistic Missile Defence and the Strategic Balance* (21 ibid. 1967)

Millar, T. B.: *On Nuclear Proliferation* (21 ibid. 1967)

Nussbaumer, A.: *Industrial Co-operation and East-West Trade* (32 ibid. 1978)

1

Radojkovic, M.: *Les Armes Nucléaires et le Droit International* (16 *ibid*. 1962)
Ranger, R.: *Arms Control in Theory and in Practice* (31 *ibid*. 1977)
Schwarzenberger, G.: *An Inter-Camp Agenda* (18 *ibid*. 1964)
Smart, I.: *Alliance, Deterrence and Defence: The Changing Context of Security* (26 *ibid*. 1972)
Yahuda, M. B.: *China's Nuclear Policy* (23 *ibid*. 1969)

(B) THE STRATEGIC BALANCE

Boardman, R.: *China's Rise as a Nuclear Power* (25 Y.B.W.A. 1971)
Boyle, Sir Dermot: *Thoughts on the Nuclear Deterrent* (16 *ibid*. 1962)
Bull, H.: *Two Kinds of Arms Control* (17 *ibid*. 1969)
Coffey, J. L.: *The Limitation of Strategic Armaments* (26 *ibid*. 1972)
Erickson, J.: *The World Strategic Balance* (23 *ibid*. 1969)
Joynt, C. B.: *Arms Races and the Problem of Equilibrium* (18 *ibid*. 1964)
Lee R.: *Safeguards Against Nuclear Proliferation* (23 *ibid*. 1969)
Martin, L. W.: *Ballistic Missile Defence and the Strategic Balance* (21 *ibid*. 1967)
Millar, T. B.: *On Nuclear Proliferation* (21 *ibid*. 1967)
Radojkovic, M.: *Les Armes Nucléaires et Le Droit International* (16 *ibid*. 1962)
Ranger, R.: *Arms Control in Theory and Practice* (31 *ibid*. 1977)
Smart, I.: *Alliance, Deterrence and Defence* (26 *ibid*. 1972)
Williams, G.: *The Strategic Nuclear Balance and the Defence of Europe* (27 *ibid*. 1973)

(C) CHINA'S EMERGENCE AS A SUPER-POWER

Adie, W. A. C.: *China and the Developed Countries* (20 Y.B.W.A. 1966)
Bell, C.: *The Containment of China* (22 *ibid*. 1968)
Boardman, R.: *China's Rise as a Nuclear Power* (25 *ibid*. 1971)
Buchan, A.: *An Expedition to the Poles* (29 *ibid*. 1975)
Erickson, J.: *The World Strategic Balance* (23 *ibid*. 1969)
Fitzmaurice, G. B.: *Chinese Representation in the United Nations* (6 *ibid*. 1952)
Frankel, J.: *The Balance of Power in the Far East* (7 *ibid*. 1953)
Keeton, G. W.: *Nationalism in Eastern Asia* (*ibid*. 1947)
Lewisohn, W.: *Basic Problems in Modern China* (3 *ibid*. 1949)
Lindsay, Lord: *Chinese Foreign Policy* (15 *ibid*. 1961)

Mahajni, U.: *Sino-American Rapprochement and the New Con-figurations in South-East Asia* (29 *ibid*. 1975)
——: *Sino-Soviet Conflict and Rivalry in South-East Asia in the Post-Vietnam Phase* (32 *ibid*. 1978)
Meissner, B.: *The Political Treaties of China and the Soviet Union in East Asia* (27 *ibid*. 1973)
Schwarzenberger, G.: *Beyond Power Politics?* (19 *ibid*. 1965)
——: *From Bipolarity to Multipolarity?* (21 *ibid*. 1967)
Wittfogel, K. A.: *The Russian and Chinese Revolutions: A Socio-Historical Comparison* (15 *ibid*. 1961)
Yahuda, M. B.: *China's Nuclear Policy* (23 *ibid*. 1969)
Yalem, R. J.: *Tripolarity and World Politics* (28 *ibid*. 1974)
Yu, G. T.: *China in Africa* (24 *ibid*. 1970)

(D) Africa and the World Powers

Bissell, R. E.: *The Ostracism of Southern Africa* (32 Y.B.W.A. 1978)
Butterworth, R.: *The Future of South Africa* (31 *ibid*. 1977)
Doxey, G. V. & M.: *The Prospects for Change in South Africa* (19 *ibid*. 1965)
Doxey, M.: *The Rhodesian Sanctions Experiment* (25 *ibid*. 1971)
Elias, T. O.: *The Economic Community of West Africa* (32 *ibid*. 1978)
Hudson, D.: *The World Council of Churches and Racism* (29 *ibid*. 1975)
Legum, C.: *South Africa: The Politics of Détente* (30 *ibid*. 1976)
——:*The Future of Ethiopia* (28 *ibid*. 1974)
Longmore, L.: *The South African Dilemma* (8 *ibid*. 1973)
Shaw, T. M.: *Southern Africa: From Détente to Deluge* (32 *ibid*. 1978)
Spence, J.: *The Strategic Significance of South Africa* (27 *ibid*. 1973)
Stent, G. D.: *Colour Problems of South Africa* (2 *ibid*. 1948)
Taylor, T.: *President Nixon's Arms Supply Policy* (26 *ibid*. 1972)

(E) Middle East

Frankel, J.: *The Middle East in Turmoil* (10 Y.B.W.A. 1956)
James, A.: *Recent Development in United Nations Peace-keeping* (31 *ibid*. 1977)
Kirk, G.: *The Middle Eastern Scene* (14 *ibid*. 1960)
Mitchell, C. R.: *Peace-keeping: The Police Function* (30 *ibid*. 1976)
Neumann, R. G.: *The Near East After the Syrian Coup* (16 *ibid*. 1968)

Parkinson, F.: *Bandung and the Underdeveloped Countries* (10 *ibid*.
  1956)
Rodinson, M.: *Israel: The Arab Options* (22 *ibid*. 1968)
Roth, S. J.: *World Jewry and Israel* (28 *ibid*. 1974)
Strange, S.: *Palestine and the United Nations* (1 *ibid*. 1949)
——: *Suez and After* (11 *ibid*. 1957)
Troutbeck, Sir John: *Stresses Within the Arab World* (12 *ibid*. 1958)

(F) LATIN AMERICA

Ball, M. M.: *Recent Developments in Inter-American Relations* (3
  Y.B.W.A. 1949)
Blakemore, H.: *Chile: Continuity and Change* (27 *ibid*. 1973)
Carnegie, A. R.: *The Law of Commonwealth Caribbean Regional-
  ism: Legal Aspects* (33 *ibid*. 1979)
Crossley, J. C.: *Agrarian Reform in Latin America* (17 *ibid*. 1963)
Ferns, H. S.: *Argentina in Travail* (29 *ibid*. 1975)
Gorinsky, C.: *Cultures in Conflict: Amerindians in New Societies* (24
  ibid. 1970)
Graber, D. A.: *United States Intervention in Latin America* (16 *ibid*.
  1962)
Hilton, R.: *Castrophobia in the United States* (18 *ibid*. 1964)
Hutchinson, G. W.: *The Coup in Chile* (29 *ibid*. 1975)
Milenky, E. S.: *The Cartagena Agreement: In Transition* (33 *ibid*.
  1979)
O'Shaughnessy, H.: *Christian Democratic Upsurge in Latin
  America* (21 *ibid*. 1967)
Parkinson, F.: *The Alliance for Progress* (18 *ibid*. 1964)
——: *Santo Domingo and After* (20 *ibid*. 1966)
——: *International Economic Integration in Latin America and the
  Caribbean* (31 *ibid*. 1977)
Salera, V.: *Economic Relations between the United States and Latin
  America* (14 *ibid*. 1960)
Strange, S.: *Cuba and After* (17 *ibid*. 1963)
Tannenbaum, F.: *The Continuing Ferment in Latin America* (10
  ibid. 1956)
Whitaker, A. P.: *The Organisation of American States* (13 *ibid*.
  1959)
Wood, B.: *The Organisation of American States* (33 *ibid*. 1979)

(G) THE EUROPEAN COMMUNITIES

Bredima, A.: *Comparative Law in the Court of Justice of the European Communities* (32 Y.B.W.A. 1978)

Curzon, G. and V.: *Neo-Colonialism and the European Economic Community* (25 *ibid*. 1971)
Geusau, F. A. M. Alting von: *The European Communities After the Hague Summit* (26 *ibid*. 1972)
Goldsmith, P. and Sonderkötter, F.: *Equality and Discrimination in International Economic Law: The European Communities* (28 *ibid*. 1974)
——: *Equality and Discrimination in International Economic Law: The European Communities and the Wider World* (29 *ibid*. 1975)
Holt, S. C.: *The British Confront their European Test* (26 *ibid*. 1972)
Parkinson, F.: *European Integration: Obstacles and Prospects* (13 *ibid*. 1959)
Scheuner, U.: *The Future of the European Community* (33 *ibid*. 1979)
Strang, G.: *The EEC Common Agricultural Policy* (33 *ibid*. 1979)

(H) OIL AND THE WORLD ECONOMY

Brown, E. D.: *Deep-Sea Mining: The Legal Regime of "Inner Space"* (22 Y.B.W.A. 1968)
——: *The Anglo-French Continental Shelf Case* (33 *ibid*. 1979)
Frankel, J.: *The Anglo-Iranian Dispute* (6 *ibid*. 1952)
Odell, P. R.: *The International Oil Companies in the New World Oil Market* (32 *ibid*. 1978)
Penrose, E.: *Monopoly and Competition in the International Petroleum Industry* (19 *ibid*. 1964)

(I) EQUALITY AND DISCRIMINATION
IN INTERNATIONAL ECONOMIC LAW

Goldsmith, P. and Sonderkötter, F.: *The European Communities* (28 Y.B.W.A. 1974)
——: *The European Communities and the Wider World* (29 *ibid*. 1975)
Kaplan, G. G.: *The UNCTAD Scheme for Generalised Preferences* (26 *ibid*. 1972)
Ramcharan, B. G.: *The Commonwealth Preferential System* (26 *ibid*. 1972)
——: *The UN Regional Economic Commissions* (32 *ibid*. 1978)
Schwarzenberger, G.: *Equality and Discrimination in International Economic Law* (25 *ibid*. 1971)
Stoiber, C.: *The Multinational Enterprise* (31 *ibid*. 1977)
Sutton, A.: *Trends in Regulation of International Trade in Textiles* (31 *ibid*. 1977)

(J) FOREIGN POLICY ANALYSIS

Aumo-Osolo, A.: *Rationality and Foreign Policy Process* (31 Y.B.W.A. 1977)

Doxey, M.: *International Organisation in Foreign Policy Perspective* (29 *ibid*. 1975)

Frankel, J.: *Rational Decision-Making in Foreign Policy* (14 *ibid*. 1960)

Morgenthau, H. J.: *The Moral Dilemma in Foreign Policy* (5 *ibid*. 1951)

Suganami, H.: *Why Ought Treaties to be Kept?* (33 *ibid*. 1979)

Williams, P. and Smith, M. H.: *The Foreign Policies of Authoritarian and Democratic States* (30 *ibid*. 1976)

(K) WORLD PORTRAITS

Bonn, M. J.: *American Statesmen* (5 Y.B.W.A. 1951)

——: *The Demise of the Adenauer Era* (18 *ibid*. 1964)

Burmeister, W.: *Brandt's Opening to the East* (27 *ibid*. 1973)

Hilton, R.: *Castrophobia in the United States* (18 *ibid*. 1964)

James, A.: *U Thant and His Critics* (26 *ibid*. 1972)

Nicholas, H. G.: *The Nixon Line* (25 *ibid*. 1971)

Pickles, D.: *France Under General de Gaulle* (16 *ibid*. 1962)

Sceats, R.: *The Continuity of French Policy* (26 *ibid*. 1972)

Tinker, H.: *Indira Gandhi: Autocratic Democrat* (33 *ibid*. 1979)

Vincent, R. J.: *Kissinger's System of Foreign Policy* (31 *ibid*. 1977)

It may also be helpful to remind readers of the Cumulative Index to Volumes 1 to 25 in the 1971 Volume of the *Year Book of World Affairs—Managing Ed.*, Y.B.W.A.

THE RISKS OF A NO-RISK SOCIETY

By

LORD ZUCKERMAN

ONE man's skin may differ from another's; so may the slant of his eyes or the shape of his nose, but otherwise all human beings, all members of the species *homo sapiens*, are built to the same pattern. If the anatomical drawings of Galen or Leonardo differ from those of today's textbooks, the conclusion we draw is not that our structure has been changing over the past few hundred years, but that these two men, great as they were, were not as skilled at dissecting and observing as we are today. Nor do we believe that when William Harvey upturned earlier views on the subject, the blood started to flow in a different way in our bodies from what it had been doing before. The conclusion we draw is that physiologists before Harvey did not understand the mechanism of the heart. We also implicitly accept that what was poison to our forebears would be poison to us, and that the new poisons we have devised since their time would also have been poison to them, just as our bullets would have killed them, and their arrows us. In short, man does not change. Poisons do not change. What undoubtedly do change—and change dramatically—are our attitudes to the scale of the hazards we face and our ability to deal with them.

This can be mainly attributed to the growth and dissemination of the kind of knowledge which now makes it so easy to imagine hazards which, even if never experienced, have become conceivable. New and highly sensitive instruments measure infinitesimal quantities of noxious compounds in our body fluids and in the air we breathe; so we worry lest we are being poisoned. We have known of accidents to vast oil tankers, and are therefore wary of their possible recurrence. Abstruse probability calculations of what might go wrong provoke nightmares about some unthinkable disaster affecting a nuclear reactor—and so we organise to delay their construction. Environmentalists are fearful lest our physical surroundings are further changed by the spread and development of extractive and manufacturing industry.

At the same time, there is a belief that modern science and technology have become so powerful that society could be provided with all our material needs and wants with no danger to man or beast. We seem to be plagued by new hazards, yet the implicit concept of a "no-risk society" has become so widespread that the

7

notion of personal responsibility has all but been submerged. Even what were once spoken of as Acts of God—for example, the damage caused by storm and flood—are events which it is assumed can be averted by governmental action.

The trouble is that a price always has to be paid when risks are eliminated. Every protective step, whether it be something positive, such as building a vast barrage across the River Thames to prevent the flooding of London, or mass inoculation with a new vaccine against a threatened epidemic, or something negative, like yielding to public pressure and refraining from building a reservoir where it would affront local environmentalists, and siting it instead at much greater cost in some remote area, deprives the community of resources which could be used for other purposes.

In the end, it does not matter who pays, whether the ordinary citizen through higher prices, or the Exchequer out of revenues either raised through taxation or invented by printing money. The basic fact is that each step taken to offset a hazard or to protect an amenity consumes resources. The standard of living might as a result seem to be raised for some people; what is certain is that the cost of living is raised for all. And since one category of hazard—for example, the risk that a drug's adverse side-effects might outweigh its direct benefits—cannot be compared on a like-with-like basis with, say, a new weedkiller which inadvertently proves toxic to some species of bird or butterfly, or some conceivable, even if improbable, disbenefit arising from the retention of lead pipes in old houses, the only measuring rod which governments could use in order to place real or assumed hazards in some sensible order of priority would be a measure of the resources that would be called for if they were to be abated. For a variety of reasons, this is not yet done, at least not on a continuing basis.

I—THE DOMESTICATION OF MAN

When our forebears began the cultural transition to life in settled agricultural communities, they must have believed that one way or another they were bettering their lot, and that they were also ridding themselves of some of the perils which beset a food-gathering and hunting existence. But to pay for the benefits of their new communal existence, they had to surrender part of what before had been their liberty. It was no longer a case of an individual doing what he wanted, when he wanted, and where he wanted. Our village ancestors had to accept a stricter discipline and had to develop a far wider loyalty than sufficed to hold together a family group. They had, for example, to learn a primitive hygiene; to learn not to foul wells and other sources of water and, eventually, even if this lesson took ages and ages, not to pollute the communal village with the midden heaps which had characterised life in the caves.

During the thousands of years which this first phase of man's social evolution lasted, the authority on which communal life depended became vested in rulers who made laws and regulations in order to maintain the stability and improve the conditions of the societies which they led. Whatever form it took, whether power was shared by a council of elders, or vested in the person of a monarch, the central authority was *ipso facto* responsible for the security of the people it governed. At one extreme it had to assure defence against possible enemies; at the other it had to do its best to see that water supplies were always available. And it had to sustain what today we call "the quality of life," both in the environmental field and in the government of the relations between individuals. Obviously what was done varied in accordance with the standard of living and the cultural level which different communities had reached. And since culture has never grown uniformly or spread evenly through the societies which make up mankind, these varied enormously. Indeed, in many parts of the world the sanitary conditions of villages, and even of towns, are not yet the equal of those of ancient Pompeii. More than that, environmental laws were sometimes far more severe than they are anywhere now. For example, it is recorded that in medieval times the lighting of a coal fire in the City of London was an offence punishable by death. Counterfeiting was also a capital offence, and at least in one country so was the adulteration of wine. It had been the custom from the days of ancient Rome to add a sweet syrup called sapa to inferior wines so as to make them more palatable and saleable. But sapa has a very high lead content, and by the seventeenth century it was well understood that lead in sufficient dose is poison. In Wurtemburg adulterating wines was therefore declared an offence punishable by death.[1] This law of 1696 appears to have been introduced in spite of the fact that it would have been difficult to enforce, not only because the chemistry of the day was too sketchy for reliable analyses of the wine, but also because of the difficulty of diagnosing lead poisoning before it was too late.

Of course, the object of the law was not to provide some form of compensation or redress for the man who drank the adulterated wine, in the sense that either he or his relatives had a claim for damages because he might have been harmed. The principle of *caveat emptor* then applied as much in the food industry as it did in

---

[1] J. Eisinger, "Lead and Man," 2 *Trends in Biochemical Science* (1977).

commerce generally. The value of the Wurtemburg law lay in its deterrent effect. Rulers, who were every bit as sensitive to the toxic effects of lead as were those whom they governed, neither wanted to be poisoned themselves nor to encourage the inadvertent poisoning of their subjects.

II—THE PROTECTION OF THE BRITISH CITIZEN

During the eighteenth and nineteenth centuries, when wealth, population and squalor were growing apace in the United Kingdom, the concern of government in the welfare of the ordinary citizen continued to develop along the same lines as it had been doing in all countries which had not become fixed in a tribal mould. In varying degrees, and with varying enthusiasm, local authorities became responsible for improving public services—water supplies, sewerage, roads, street-lighting and even fire services—while the main concerns of central government continued to be the defence of the realm, the maintenance of law and order, and preventing the Exchequer from being cheated. Presumably because the Crown was also concerned to protect the well-being of its subjects, whose contentment was clearly a condition of social stability, there was also a law as far back as the thirteenth century which was ostensibly designed to protect the consumer against short weight and the adulteration of foodstuffs, for example, the watering of milk, or, when tea started to be imported, the addition of exhausted leaves to fresh tea, which was then glazed with black lead.

But this law, like various similar statutes that were passed until well into the nineteenth century, and which it was the duty of the craft guilds to monitor was, as Giles has pointed out,[2] all but useless. Effective protection of the British consumer did not come about until the passage of the 1875 Sale of Food and Drugs Act. This laid down for the first time that "no person shall sell to the prejudice of the purchaser any article or any thing which is not of the nature, substance or quality demanded by such purchaser." The burden of implementing the new regulations fell on local authorities who at the start had to turn for help to the Government Chemist, a central office which had been established in 1842, and whose first task had been to help the Department of Customs and Excise in its efforts to prevent the adulteration of tobacco. Starting with the 1875 Act, and its successors of 1928, 1938, and finally with the Food and Drugs Act of 1955, British citizens are now legally protected, not only against being cheated by those from whom they buy, but also from

---

[2] R. F. Giles, in *Food Quality and Safety. A Century of Progress*, H.M.S.O. (1976).

being poisoned by dangerous food additives and unsafe drugs. The Medicines Act of 1968, the Trade Descriptions Act of 1972, and the Fair Trading Act of 1973 have since been added as further measures of consumer protection.

These recent Acts, as well as the 1955 Food and Drugs Act, reflect a sharp change in public attitudes to the risks associated with modern industrialised societies. Almost everywhere in the West, people have been encouraged since the end of the Second World War to demand far more in the diminution of the hazards of life than just legal protection against contaminated or adulterated food. Spurred on first by dreams of social justice or equality, and then by the competitive bids of rival political parties, our expectations of higher standards of living, of greater personal security, of the elimination of a host of presumed perils which our fathers or grandfathers accepted without question, have continued to rise. Correspondingly, those by whom we are governed have to steer a middle course between diverse and often conflicting social pressures. Security of employment has now become a right. So have unemployment benefits and pensions. The best education and medical service must be accessible to all, and at the same time military services must be adequate and up-to-date. A vociferous lobby of self-styled ecologists wants artificial fertilisers banned; another insists that the energy problem be solved without resort to nuclear power; and a third requires an assurance that no drug, old or new, will have adverse side-effects. And, of course, if anything goes wrong, if any individual is harmed, there must be compensation.

The unrestrained pressures which develop within our democratic electoral system inevitably have the effect that both the government in power, as well as the alternative government or governments waiting in the wings, promise the electorate more and more. A not unforeseeable consequence has been that over recent years, in a period which began with golden hopes of increasing prosperity and social harmony, and which today can hardly be said to be characterised by the latter, the public sense of priorities about hazards has become more and more unreal, and the government's tasks in meeting ever-rising expectations increasingly difficult.

III—THE COST OF PROTECTION

Not one of the risks which beset modern industrial society— whether it be lead or sulphur in the atmosphere, or the possibility of adverse side-effects from some new drug—can be eliminated or reduced without paying a price. As I have stated, it matters not at all whether it is the Chancellor of the Exchequer, or the private manufacturer, or the consumer who has to bear the cost. The diversion of resources to make life safer in any one respect inevitably means that less is available for other social purposes.

For example, it now takes millions of pounds to develop a new pesticide or drug, and about half of the money has to be spent on statutory safety and environmental tests. The cost of satisfying safety regulations is becoming so high that it seriously reduces the amount of money that should be available for further research. It is therefore not at all surprising that the number of new crop-protection compounds that are submitted for approval to the World Health Organisation has declined precipitously over recent years. Moreover, since no manufacturer can be certain that a novel product will satisfy the additional regulations that seem to be imposed every year by countries which might otherwise be importers, it is also not surprising that some companies are hesitant about accepting the risk of embarking on new developments.

On top of all this, there is also the matter of liability. At least one major pharmaceutical firm has ceased its research and development activities because of the vast sums that have had to be paid out in compensation to people who were adversely affected by a product it put on to the market. All in all, the whole process of development in the chemical industry is being slowed down, in spite of the fact that effective agrochemicals and drugs are vital if the production and distribution of food in the world is to increase at a rate commensurate with need, and if improvements in world health are to be sustained.

IV—SOURCES OF DISQUIET

Obviously it would be criminal not to do everything that is reasonable to ensure that new chemicals that come on to the market are safe. Paradoxically, however, hard experience shows that the question of what is reasonable has no rational answer. In imposing new and more stringent safety regulations, governments and international organisations alike are doing what seems to be necessary. Sometimes, however, they are also over-reacting to irrational public pressure. Small groups of activists in the modern environmental movement have been so successful in generating public fears, and then in stimulating governmental action, that not surprisingly they are encouraged to press on with their crusades. The media, too, are quick to seize on new stories about the hazards of industrialised societies, and journalists are well-skilled in dramatising issues out of all proportion to their relative importance. It is ironical that the words "mercury" and "lead" seem to have become better known as environmental poisons than for the parts which the two elements that go by these names have played in helping to build the framework of the well-appointed world into which we who are alive today have been born. There is no glamour or drama to that story.

Instead we listen to endless warnings that children are at risk, and adults too, because of lead in the air that we breathe and in the water which we drink. We hear about fish being contaminated with mercury and then poisoning us. But is the emphasis given to these stories justified? Is the risk of generalised lead-poisoning or mercury-poisoning all that significant relative to the others which we run? Clearly we cannot expect members of the British Campaign Against Lead in Petrol to provide dispassionate answers to such questions. A recent article by John Mathews,[3] a post-graduate student who is connected with this organisation, and who was proclaiming his fears, was not surprisingly dismissed by another writer—who could claim to speak with at least as much authority—as being not a scientific analysis but a piece of propaganda, written in the style "typical of that used by crusading environmentalists."[4]

Messages about the need to eliminate this or that hazard always run the risk of back-firing. In July, 1977, the BBC put on a television programme about the adverse side-effects of the drug Eraldin, a pharmaceutical which had been marketed as a medicine for heart troubles after it had undergone the statutory tests of safety. In the course of the lengthy presentation, a number of people who had been concerned in developing and authorising the use of the drug, and others who could speak for those who had suffered from its side-effects, were interrogated. But realising that the general impression which the programme left was likely to scare thousands of people who were taking other drugs to alleviate their cardiac disorders, the presenter—almost as an after-thought—had to end his programme by warning his viewers not to be panicked to the point of giving up other medicinals which might have been prescribed for dealing with their troubles. One can only hope that his advice was taken, and that the numbers of those who inadvertently suffered because of the fears which the programme generated were fewer than the unfortunate victims of Eraldin's side-effects. It is so easy to overdramatise the occasional drug-disaster, and to be silent about the benefits which we have all derived from modern pharmaceutical science—and indeed from medical science generally.

Our health authorities, as well as some members of the public, appear to be living with another such problem today. In some areas of the United Kingdom whooping cough seems to have re-emerged

---

[3] J. Mathews, 75 *New Scientist*, August 11, 1977, p. 348.
[4] G. S. Parkinson, 75 *New Scientist*, September 15, 1977, p. 692.

and to be reaching epidemic proportions. Because of the publicity given a few years ago to a few sad cases of brain damage which it was suspected could be associated with the whooping cough vaccine, the number of children to whom it has been administered has recently fallen dramatically. Who now decides which is the greater risk—the possibility of a widespread and serious epidemic or that of a minute number of further cases of adverse side-effects? And if the medical authorities now decide that vaccination is the lesser evil, how do they impose their decision on parents?

It is not just that we have been made fearful in recent years of what we put into our mouths or breathe into our lungs. We have also had our fill of warnings of more remote dangers. For example, in recent years we have heard a great deal about the hazards of aerosols, and about the effect they might be having on the ozone layer of the stratosphere. Some might have believed that the skies were about to fall in. Was the kind of publicity given to this matter justified? In my view the answer is "no." While publicity about the possibilities of danger should never be suppressed, I firmly believe that premature speculation about such conceivable dangers only becomes cause for panic and meat for unfruitful political dispute when the matters concerned have not been properly sorted out—in public if needs be—by those with sufficient professional knowledge to reach a consensus.

It is not just the "environmental" extremist or the enthusiastic journalist who sharpens our fears about the hazards of the life into which we have been born. Scientists who speak with authority on particular issues also sometimes play a powerful part in stoking the fires of public disquiet. For example, we have been told lately of the likelihood that many kinds of cancer can be associated with the emission into the atmosphere of toxic industrial chemicals, and that regulations should be imposed to stop this form of pollution. In a recent number of *Daedalus*, Lewis Thomas,[5] who seems to share this view, has written that "the major diseases of human beings have become...ultimately solvable," and that it consequently follows that "it is now possible to begin thinking about a human society relatively free of diseases." But even if he and other distinguished scientists who wish to eliminate cancer by preventing industrial pollution are right, why do they not tell us the price that we would have to pay for the benefits which they proclaim, or what it is we would die of when all disease has been eliminated?

Recently there was an assertion by a single medical scientist, well-publicised in the Press,[6] that heart disease could be correlated

[5] L. Thomas, *Daedalus* (1977), p. 163.
[6] J. Segall, 31 *British Journal of Preventive Social Medicine* (1977), p. 81.

with the drinking of milk. I do not know the qualifications of the author of this scare story, nor can I judge the authority with which he speaks. For all I know, his statistical expertise might also have been equal to the unexacting task of correlating heart disease with the eating of bread. But what matters is the likely reaction of some average citizens to the story. Will they dismiss it or start discouraging their families from drinking what must be the most ancient constituent of man's diet?

Modern man is no more immortal than were his pre-industrial ancestors, or for that matter the tens and tens of thousands of animal species which disappeared from the face of the earth long before *homo sapiens* emerged. The fact is that the vast improvement in standards of health and the decline in mortality rates which have occurred in all industrialised societies during this century were associated with the development of modern industry, and in particular of the pharmaceutical and agrochemical industries. If we need to be reminded of this fact, we have only to compare our condition today with that of peoples in the Third World. Clearly, everything that can reasonably be done to prevent environmental pollution by industrial chemicals should be done. But the price might well prove too high if what could happen is that sections of modern industry are discouraged from trying to develop because of the prohibitive cost of conforming with over-exacting environmental regulations. In theory, this would mean a slow but eventual return to the conditions of our forefathers. What is implied is by definition a reversal of the selective processes which have raised our species to its present standard of living.

V—THE PRIORITIES OF HAZARDS

Whatever the forces which now power the drive to reduce the risks faced by man in modern society, it is therefore essential that we try to achieve a sense of reality about the hazards which we face. They are not always what one reads in the Press or hears on the radio or television. Some are real, but others are certainly illusory. A few of the real ones may be short-term and urgent, but most are medium-term, and some very, very long-term. We also need to be reasonable about the part which governments on the one hand, and we, the governed, on the other, can play in bringing about their reduction. For example, over recent years governmental agencies, as well as highly authoritative institutions such as the Royal College of Physicians, could not have done more than they have to publicise the fact that the incidence of lung cancer is correlated with the smoking of cigarettes. But in spite of all the anti-smoking propaganda, there is little indication yet that significantly fewer cigarettes are being smoked than before. What more can the government do, given that smoking cannot be made a criminal offence—any more than can over-eating?

And what about dangerous driving? Every year some 7,000 people are still killed on our roads, and almost 400,000, so we are told, injured. As has been said,[7] people seem to be reconciled to a carnage of over 1,000 killed or injured every day, in the same way as they once were to typhus. There are penalties for a variety of driving offences, and there is also no end to official admonitions about the need to drive carefully. We are warned that governmental regulations will soon be introduced to make the wearing of seat-belts compulsory. Such a step may reduce the carnage of the roads, but is there much reason to suppose that it will stop?

In no modern society would anyone question that it is the responsibility of the central authority to assure such matters as defence or access to wholesome water supplies or the disposal of household waste—for all of which, of course, we pay through taxation. It is obvious, too, that there have to be governmental procedures to assure the safety of drugs and food additives. But yet when it comes to formulating standards of safety, or to matters such as product-liability, we almost inevitably find ourselves in a grey area, as we also seem to be in matters such as compensation for injury.

V—Whose Responsibility?

It seems to be a normal reaction for a man who has suffered an injury, either to his person or to his property, to try to pin the blame on someone else—and preferably on someone from whom some compensation can be exacted. It does not matter whether the "someone" is an individual, or a company, or a public authority. Legal rights for compensation now vary from country to country, and it seems to be a general belief that they are most extreme in the United States where, for example, the insurance premium that medical men have to pay as a protection against charges of malpractice is sometimes so high that rumour has it that many doctors have been driven out of practice. But the area in which compensation can be sought now seems to be widening fast in all industrialised countries. I was brought up to believe that it was my fault if I was hurt when I tripped over a badly-laid paving stone. Today I would not be surprised to learn that I had a claim for damage against the public authority concerned. I am told that if I were riding a bicycle and the

---

[7] Lord Ashby, 74 *New Scientist*, May 19, 1977, p. 398.

handlebars failed and an accident ensued, it would be better to have this happen in France rather than here. In France one would claim immediately from the manufacturer; in the United Kingdom, if one were seeking compensation, one would have to start a slow process against the retailer. Not surprisingly, circumstances also still determine where liability rests. For example, only a few years ago a considerable hole suddenly appeared in the motorway between Birmingham and Wolverhampton as a result of subsidence over some old coal workings. It is ironical to think that if a car had been driving over the site at the moment when the hole appeared, and had suffered an accident, the highway authority would have been liable for damages. But if, because of dangerous driving, the owner of the car had been involved in an accident at that precise spot the day before, he—and his insurance company—would have had to bear the cost.

The legal burden which employers had long borne for assuring safe conditions for their workers was much increased by the British Government's 1974 Health and Safety Act. As a result, the responsibilities of the factory manager, or even of scientists who are responsible for managing a research laboratory, are far more demanding now than they were even a few years back. Gone, indeed, are the days when the death of a technician who was helping in experimental work on some virus was treated merely as a highly regrettable accident.

On the other hand, now that the cost of abiding by all the provisions of the new Act have become obvious, it seems that certain relaxations are being allowed in its implementation. Yet at the same time, one of the recommendations of Lord Pearson's Royal Commission on Civil Liability is based on the concept of "no fault liability." If it is accepted, people hurt in motor accidents or injured in the course of their work would be compensated regardless of any proof of negligence. Who in the end pays for all this would seem a mystery. But one thing is obvious. In so far as they increase costs—however widely these are spread—more stringent rules about liability do not benefit the community, however much they may be to the advantage of the individual who has suffered, or to that of his family.

What is equally obvious, and the point needs to be made again, is that there is no single scale against which to equate all the diverse hazards which the individual or governments face in our increasingly complex social world, and no easy way of arranging them in one order of priority in terms of risk. Individuals are clearly irrational in the way they treat the apparent hazards to which they are exposed, and it is not surprising therefore that in recent years the decisions of governments, in response to public pressure, have sometimes seemed the same. The subjective element, whether it be animated by self-interest or by some belief in the common good, will never be eradicated from decisions about the balance of risk.

VI—No One Scale of Hazards

The ability of public and government alike to live with the fact that every year thousands of people will be killed or maimed on our roads, and that this toll of injury implies an enormous loss to the community, seems to make no difference to our consideration of other hazards. For example, those who have some knowledge of the safety record of the nuclear industry are in no doubt that on any quantitative assessment, the health hazards associated with, say, an extension of the Windscale reprocessing plant, could hardly be as serious as the continued increase in the number of cars or lorries on our roads. But a vague fear on the part of certain sections of the public that Windscale might be a worse risk, coupled with the likelihood that the availability of plutonium could be a spur to the proliferation of nuclear weapons, forced the British Government to hold an elaborate inquiry into a proposed extension of the Windscale reprocessing plant. We know the outcome of the inquiry, but we still cannot predict what decision the Government will feel constrained to take on the Committee of Inquiry's positive recommendation—extend the plant.[7a] From the Government's point of view, and indeed from that of the Opposition, doing something to restrict the volume of traffic is much more of an immediate and generalised electoral hazard than building a new nuclear plant or extending an existing one; whereas from that of the public, or that part of the public which has concerned itself with the matter, impeding the growth of the nuclear industry costs nothing. In order to achieve their short-term objectives, the anti-nuclear lobby, for example organisations such as the Friends of the Earth, are prepared to minimise the force of the essential proposition that, on any dispassionate assessment of such facts as there are, the day will come when if not they, then certainly their children, will not be able to do without nuclear energy. However noble their present motives, such bodies are not concerned—or seem not to be concerned—with the needs of future generations. That is for tomorrow.

The public is no doubt aware that "fatal accident frequency rates" have been calculated for various industries and occupations. Imperial Chemical Industries follow an order of priorities in the elimina-

---

[7a] This recommendation has since been accepted.

tion of hazardous processes.[8] But our knowledge of their nature provides no guarantee that there will never be another Flixborough or Seveso, or, for that matter, another dust explosion in some giant grain silo. Moreover, however remote, however improbable the risk that the unimaginable accident might happen in, for example, a nuclear reactor, some people will never rest satisfied with official assurances. They are not going to be persuaded by being told that the hazards associated with the construction industry, or with coal-mining, or with conventional power stations, are much more real and much more dangerous to life than the risks associated with nuclear power stations. It is the word "nuclear" that matters, as does, in a different context, the word "cancer." Facts, or assessments agreed by, say, an overwhelming majority of those competent to speak on such matters, seem powerless in the face of emotionally-held belief.

Another difficulty in the way of a rational appraisal of the problem of hazards is that estimates of probabilities do not tell us when an accident will happen, or who will be affected, or how he will be affected. Nor do they tell governments, and because governments have to deal separately with risks as they become apparent, governmental priorities, when viewed in retrospect, cannot but sometimes seem strange.

For example, in 1953 an unusual combination of tide and wind forced the waters of the North Sea southwards along the East Coast and on to the northern shores of the European mainland. There was considerable flooding and more than 300 people living along the coast between the Humber and the Straits of Dover lost their lives. A Committee was immediately set up under the late Lord Waverley to consider the improvement of our sea defences and the organisation of a system of coastal stations to warn about the imminence of any recurrence of similar floods. The Committee reported in 1954 and one result of its recommendations was that the banks of the Thames Estuary were raised and strengthened. Schemes for the protection of Central London were also examined. The threat of a tidal surge, which was increasing due to relative changes in land levels, also meant that in extreme conditions areas of the capital itself could be inundated and thousands of people put at risk. Calculation showed that the likelihood of such a disaster happening was extremely remote, but the fact that it could not be ruled out made a later government decide that a costly barrage—not yet completed—had to be built across the Thames. I can hardly imagine any government doing otherwise, and so risk being condemned by a

---

[8] T. A. Kletz, 74 *New Scientist*, May 12, 1977, p. 320.

future generation which could declare that because of the failure of the government to act, thousands of people had been drowned in their homes. But at the time there was little public interest in the decision.

Recently the government has also had to take certain steps to guard against the risk that rabies will be introduced into Great Britain and that it could become endemic, as it is on the European mainland, with all the consequences of which we have been warned. As a result of the recommendations of the 1971 Waterhouse Committee, procedures to prevent the illegal importation of dogs and other possible carriers of the virus were considerably tightened. Airports and harbours now display dire warning notices, and people who have been discovered contravening the regulations have been heavily fined. Yet the government did not feel that it could accept one of Waterhouse's important recommendations—that in order to reduce the risk of the disease being brought into this country, there should not only be a limited number of recognised points of entry for potential carriers, but that these should be provided with adequate arrangements for holding animals *under the control of a fully-trained veterinarian*. I am sure that the major reason for the failure to implement this recommendation was cost. But supposing that one day rabies did become established in the United Kingdom, and that it could be proved that a carrier or some carriers had managed to get into the country through lack of vigilance at an airfield or port? What judgment would then be made of the decision of "x" years back not to implement this particular Waterhouse recommendation? Today the man in the street seems totally uninterested in the subject, far less than he seems to be in the possibilities of lead or asbestos poisoning, about which the media are so ready to sharpen fears. But if ever rabies were to become endemic, there can be little doubt that some sections of the public would then be only too ready to turn on the government for what would be called foolish parsimony. Millions could be made available for a Thames barrage, one can hear it said, but not a few thousands to pay for a handful of veterinarians. Government can rarely win in these matters.

John Dunster,[9] the Deputy Director of the Executive which was set up after the passage in 1974 of the Health and Safety at Work Act, has rightly reminded us that in modern society some people always have to risk their health and lives for the benefit of others. This is obviously true. But theoretically there are also situations when not just some of us, but all of us, are at risk. The ordinary man is powerless when it comes to some of the remote risks to which

[9] J. Dunster, 74 *New Scientist*, May 26, 1977, p. 454.

mankind may be exposed; for example, an all-out man-made nuclear exchange, or some violent God-made climatic change. Governments are hardly in a stronger position than are individuals in dealing with potential hazards such as these; and, as recent strikes of workers in some branches of the public services—for example, the fire service—show, they can be severely hampered even in countering the everyday hazards against which it is their responsibility to guard.

VII—FANCIES ABOUT HAZARDS

There can never be complete knowledge about the risks to which we are now exposed, or about the new ones that tomorrow will bring. There cannot be absolute safety. There cannot be such a thing as a no-risk society. And for this very reason, we should try to be as objective as possible about the facts of such definable risks as those to which we are or may be exposed, and so far as possible to behave rationally about them.

But discovering the facts, and getting general agreement about them, particularly by those who are determined to believe otherwise, is never easy. Some amateur environmentalists hold as a matter of faith that most, if not all, agrochemicals are inimical to wild life and to the microfauna of the soil. For example, it is a common belief that artificial manures have highly deleterious effects on soil fauna. Yet a recent public publication[10] of the Commonwealth Agricultural Bureaux shows that this is the reverse of the truth. We read that "although certain formulations may adversely affect a specific group of animals, manures and fertilizers generally increase numbers and species of the soil fauna." We are also told that "temporary reductions in faunal populations are usually counterbalanced by large increases at a later date."

A powerful cause of the reaction against modern agrochemicals was the fact that certain species of bird suffered badly during the post-War years when pesticides first came into extensive use. For example, the peregrine falcon and the sparrow hawk declined in numbers, almost certainly because of the build-up of toxic chemical residues in the food chain of which they are part. On the other hand, the general ornithological scene has changed far less because of the use of agrochemicals than it has from the drainage of land, from the removal of hedges, and from climatic change. For example, it was inclement weather—not the use of agrochemicals—which in 1963 decimated the wren population. Happily the wren has since become

---

[10] V. C. Marshall, *Effects of Manures and Fertilizers on Soil Fauna: A Review*. Commonwealth Agricultural Bureaux (1977).

one of Britain's commonest birds. Among other species that have spread in recent years are the hen-harrier and the bearded tit. Correspondingly, neither pollution in general nor the use of modern pesticides in particular was responsible for the post-War decline in the numbers of some species of bird, for example the puffin, and of certain butterflies. And in the light of all the fears that were generated by Rachel Carson's *The Silent Spring*,[11] and possibly because of the action to which they led, it is reassuring to learn that in recent years gains seem to have outnumbered losses. *The New Dictionary of Birds*[12] tells us that many more species disappeared in the first half of this century, when there was no modern agrochemicals than have since. No bird has provedly become extinct since 1945.

But how are authoritative scientific statements such as these to be got across to those who are determined to think otherwise? It will correctly be argued that the "best" scientific view about any matter implies no more than the prevailing consensus about the significance of a family of related observations which have satisfied adequate tests of verification. The standing and reputation of the scientists by whom the view is shared may help impart to it a certain authority. But whatever else, its validity is neither established by a show of hands, nor does the "best" view necessarily imply unanimous acceptance. Dissent from doctrine is an essential part of the process of developing new scientific knowledge, or of gaining a new scientific understanding, with the proviso that if a dissenting view is to carry weight within a scientific context, it should not be coloured by value judgments that are extraneous to the scientific process. This does not mean that scientists do not have as much right as the next man to express views about the social implications of scientifically-agreed facts. But as the controversy over lead in the environment shows, scientists run the risk of being dubbed crusaders rather than scientists once they become more concerned to get their message about action across than they are to achieve agreement about the scientific facts. For example, a recent article[13] tells us that earthworms are a possible environmental hazard because they can absorb large amounts of lead which then get into the food chain. What the paper did not provide its readers was any indication of the relative significance of this contribution to the total amount of lead that is found in the "food chain," nor any indication of any harm which it has done to any species of animal—leave alone man. Here is an instance of the presumed specialist conveying vague feelings of disquiet. Why

---

[11] Rachel Carson, *The Silent Spring* (1963).
[12] A. L. Thomson (ed.), *A New Dictionary of Birds* (1964).
[13] M. Ireland, 74 *New Scientist* (1977), p. 486.

then should the amateur environmentalist ever feel inhibited in going one better?

As one measure to assure the safety of the public, and to protect them against quack doctors and quack remedies, no one is authorised to practice medicine in any civilised society unless he has the requisite qualifications for his name to be included in an official medical register. Eyebrows would undoubtedly be raised if, say, a professional physicist or civil engineer were to take it upon himself to diagnose cancer of the lung, or hepatitis in one of his colleagues. And if his "patient" were to die, he would certainly be debarred legally from signing the death certificate.

But there is no convention, and certainly no law, which constrains someone who is not medically qualified from behaving like a practitioner of social medicine. However much they may know about methods of detecting minute quantities of the element, few of the scientists who have contributed to the debate about the dangers to health of lead or mercury in the environment have any medical qualification. And not one of those who have been most vocal or literate on the subject seems to have provided any indication of the importance of either as a cause of human misfortune relative to the numerous diseases which are more obvious—and, one may suspect, more significant. It is again the dramatic story which counts, not the commonplace. And it is therefore not at all surprising that the way these matters are presented makes it all but impossible to persuade the environmental propagandist, leave alone the average citizen, that the medical profession does not know enough about environmental poisons, or the biologist about the factors which determine "natural" changes in the populations of wild creatures, or about the extent of these changes themselves, to judge the significance of any new apparent medical hazard or any sudden change in the numbers of some species of bird which one might be inclined to attribute to the introduction of, say, a new agrochemical.

VIII—STATUTORY COMMITTEES

The "environmental" and "ecological" enthusiasts who have today captured the limelight which once bathed other groups of reformers or would-be watch-dogs of man's well-being, have undoubtedly served some useful purpose. But it is hardly as useful a one as that of those long-standing professional bodies which past British governments have set up to protect the consumer, and whose workings have been constantly improved in the light of experience. We have the Food Standards Committee which advises Ministers on matters relating to the composition, labelling and advertising of food. There is the Food Additives and Contaminants Committee which advises on the level of contaminants that can be permitted in foodstuffs and on the need and safety of additives. Both are independent bodies. They conduct their reviews in whatever way they deem appropriate, and anyone can comment on their recommendations once they are published—not only individual consumers, but also manufacturers, distributors (whether at home or abroad), enforcement authorities, or scientific bodies. Only then do Ministers decide on the regulations which need to be prepared by their departments.

In the case of agricultural chemicals, the British public is protected by what is called The Pesticide Safety Precautions Scheme. This is an arrangement that has now operated on a non-statutory basis for over 20 years, although certain associated safeguards—for example for workers—have been made statutory. Once again, the success of the scheme derives from its independence. Although not legally binding, what is formally agreed becomes a lasting concordat between the agrochemical industry and government. A clearance by The Pesticides Safety Precautions Scheme is a seal of safety so far as industry is concerned, while government at the same time is assured that it is providing for the necessary protection of people and their environment without having instituted the controls of a statutory régime.

A third Committee deals with the Safety of Medicines. This body derives its authority from the Medicines Act of 1968. After a new drug has been tested in the usual way in laboratories and under controlled hospital conditions, the Committee has to advise on the drug's safety before it can be cleared for use by the medical profession. Once on the market, the Committee then becomes the recipient of what are called "yellow cards" on which doctors and practitioners are invited to record any adverse effects which they may have noticed from the use of the new pharmaceutical.

No procedures can guarantee absolute safety, and the British system, as represented by these three Committees, differs considerably from the corresponding one which operates in the United States under the overall control of the Federal Food and Drugs Administration, better known as the FDA. In comparison with our own, the FDA's mode of operation is both absolute and statutory, either when dealing with pharmaceuticals, or with herbicides and pesticides which might leave some residue in harvested material that ultimately enters into human consumption. Before any new chemical compound is passed for use, it has in theory to satisfy the 1958 Delaney Amendment to the 1938 Food, Drug and Cosmetic Act. This means that it is necessary to prove that whatever its nature, the new substance cannot cause cancer in man or animal. This is one of those cases where the law has to behave like the proverbial legal ass since what is called for by an Act of Congress is more or less equivalent to a demand that a negative be proved. This is an impossible condition. No scientist could declare that the circumstances in which he tests a new chemical compound are necessarily the only ones in which it could be tested, or that if he went on testing, none of his test animals would ever develop a cancerous growth. Moreover, in the final analysis, animal tests for toxicity do not necessarily tell us what is carcinogenic or toxic to man—as the story of Eraldin shows.

Obviously the rigid and absolute system of the United States is easier to operate than the United Kingdom's more flexible and pragmatic procedures. Dr. Alexander Schmidt,[14] until recently the head of the FDA, has pointed out that the intent of the original Delaney clause was to prevent "any exercise of scientific or regulatory judgment." But whatever the intent, the American scheme would also seem, like the corresponding environmental laws in the United States, to be a greater obstacle than the British to new development, and also one which is more prone to open the door to legal disputes about matters toxicological, and to judicial, as opposed to scientific, judgment. In the field of safety, most people would, I feel sure, prefer to rely on the scientist.

Clearly no one wants another thalidomide disaster. Nor do we want the kind of tragedies which occurred in the United Kingdom before statutory regulations were introduced in order to control the use of organophosphorus compounds in agriculture. But it is legitimate to ask whether it was because the Americans had a presumably safer system than the British that they were saved from the ill-effects of thalidomide. Or could it have been the case that, given different circumstances and timing, a British official—regardless of the nature of the system within which he operates—might have advised against the use of the drug? In any event, neither the British nor the American system, nor any other conceivable system, could guarantee that there will never be another tragedy like that associated with thalidomide, unless, of course, there were a total stop to the development of new pharmaceuticals. Even then, those already in use would, I am sure, come under suspicion.

IX—Absolute or Flexible Standards?

In the end, the question to which one is driven is, which safety system—statutory or non-statutory—is most useful in balancing risks? The banning of some new drug or food–additive or

---

[14] A. M. Schmidt, in *Food Quality and Safety. A Century of Progress*, H.M.S.O. (1976).

agrochemical might well prevent a certain amount of harm; equally, the denial of its use could result in a far greater social loss. There is also the question of direct cost. Some figures which I have been given suggest that in order to protect themselves from the toxic effects of drugs and food-additives the American public is prepared to spend each year per head of population well over 10 times what we in the United Kingdom spend.[15] One might well ask whether it is really buying so much extra protection.

But there are more serious objections to absolute and statutory standards in the control of toxicity. They presuppose a depth of knowledge about toxicological and environmental matters which seems almost like a scientific conceit. If taken in sufficient quantity, probably anything is poison. But, to invert the ancient adage, what to one man is poison, can be another's meat. Above all, what can be afforded in protection by one country may be totally inappropriate for another—and particularly by countries of the Third World. The harm that a particular seed-dressing might cause environmentally in the United Kingdom would be trivial to the human good it could do in others—particularly in those where need is greatest. Equally, while the United States could afford to put a ban on the use of DDT, the temporary suspension of its use in Ceylon cost thousands of lives when malaria reappeared in raging epidemic form in the early 1960s.

The present trend within the Common Market countries is towards the American system and to the imposition of uniform and absolute standards, for example, in the quality of the water we drink, or in that of the seas in which we bathe. My own view is that this is a move in the wrong direction. Clearly there may be occasion for toxicologists in all countries to agree firmly that a drug or agrochemical is too dangerous to be licensed at all. But this is the unusual case. The more frequent question is how much of a substance which would be toxic if ingested in quantity should be allowed to reach the consumer. The final decision in such matters must be political. But before decisions are taken, politicians should insist that better attempts should be made than have been hitherto to achieve international consensus on the scientific facts. Why, one might well ask, do we not hear of comparative studies that could tell us which kind of national system for the control of safety is in general the most effective—I say in general because isolated tragedies like thalidomide do not give an adequate answer. It is not just cynicism which prompts one to ask why the United Kingdom decided to ban the "doctoring" of cattle-cake with antibiotics years ago when the

---

[15] S. Zuckerman, in *Food Quality and Safety. A Century of Progress*, H.M.S.O. (1976).

Americans, who are supposed to be so much more severe in these matters, waited until only a few years back before doing the same. Why should the world be now kept in doubt while the United States puts back its threatened decision to ban the use of saccharin—all because of some controversial evidence about the rare incidence of bladder cancer in test rats? Why did other countries have to follow the American decision to ban cyclamates? Who then worried about the diabetics who did not carry American passports?

All members of the human species, as I have said, have the same anatomy, the same physiology, and the same sensitivity to poisons. But our social needs are different, and it is on this issue too that politicians should focus when considering whether the facts which only scientists can provide about toxicity or about enduring environmental damage imply the need for absolute uniform standards. What is more, the imposition of absolute environmental or toxicological standards by one country, or a group of countries, can result in non-tariff barriers to trade in a world which can hardly afford any such artificial restrictions to commerce.

The world is far from ready for the application of uniform environmental and consumer standards. With their differing national traditions and physical conditions, and with their, one hopes, transitory divergent economic interests, the nine countries of the European Economic Community have already discovered how difficult it is to standardise in these matters. Even the vastly wealthy United States cannot afford all the schemes to protect against hazards, and all the measures of environmental protection and conservation, which enthusiasts dream up.

Nonetheless, however halting our steps, and however long it takes us to get there, uniform and high consumer standards are inevitably the goal towards which the world is moving. It is far too soon to consider the establishment of an international political forum where effective discussion could take place about the priorities which should be accorded, and the measures which should be taken to counter the common hazards which beset the whole human species. But it is certainly not premature to encourage far more international collaboration in the examination of these matters than now takes place at the technical level. Tests to satisfy toxicological and environmental standards are very costly, and the need for industrial secrecy does not apply, or should not apply, at the level where toxicological knowledge is being sought. The information such researches yield is of interest to all men. For a start, it would save endless trouble, as well as scarce resources, if work at this level were therefore carried out on an international basis. The researches should be supervised by an internationally accepted body of experts, which would not only have the responsibility of affirming publicly that experiments were adequately designed and conducted, but also that of commenting on the results.

When technical assessments are made in a national context about possible social hazards and about the relative toxicity of any new drug or any new food additive or agrochemical, those responsible should take into account not only their national interests, but the balance of risk in the world as a whole. Population growth still remains one of the most serious problems that mankind has to face. Starvation still haunts large parts of the world. The expectation of life in the poorer parts of the world may be 10, 20, years less than in the richer. Enthusiasts in advanced countries divert attention from the real issues if their fear of some possible localised adverse environmental effects of, say, a new pesticide leads to the banning of its use, when it could make a significant difference to food output in a needy part of the world. Food surpluses to protect against mass starvation cannot be built up without the use of pesticides and herbicides which are made by modern chemical plants. About one-third of the world's present harvest is still being lost to pests of one kind or another.

In order to offset the dramatic and isolated presentations about hazards with which we are accustomed to being fed by the media, or which are voiced by dedicated but narrow-minded specialists, there should be the most open publication possible of the conclusions of deliberations on these matters by bodies of properly qualified inter-national experts. Today we read only too often that so-and-so, a scientist, or so-and-so, a doctor, believes that raw material "x," or process "y," or product "z," should be banned because of some hazard or other. What the public does not know is that the said scientist, or doctor, may often be speaking only for himself, and that his views could be shown to be out of balance or even false by those who are the leaders of the subject.

At the national level there is something more that could be done. Governments, as I have said, normally have to decide what to do about particular hazards when they suddenly become matters of public concern. In the United Kingdom, those which relate to food production and to drugs are dealt with by two different Depart-ments of State. Nuclear hazards are the concern of two other and separate Departments. The hazards of floods and fires are the responsibility of yet another Ministry, of the roads, of still another.

Not surprisingly, Department X is mainly concerned with its own business, and cannot spare precious time to worry about what Department Y is proposing to do about some potential hazard which is its responsibility. But dealing with any hazard means the diversion and mobilisation of national resources. And that is not something which as a rule can be dealt with separately by individual Departments. The government as a whole may agree to do all that seems necessary about a particular hazard; or to do only as much as current resources permit; or sometimes, perhaps, not to do anything effective at all. But whatever is decided, it is not long before the issue becomes overlaid by other problems.

To help prevent the actions of government from becoming unduly affected by gusts of public emotion, some independent but inter-departmental body should be given the responsibility of keeping under continuous review an "active" list of matters which for one or other reason, being regarded as hazards, have to be dealt with separately by different departments of state. Since there is no com-mon scale which makes it possible to equate risks of a totally different kind (*i.e.* adverse environmental effects of DDT cannot be compared with the danger of being killed on the roads or the risk of being drowned in one's bed through the flooding of the Thames), such a body should be charged with the comparison of risks in terms of the money that would have to be spent in their reduction. It would be its duty to advise whether there was more social benefit in spending £x million on one rather than another programme of improvement, taking into account not just the most urgent issues that have cropped up, but others which may have been forgotten, or which may have been dealt with only partially. The Hazards Committee should not be a body of "experts" but a group of sophisticated individuals able to understand the recommendations of committees which deal in a specialised way with different categories of risks. Obviously its members should be men who, because of the spread of their experience, command the confidence of the public as well as that of government. They would also be advising whether the social value of banning some new drug or agrochemical because of its rare but deleterious side-effects in an advanced country compensates for the losses which a poorer coun-try would suffer if a ban were imposed on its use. And it should be a public body which would issue annual reports on the whole spec-trum of hazards in terms understandable by the literate but non-specialist citizen.

Such a committee could not rid us of all the hazards that crop up in our advanced societies, any more than our primitive ancestors were able to banish those by which they were beset. But it could certainly help to get our priorities right in terms of the sacrifices we are prepared to accept in dealing with them. As I have implied, the concept of a no-risk society is an idle dream, an affliction of the advanced world, not of the Third World, where the larger part of mankind lacks what citizens of the Western world regard as necessities. While we do what we can to reduce the hazards we ourselves face, we need to be wary lest, in our efforts to help ourselves, we do a greater hurt to our less-favoured fellow creatures, and indeed, to our children.

THE SCOPE AND LIMITS OF DÉTENTE

By

LORD HOME

ONE of the tiresome things about even the simplest words is that they mean entirely different things to different people. To anyone in a Western democracy "détente" implies a degree of co-operation between two parties to achieve some mutual advantage. But to a Russian Communist it means nothing of the sort. He is compelled by an ideology to believe in the "ultimate victory" of Communism over every other way of life, and everything—even "détente"—has to be seen as a contribution to that end. So Mr. Brezhnev says: "détente with the West in no way signifies the end of the ideological struggle. On the contrary we should be prepared for the intensification of it." "Victory"—"struggle": Those words could not be used by a Westerner in the context of détente, but to a Russian Communist there is no contradiction at all.

The difference becomes more significant and more disturbing when it is recognised that on the way to "ultimate victory" the Communist doctrine includes the use of force. This was stated in plain terms only a few years ago by the Secretary-General of the Communist Party in the Soviet Union. He wrote: "We do not desire to use force, but we cannot allow the lack of it to stand in the way of our political aims."

These definitions of objectives and ways and means are underlined on the ground. The Berlin Wall, which would be a blot on any period of history, is still there, while Czechoslovakia is still occupied by Russian troops. It is instructive to recall the words of Mr. Malik, the Soviet representative at the United Nations in 1968. Speaking to the Security Council he said: "The entry of these units is temporary, and they will, of course, be withdrawn as soon as the Czechoslovak Soviet Republic finds these units to be unnecessary." Ten years later the forces are still there. "Temporary" is another word which has a different meaning to a Russian and to a member of a Western democracy. So it seems that any country outside the Soviet Union can be a "political aim" and must calculate that force may possibly be used against it in the context of ultimate victory for Communism.

The Soviet Union has recently put some of her latest war planes into Cuba and she has warned the United States against interference in Iran. There may or may not be nuclear weapons on the MIGs, and certainly the Americans have no intention of intervening in Iran's

31

internal affairs. But the trouble is that the Soviet leaders are capable of such provocative action, and one of their regular techniques is to accuse others of doing what they mean to do themselves.

If the Russians desired Communism for themselves no one would object, or if the ideology were merely a contest of dialectics it could be a matter of friendly disputation, but it is in fact for export. The anxiety of the countries of Western Europe is greatly increased by the Soviet Union's large forces on the eastern frontier of Western Germany, and their massive reinforcement with conventional weapons in the last few years.

It seems to be certain that, as soon as the Soviet Union reached parity with the United States in nuclear weapons, the Soviet Chiefs of Staff advised a shift in Soviet strategy. The argument will have run like this: with the attainment of parity in intercontinental missiles, nuclear war has become incredible, no one will dare to start it; therefore the Soviet Union's political aims are more likely to be attained by the constant pressures which can be applied here and there by massive and mobile military strength in "conventional" arms.

No figures are accurate for long, but here are clear indications of the weight of the Soviet's conventional military effort. The military budget is running at 15 per cent. of the Soviet Union's Gross National Product—nearly three times the average of the contributions made by the members of the NATO alliance. In 1967 the tank force was 34,000—now it is 50,000. The deployment of main-line battle tanks on the European front is Warsaw Pact: 21,000—NATO: 7,000; the quantity of conventional artillery is Warsaw Pact: 10,000—NATO: 2,700. There is as much again in men and hardware inside the Soviet Union within easy reach of the front. By sea the expansion of the submarine fleet—many being nuclear-propelled—is just as rapid, the whole amounting to forces which are, in the words of the allied Heads of Government, "far in advance of anything required for self-defence."

It was the drive put into the Warsaw Pact reinforcement and rearmament which led Dr. Solzhenitsyn to say on his arrival in Europe that war between the Soviet Union and the West was now inevitable. The Chinese have endorsed that point of view, placing the completion of the Soviet's rearmament plan for superiority in the early 1980s, with the war to follow shortly thereafter. Without accepting either the thesis or the time-scale, it is certainly true that there is a wide discrepancy in military strength between East and West. The Soviet Union means to retain the gap in the knowledge that the nature of modern weapons is such that it will not be easy for the democratic countries to bridge it quickly. The Soviet negotiators at the recent disarmament conference in Geneva made that clear beyond doubt. Their interest in a second SALT treaty was predictable, and from the point of view of the Western allies it was a good thing for some agreement to be reached. There ought to be a mutual interest in saving money. But despite agreement being reached, both the Soviet Union and the United States will retain a massive overkill in terms of nuclear power, and the thesis of the Soviet Union's military leaders could still be valid.

There is another aspect of the Soviet Union's foreign policy which sharpens apprehension. It is part of their pursuit of "political aims" with a view to "ultimate victory." It derives directly from the teaching of Marx that the capitalist societies must be undermined and removed from the world scene.

The French and then the American presence in South-East Asia gave the Soviets the opening. There they set up a prototype of war at secondhand. The North Vietnamese were ready to be the cat's-paw, the prize for them being domination of South Vietnam and Cambodia; the prizes for the Soviets being first, chaos out of which would emerge governments in South-East Asia favourable to them and, secondly, the loss of credibility by the rest of the world in United States foreign policy should they have to withdraw their presence under pressure. The Soviets' campaign was clever. They pushed heavy armaments into North Vietnam over a long period of time, and when opinion in the West became too excited over their activities, they used truces and treaties as tactical moves to distract attention from their real purpose. It was a classic operation according to the "Red Book" of Communism.

Now, having tasted success, the Soviet leaders are pursuing war by proxy in Africa. The targets there are to expel European influence and then to bring revolution into Rhodesia and South Africa. It was Mr. Zhou Enlai who said that the continent of Africa was "ripe for revolution"—it is the Russians who are taking him at his word. To enlist Cuba was diabolically clever. Castro is a fanatical Communist, eager to retrieve a reputation which has been tarnished in South America. Cubans are judged by the Third World to have been dominated by the United States. Cubans are coloured and would therefore automatically be looked upon by Africans as friends and liberators. They were the ideal tool for war at secondhand from which Communist Russia could gain a favourable spin-off.

East German officers have been in Angola, Ethiopia and Mozambique in order to emphasise the solidarity of the Warsaw Pact as the protector of the poor, the oppressed, and above all the coloured. Care for the local inhabitants is as bogus as it was in Vietnam and Cambodia, where, once the Soviet Union's "political aims" were secured, the people were left to rot, but no African would believe such a tale.

Angola is near to Namibia. The Horn of Africa gives options towards the Gulf or into Somalia, while Mozambique is on the road to Rhodesia, and Rhodesia to South Africa. That is one prong of "political" advance. The other is Afghanistan, Pakistan and Iran. The eye of the Soviet is always on oil, for the Russians know that for the next 30 years the United States will be dependent on the Gulf area for a large part of its supplies; while Germany will be even more so, and all Western Europe is very vulnerable.

It is arguable that the Soviet Union is not deliberately following a course of Empire-building regardless of all the consequences. But there can be no doubt at all that wherever there is a weakness in a country which may be exploited, or a vacuum in the field of power, that she is ready to take advantage of it at the drop of a hat. Any instability anywhere is, by definition, something which is unsettling and harmful to the West so that, while the Soviets are so active in so many places of concern to the democracies it is difficult to settle down and to talk détente. Not that the Western world has not tried. The Helsinki Conference was meticulously prepared with a view to improving the contacts and relationship between East and West, and it was followed after a two-year interval for thought by one in Belgrade, which sought advance on the same themes. Progress was meagre, and on the subject of human rights disappointing in the extreme. The Soviets turned détente into an exercise in frustration.

It is possible that, ever since the Revolution of 1917, the leaders of the Soviet Union have been pursuing a plan designed to give them world domination? It is probable that their intentions were not so formed in the early years, but there is a lot of hard evidence that since the War they have been consistently engaged in just that.

In 1945 with the signing of the United Nations Charter, there was a chance for the countries of the world to break with the tradition that peace could only be held by a balance of power, and to substitute for it the concept of Collective Security. The Allies, who had won the war against Hitler's Germany—France, The United Kingdom, China, the United States and the Soviet Union—all signed the Treaty at San Francisco which was designed to enable the Big Five to keep the peace, while an International Police Force could be organised as a permanent instrument for peace-keeping. The climate was ready for such an experiment, for the world had lately witnessed the devastation of the Hiroshima nuclear bomb, unlike the early experiment of the League of Nations, the Soviet Union and the United States were both members of the United Nations Security Council.

With the benefit of hindsight it was clearly naïve to believe that peace is a state of normalcy for man, but why did the Soviet Union wreck the chances of that Collective Security which could have guaranteed the safety for which she yearned? Why did she use the veto in the Charter on peace-keeping resolutions so recklessly (over 30 times in the first nine years) when she could so clearly have been a beneficiary? Her attitude seems to have derived from a pathological suspicion of foreign entanglements, dating from tsarist times, to which was added the Marxian teaching that the capitalist societies were the principal enemies to be undermined and destroyed. Co-operation for joint peace-making in the minds of Soviets would have meant shared decisions, and this they regarded as an infringement of the Soviet Union's sovereignty.

Confirmation for that line of reasoning comes from the second chance of co-operation with the West which the Soviets spurned. It was Marshall Aid. It represented a generous offer by the United States to help in the rehabilitation of the economies of her wartime allies which had been badly dislocated by war. The Soviet Union was fully entitled to reject aid and to rely on her own effort to accomplish her recovery, but it was the nature of the refusal which was revealing. It was that the acceptance of mutual aid would amount to an "unacceptable interference with the sovereignty of the Soviet Union."

Co-operation in schemes for assisting development in the Third World was curtly dismissed and the International Bank and the International Development Agency had to get on without the Soviet Union's help. So from the start there was little encouragement to the West to persevere. Ought this to have come as a surprise to the democracies? The answer is "No." Russia's policy for close on two centuries has been entirely consistent. The leaders have chosen to act on their own, and they have pursued expansion at other people's expense. The objectives of Peter the Great were virtually the same as those of Chairman Brezhnev. The continuing occupation of Eastern Europe; the retention of the islands which they should have returned to Japan long ago; the absorption of the Baltic States; the recent establishment of control in Afghanistan; and the actions in Asia and Africa are all of the same pattern which can only be labelled "Imperialism."

After two world wars and the devastation which they caused the people of the Western democracies find it almost impossible to believe that the leaders of the Soviet Union can mean what they say—let alone do it. This undiscriminating tolerance is an amiable characteristic, but it is dangerous. Hitler, Castro and Nasser all foretold exactly and publicly their plans for expansion and nobody took any notice. The penalties of the neglected warnings were duly paid in blood and tears. Once again the democracies have been warned.

What should the West do? How should the democracies respond to this difficult and potentially dangerous situation? The first necessity is so to add to the strength of the NATO alliance that the Soviet High Command are convinced that aggression in Europe cannot pay. That means that the West must never give the Soviet leaders any excuse to believe that, should they launch an attack with conventional weapons on Western Germany or any other ally, tactical nuclear weapons would not immediately be used in response. Doubt in the mind of the Soviets is paradoxically the best guarantor against war. It means, too, that NATO should increase its conventional forces and weapons so as to reduce the present discrepancy in relation to the Warsaw Pact.

Taking the overall balance of strength between the Western alliance and the Eastern bloc, aggression would seem at present to be marginally unattractive. It has to be made even more so and action is urgent. It means too that the politicians of the West should never make a concession to the Communists without exacting a *quid pro quo*, nor allow them to win a dialectical argument, for that is immediately interpreted as a weakness. Neither should credit be given to the Soviet Union for projects which could contribute to its military effort. Expenditure now to deter will pay a high dividend. The West too will do well to cultivate diplomatic relations with China. They are Communists, but they have the liveliest appreciation of the dangers of Soviet imperialism. The Chinese armies are trained for defence, and in guerrilla tactics, and could not attack the Soviet Union, but in the event of a war with the West many Soviet divisions and much weaponry would have to be kept deployed on the Soviet Union's eastern frontier.

The full Communist plan for world revolution has not caught on and some of the Soviet Union's plans for expansion have failed, at any rate for the time being. Egypt was nearly engulfed and escaped only in the nick of time. Soviet colonialism is clumsy, and in time it becomes apparent that they care nothing for the well-being of indigenous peoples. Ethiopia, South Vietnam and Cambodia tell their sordid and harrowing tales. It is likely that the countries of Asia and Africa will in their misery begin to contrast the performance of the United Kingdom, France and the Netherlands which granted independence, to that of the Soviet Union which strengthens its grip. Sooner or later the cry for freedom will be raised; large areas of Angola are already in revolt, but for the present, force talks.

Dr. Solzhenitsyn's warning to the democracies about the momentum of Russia's armament and of their imperialist designs was certainly timely. For 30 years the West has stood firm and gained time, and there has been no war in the European and Atlantic area. Perseverance can still prevent conflict, but it will require an extra act of will. Is it there? Dr. Solzhenitsyn's second anxiety was whether the morale of the democracies could be sustained at a level which would resist the relentless pressures which Communism would bring to bear upon them. His pessimism has increased in recent years. Allowance has to be made for the fact that, during many years of harsh conditions in a Soviet prison, he must have concluded that, by comparison with the Soviet Union, life in the Christian democracies would be something akin to paradise. Some disillusion was bound to follow.

Nevertheless, the democracies should not be complacent about the principles which underpin their free societies, and on which European and Atlantic civilisation was built. The Christian religion; the elected parliaments; the common law; the self-disciplined society; respect for the individual: all these have buttressed democracy, and are virtually inseparable from its history and its future. Indeed as lately as the 1940s millions were ready to fight and to die for them.

Today many of these traditional values are in question, and in the permissive society it sometimes seems that there is nothing to take their place. If this were true the outlook would be bleak, for a nation with no values would have no chance to stand against the Communist whose ideology is a crusade. But when pessimism looks like taking charge events reveal a very different picture. The Queen's Jubilee year demonstrated that millions could recognise basic values when they saw them. The recent response in Europe to the election of the Pope showed a reaction by millions that values matter to them. This public witness should not be ignored by any Power, however great, which might be tempted to subvert, over-bear and destroy. The Kaiser and Hitler both made the mistake of believing the young generation to be effete with consequences which were dire for themselves and their countries. The British people are not articulate, nor do they wear their values on their sleeve, but it would be a grievous error if the Soviets were to believe that they could take advantage of that reticence. In the days following the war, when the Soviet looked like turning nasty, the response of the British Foreign Secretary, Ernest Bevin, was "I won't 'ave it." Unsophisticated, a gut reaction, but I believe it is enduring.

There is a theory advanced by Professor Toynbee and others that two philosophies in confrontation will absorb much from each other. To some extent that has been true of Communism and of

Democracy. The West has adopted throughout parts of its economy the practice of State intervention, ownership and control. Change is much slower in the Soviet Union because, under the rigid application of the ideology, no individual or group of individuals can initiate change. Nevertheless, there are signs which the careful observer may note. Credit is accepted as necessary for industrial expansion. The consumer is beginning in a very small way to call the tune. In the last 10 years, for example, shape (style is not yet the appropriate word) and colour have been introduced into women's clothing; while the dissidents, small in number as they are, are voicing the need for human rights. This is true, not only of the Soviet Union, but of the countries of Eastern Europe as well.

It is useless to expect that there will be rapid change; Communism does not dare officially to admit free discussion lest it become the thin end of the wedge which would prize the Communist system wide open. Communists are, as President Carter detected, particularly vulnerable on human rights. Here the West is in a dilemma as to how far to press this issue. The Charter of the United Nations included the rule that there should be no interference by one country in the internal affairs of another. The authors foresaw, and rightly, that unless this precept was accepted the result would be international chaos.

That the Soviets are the first to flout the rule does not prevent them from quoting it in favour of themselves. When they claim that Jews or "dissidents" are breaking laws which apply to all other Soviet citizens and are internal to the Soviet Union, they have a point in terms of the content of the Charter. Any direct intervention by the West to humanise the legislation, or stir up active opposition to inhuman interpretation of the laws is clearly out of the question, if only because the Soviet authorities would stamp out any organised opposition with ruthless disregard for rights and life. Nevertheless there are certain moral issues which in these days of rapid communications cannot be swept under the carpet, and elementary human rights is one of them. The Belgrade Conference revealed that the Soviet leaders were stubbornly opposed to any modification of their present practices. So long as they persist in that negative attitude it will be that much more difficult to arrive at true détente.

Is it possible that Euro-Communism might be the side road by which détente is eventually reached? Could it be that the Communists of Italy and France are ready to dilute their ideology to a point where it could come within the ambit of the ethics and principles of democracy? The phenomenon being new, it is difficult to measure its relevance, if any, to détente. The elements in the tests to be applied have been suggested by the Institute of International

Studies: independence from Moscow; commitment to European integration; acceptance of democratic pluralism; the democratisation of the party structure; readiness to accept an adverse vote. One has only to glance at these conditions to realise how far away is the key which will unlock the door between Communism and Democracy, and between East and West.

So far comment can only be provisional and tentative. For example, all the Euro-Communists are firmly anti-NATO, and when they have pronounced on international issues they have invariably lined up behind the Soviet Union. In Portugal, when the Communists entered the government, they preserved the Marxist-Leninist Party intact. Neither in Italy nor in France is the structure of the parties democratic. It has to be said, too, that there is no evidence to suggest that the Euro-Communists would be as happy to lose power through compromise as they have been to gain it by their traditional policies. The only safe response for the present must be vigilance in pursuit of co-existence. This development of Euro-Communism may be the trap which is part of the dreary old story, or it might be the pointer to the dilution and breakdown of doctrine. It is important that the West should accurately and intelligently interpret the signs.

So how does one sum up the prospects for détente? The first conclusion, in the absence of mutual and balanced disarmament, must be to redress the disparity in "conventional" strength to a point where the Soviets are bound to conclude that the risk of military adventure is too high. That, paradoxically, is a contribution to détente as it can compel the Soviets to take it seriously. The present NATO timetable for increased forces and arms should be telescoped so that this goal is achieved in the shortest possible time. The military programme is within our means. Meanwhile, the Soviet leaders must be given to understand that should they commit aggression in Europe it would be inevitable that the tactical nuclear weapon would be used in defence. From that they are likely to draw the realistic and the right conclusion.

On the periphery, where British interests may be threatened, we have to recognise that we have not the power which we had in the days of Empire and the authority which went with it. But because we have less power and less influence it would be a cardinal error to conclude that we have none.

The democracies of Europe and of the North Atlantic have much to offer. The knowledge that the NATO alliance has no intention of yielding to force will in itself give courage to others. They need have no doubt that the allies have enough wealth and will to face up to the rearmament on the scale which is necessary to convince the Soviet

Union that war cannot pay. There will also be a reaction against the callous cruelty which has followed the Revolution which the Communists have inspired.

In Asia and Africa the democracies will have the chance to prove themselves to be sympathetic friends standing for ethical standards of probity in international dealing, setting an example in human rights and freedom which is real and has meaning. The contrast between Communism and liberty will not be missed by the Third World. The democracies have to practice what they preach, and there are still some weak links in the chain. But if they are seen to support parliaments which derive their authority from adult suffrage, and if they set an example of self-discipline within the law which is the guardian of the freedom of the individual, then others will make the comparison and mark the virtue in the democratic process. Above all, if the democracies use their power with discretion, that will point the contrast with those who use it to dominate.

The Commonwealth, which succeeded the British Empire, is an experiment in the early stages of positive co-operation and it is on that pattern that countries can associate within the real meaning of the word détente. The European Community and the Commonwealth are both milestones on the approach to neighbourly co-operation. It will be a long time before the leaders of the Soviet Union even begin to think in such terms.

In the meantime they will continue to present to the West the most difficult of all problems—how to conduct policies of reconciliation when the other negotiator insists on talking in terms of subversion, revolution and force. As Sir Terence Garvey has written lately: "The Russians, assuming they wish to impress us with their good faith, are their own worst enemies." They leave no option to the West but to add to the military strength of NATO, for the democracies have no intention of allowing a situation to develop where there would be no choice but to fight a rearguard action; nor to be content with a situation where the only context in which the democracies can pursue détente is that of the strict *quid pro quo*. Our efforts to arrive at détente will continue, whatever the frustrations.

There is a risk in matching strength with strength. It is forced on the democracies by the Soviets. But it is necessary, for it is only when it is clearly understood by the Soviet leaders that there will be no surrender, that détente will begin to mean the same to them and to us.

THE STRATEGIC BALANCE

By

FRANK BARNABY

A GREAT deal was said and written about strategic nuclear weapons during 1978 and 1979. This interest arose mainly because the United States and the Soviet Union were busily trying to negotiate a new treaty (SALT II) limiting these weapons. A SALT II treaty had, in fact, been expected ever since President Ford and General Secretary Brezhnev signed the so-called Vladivostok accords in December 1974 which were meant to be the basis for a new treaty. For more than four years we were told that a treaty was just around the corner. No wonder that the credibility of optimistic forecasts remain low.

There were, however, good reasons to believe that both parties were trying their best to succeed. That both Mr. Brezhnev and Mr. Carter genuinely wanted a SALT II treaty could hardly be doubted. Both leaders, particularly the Soviet one, were politically committed to such a treaty. And both knew that political détente was unlikely to survive for very long once it became clear that no treaty was forthcoming. Soviet feelings on this issue amounted almost to an obsession. So much importance was attached to it that, for example, a meeting between the American and Soviet leaders was, to say the least, unlikely unless they could sign a SALT treaty on the occassion.

But a signed treaty was not the end of the matter. It seemed that President Carter was likely to have great difficulty in drumming up the two-thirds majority he needed in the Senate to get the treaty ratified. This exercise became even more difficult after the previous November's congressional elections. At least six pro-SALT Senators were defeated; there is now formidable opposition to SALT II in Congress.

The debate about the desirability of limiting strategic weapons, usually based more on emotion than fact, often hinges on whether or not a balance exists between the strategic nuclear arsenals of the United States and the Soviet Union. Few on either side question the sense of the concept of such a strategic balance in today's world. But before considering this, some details of the SALT process will be given.

I—A SALT II AGREEMENT

On October 3, 1977, the five-year United States-Soviet interim SALT I agreement limiting strategic offensive weapons, expired.

41

Under this agreement the United States is limited, for example, to 1,000 intercontinental ballistic missiles (ICBMs) and 710 submarine-launched ballistic missiles (SLBMs), and the Soviet Union to 1,408 ICBMs and 950 SLBMs (Table 1). Shortly after the interim agreement expired the United States and the Soviet Union stated that they would, for the time being, keep to the terms of the SALT I agreement.

A second component of SALT I was a treaty, of indefinite duration, limiting anti-ballistic missile systems (the ABM treaty). Both the United States and the Soviet Union were limited to 100 ABM launchers and interceptors at each of two sites. A second ABM agreement entered into force in 1974 limiting the United States and the Soviet Union to one ABM site of 100 launchers and interceptors. The treaty also prohibits the establishment of a radar base for nationwide missile defence and providing anti-aircraft missiles with the capability to counter strategic ballistic missiles. The ABM agreement has so far been unaffected by the expiration of the interim agreement.

Table 1
SALT I ceilings on United States and Soviet Offensive Strategic Weapons

Weapon system	United States	Soviet Union
ICBM launchers	1,000–1,054, depending on whether old ICBMs are replaced by SLBMs	1,408–1,618, depending on whether old ICBMs are replaced by SLBMs; a sub-limit of 308 was placed on modern "heavy ICBMs"
SLBM launchers	710, provided that 54 Titan II ICBMs are withdrawn	950, provided that 210 SS–7 and SS–8 ICBMs are withdrawn
Ballistic missile submarines	44, provided that 54 Titan II ICBMs are withdrawn	62, provided that 210 SS–7 and SS–8 ICBMs are withdrawn

An effective missile defence system has yet to be developed. Nevertheless, the Americans began the construction of an ABM system—based on the most advanced radars and computers, and missiles with high accelerations—to protect an ICBM site at Grand Forks, North Dakota but later abandoned it. And the Soviet Union has deployed 64 ABMs around Moscow.

Research on ballistic missile defence systems is actively under way. That the ABM treaty did not prohibit such research greatly reduces its effectiveness. In fact, the most noteworthy thing about the treaty may be the considerable technical detail contained in it.

A SALT II treaty based on the Vladivostok accords would limit both the United States and the Soviet Union to the deployment of 2,400 strategic delivery systems—strategic bombers, ICBMs and SLBMs. Of this total, no more than 1,320 ICBMs and SLBMs would be permitted to carry multiple independently-targetable re-entry vehicles (MIRVs) (Table 2). The Soviet Union interprets the Vladivostok accords as covering all strategic missiles, but the United States interpretation is that only ballistic strategic missiles are included. Because the United States wants to deploy modern cruise missiles, which are not ballistic, the dispute has been a major obstacle to a SALT II agreement.

Table 2
United States and Soviet Strategic Delivery Systems, Levels and Limits

Weapon system	June 18, 1979 levels USA	USSR	1974 Vladivostok limits	SALT II limits[1]
Heavy ICBMs	54	308	308	308
Other ICBMs	1,000	1,090		
SLBMs	656	950		
Long-range bombers	300[1]/576[2]	576[3]		
Total strategic nuclear delivery systems	2,286[3]	2,504[3]	2,400	2,250
MIRVed ICBMs	550	608		820
MIRVed SLBMs	496	144		
Total MIRVed missiles	1,046	752	1,320	1,200
MIRVed ICBMs +SLBMs + aircraft with long-range cruise missiles				1,320

[1] Estimate of number of strategic bombers in fully operational (intercontinental) status, excluding aircraft used for training, aircraft in storage, mothballs and reserves.

[2] Total number to be used in SALT II limit unless some are destroyed.

[3] Number to be compared with SALT II limit.

Source: SIPRI data.

Another problem has been whether or not to classify the Soviet Tupolev Backfire bomber—a supersonic swing-wing aircraft with a 2,500-nautical mile unrefuelled operational radius—as a strategic bomber. A third issue has been the verification of the number of deployed ICBMs equipped with MIRVs. Such verification, without on-site inspection, is virtually impossible and, if MIRVs are to be restricted, any deployed ICBM of a type which has been tested with MIRVs has to be assumed to be carrying them.

In March 1977 United States Secretary of State Cyrus Vance discussed, in Moscow, with President Leonid Brezhnev a set of proposals, different from those in the Vladivostok accords, on which the new Carter Administration wished to base a SALT II treaty. Reportedly, the main proposal was that the total number of strategic bombers, ICBMs and SLBMs should be limited to between 1,800 and 2,000, rather than the Vladivostok limit of 2,400. The total number of MIRVed ICBMs should be between 1,100 and 1,200 instead of 1,320. And the number of MIRVed ICBMs should be limited to 550. The number of so-called "heavy ICBMs" deployed should not exceed 54 Titan IIs for the United States and 150 SS-9s and/or SS-18s for the Soviet Union.

It seems that it was also proposed that no cruise missiles with ranges over 2,500 kilometres should be deployed and that cruise missiles launched from aircraft other than strategic bombers should have ranges limited to 600 kilometres. The Backfire bomber seemingly was to be excluded from an agreement, subject to certain unspecified conditions. The modification of existing ICBMs and the deployment of new types, including mobile ICBMs, was apparently not to be allowed. The number of flight tests of existing ICBMs and SLBMs was to be limited to six per year.

The Soviet Union rejected these United States proposals. Reportedly, the Soviet counter-proposal was to negotiate a SALT II treaty according to the Vladivostok accord, including cruise missiles. There were speculations on the effect of the human rights issue on the Soviet attitude, but there is little doubt that the United States proposals were so far-reaching as to take the Soviet Union by surprise. Moreover, they were probably seen as more favourable to the United States than to the Soviet Union. In fact, at that time the intentions of the new Carter Administration regarding arms control may have been obscure to the Russians.

One probably specific Soviet objection to the Carter proposals was the low numerical limit set on Soviet heavy ICBMs. The United States is concerned that MIRVed warheads delivered by such ICBMs will soon threaten the United States land-based ICBM forces. The limit on the number of ballistic missile tests would have seriously restricted Soviet improvements in missile accuracy—an area in which the Soviet Union is significantly behind the United States. The Soviet Union also probably wanted more restrictions on cruise missile deployment—the Soviet Union is less advanced than the United States in modern cruise missile technology.

In negotiations in May 1977 Secretary of State Vance and Foreign Minister Gromyko agreed on a general framework for SALT II which appeared to satisfy both the Soviet desire for retaining the spirit of the Vladivostok accords and the American desire for reductions in the Vladivostok limits on strategic offensive weapons. The agreed SALT II framework has three components. First, a treaty lasting until 1985. Secondly, a short-term protocol—lasting until the end of 1981—dealing with what are called "contentious issues not yet ready for long-term solution." Thirdly, a joint statement of principles for SALT III.

The new treaty establishes equal limits for the Soviet Union and the United States on the total number of strategic nuclear delivery systems. An initial total of 2,400 strategic systems (the Vladivostok limit) will be reduced to 2,250 by 1981. Within this total, there is a limit of 1,320 on the total number of ballistic missiles (strictly speaking to treaty limits launchers rather than missiles) equipped with MIRVs and bombers armed with long-range cruise missiles. The new agreement will limit the number of MIRVed land-based ICBMs and SLBMs to 1,200. A further limit of 820 is placed on MIRVed land-based ICBMs. The Soviet Union is allowed 308 heavy ICBMs of the SS-18 type. There is an agreement to exchange data on the numbers of strategic weapons systems in constrained categories. Given the Soviet habit of extreme secrecy about their strategic (and other) weapons this agreement to exchange data is a considerable breakthrough.

Within these numerical limits, each side is free to determine the structure of its strategic nuclear forces. The equal numerical limits and the freedom to mix strategic systems within them is meant to provide for "equivalence" given the differences in the make-up of the Soviet and American strategic nuclear forces.

The treaty includes very detailed technical descriptions of strategic nuclear weapon systems, restrictions on certain new strategic weapons, and provisions to improve verification.

The protocol will allow the flight testing of cruise missiles to unlimited range but will ban the deployment of ground- and sea-launched cruise missiles capable of a range greater than 600 kilometres. There will be no maximum on the range permitted for deployed air-launched cruise missiles. The deployment of mobile ICBM launchers will be banned for the period of the protocol and so will the flight-testing of ICBMs from such launchers. The flight-testing and deployment of new types of ballistic missiles will also be limited. The treaty will provide for the advanced notification of certain ICBM-test launches. SALT II will not affect the continued nuclear or conventional co-operation with allies.

The Soviet Backfire bomber will not be counted as a strategic bomber within the limit of total strategic delivery vehicles, but the Soviet Union will be prohibited from deploying the Backfire as a strategic bomber against the United States and the rate at which the aircraft may be produced in future stipulated.

The cruise missile ranges refer to maximum ranges, that is, the maximum great-circle distances between launch points and targets. Because a cruise missile may make many deviations in its course—to avoid obstacles and defended areas, for example—the actual distance flown may be much greater than this range. Verification of a cruise missile range limitation would be exceedingly difficult to achieve by "national technical means," as far as deployed missiles are concerned. About all that could be observed from satellites would be the ranges over which cruise missiles are tested.

The statement of principles for SALT III included commitments to further reductions, more comprehensive qualitative constraints on new systems, and provisions to improve verification. Given the difficulties in agreeing on the details of SALT II, this premature concern about SALT III indicated the professional optimism of the SALT negotiators.

By the end of 1978 only two or three technical obstacles to a SALT II treaty remained. Even these were not significant and appeared to include the number of cruise missiles allowed in each aircraft carrying them and the number of MIRVs allowed on new strategic ballistic missiles. By the time Secretary of State Vance and Foreign Minister Gromyko met in Geneva in December 1978 to discuss SALT issues, 95 per cent. or so of an agreement had been completed in a joint draft treaty more than 60 pages long. The main obstacles were again political. This time the Soviet Union probably dragged its feet because of annoyance about the normalisation of relations between the United States and China. But after some further negotiations, the SALT II treaty was signed by Presidents Brezhnev and Carter in Vienna on June 18, 1979.

The United States currently admits to having 1,710 ballistic missiles (1,054 ICBMs and 656 SLBMs) of which 1,046 (550 ICBMs and 496 SLBMs) are MIRVed. About 300 B-52s are assigned strategic roles (although 576 B-52s exist) (Table 3). The Soviet Union is thought to have 2,345 ballistic missiles (1,398 ICBMs and 947 SLBMs) of which 353 (321 ICBMs and 32 SLBMs) are MIRVed (Table 4). Perhaps 140 Soviet long-range bombers are assigned strategic roles. The Soviet Union appears to be scrapping its oldest ICBMs (SS-7s and SS-8s).

Although the United States is developing the M-X mobile ICBM, it has not officially announced plans to increase the number of its MIRVed ICBMs above the current level of 550. The first Trident strategic nuclear submarine is scheduled to be operational in 1981. Others may become operational at a rate of four every three years.

Table 3
Current United States Strategic Delivery Capability

Vehicle	Number of vehicles deployed	Number of warheads per delivery vehicle	Total delivery capability No. warheads	Total yield per delivery vehicle Mt	Total delivery capability Mt
MIRVed vehicles					
Minuteman III	550	3	1,650	0·51	280
Poseidon C-3	496	10[1]	4,960	0·4	198
Sub-total	1,046		6,610		478
Non-MIRVed vehicles					
B-52	300[2]	11[3]	4,300[4]	12[3]	3,800[4]
Titan II	54	1	54	7·5	405
Minuteman II	450	1	450	1·5	675
Polaris A-3	160	3	480	0·6	96
Sub-total	964		5,284		4,976
Total	2,010		11,894[5]		5,454

[1] Average figure.
[2] Estimate, excluding aircraft used for training, aircraft in storage and reserves. Currently 478 B-52s can be made ready for flight in a relatively short time. Ninety-five others are in deep storage.
[3] Excluding the nuclear-armed short-range attack missile (SRAM). Maximum loading. Current operational loading is said to be 4 bombs, each of about one mega ton, per aircraft.
[4] Including SRAM. Maximum loading.
[5] Of these, 7,274 are independently targetable warheads on ballistic missiles.
Source: SIPRI data.

Table 4

Soviet Strategic Missile Delivery Capability, September 1978

Vehicle	Number of vehicles deployed	Number of warheads per delivery vehicle	Total delivery capability No. warheads	Total yield per delivery vehicle Mt	Total delivery capability Mt
MIRVed vehicles					
SS-17	70	4	280	2	140
SS-18	54	8	432	4	216
SS-19	230	6	1,380	3	690
SS-N-18	32	3	96	0·6	19
Sub-total	386		2,188		1,065
Non-MIRVed vehicles					
SS-9	192	1	192	20	3,840
SS-11	730	1 or 3	1,530[1]	1 or 0·6	650
SS-13	60	1	60	1	60
SS-18	62	1	62	20	1,240
SS-N-5	21	1	21	1	21
SS-N-6	528	1 or 2	700[1]	1 or 0·4	430[1]
SS-N-8	354	1	354	1	354
SS-NX-17[2]	12	1	12	1	12
Sub-total	1,959		2,931		6,607
Total	2,345		5,119[3]		7,672

[1] Estimate.
[2] MIRV capability.
[3] Of these ballistic missile warheads, 4,147 are independently targetable.
Source: SIPRI data.

Table 5

Probable United States Strategic Delivery Capability in 1985, With or Without SALT II

Vehicle	Number of vehicles deployed	Number of warheads per delivery vehicle	Total delivery capability No. warheads	Total yield per delivery vehicle Mt	Total delivery capability Mt
MIRVed vehicles					
Minuteman III	550	3	1,650	0·51	280
Poseidon (C-3 and C-4)	640	10[1]	6,400	0·4 or 0·8	350
B-52 with ALCM	80	20	1,600	4	320
Sub-total	1,270		9,650		950
Non-MIRVed vehicles					
B-52 (penetrating)	220	11[2]	3,420	12[2]	2,840[3]
Titan	54	1	54	7·5	405
Minuteman II	450	1	450	1·5	675
Polaris	64	3	192	0·6	38
Sub-total	738		4,116		3,958
Total	2,058		13,766[4]		4,908

[1] Average.
[2] Excluding SRAM. Maximum loading. Operational loading per aircraft may be 4 bombs, each of about 1 Mt.
[3] Including SRAM. Maximum loading.
[4] Of these, 8,618 are independently targetable warheads on ballistic missiles.
Source: SIPRI data.

The deployment of air-launched cruise missiles is planned to begin in late 1982, perhaps at the rate of about 40 per month. Therefore, 80 B-52Gs could be armed with 20 missiles each by the end of 1985, the number allowed by SALT II.

The Soviet Union has deployed MIRVs over the past three years at an average rate of about 100 per year. The Soviet Union may, therefore, increase its MIRVed ICBM force to 820 by 1985.

According to current deployment plans, the United States, for example, will in 1985 probably have 550 MIRVed ICBMs, 496 MIRVed SLBMs on 31 Poseidon nuclear submarines, 144 MIRVed SLBMs on six Trident submarines, and 80 B-52G bombers each equipped with 20 cruise missiles. (The present plan is eventually to arms all 173 B-52Gs with cruise missiles.) These strategic delivery systems could deliver about 10,000 nuclear warheads—1,600 by cruise missiles, about 1,600 by land-based ICBMs and about 6,400 by SLBMs. Single-warheaded ICBMs, the remaining SLBMs and the other strategic bombers could deliver an additional 4,000 warheads (Table 5).

United States ICBMs, SLBMs and strategic bombers currently deployed can deliver about 12,000 nuclear warheads (Table 3). The total of 14,000 United States strategic nuclear warheads which may be deployed in the mid-1980s therefore still represents a significant increase in the size of the United States nuclear arsenal.

It is evident that the SALT II treaty will not greatly affect quantitative increases in the United States nuclear arsenal. Similarly, the size of the Soviet nuclear arsenal seems likely to increase considerably.

But qualitative improvements in nuclear warheads are more likely to increase the probability of a nuclear world war than quantitative increases in nuclear arsenals. The latter have for a long time been so huge as to make further increases meaningless, at least from the military and strategic points of view. SALT II will not significantly affect planned qualitative improvements in strategic weapons.

II—Qualitative Improvements in Nuclear Weapons

The most dangerous current developments in nuclear weapons include: the continuous improvement of the accuracy, reliability, and other characteristics of warhead delivery; mobile land-based missiles to carry these super-accurate warheads; cruise missiles; and miniaturised tactical nuclear weapons, including enhanced-radiation reduced-blast weapons—the so-called neutron bombs.

Some of the strategic nuclear weapons now being developed or deployed are very dangerous in that they have war-fighting characteristics—in particular very accurate warheads for ballistic missiles, such as the Mark-12A warheads for the United States Minuteman III (now being deployed); mobile ICBMs, which have been developed by the Soviet Union and are in the initial stages of development in the United States for deployment in the 1980s; and long-range, land- or sea-based modern cruise missiles (being developed by the United States).

Future land-based mobile ICBMs may be awesome weapons. For example, the United States M-X, a $40,000 million weapon system, will probably carry ten manoeuvrable re-entry vehicles (MARVs) with terminal guidance[1] giving Circular Error Probabilities (CEPs)[2] of a few tens of metres. SALT II allows each side to flight-test and deploy one new type of ICBM during the lifetime of the treaty. This missile can be equipped with a maximum of ten MIRVs.

One deployment scheme for the M-X missile is the Multiple Aim Point deployment (MAP). Under MAP an ICBM could be moved between, and launched from any one of, many covered silos. The Soviets would then have to attack all of many holes to be sure of knocking out the missile. The scheme would, to be effective, involve the use of literally many thousands of new holes. The environmental objections to MAP are clear. Another possible deployment scheme being considered is that M-X missiles should be carried on and launched from cargo aircraft.

In the United States, the development of MARVs is under way also for future SLBMs, such as the 6,000-nautical mile range Trident D-5. This missile, in the first stages of development, is planned for eventual deployment in Trident strategic nuclear submarines. Two of these ships, to be equipped with 24 SLBMs each, are under construction. Initially, Trident submarines will be armed with the 4,000-nautical mile range C-4 SLBM now being tested, each carrying up to eight 100-kt MIRVs. The C-4 will have nearly double the range of the current Poseidon C-3 SLBM and a CEP of about 500 metres. These missiles will be back-fitted into some Poseidon submarines beginning in October 1979.

---

[1] Terminal guidance uses some system (*e.g.* lasers or radar) to guide the warhead, after re-entry into the earth's atmosphere, on to its target.

[2] Circular Error Probability (CEP) is the radius of a circle around the target, within which 50 per cent. of the weapons aimed at the target will fall. The current United States Minuteman III, the world's most accurate ICBM, has a CEP of about 350 metres. The NS-20 guidance system reduces this to about 200 metres. Using the Advanced Inertial Reference System (AIRS), being developed for the MX ICBM, CEPs of 60–120 metres may be achieved. And terminal guidance could reduce this to 15 to 30 metres.

The Trident programme is enormously expensive—each submarine will cost over $1,700 million and the total programme costs will probably exceed $30,000 million.

The Soviet Union is also increasing the accuracy of its strategic nuclear warheads. A mobile intermediate-range ballistic missile (the SS-20), armed with MIRVs, is already being deployed as a tactical nuclear weapon for use in, for example, Europe. According to United States sources, a new generation of Soviet ICBMs for possible deployment in the 1980s is under development.

Whereas the high-quality strategic nuclear weapons described above are so expensive that only the United States and the Soviet Union can contemplate their large-scale deployment, the cruise missile is cheap enough to make it a potential strategic system for medium and even small Powers. The development of modern cruise missiles, therefore, has far-reaching consequences.

III—Cruise Missiles

These missiles are small, pilotless aircraft powered by air-breathing jet engines. In contrast, ballistic missiles are powered by rocket engines.

Cruise missiles date back to the German V-1 or "buzz-bomb" of the Second World War. Soon after the war, the United States and the Soviet Union began developing these missiles and produced a variety of types (surface-to-surface, surface-to-air and air-to-surface) for both short-range (tactical) and long-range (strategic) applications.

In the early 1960s, United States long-range surface-to-surface cruise missiles were replaced by ballistic missiles. However, some cruise missiles—for example, the 1,000 kilometre range nuclear-armed Hound Dog air-to-surface missile, first deployed on B-52s in 1960—have remained in use.

In 1962, the Soviet Union deployed the SS-N-3 Shaddock—a 450-kilometre range cruise missile carrying a nuclear warhead—and some short-range types (mainly naval air-to-surface missiles). Current Soviet cruise missiles also include the 60-kilometre range SS-N-7, the 750-kilometre range SS-N-12 surface-to-surface naval missile, and the 550-kilometre range AS-6 air-to-surface missile developed for use in the Backfire bomber.

In 1972, the United States interest in cruise missiles revived, probably as a "bargaining chip" for SALT. A number of technological advances favoured cruise missile development. The most important by far was the combination of the miniaturisation of computers with accurate data about the co-ordinates of potential targets. Very small but accurate missile guidance systems could thus be developed. For example, the McDonnell Douglas Terrain Contour Matching (TERCOM) system, which weighs only 37 kg., can guide a cruise missile to its target with a CEP of a few tens of metres. TERCOM uses an on-board computer to compare the terrain below the missile (scanned with a radar altimeter) with a pre-programmed flight path. Very accurate maps, obtained by satellite mapping, allow the positions of targets and the contours of flight paths to be obtained with great accuracy. Targets could not be located accurately enough from earlier maps to make effective use of the new cruise missile guidance systems. Very small jet engines were also available. For example, the Williams Research Corporation produces a turbo-fan engine weighing only about 60 kg., and generating a thrust of about 275 kg.

Using these new technologies, cruise missiles are being developed in the United States to be launched from air, sea and ground platforms. The most important is the air-launched version.

The air-launched cruise missile (ALCM) being developed by, for example, Boeing is designed to be carried by B-52 bombers. The plan is that each B-52 should carry 20 missiles.

The ALCM is designed to cruise at a speed of about 450 kilometres per hour, have a range of about 2,500 kilometres have a very small radar image, and fly at very low altitudes (a couple of hundred metres over rough terrain and a few tens of metres over smooth ground). The missile is difficult to detect and destroy. Defence against the missiles would thus be both difficult and costly, particularly if they were launched in large numbers. Effective detection of ALCMs would probably involve look-down radars carried in sophisticated Airborne Warning and Control System (AWACS) aircraft. To patrol a long frontier would require a fleet of such aircraft—a very costly undertaking. A large number of long-range interceptor aircraft would also be required to operate with AWACS to intercept and destroy the incoming missiles, which would also be extremely costly. A defensive system against cruise missiles is generally more expensive than the cruise missiles themselves. And this may be the main point in deploying the weapons.

Apart from their high accuracy and relative invulnerability, cruise missiles are quite cheap. In a production run of, say, 2,000 missiles, the unit cost (including development costs) is likely to be about $750,000 (much less than the cost of a modern main battle tank). It is then perhaps not surprising that countries other than the United States and Soviet Union are interested in cruise missiles. The United Kingdom and France, for example, are considering these missiles as potential cheap replacements for their strategic nuclear weapons as these become obsolete in the 1980s. Most industrialised countries (and possibly some Third World ones) are technically capable of producing cruise missiles indigenously. But what is often lacking is a precise knowledge of the co-ordinates of potential targets and accurate information about the flight path to navigate to their co-ordinates with the full effectiveness of the missile's guidance system.

The proliferation of cruise missiles, particularly among NATO countries, could have far-reaching effects. The Soviet Union would probably react strongly against it, particularly if the Federal Republic of Germany were involved. The Soviet Union would also argue that it would complicate arms control and disarmament negotiations.

If cruise missiles do proliferate widely, they may turn out to be the most far-reaching military technological development ever. It is ironic that the modern versions of these weapons were initially developed by the Americans not for deployment but to provoke the Soviets to make concessions in a strategic arms limitation treaty. There is little doubt that improved versions of cruise missiles will, in future, be developed in rapid succession.

IV—STRATEGIC BALANCE

Soviet and American strategic nuclear forces differ in many ways. Those of the United States contain, for example, about twice as many warheads as those of the Soviet Union. But Soviet warheads generally have much greater explosive power than American ones so that the Soviet strategic nuclear forces can deliver about 60 per cent. more megatonnage than the United States ones. In terms of equivalent megatonnage[3] the Soviet forces are nearly twice as powerful as their American counterpart.

The composition of the forces also differs markedly. The Americans have many more strategic bombers than the Soviets; the Soviet force is almost entirely a missile force. The Soviets have considerably more ICBMs and SLBMs than the Americans. But the Americans have many more MIRVed missiles.

United States missiles are more accurate and reliable than Soviet missiles and United States strategic nuclear submarines are superior to their Soviet counterparts. In fact, American military technology is generally of higher quality than Soviet military technology. But

---

[3] Equivalent megatonnage, a measure of the urban area destructive power of a nuclear weapon which takes into account the fact that the destructive power does not increase proportionally with increases in explosive power, is expressed as N multiplied by Y to the 2/3 power, where N is the number of weapons of explosive power Y.

what seems to worry some Americans is that in some respects they have lost the quantitative advantage they once had over the Soviets. The number of Soviet ICBM launchers, for example, overtook that of American ICBM launchers in 1969. The number of Soviet modern strategic nuclear submarines and SLBM launchers surpassed those of the Americans in 1975. And the Soviet have had a greater number of strategic delivery systems since 1973. This loss of advantage, meaningless though it may be in any military or strategic sense, is of great concern to those who demand superiority in all possible respects.

Because of their differences, meaningful comparisons of the two strategic nuclear forces are extremely difficult. The problem is compounded by such differences as those of a geographical nature between the United States and the Soviet Union, those concerning the degree of urbanisation of the two societies and in the siting of cities, and those involving the patterns of industrialisation. A nuclear attack with a given number and size of warheads would have different effects on each country.

The statistics can be, and are, used to support any theory about the relationship between the two strategic nuclear arsenals. What is usually ignored is the fact that both arsenals are so huge that even large differences have (or ought to have) little meaning.

Operational American and Soviet strategic nuclear forces are probably loaded with a total of about 14,000 nuclear warheads with a total explosive power equivalent to that of about 10,000 million tons of TNT. In addition, the two super-Powers probably have about 50,000 tactical nuclear warheads, each on average four times more powerful than the atomic bomb that destroyed Hiroshima. So-called tactical nuclear weapons, therefore, add an explosive power equivalent to that of 2,500 million tons on TNT to make a grand total of about 12,500 million tons—the equivalent of about 1 million Hiroshima bombs or over three tons of TNT for every man, woman and child on earth.

In a nuclear world war most nuclear weapons would presumably fall in the northern hemisphere, although some are almost certainly aimed at targets in the southern hemisphere, such as communication bases, and so on. There are at most 400 cities in the northern hemisphere big enough to warrant a nuclear warhead. Assuming that about one-half of the warheads are targeted on cities then, on average, each city would be bombarded by the equivalent of roughly 15 million tons of TNT. Each city, in other words, would be hit by the equivalent of about 1,500 Hiroshima bombs. The nuclear warheads dropped on *each city* would, on average, be equivalent in explosive power to more than five times the total explosive power of all the bombs dropped by the allies throughout the Second World War.

In a nuclear world war the bulk of the urban population in the northern hemisphere would be killed instantly by blast alone. Most of the survivors and the bulk of the rural population would soon die from the effects of the radiation from radioactive fall-out. And so would millions in the southern hemisphere.

The after-effects of a nuclear world war are unknown. There could be dramatic changes in the global climate. The ozone layer in the stratosphere which protects life on earth from excessive exposure to ultra-violet radiation could be severely reduced. And there could be severe long-term genetic effects from the exposure of survivors to radiation. The total consequences of these and other effects are simply not predictable. No scientist can show that Mankind would survive a nuclear world war in which all, or a significant fraction, of the weapons in the nuclear arsenals were used.

Given the characteristics of currently-deployed strategic nuclear weapons, the concept of a strategic balance at such enormous levels of destruction has little use, at least militarily or strategically. The concept loses its meaning once the nuclear arsenals are significantly larger than the minimum size required for nuclear deterrence. A single United States Poseidon strategic nuclear submarine carries enough nuclear warheads to destroy every Soviet city with a population of more than 150,000. The United States Navy has 31 such submarines. Surely the United States (and the Soviet Union) could reduce its strategic nuclear submarine fleet by, say, one-half without any meaningful effect on its current military strength or deterrent posture, and scrap its ICBM force and strategic bombers. What is the point of being able to destroy the enemy society more than once? What is the point of dropping nuclear warheads on a land which has already been reduced to a radioactive desert?

The argument usually made by political leaders for worrying about the "strategic balance," whatever this is perceived to mean, even when the destructive power of nuclear forces has long surpassed any rational level is the potential effect of "nuclear inferiority" on one's allies. If the Soviets are perceived to have a nuclear force significantly stronger in some respect than the Americans, the argument goes, then the West Germans, for example, may become so concerned as to succumb to Soviet pressures. "Finlandisation" is the term most frequently used in this context.

But the real explanation for the size of nuclear arsenals is probably related to such factors as interservice rivalry, political compromises between the demands of doves and hawks, local pressures for maintaining defence industries. In other words, the size of the nuclear arsenals is not determined by such considerations as a rational assessment of external threats, or of the number of nuclear weapons required for nuclear deterrence or to prevent nuclear blackmail.

The nuclear arms race between the United States and the Soviet Union has moved from a race for quantity to one for quality. The new emphasis threatens world security much more than the old. Qualitative improvements in nuclear weapons come about mainly through the sheer momentum of military technology, fuelled by military research and development. For the past 30 years or so an enormous effort has been put into military research and development. Currently about $30,000 million is spent annually on this activity, significantly more than is spent on peaceful research. And military research and development employs more than one-half of the world's research physical and engineering scientists. An effort of this magnitude cannot help but produce spectacular results. To take just one example. Since the Second World War nuclear warheads have developed from the Hiroshima atomic bomb, which weighed about 4,000 kg. and had an explosive yield equivalent to that of about 12,500 tons of TNT, to today's United States Minuteman III MIRVed warhead, which weighs about a mere 100 kg. and has an explosive yield of about 200,000 tons of TNT.

Once military technology makes a weapon available, strong pressures build up for its development and deployment. In this way, almost all conceivable technological advances are used for military purposes. Military technology has now reached the stage at which weapons are being developed with characteristics suitable for fighting, rather than deterring, a nuclear war. Apart from the offensive strategic nuclear weapons with the characteristics which are described above, research is underway in ballistic missile defence systems, and in anti-satellite and anti-submarine warfare techniques. A breakthrough in these areas, which is probably only a matter of time given the effort being devoted to them, would significantly increase the probability of a nuclear war.

Unless military technology is brought under control, the day will almost certainly come when political and military leaders perceive a chance of making a successful first-strike. To be perceived as successful, a first-strike need not result in the total destruction of the other side's retaliatory forces. One side may perceive that it can destroy enough of the enemy's forces to limit the death and destruction it suffers in a retaliatory strike to a level considered "acceptable" for a given political goal. One side may, in fact, be tempted to make a first-strike just because it has developed and deployed weapons with first-strike capabilities. This could happen, perhaps in

Table 6

United States and Soviet Strategic Nuclear Forces, 1967–1979

	1967	1968	1969	1970	1971	1972	1973	1974	1975	1976	1977	1978	1979
Modern strategic nuclear submarines													
USA	41	41	41	41	41	41	41	41	41	41	41	41	41
USSR	—	—	8	14	21	27	34	41	46	52	57	62	64
ICBMs													
USA	1,054	1,054	1,054	1,054	1,054	1,054	1,054	1,054	1,054	1,054	1,054	1,054	1,054
USSR	720	900	1,177	1,487	1,527	1,527	1,547	1,567	1,587	1,547	1,447	1,400	1,398
SLBMs													
USA	656	656	656	656	656	656	656	656	656	656	656	656	656
USSR	27	59	152	248	360	459	567	651	711	791	867	947	979
MIRVed missiles													
USA	—	—	—	26	222	402	630	752	950	998	1,030	1,046	1,046
USSR	—	—	—	—	—	—	—	—	—	110	208	—	588
Total nuclear delivery systems (long-range bombers and missiles)													
USA	—	—	—	2,210	2,141	2,092	2,092	2,092	2,031	2,010	2,010	2,010	2,010
USSR	—	—	—	1,875	2,027	2,126	2,254	2,358	2,438	2,478	2,454	2,487	2,517

[1] Operational.
Source: SIPRI data.

spite of the political leadership's reluctance to trigger off a nuclear war, in order to prevent the other side from eventually getting a similar capability.

We have recently seen a growing tendency to move from nuclear deterrent strategies based on counter-city weapons to counter-force strategies based on accurate nuclear warheads. Interest in civil defence and the protection of heavy industry from nuclear attack is intensifying. These are just the moves to be expected as the super-Powers develop and deploy nuclear weapons with war-fighting capabilities. The sooner it is realised that the probability of a nuclear world war is increasing irrespective of such out-moded concepts as a "strategic balance," the better.

VALÉRY GISCARD D'ESTAING

By

B. J. CRIDDLE

VALÉRY GISCARD d'Estaing, advocate of an "advanced liberal society" and a "confederal Europe" was elected third president of the French Fifth Republic in May, 1974. He succeeded to executive power with certain generally formulated objectives and a reputation for efficiency, brilliance and moderation. Unlike his two predecessors, however, his freedom to impose his policies in either domestic or foreign affairs was to be severely circumscribed by the lack of a reliable parliamentary base and by the worst economic recession since the Second World War. In consequence many expectations generated by the election of a "reformist," non-Gaullist president came virtually to nothing in the first five years of a seven-year term.

In 1976 Giscard wrote that "the taste for assuming responsibilities and the capacity for exercising them are not things we are born with: they are developed by education and apprenticeship; they atrophy when they are not used and when we let things slide."[1] It is certain that in his own quest for power Giscard let nothing slide: how far, however, his taste for power derived more from education than inheritance was less easy to determine since he had been amply endowed with both. Descended through his father, an *inspecteur des Finances*, from an eighteenth-century admiral guillotined during the Terror; and through his mother from a Bourbon monarch, a minister of the July monarchy, and a succession of Third and Fourth Republic conservative politicians—from one of whom he was to inherit a parliamentary seat—it is hard to see how Giscard could have avoided a career of public prominence. A schoolboy when France fell in 1940, he enlisted in a tank regiment at the Liberation, was decorated and proceeded with distinction through both the École National d'Administration and the École Polytechnique, followed his father into *l'inspection des Finances*, and married a member of the industrially-powerful Schneider family. Thence into ministerial *cabinets*, notably that of Premier Edgar Faure in 1955, and into parliament the following year at the age of 29, as an *indépendant*. In 1959, having supported the recall of de Gaulle, he entered the Debré Government as junior minister at the Ministry of Finance, and in 1962 became at 36 the youngest Minister of Finance

---

[1] Giscard d'Estaing, *Démocratie française* (1976); English edition: *Towards a New Democracy* (1977), pp. 65–66.

since another conservative, Poincaré, in the 1890s. In 1962 he formed a small parliamentary group of *Républicains indépendants* who decided to continue support for de Gaulle and his Prime Minister, Pompidou, beyond the end of the Algerian war, and the introduction of universal suffrage for presidential elections. Thereafter the *Républicains indépendants* were a crucial *force d'appoint*—necessary (from 1962–68) to the Gaullists in providing the margin of votes needed for a majority in the National Assembly.

A seemingly inexorable rise was halted temporarily in 1966 when Giscard was sacked from the Finance Ministry, mainly in order to placate Gaullist ire after de Gaulle's less than convincing victory in the 1965 presidential election. During the following three years Giscard—out of office—concentrated on projecting a more distinct political personality; and the roots of the trouble after 1974 between Giscard and the Gaullists date from this period. The *Républicains indépendants* were transformed into a party with the intention of promoting Giscard's ambitions; the relationship with the Pompidou Government was defined by a conditional "oui, mais"; as chairman of the finance committee of the National Assembly Giscard criticised the budgets of his Gaullist successor, Debré; following de Gaulle's declaration in Canada—"Vive le Québec libre"—he attacked "the solitary exercise of power"; and, finally, in 1969 by refusing to support de Gaulle in the unsuccessful referendum on Senate and regional government reform contributed significantly to the general's defeat and premature retirement. Support for Pompidou in the 1969 presidential election ensured return to the Finance Ministry, and by the time Pompidou died five years later Giscard had presided for a total of nine years over what many observers were calling an "economic miracle," comprising annual growth rates of 6 per cent. and rapidly rising living standards. No other non-Gaullist politician of the Fifth Republic had for so long as important a ministerial function or established as great a reputation for unrivalled competence and success.

Victory in 1974, therefore, seemed almost a natural culmination to what had gone before, if assisted somewhat by Gaullist division and the failure to produce a credible alternative to Giscard from inside the government alliance. It was, as Giscard was keen to point out, the victory of a man rather than of a movement or a party ("Alone, without a party, I defeated the other parties combined"); an outsider who had deliberately avoided absorption into a Gaullist party he judged by its very nature to be a transient force. "For me," Giscard has said, "Gaullism was de Gaulle—and for de Gaulle, Gaullism was de Gaulle";[2] Gaullism without de Gaulle was as

---

[2] Interview on BBC television, May 25, 1977.

absurd as Bonapartism without Napoleon.[3] This view of Gaullism as merely an emergency or crisis-solving phenomenon, with appeal at a time of national demoralisation, implied, for Giscard, a strategy of *attentisme* and the preservation of a more traditional conservative pole towards which would move both Gaullist voters as the Gaullist power of attraction declined, and those voters of centre and right who had, with Giscard, resisted incorporation. What precisely it was to which the voters would be moving back—by what doctrines or programmes they would be attracted—has been disputed. Pompidou, for example, is said to have observed that the *Républicains indépendants* had "pratiquement pas d'hommes et encore moins d'idées,"[4] whilst to another Gaullist "le giscardisme est une ambition et non une pensée."[5] What Giscardism is—beyond being "an ambition"—is a modern representation of the Orleanist liberal tradition, the moderate right that "eschews demagogic and authoritarian dictatorship either of the masses or of a man; ... rooted in bourgeois values ...," favouring "order and stability; common sense rather than utopia; reproving adventure—interior or exterior; fundamentally opposed to extremism."[6] In the post-War context this right has been in competition with the Gaullist/ Bonapartist right—whose anti-parliamentary, plebiscitarian and charismatic inclinations are at odds with the more middle of the road conservation just described, and arguably are inappropriate to conditions in a "legal rational" polity other than as a crisis-resolving expedient. Giscardian conservatism, more moderate, less exciting, more run-of-the-mill, is on the other hand temperamentally equipped to be the conservatism of a stable policy. It has since the middle 1960s been identified by three adjectives: centrist, liberal and European.[7]

I—CENTRISM

Centrism is implied in the rejection of extremes. Following his celebrated injunction that "France must be governed from the centre," Giscard, in *Démocratie française*, argued that the traditional ideologies of left and right—Marxism and traditional liberalism—no longer provide explanations that make possible the analysis

---

[3] O. Todd, *La marelle de Giscard* (1977), p. 385. For other interim biographies of V. Giscard d'Estaing see: F. Lancel, *Valéry Giscard d'Estaing* (1974); and A. Pautard, *Valéry Giscard d'Estaing* (1974). See also B. Lecomte and C. Sauvage, *Les Giscardiens* (1978).

[4] P. de Saint Robert, *Les septennats interrompus* (1977), p. 113.

[5] *Ibid*. p. 18. See also "Le giscardisme," *Pouvoirs*, Nr. 9, 1979.

[6] R. Rémond, *La droite en France* (1968), 2 Vols., p. 283.

[7] J.-C. Colliard, *Les républicains indépendants* (1972), pp. 314–319. See also on the period before 1974: P. Viansson-Ponté, *Après de Gaulle Qui?* (1968); M. Cotta, *La Vie république* (1974); M. Bassi and A. Campana, *Le grand tournoi: naissance de la Vie république* (1974).

of reality, and therefore provide no guide to action. Both ideologies are characterised as "a quasi-religious form of compensation at a time when faith in traditional religions has dwindled."[8] Marxism is rejected in terms expected of a conservative: its pseudo-scientific nature; its reduction of all history to class war, and its belief in the "redemptive" role of one particular class. Traditional liberalism, more interestingly, is praised but then blamed: praised for upholding political freedoms and engendering economic growth; but blamed for believing only in economic man and failing to meet "the desire for justice." Liberalism is also blamed for being insufficiently liberal in its encouragement of competition. From political theory Giscard proceeds to sociology and identifies a "large and expanding amorphous central group" in the electorate that rejects the confrontation between the classes (bourgeois and proletarian) expressive of the traditional ideologies. Extending from skilled workers and technicians to managerial categories this group is neither bourgeois in the proper sense—though it is sometimes described as the "advanced bourgeoisie"—nor proletarian in the sense of being culturally and socially isolated. It is seen by Giscard as the "sociological centre," and upon this extending raft of voters—growing with the expansion of the tertiary sector of the economy—he seeks to establish an electoral base, an unlikely objective for a man seen by many left-wing politicians as the incarnation of the French bourgeoisie. To such observers Giscard in seeking to occupy this "centre" ground is no more than making a virtue of necessity.[9] The electorate of the Gaullist-conservative coalition has been shrinking for the past 10 years: it now reflects a disproportionately heavy reliance upon the support of certain socio-economic groups, notably the peasantry and petite bourgeoisie, that are themselves in steep decline, and a lack of penetration of the expanding middle managerial and white-collar groups,[10] only two in five of whose voters supported Giscard in 1974 and the government parties in the 1978 general election. In 1969 Pompidou won the presidency with 58 per cent. of the vote; but in 1974 Giscard was reduced to a mere 51 per cent. and that despite the incorporation in his alliance of all small centre parties previously maintaining a pretence of independence. The bipolarisation of opinion—encouraged by presidentialism and electoral laws—has cut France neatly in two, with much of the dynamic "centre" in which Giscard is interested gravitating towards the moderate (socialist) part of a left alliance, which until the

---

[8] Giscard d'Estaing, *op. cit.* in note 1, above, p. 31.

[9] See J.-P. Chevènement, "Perspective et realité du Giscardisme," *Le Monde* May 13, 1978.

[10] See H. R. Penniman (ed.), *France at the Polls: the Presidential Election of 1974* (1974); and Louis Harris poll, *L'Express*, March 13, 1978.

Communists decided on a less collaborative strategy in 1977 had established great credibility. It is in order to angle for the support of those new socialist voters that the second Giscardian theme—liberalism—is invoked.

II—LIBERALISM

Liberalism is a two-edged sword: political liberalism, implying "reform" and "social justice," and economic liberalism, implying free play of market forces, are potentially in conflict. As if aware of this Giscard once said that he was "a liberal, but not liberal in the sense that economists mean 'liberal': for me to be liberal is to be in favour of a political, economic and social evolution founded principally on the transfer to individuals, either singly or in groups, of responsibilities for decision-making, behaviour and choice."[11] By this definition Giscardian liberalism is another word for pluralism, a very strong theme in his book, where he argues for a decentralisation and distribution of power in politics, administration, the media, and also in economic life, where competition is preferred to State or private monopoly; where the State's role is not to nationalise but to intervene to establish and maintain competition; and where vigorous trade unions and consumer organisations exist as "counterweights" to company power.[12] The problems with doing more than talk about this vision are twofold: first, there is the absence of a liberal tradition in a country with a reputation for *dirigisme* and the belief that "pluralism" is an essentially non-gallic idea. Giscard himself has acknowledged that the thought of the liberal de Tocqueville, for which he has great respect, has always been isolated in France. Secondly, there is the possibility that the one sort of liberalism (political) will be negated by the impact of the other (economic).[13]

Giscardian political liberalism has taken two forms: institutional reform and innovation in social policy. On the institutional side, Giscard's goal is a "pluralist democracy," where there exists a "reasonable cohabitation" between government and opposition; where rivalry is "not a war but merely a competition," and where the competition is not "unnecessarily dramatic"; where the institutional structures themselves are not part of the political debate; and where governing responsibilities are entrusted now to one party, now to another—this form of alternation being in the nature of

---

[11] Todd, *op. cit.* in note 3, above, p. 433.
[12] Giscard d'Estaing, *op. cit.* in note 1, above, pp. 81–90.
[13] See P. de Saint Robert, *op. cit.* in note 4, above, pp. 166–168.

advanced democratic societies.[14] Whilst acknowledging that this Anglo-Saxon or North European model of an harmonious polity fits uneasily a country "where political life has always been heightened by Mediterranean passion and a Latin liking for absolutes,"[15] Giscard has nonetheless sought "reasonable cohabitation." Presidential grandeur has been reduced: relations with the Press made less formal; censorship of Press comments on the President relaxed; invitations for talks at the Elysée Palace have been issued to Opposition leaders (and, in 1978, accepted); presidential patronage has been extended to prominent members of the non-communist left (notably to a left-Radical, appointed to head a study into unemployment). But all significant reforms requiring the parliamentary approval of the Gaullists who comprised before the 1978 elections 60 per cent. of the government's parliamentary support, and still more than half after the elections, have either been rejected—*viz.* attempts to give the Constitutional Council the power of judicial review, and to reduce the presidential term from seven to five years; or opposed—*viz.* the introduction of finance for political parties and a return to a system of proportional representation in local elections. Moreover, the only significant move accomplished towards the liberal goal of decentralisation—the revival of the office of Mayor of Paris—rebounded on the President when his own candidate for the post was defeated by the Gaullist, Jacques Chirac.

In social reform, as in institutional reform, performance lags well behind promise. The solid achievements: votes at 18; a minister for women; easier access to divorce, abortion and contraception, are all reforms of a sort that involve little more than a synchronisation of the law with changed moral attitudes (a process taking place in most West European countries), though they are reforms that tamper seriously with the taboos of Giscard's ageing bourgeois electorate, and were indeed diluted by parliamentary pressure. Other celebrated initiatives for creating greater social justice and "the abolition of privileges,"[16] announced with much publicity by Giscard, included capital gains tax; increased profits tax; higher income tax on upper income groups; restrictions on property development as well as the more usual measures to help lower income groups—improved severance pay, higher pensions, *etc.* Taken at face value, these reforms suggest that the old adage about socialists campaigning on the left and governing on the right had been reversed. More sceptically it was suggested that the reforms were cosmetic attempts to hide the harsh reality of the government's

---

[14] Giscard d'Estaing, *op. cit.* in note 1, above, p. 133.
[15] *Ibid.* p. 134.
[16] Giscard d'Estaing, *Le Figaro*, May 21, 1975.

draconian Fourcade and Barre "stabilisation" plans. These were intended to put the balance of payments in the black, stabilise the value of the franc and curb inflation; and with an electoral victory behind it in 1978 the Barre Government administered a very stiff dose of economic liberalism by freeing industrial prices from an elaborate web of controls built up since the war, and removing public sector subsidies. Barre's reassurance that this was less economic liberalism than the putting of "a few pike among the carp to prevent the latter from getting a muddy taste" could not conceal the fact that there was something contradictory or maybe Machiavellian in a situation where the President spoke publicly of "reforms" whilst his Prime Minister turned the inflationary screw. Of reforms one commentator has suggested that "one by one the great changes so noisily announced, so bitterly debated that many are those who think they were passed, have been adjourned, cancelled, abandoned."[17] Certainly this is true of all attempted reforms that hit at the pockets of Giscard's own constituency, where dilution, if not complete abandonment, of reforms was the rule.

The Giscardian quest for a centrist reputation via liberal reforms foundered on the very traditionalism of, first, a parliamentary majority elected to support the Gaullist Pompidou in 1973, and then, after 1978 one that still had too many Gaullists in it. Since 1974 Giscard has sought to counter the weight of the Gaullists in his alliance, first by trying to coalesce the small parties loyal to him (Radicals, Social Democratic Centrists and his own—since 1977—Republican party), an objective partially obtained when the parties came together to fight the 1978 elections; secondly, by denying the Gaullists patronage, and thus destroying part of their *raison d'être*. He kept a Gaullist prime minister, in an attempt to colonise the party between 1974 and 1976, but reduced Gaullist representation in Cabinet to a few, mostly second-rank ministries, occupied by second-rank Gaullists, and imposed in 1976 a non-Gaullist premier. The consequence of all this is, compared with the late 1960s, an ironic reversal of roles, with the President on the sharp end of a Gaullist *"oui, mais."* The parliamentary liberal Giscard who believes that "it is in the nature of our institutions that the government should persuade parliament that its plans are sound and strive to obtain parliament's approval for them,"[18] has found himself echoing the testy remark made by de Gaulle in 1968 ("A government does not negotiate; it gives orders") when confronted by a Gaullist parliamentary rebellion in April 1977: "It is not," he

---

[17] P. Viansson Ponté, *Le Monde*, January 1, 1976. See also H. Madelin, "Le libéralisme de Giscard," *Projet*, December 1975, pp. 1157–1170.

[18] Giscard d'Estaing, *op. cit.* in note 1, above, p. 132.

said, "the National Assembly that governs France; that is the difference between the Fourth and Fifth Republics." Whilst that is a statement of constitutional doctrine from which no Gaullist could dissent, there is among the Gaullists a deep visceral distrust of Giscardian liberalism, and of a "less independent" foreign policy; between the two "clans" there is the temperamental contrast of "French" Gaullism and—arguably—more "Anglo-Saxon" Giscardism; and on the Gaullists' side are the presidential ambitions of Jacques Chirac which can be served only by the undoing of Giscard.

There was also much disagreement on strategy before the 1978 elections, which all pollsters predicted the left would win. Giscard's strategy was, first, to strive for left-wing votes through his reform programme, and, secondly (when that failed), to refuse to threaten the constitutional and social crisis which the previous Gaullist presidents had said would be the consequence of a left victory. From mid-1976 onwards Giscard made clear he would not resign if the left won a majority in parliament. In Chirac's eyes this compounded one error with another. The first was the attempt vainly to appeal to left-wing voters with reforms that seemed only to antagonise the government's existing clientele. (The fact that de Gaulle, and the Gaullist Premier Chaban Delmas in the early 1970s, had followed much the same strategy was ignored by Chirac).[19] The second was Giscard's implication that he would remain as president with a government acceptable to parliament, *i.e.* a left-wing one. Here loomed for Gaullists the spectre of, at least, a brokerage-role-playing president of the Fourth Republic sort, and at worst the prospect of Giscard achieving out of existing political divisions a parliamentary alliance consisting of his own supporters and the socialists—a conjunction of centre-right and centre-left, "governing France from the centre," with the Gaullists left stranded in opposition. To counter these possibilities the Chiracian confrontational strategy was to ensure a government victory in 1978 by polarising the fight into Left and Right to firm up the government's electorate and to tar the Left opposition with the Communist, collectivist brush.

The clash between the rival right-wing clans is not taken seriously by everyone. The Communist leader Marchais, for example, sees it as a mere prefabricated electoral ruse.[20] To gather as broad an electorate as possible in order to save its power the bourgeoisie presents two faces—one liberal, the other authoritarian and populist. It even runs these rival candidates against each other in the first round of elections (in 1978 in all but a few constituencies) on the

---

[19] On electoral strategies see M. Bassi and A. Campana, *op. cit.* in note 7, above, p. 58.
[20] G. Marchais, *Le Monde*, January 26, 1977.

assumption that two rods catch more fish than one, and thus facilitate victory for either clan's candidate at the second round confrontation between united right and united left. To some extent in support of the Communist view that Giscardian-Gaullist rivalry is no more than the rivalry of *blanc bonnet* and *bonnet blanc* are the electoral data that reveal a virtually exact correspondence—in socio-economic composition—between Giscardian and Gaullist electorates.[21] On the other hand it does seem prudent to consider the opinion of other Marxist observers[22] who acknowledge the Giscard-Chirac conflict as being the reflection of strains between the modern or "advanced" and the "traditional" sections of the bourgeoisie; where tensions are unleashed if the interests of the former in liberalised morals, deaccentuated nationalism and greater social justice are preferred to those of the conservatism of the traditionalist elements. A president who seeks to appeal to this broad constituency by saying, as Giscard did in July 1974, that he was "a traditionalist who likes change," is likely, given an economic crisis that precludes the intended appeal to the new strata, and correspondingly accentuates the dead-weight of the older system of alliances buttressing bourgeois power, to end up having to cohabit with a traditionalist electorate that resists the modernising thrust towards an "advanced liberal society."

III—EUROPE

If after five years in office little headway has been made towards centrist and liberal goals, what of the "European" objective? It has been suggested that if governing from the centre is unobtainable domestically in a system of bi-polarised politics, how much more possible is a foreign policy that seeks in a bi-polar international system to play off, when convenient, one super-Power against another.[23] With variations this has been the traditional foreign policy since the war; and the vehicle with which the anti-super Power, or anti-bloc, preoccupation has been expressed has been in one form or another "Europe."[24] In the 1940s it was through European organisations that economic recovery and West German integration was to be assured and German reunification prevented; in the 1960s it was through the Europe of the Six that French dominance was to be exercised, an international role for France

---

[21] Louis Harris poll, *L'Express, loc. cit.* in note 10, above.

[22] J.-P. Chevènement, *op. cit.* in note 9, above; and R. Debray, *New York Times*, May 24, 1975.

[23] A. Fontaine, *Le Monde*, December 31, 1975.

[24] See E. Weisenfeld, "Les grandes lignes de la politique étrangère de la France," *Politique Etrangère* (1975), pp. 5–18.

established and French agriculture given vast subsidies and assured markets; in the 1970s it is through the trading links of the Community that further French industrial growth is to be achieved and recovery from economic recession sought.

Giscard came to office with a much vaunted reputation for favouring a "confederal Europe" and an inclination revealed in his early presidential declarations to emphasise interdependence and conciliation in foreign policy. Of four characteristics identified by him as defining French foreign policy the first was understandably "sovereignty" in decision making. The other three all implied a collaborative pragmatic approach: first, that problems being world problems required worldwide solutions; secondly, that concerted action must have precedence over confrontation; and thirdly, that since France wants a liberal domestic policy she must also have a "liberal external policy and image."[25] Whilst this definition might imply no more than a traditional pragmatic mix of independence and interdependence in accordance with calculations of French national self-interest,[26] it was Giscard's first prime minister, Chirac, who announced in 1974 that French foreign policy was to be "liberal, European and courteous," and Giscard himself who added in 1976 that "to assert its independence France does not have to be cantankerous."[27] At the same time Giscard could not fail to take account of a contrary sentiment voiced by Pompidou's last foreign minister, Michel Jobert: "Woe the day when foreign Powers can rejoice that France has become amiable again." In foreign policy—more than in domestic affairs where the disagreements between Giscard and the Gaullists are less severe—the President, despite the absence of legislative constraints on foreign policy, has had to take account of Gaullist prejudices, the more so once Chirac cut loose in 1976 and proceeded to cast around for sticks with which to beleaguer the Giscard presidency, and to promote his own ambitions.

It is a hallmark of the sort of polity Giscard wishes France were not, that foreign policy is politicised and possesses significance for internal political alignments. During the Fourth Republic for example there could be no alliance of parties of the left as long as fundamental disagreements existed over foreign policy; and, since the passing of the broad consensus that formed around de Gaulle's chauvinistic and ambiguous foreign policy, it is—on right as well as left—to their conflicting foreign policy attitudes that ostensibly

---

[25] Text of presidential press meeting, October 24, 1974; French Embassy, London.

[26] See S. Serfaty, "The Fifth Republic under Giscard d'Estaing: steadfast or changing," *The World Today*, March 1976, p. 98.

[27] Giscard d'Estaing, *op. cit.* in note 1, above, p. 142.

allied parties turn when seeking ammunition for the war of supremacy taking place inside each alliance. Giscard moreover, being by
experience first an economist, and only second a diplomatist, in
contrast to de Gaulle is more inclined to see external policy as being
at the service of domestic political objectives. Thus if French industrial modernisation and growth are the major goals then the foreign
policy has to be one that, to cite one example, assures for a country
lacking indigenous raw materials imported energy supplies.
Furthermore there is no doubt that one way to reach the kind of
centrist conjunction in domestic politics favoured by Giscard is to
play on those issues of foreign policy where centre left (socialist) and
centre right (Giscardian) opinion tends somewhat to converge—on
defence; the EEC; the Atlantic alliance, *etc*. Failing attainment of
this maximalist objective, focus on certain foreign policy
issues—such as direct elections to the European Assembly—might
serve at least to split moderate from chauvinistic Gaullists and thus
contribute to the decline of Chirac's party.

It is, however, important to distinguish between the character of
Gaullist foreign policy in the general's heyday (the partial withdrawal from NATO; the Phnom Penh speech; the provocative
encouragement to French Canadian separatism) and that of the
final period, after the internal and external crises of 1968 which
required de Gaulle to revise his foreign policy whilst preserving part
of the vocabulary which had popularised it.[28] Shorn of its largely
verbal excesses Gaullist foreign policy thereafter represented little
more than a legitimate concern for safeguarding French interests,
with there being three areas only in which scope was provided for
independent action: Europe; relations with the Third World—especially francophone Africa and the Arab States; and relations with
the United States.[29] Under Giscard these have continued to comprise the essential preoccupations of French foreign policy, with—in
the light of the oil crisis—the paramount concern being to cover all
deficits in foreign trade.[30]

Some of Giscard's actions have however been seen as positively
Gaullian in a more traditional sense. In May 1977 he refused to
attend a heads of government summit dinner to which the President
of the European Commission was invited—an action suggesting a
preference for a *Europe des états*. In November 1977 there was the

[28] G. de Carmoy, "The Last Year of de Gaulle's Foreign Policy," 45 *International Affairs*, Nr. 3, July 1969, p. 433.
[29] See D. Pickles, "The Decline of Gaullist Foreign Policy," 51 *International Affairs*, Nr. 2, April 1975, pp. 220–235.
[30] See M.-C. Smouts, "French Foreign Policy: the Domestic Debate," 53 *International Affairs*, Nr. 1, January 1977, pp. 36–50.

lavish welcome accorded to Québec premier René Levesque, and Giscard's remark that the Québecois "are a people and they naturally want their quality and prerogatives to be recognised"; Trudeau when asking what this implied was told that French policy was one of "non-indifference and non-interference." In September 1978 the decision was announced to start manufacture of a sixth atomic submarine despite previous warning from the (Gaullist) defence minister about potential obsolescence. In 1977 and 1978 there was a good deal of French military intervention in Africa, most importantly in the Shaba province of Zaire, of which action Giscard observed: "very often the wish is expressed that we should have an independent policy. Here is one." And there has also been contact via the foreign minister with the Palestine Liberation Organisation (PLO) leader Arafat in 1974 and the controversial release of the Arab terrorist Abu Daoud in January 1977.

These instances of latter-day Gaullism are to be explained in two ways: first, they were placatory. Whilst Gaullism in government before 1974 was pragmatic and of necessity less chauvinistic, Gaullism after 1974, and especially after 1976, denied any significant governmental responsibilities, reverted to a baser type. With the need to ensure parliamentary support for his programme, and with the degree of doubt existing before the March 1978 elections about the chances of the government beating the left alliance, the contribution made by foreign policy in promoting harmonious relations between Giscardians and Gaullists was more important than the more radical and risky ideas either of breaking the unity of the Gaullist party in order to "giscardise" the coalition or of pursuing a new majority including socialists. Secondly, and of more fundamental importance, assertions of "independence" in foreign policy reflect a single-minded pursuit of French trading interests.

The pro-Arab policy underlines France's extreme vulnerability to oil-blackmail through chronic dependence on imported energy supplies, which in the 1960s provided a cheap fuelling of industrial growth. Moreover, the extent of dependence on energy and raw material imports and the lack of monetary resources are such that a serious trade deficit would exist were it not for the lucrative arms trade France has with the Third World—by 1973 accounting for as much as a quarter of her exported capital goods trade,[31] and making her after the Soviet Union and the United States the world's third biggest arms supplier. French military involvement in Africa—as arms supplier, military adviser and as active participant in civil wars in a number of States—reflects the vast commercial interests that are at stake. Giscard has understandably sought to share the burden

---

[31] D. Pickles, *loc. cit.* in note 29, above, p. 227.

by proposing in 1978 an equivalent of a Marshall Aid plan (with a 40 per cent. United States contribution) and an African intervention force backed by Western support to ensure stability, to guarantee the Northern industrial world the Southern world's raw materials (the "North-South dialogue"), and to hold back Soviet penetration at a time when the United States seeks, after Vietnam, to avoid major commitments. It is certainly not correct to see French over-involvement in Africa as a Gaullist spasm; indeed Gaullist politi-cians have criticised the lack of independence in the policy reflected in Giscard's call for the United States to provide help in Zaire, and made the unjustified suggestion that Giscard was acting as a proxy for the Americans in Africa. As far as Franco-American relations are concerned they have tended to centre largely on economic questions: trade barriers; the unstable dollar and fears for its effect on oil prices; the United States attempt to prevent French sales of nuclear energy plants in the Third World; Concorde landing rights. In July 1977, in a Gaullist-sounding interview in *Newsweek*, Giscard criticised Carter for endangering détente with the Soviet Union by his preoccupation with human rights, but in effect relations with an American administration uncharacteristically reticent about its world role, have been relaxed to a degree worrying to Gaullists who see Giscard as an "Atlanticist"[32] in the process of stealthily recom-mitting French defence forces to NATO's integrated command, and accepting the 1976 Jamaica Agreement on dollar supremacy in the international monetary system.

The priorities in Giscard's foreign policy have been reflected in the choice of the three foreign ministers (all civil servants) since 1974, two of whom have been European experts and the other a Third World specialist. The latter, de Guiringaud (1976–78), con-centrated on strengthening French economic links with the Third World, the southern part of the North-South dialogue initiated by Giscard. The appointment of the two "European" ministers, Sauvagnargues (1974–76) and Francois-Poncet (1978–   ), equally reflected a preoccupation with economics: more European collab-oration in order to boost trade within the Community and between it and the Third World. The appointment as prime minister of Raymond Barre, economist, ex-EEC commissioner and ex-trade minister, served also to underline the priorities. Giscard's commit-ment to European collaboration is longstanding but pragmatic. The European label was adopted in the 1960s in part to express a rejection of the worst excesses of Gaullist chauvinism, to highlight

---

[32] See M.-C. Smouts, "Du Gaullisme au néo-atlantisme: les incertitudes françaises," in A. Grosser (ed.), *Les politiques extérieures européennes* (1976), pp. 87–113.

Giscardian identity, and to seek the support of three million centrist electors who had in 1965 voted for the pro-European presidential candidate, Lecanuet. The "confederal" Europe envisaged is very much a *Europe des états*. In 1974, as chairman of the Community's Council of Ministers, Giscard proposed the establishment of a "European Council" where heads of government would meet periodically to review the progress of the Community; encouraged regular bilateral inter-governmental meetings; and unsuccessfully suggested a European directorate of the four largest EEC States.

It was from bilateral summitry of the type favoured by Giscard that the Schmidt-Giscard proposals for a European monetary system emerged in 1978, with the intention of linking European currencies together so that the EEC might as a bloc attack the inflation problem and help create stable conditions for the growth of world trade. In an elegant discourse on the state of the world economy in July 1978, identifying seven poles of economic activity—four in the industrialised north (North America, Europe, the Soviet bloc and Japan) and three in the south (the oil producers, the non-oil producers and the industrialising)—Giscard argued that of the northern blocs, Europe was the only one with internal monetary instability despite the fact that the greater part of its foreign trade was conducted within the bloc. Monetary stability, he believed, would protect half the bloc's trade from currency fluctuation and create additional incentives for expansion.[33] Whilst the linking of a relatively weak currency like the franc with the Deutschemark carried risks for France, Giscard was hopeful that the system would help stimulate the economy of Western Germany (France's largest single export market), force the French economy to compete, lead to a stable franc and help to impose wage and price discipline on industry and trade unions in France. Giscard's particular ambition for France as declared in late 1978, was to overtake Western Germany in economic development by the last decade of the century. It would not be good, in his opinion, for Europe to be dominated by one great economic Power, but for there to be two countries of comparable influence: Western Germany and France.[34] Europe as a Franco-German condominium, if not as a theatre for French dominance, appeared to be the nature of Giscard's "confederal Europe": *plus ça change*.

IV—Prospects

Just as in domestic affairs Giscard has had perforce to govern less from the centre than from the right, and to implement legislation

---

[33] *Le Monde*, July 13, 1978.
[34] *Le Monde*, October 18, 1978.

less "liberal" than he would have wished, so in foreign policy he has not unexpectedly—by the nature of French interests and in quest of his goal of French economic success—employed unilateral action outside the European arena and concentrated upon inter-governmental action within it. What is different is an absence of the expression of anti-Community prejudices. Before Chirac left the premiership in 1976 much the same was true of the Gaullist leadership. In December 1975, as Prime Minister Chirac said, of direct election of the European Assembly, that "cette élection est un élément de la nécessaire construction européenne."[35] After leaving office and refashioning the Gaullist party as an instrument of his own ambition, however, the European election issue was drummed up into a Gaullist *cause célèbre*: the Community became "un con-glomérat où se diluerait la force française" and the French proponents of direct election "le parti de l'étranger."[36] The process of parliamentary ratification of the European elections bill was made difficult by Chirac and ultimately only secured, as constitutionally it could be, without a vote.[37] It was on this issue that foreign and domestic politics appeared to converge. Denied by Gaullist recalcitrance a secure parliamentary majority, Giscard's European policy was encouraging domestic realignment of centre against extremes. Opposition to the European elections came from Gaullist and Communist parties and support from Giscardian and Socialist parties, though a good deal of influential Gaullist opinion was favourable and a significant section of the Socialist party hostile.

Broadly speaking, however, Giscard's elusive centre appeared in prospect as a strange alliance of Gaullists and Communists which took up, for want of something better, an ultra-nationalist cause in order to stave off the threatened decline of their two parties. Moreover, the proportional representation electoral system adopted for the European elections in 1979 was one which would do away with the necessity for alliances of left and right, and instead allow the measurement of support of each of the four political currents. Proportional representation, were it to be extended to French general elections, would—given the strains within left and right—unfreeze the blocs and produce a politically-fragmented par-

[35] *Le Monde*, December 12, 1975.
[36] Chirac in *Le Monde*, August 19, 1978 and December 8, 1978.
[37] On the debate about elections to the European Assembly see: R. Chiroux, "Les partis politiques et l'élection du Parlement européen," 80 *Revue politique et parlementaire*, Nr. 876, Sept.-Oct. 1978, pp. 28–45; M. Leigh, "Giscard and the European Community," 33 *The World Today*, Nr. 2, February 1977, pp. 73–79; J. C. Hollick, "Direct elections to the European Parliament: the French Debate," 33 *The World Today*, Nr. 12, December 1977, pp. 472–480; H. Madelin, "Elections européennes, les habiletés du giscardisme." *Projet*, Nr. 114, 1977, pp. 459–466.

liament through which the President would "divide and rule." It would also, however, in all probability, by freeing Communist and ultra-Gaullist forces from the constraints imposed upon them by electoral alliances with more moderate parties, exacerbate centrifugal forces. Centre-placed governments imply excluded extremes, and the moderate, reformist, unchauvinistic democracy imagined by Giscard is the more likely to proceed from a bi-polar system incorporating extremes than from a tri-polar one excluding them. It is also more likely to proceed from a successful economy that facilitates the removal of social injustice without the confiscation of privileges. To the extent that a reformist image has facilitated popular acceptance of sacrifices on behalf of an economic growth, to be attained in part by inter-governmental collaboration, Giscard has not been entirely unsuccessful, but there remains real doubt that "Anglo-Saxon" political attitudes and practices of the sort respected by the President can be made to stick, in the precise way he seeks to make them stick, as long as significant elements at élite level (the present Gaullist leadership) and the Communist party are unprepared to endorse them.

Towards the end of his book Giscard writes of the need for society to find "the energy to improve what must be improved, the maturity to debate essential questions, the patience to put reforms in hand and the perseverance to complete them. We need a lion's strength and a fox's patience."[38] De Gaulle had both; Pompidou certainly in his best years had the latter; whether Giscard is a sufficiently adept Machiavellian man of action remains to be seen.

---

[38] Giscard d'Estaing, *op. cit.* in note 1, above, pp. 147–148.

FOREIGN INTERVENTION IN AFRICA (I)

By

COLIN LEGUM

DEVELOPMENTS since 1975 have made it clear that Africa has become an important testing ground for the foreign policies of the Western Powers, China, the Soviet bloc and Cuba. The continent's leaders, for the first time, seriously faced up to challenge of foreign intervention in their affairs at the Heads of State summit of the Organisation of African Unity (OAU) held in Khartoum in July, 1978.[1]

The debate at the Khartoum summit was remarkably different from similar Pan-Africanist meetings just 20 years earlier: then Ghana was leading black Africa into its decade of independence, and the mint-fresh leaders were setting themselves two foreign-policy objectives—to stay out of the conflicts between the major Powers, and to prevent any future foreign interference in their continent's affairs. These aspirations found expression in the concept of nonalignment, and in the slogan "Hands off Africa."

I—AFRICAN PERCEPTIONS OF FOREIGN INTERVENTION

The Khartoum summit showed that the continent's leaders were no longer as confident of their ability to stop all foreign meddling in their affairs as they had been in the 1960s; nor was there any longer even a consensus about whether or not all forms of external intervention were undesirable. The main disagreements at Khartoum were over what constituted acceptable or unacceptable external intervention, and over which of the foreign Powers were responsible for the threats to the continent's stability. Three distinctly different attitudes were expressed at the summit. One minority attitude (representing perhaps eight of the OAU's 49 member-States)[2] strongly endorsed the role of the Soviet bloc and Cuba in all the current conflicts in the continent. A second minority attitude (representing about a dozen of the member States)[3] condemned all forms of

---

[1] For a fuller discussion of the Khartoum summit of the Organisation of African Unity and for the resolutions adopted see Z. Cervenka and C. Legum, "The OAU's Year in Africa," XI, *Africa Contemporary Record* (1978–79).

[2] The OAU member States which fall into this category are Angola, Mozambique, Ethiopia, Guinea-Bissau, Cape Verde, Sao Tome and Principe, Benin and Congo People's Republic. However, both Angola and Mozambique also endorsed Western involvement through the initiatives they took in Rhodesia and Namibia.

[3] The leading members in this group are Egypt, Morocco, Sudan, Ivory Coast, Senegal, Zaire, Togo, Liberia, Tunisia, Somalia.

Soviet/Cuban intervention and favoured greater Western involvement in opposition to the policies of Moscow and Havana. A third attitude (representing the majority of OAU members) remained true to the principles of nonalignment; but they qualified their opposition by endorsing foreign intervention in particular situations. This majority view—as expressed in a major policy statement made at the Khartoum summit by Nigeria's head of State, Lieutenant General Olusegun Obasanjo—is contained in the following key passages taken from his speech:

"In the context of foreign intervention in Africa, there are three parties involved. There are the Soviets and other socialist countries, the Western Powers and we, the Africans. If the interests of Africa are to be safe-guarded, there are certain considerations which each of the parties must constantly bear in mind. To the Soviets and their friends, I should like to say that having been invited to Africa in order to assist in the liberation struggle and the consolidation of national independence, they should not overstay their welcome. Africa is not about to throw off one colonial yoke for another. Rather, they should hasten the political, economic and military capability of their African friends to stand on their own."

"We recognise that African countries are unequal partners in an interdependent world community and we shall, therefore, continue to need external assistance of all kinds for many years to come. But in the effort to develop our economies and improve the quality of life of our peoples, we must be the prime determinants of our destiny. We, in Africa, need massive economic assistance to make up for the lost ground of the colonial era, not military hardware for self-destruction and sterile ideological slogans which have no relevance to our African society. The longer we continue to be spoon-fed by other Powers, the longer we delay our indigenous capacity to learn and improve from one level to another. The Soviets should, therefore, see it to be in their interest not to seek to perpetually maintain their presence in Africa, even after the purpose for which they were invited has been achieved. This way they run the risk of being dubbed a new imperial Power as indeed they are already being called, even by those with whom they have had long association. Let the Soviets and their collaborators heed this timely counsel."

"To the Western Powers I say that they should act in such a way that we are not led to believe they have different concepts of independence and sovereignty for Africa and for Europe. A new Berlin-type conference is not the appropriate response to the kind of issues thrown up by the recent unfortunate Kolwezi episode. Paratroop drops in the twentieth century are no more acceptable to us than the gunboats of the last century were to our ancestors. Convening conferences in Europe and America to decide the fate of Africa raises too many ugly spectres which should be best forgotten both in our, and in the Europeans', interests. The détente which the Western nations seek with the Soviets in Europe cannot be effective without extending it to include Africa as well. The Western nations' primary interest in Africa is our raw materials. But they should begin to see the market Africa offers to their manufactured goods as even more important since they can develop substitutes for raw materials, but not for markets. If they saw Africa primarily as a market rather than a source of raw materials, they would realise the importance of ensuring that they do not disturb our peace and stability."

"Conflicts and their effects cannot be contained within easily definable boundaries and it is in the interest of all concerned to avoid them, let alone initiate and encourage them. We totally reject as an instrument of neocolonialism any collective security scheme for Africa fashioned and teleguided from outside Africa for the economic, political or military interest of any super-Power bloc. It is an insult to the dignity and intellect of the African man."

"We African leaders must also realise that we cannot ask outside Powers to leave us alone while, in most cases, it is our own actions which provide them with the excuse to interfere with our affairs. We must begin to depart from the diplomatic habit of closing our eyes to what should be deprecated, simply because it is happening in an African country, or because it is being committed by a fellow African leader. We must have the courage to tell ourselves what is unjust and what is immoral, so that we can ensure amongst ourselves certain minimum levels of decent leadership and good government for our people; nothing that is morally wrong and grossly unjust can be politically right within any society and no less an African society. For as long as we neglect the true interest of the generality of our peoples, so long will other Powers find it easy to interfere in our internal affairs and divide our peoples. There is no better defence against external forces than the government which endeavours to carry the majority of the population along with it and treats its people fairly decently. We must not allow the East and the West to divide us and set us against ourselves under any guise."

Some of the major points contained in the Nigerian leader's speech were made even more sharply by Tanzania's President Julius Nyerere[4]: "We regret, even while we recognise its occasional necessity, that an African government should ask for military assistance from a non-African country when it is faced with an external threat

---

[4] Statement made in Dar es Salaam on June 8, 1978; for fuller text see *Africa Currents*, Nr. 12/13, 1978.

to its national integrity. We know that a response to such a request by any of the big Powers is determined by what that big Power sees as its own interest. We have been forced to recognise that most of the countries acknowledged as world Powers do not find it beneath their dignity to exacerbate existing and genuine African problems and conflicts when they believe they can benefit by doing so. We, in Tanzania, believe that African countries, separately and through the OAU, need to guard against such actions. But we need to guard Africa against being used by any other nation or group of nations. The danger to Africa does not come just from nations in the Eastern bloc. The West still considers Africa to be within its sphere of influence, and acts accordingly. Current developments show that the greater immediate danger to Africa's freedom comes from nations in that Western bloc. We reject the right of West European countries to dominate Africa, just as much as we would reject attempts by Eastern bloc countries to dominate Africa. In particular, we want it to be clear that Tanzania resents the arrogance and the contempt of those who purport to set up a Pan-African Security Force, or an African Peace Force, on behalf of Africa. Either Africa will do that for itself, or there will be no Pan-African Force defending the freedom of Africa, only something calling itself by some name which is an instrument for the renewed foreign domination of this continent."

General Obasanjo's strictures about the share of responsibility Africans must themselves shoulder for inviting foreign involvement was strongly reinforced by Guinea's President Sékou Touré in his address to the Khartoum summit: "We Africans are more responsible for our misfortunes than imperialism."

A totally different view from that of the Nigerian and Tanzanian leaders was expressed by Senegal's President Leopold Senghor, who reflects the views of a dozen or more African presidents belonging to what might loosely, but accurately, be described as an "anticommunist grouping." In an interview,[5] Senghor said: "The West is illogical. If it wants us to defend ourselves against the forces of external aggression, against the forces of international communism, it must give us the means to do so. Otherwise it can sit back and watch Africa fall to international communism. The West doesn't want that to happen, but it also doesn't want to spend money to aid us. What we're experiencing at present is the first phase of World War III—and the East has the edge on us because it has definite objectives and is prepared to commit very efficient, modern and expensive means towards attaining them."

---

[5] *Newsweek*, June 9, 1978.

A useful way of examining the role of foreign Powers in Africa is first to identify the major developments within the continent which have led to greater involvement by outside Powers pursuing their own national interests. The three situations which have most commonly resulted in increased foreign intervention are:

(a) *Inter-African disputes*. These have frequently led to governments wishing to strengthen their military, economic and diplomatic position enlisting the support of an appropriate foreign Power. Examples of these are: Somalia's alliance in the 1960s with the Soviet Union against Haile Selassie's Ethiopia, which introduced the Soviet factor into the Horn of Africa; the decision by Haile Selassie's successors to invite Soviet/Cuban support when faced with troubles at home and by aggressive neighbours on their borders; the decision of the MPLA to appeal for Soviet/Cuban military support to buttress its claims to being the legal government, and to consolidate its power in the Angolan struggle in 1975/76; Chad's enlistment of French military aid to resist the Libyan-supported rebellion by FROLINAT; Libya's decision to enter into a multi-billion-dollar arms agreement with the Soviet Union because of Colonel Gadhaffy's conflict with Egypt's President Sadat; President Seso Seko Mobutu's appeal for French, Belgian, American and Chinese aid to repel invasions into Zaire from across Angola's border. This list could easily be extended.

(b) *Armed liberation struggles in Southern Africa and the Horn of Africa*. Pitted against strong adversaries, the liberation movements have invariably sought foreign aid, mainly military, to assist them in their struggle. Virtually all foreign military aid for the anti-Portuguese liberation movements and for those in the rest of the sub-continent came from the Soviet bloc, Cuba, China and Yugoslavia. The support for the Eritrean liberation movements came largely from Arab States, but also from Cuba and, for a time, from the Soviets and China.

(c) *Insecurely-based, often unpopular, régimes struggle to maintain themselves in power*. They seek out one or more strong foreign allies willing to provide both military and economic support. Examples of this were General Idi Amin's régime in Uganda, which had then obtained Soviet and Arab support; President Mobutu Sese Seko's régime in Zaire which secured American, French, Belgian, Chinese and North Korean support; and a number of the francophone African States who have relied heavily on French aid.

II—THE CHANGING PATTERN OF FOREIGN INTERVENTION

The formal withdrawal of the Western colonial Powers (other than

Portugal) from the continent in the 1960s opened the way for the Soviets and Chinese to develop normal diplomatic and economic links with the new African States. This development had caused some early anxieties in Western (mainly conservative) circles about the danger of "communist penetration" of Africa. It is interesting to recall the almost hysterical Western reactions in 1961 to the first African visit by China's then Foreign Minister, Zhou Enlai, and especially to his statement in Mogadishu that "Africa is ripe for revolution." Today, it is the Soviets who are seriously concerned about Chinese policies in the continent.

After a relatively brief period, though, the Soviets' initial impact on Africa began to wane as they discovered that there were no easy pickings to be had in the immediate wake of the Western withdrawal, and as the new African leaders found that their Western connections often had more to offer than the communist world, and because of disillusioning experiences in their contacts with, especially, the Russians. The Soviets chose instead to concentrate their main efforts on Egypt as the fulcrum of their Middle Eastern strategy, while taking a much longer-term view of their opportunities in Africa. China's main interest was centred mainly in East Africa, where they developed a particularly close friendship with President Julius Nyerere's Tanzania. By the end of the 1960s Western anxieties about a possible "Soviet takeover" of Africa had lessened considerably and, by the early 1970s, it seemed as if Africa was to be allowed to stay out of the mainstream of international rivalries. Western commitments to, and interests in, the continent diminished to the point that it became the fashion of the day to dismiss as "Africa bores" those who continued to try and arouse interest in the problems which had remained unresolved at the time of the major Western Powers' withdrawal—*e.g.*, Portugal's continuing colonial rule, and the race policies of the white minority régimes in Southern Africa.

This picture changed dramatically in 1974 because of two historic events which occurred within a few months of each other. In February, 1974, units in the Ethiopian army began a mutiny in Negelle, a remote outpost of the empire, which spread so rapidly that it became known as the "Negelle fever"; it toppled the aged Emperor Haile Selassie from his throne, hastened the disintegration of the ancient empire, and upset the long-established balance of power in the Horn of Africa.

The second event was the army *coup* in Lisbon on April 24, 1974, when the Caetano régime was overthrown and over four centuries of Portuguese colonialism was brought to a close. Its major consequence was to change the power structure in Southern Africa.

Thus, two strategically important areas of the continent—both of which had served the interests of Western security for centuries—were suddenly (if not altogether unexpectedly) destabilised. Neither of these decisive changes was caused by Soviet or Chinese policies; nevertheless, the result was to throw the Western Powers on the defensive because they had lost their traditional friends and allies in both regions. The new situation favoured Soviet strategy.

South Africa's Prime Minister at the time, John Vorster, was the first to recognise the significance for the sub-continent of the collapse of Portuguese colonialism. In a famous speech to his parliament in October, 1974, he announced that South Africa had come "to an important crossroads" in its history. He embarked on a diplomatic initiative to try and establish a new relationship with black Africa, warning that "the alternative to peace in Southern Africa is too ghastly to contemplate." Although his efforts to reach some understanding between black Africa and South Africa looked reasonably promising at one stage, they finally foundered on the battlefields of Angola, after the South African army's intervention in August 1975 on the side of Jonas Savimbi's Union for the Total Independence of Angola (UNITA) and Holden Roberto's Front for the National Liberation of Angola (FNLA), against Dr. Agostinho Neto's Popular Movement for the Liberation of Angola (MPLA), which attracted the military and political backing of the Soviet bloc and Cuba.

The successful Soviet/Cuban military intervention in Angola was significant for a number of reasons. (1) It demonstrated the military thrust capacity which the Russians had developed, enabling them to intervene effectively in a conflict over 5,000 miles distant from their own territory. (2) It was the first time, since the start of the decolonisation process in Africa, that foreign troops were used on a massive scale as combatants to decide the outcome of an African conflict. Up to 20,000 Cuban troops were committed in Angola at the peak of the fighting. (3) It not only assisted a Marxist-Leninist régime to win power in Africa, but it left the new régime dependent on continuing Soviet/Cuban support to maintain itself in power.

This military intervention in Angola was justified by the Soviets and Cubans principally on the ground that the MPLA had requested their assistance to help repel the invasion of their country by the South African army. South Africa justified its intervention for the opposite reason: that they had been invited to send in their troops by UNITA and FNLA, as well as by certain unnamed African governments, to counter Soviet/Cuban military intervention. The chronology of the deployment in strength of the foreign military forces leaves no doubt that the Soviet/Cuban military role pre-dated that of the South Africans.[6] Nevertheless, it was the fact of South African military intervention which swung the balance of opinion within the OAU in favour of the communist intervention. Up to September 1975 a virtual consensus had prevailed within the OAU in support of a policy which, *inter alia*, opposed all foreign intervention in what was regarded as a purely African domestic affair.

The events in Angola forced the OAU to face up to the risk of massive foreign intervention in an African conflict. It found itself split exactly in half when a special summit of African Heads of State was called to discuss the issue in January 1976. Twenty-two African governments voted to endorse the role of the Soviets and Cubans in Angola, the great majority of them basing their decision purely on the ground of South Africa's military involvement. Their decision was clearly of major importance to the Soviet bloc in planning their next major act of military intervention—in the Horn of Africa—two years later.

One clear conclusion that can be drawn from the African reaction to the events in Angola is that when the OAU is faced with any situation involving South Africa on one side, and the Soviet bloc on the other, they will choose the latter. This conclusion is important in considering the circumstances under which foreign military intervention is likely to win a wide measure of African endorsement in the sub-continent. Since the OAU regards the white minority régimes—especially South Africa's—as their principal enemy in the continent, it is fairly certain that a majority of its member States would welcome foreign intervention from any quarter assisting those struggling against the South African and Rhodesian régimes. Indeed, the OAU has already asked foreign Powers to provide arms and other forms of assistance for the movements recognised by its African Liberation Committee (ALC). However, the OAU has so far carefully limited the request for military support only to the supply of weapons and training; it insists that all such aid should be channelled through the ALC. Only the Soviet bloc countries, China and Yugoslavia have, as yet, contributed arms for the Southern African liberation movements. A number of Western countries (notably the Scandinavians and, to a much lesser extent, the United Kingdom and the Netherlands) have contributed aid classified as being for "humanitarian purposes." The OAU has expressed its regret at the refusal by Western countries to support the armed struggle for two reasons: because it indicates a refusal by the West to accept the necessity of armed struggle as an *element* in the liberation

---

[6] For a discussion of the chronology of the arrival of Soviet/Cuban and South African forces see C, Legum and T. Hodges, *After Angola: A Study of International Intervention* (1976).

process; and because it makes the liberation movements completely dependent on Communist countries for their weapons.

Although the OAU actively discourages foreign Powers from using their support for the liberation movements as a means of promoting their rival interests, its efforts have been far from successful. Of the four major Communist centres—Moscow, Havana, Peking and Belgrade—only the latter two have complied with the OAU requirement that all their military aid should be channelled through the ALC. The Soviets and Cubans consign only a part of their arms through this channel; the rest is delivered directly to the liberation movements they favour. Furthermore, because sharp rivalries exist between liberation movements themselves (*e.g.*, the African National Congress and the Pan-Africanist Congress of South Africa, and the two wings of the Patriotic Front of Zimbabwe), they have increasingly oriented themselves towards either Moscow/ Havana or Peking. Thus, the element of foreign Power rivalries—especially, but not only, in the Communist world—has already been introduced into the Southern African liberation struggle.

As in Angola, the Soviets and Cubans succeeded in winning broad endorsement from black African States for their massive military intervention in the Horn of Africa. In this case they based their intervention on three separate grounds. First, that it was in response to a request from a sovereign government (the Ethiopian military régime). Secondly, that they went to the assistance of an independent African State to resist military aggression against its borders by a neighbouring State (Somalia) which—contrary to the OAU Charter—was seeking to alter the established borders by force. Thirdly, that they were helping to prevent the break-up of Ethiopia by opposing the secessionist ambitions of the Eritrean liberation forces; this, too, was represented as being consistent with the OAU Charter, which implicitly opposes all secessionist movements.

It is not my purpose here to rehearse the arguments over the legitimacy of the Somali/Ethiopia border, or over the Eritreans' right to self-determination; what is immediately relevant to this discussion is that the great majority of the OAU's members is strongly against the idea of a Greater Somalia being created by violent methods, while a somewhat smaller majority views the Eritrean struggle as a threat to the integrity of an African State. All the OAU members acknowledge the sovereign right of its members to make their own decisions about the source of their military support. Thus, on all three grounds, the Soviet intervention won the broad support of the OAU.

It is necessary, however, to point out in passing that the issues raised by the Soviet/Cuban intervention in the Horn of Africa are by no means as clearcut as might be assumed from the reasons they have given for their military involvement. At least three major questions require further consideration. The first is whether the Ethiopian military régime was, in fact, the effective sovereign government of Ethiopia at the time it sought the support of the Soviets and Cubans. It described itself (as it still does) as the Provisional Military Administrative Committee (PMAC)—a recognition that it still lacks legitimacy. That legitimacy has been denied to it by a great number of Ethiopians—not just by the Ogadeni Somalis and the Eritreans, but also by other regional and nationalist opposition movements, as well as by several Marxist groups. It was only because of foreign military support that the PMAC was able to maintain its hold on power (military rather than political); thus, if it should succeed in the end, the PMAC will have secured its claim to legitimacy largely (if indeed not entirely) thanks to foreign military intervention. It is therefore by no means clear that the régime led by Lieutenant Colonel Mengistu Haile Mariam was (or is) the "legitimate government of a sovereign State."

The second question touches on the right of self-determination. If all secessionist movements are automatically seen as infringing the OAU Charter, how can the universally-recognised right of self-determination be exercised in Africa? Eritrea provides one of the few exceptional examples in the continent of a territory whose modern status was decided within the framework of the United Nations. Its internationally-recognised status was violently destroyed by the régime of the late Emperor Haile Selassie. Do the Eritreans have no right of redress, except by agreement, achieved non-violently, with the government in Addis Ababa? And if the Ethiopians were to continue to refuse to listen to peaceful arguments—as they have always done in the past—is the case of Eritrean self-determination to remain unconsidered?

The purpose of putting these questions in this sharp form is not to try to justify the claim of the Eritreans to independence, but to suggest that the vital principle of self-determination requires a better answer than just to knock down the Eritrean case by saying that "secessionism" is a sin against the OAU Charter. Nor is it entirely irrelevant to recall that in the days of Haile Selassie's rule, the Soviets and Cubans were among the strongest upholders of the Eritreans' claims to self-determination.

The third question arises from a closer consideration of Soviet aims in Ethiopia. Apart from the reasons which the majority of OAU members have accepted as justifying Soviet/Cuban military intervention, Moscow has also consistently put forward another reason for this intervention—a reason which runs smack against

OAU policies—as well as against the interests of the Western Powers and of China. From September 1974—when the PMAC dethroned the late Emperor and announced that it was embarking on a new course—the Soviets proclaimed it to be their "international duty" to help the "Ethiopian revolution" to succeed against its "feudal and imperialist enemies," and to assist in its consolidation. This objective was formally set out in a joint communiqué[7] by the First Vice-President of the Soviet Union, Vasiliy Kuznetsov, and the Ethiopian leader, Colonel Mengistu, in Addis Ababa on September 20, 1978: "In the USSR, the Ethiopian revolution is regarded as a component part of the world revolutionary process. The Soviet Union will continue to give all-round assistance to the friendly people in Ethiopia in attaining their noble aims."

What this plainly means is that the Soviets' role in Ethiopia is not confined only to helping "repel foreign invasion" and to supplying normal military aid as between two friendly States; its aim is to promote and consolidate a communist revolution. The Soviet bloc has gone so far as to provide Marxist cadres to teach the Ethiopian military régime *how* to create an Ethiopian Popular Marxist Organisation! The actual nature of the Soviet-Ethiopian alliance is further elaborated by other references in the joint communiqué referred to above: Support for the victory of the April 1978 "revolution in Afghanisation"; denunciation of "the interference of NATO member-countries, with the United States at the head, into the affairs of the African continent"; denunciation of "the Great Power hegemonism and the expansionist policies of the present Peking leaders...." The Addis Ababa régime also supported the overthrow of the Pol Pot régime in Kampuchea, and criticised China's interference in the affairs of Vietnam. Another significant element in this alliance is Ethiopia's decision to become an associate member of COMECON.

It is clear, then, that the Soviet involvement in Ethiopia goes far beyond the three objectives which made its initial military intervention acceptable to a majority of African States.

But what is the actual Soviet interest in Africa? This question cannot be considered separately from the interests and involvements of the other major Powers.

III—The Western Interest in Africa

The West's residual interest in the continent at the end of the colonial period was essentially economic and strategic. Having lost

---

[7] Radio Addis Ababa; September 20, 1978.

direct control over their former colonies' resources and markets, the West European nations—especially Britain, France and Belgium—were faced with the problem of how to maintain their markets and to retain access to the continent's resources. Some of the methods they adopted smacked of "neo-colonialism" to the newly-independent African States—an allegation directed especially against France over the new institutions created in the francophone African community. More recently, this suspicion has fastened most acutely on the role of the multinational corporations which have been invited to play an increasingly larger role by the more advanced African countries—including the most radical among them—since their independence.

Although the Communist Powers' economic share in African markets has grown since the 1960s, it still remains relatively small because neither the COMECON countries nor China have as yet proved to be serious competitors to the Western industrial nations. In fact, the largest beneficiaries from the ending of Africa as "a captive market" for the former colonial Powers have been the United States, Japan and West Germany; and the sharpest rivalries for the African markets exist among the Western nations themselves. Unlike the United Kingdom, France has tried to use its political ties with its former colonies, as well as its aid programmes, to maintain and expand its sphere of economic interest. French post-colonial policy has been decidedly more aggressive—and adventurous—than the other former colonial Powers. The United Kingdom, for example, has made not the least attempt to use the Commonwealth of Nations as an economic instrument. A significant element in French policy has been its willingness to maintain defence treaties (and even military bases) with some of its African associates, such as Morocco, Ivory Coast, Senegal and Gabon. This aspect of French policy explains why some African countries (for example, Zaire) have turned to Paris for military support in times of trouble. It also accounts for the initiative taken by the Franco-African Conference in Paris in May 1978 to consider the idea of an Inter-African Military Force capable of intervening when African States face threats of external aggression. Although this idea attracted strong support from a number of African countries, it also encountered the strong hostility of leaders like Tanzania's President Nyerere (see above).

Perhaps the most significant West European attempt to establish a new kind of relationship with the former colonies is the Lomé Treaty signed in 1975 between the European Economic Community and 46 countries from Africa, the Pacific and Caribbean Islands (the so-called APCs). Unlike the Yaoundé Agreement, which it replaced, the Lomé Treaty does not treat the APCs as associates; it is an agreement between independent sovereign States covering a wide area of common interests in trade and aid. One of its more notable features is the Export Earnings Stabilisation System (STABEX) for commodity exports to the EEC.

Another notable development of EEC policy has been the beginning of a common West European approach to the problems of Africa—and especially towards Southern Africa. The Community's Foreign Ministers have already succeeded in reaching a consensus on a number of important issues such as over a proposed Code of Conduct for West European firms doing business in South Africa, a joint approach to South Africa over apartheid and, even, agreement to study contingency plans for a possible selective boycott against South Africa if the situation should continue to deteriorate.

The United Kingdom inherited two particularly difficult problems from its colonial past: the unresolved crisis in Rhodesia, produced by the Smith régime's Unilateral Declaration of Independence in 1965; and a considerable stake in South Africa's economy. Both have proved to be highly embarrassing at a time of greater international involvement in the increasingly violent conflicts in the sub-continent. The United Kingdom's apparent inability (or, in African eyes, reluctance) to end the Rhodesian rebellion has troubled its relations with African governments and, in particular with its fellow members in the Commonwealth. However, much more complicated issues are raised for the United Kingdom—as well as for other Western nations—by their considerable involvement in South Africa's economy. The Africans, almost without exception, see this Western interest in the apartheid Republic's economy as buttressing its system of apartheid.

Because the Soviet Union and China have no special interests of their own to defend in Southern Africa, they stand to gain by committing themselves to the cause of those challenging the region's *status quo*; the situation is much more complicated for the Western Powers. Although they have long since lost their political hegemony over the sub-continent, their economic involvement places constraints on their actions in dealing with the Pretoria régime. The result is that Western policies towards South Africa are seen as being, at best, ambiguous by Africans and, at worse, as colluding in maintaining a system of racial oppression.

As the conflict over Southern Africa moves towards a climacteric, the dilemma facing the Western Powers is bound to become extremely acute. Failure to produce a convincing policy would undoubtedly contribute substantially to the erosion, or even complete loss, of Western influence and interests in that strategically and economically important part of of the world.

So long as the Soviets showed no great interest in obtaining strategic vantages in Africa and the surrounding oceans, the NATO Powers seemed content to accept the diminution of their military position in the post-colonial situation, especially since the balance of strategic advantage remained strongly in their favour. But that balance began to change with the collapse of Portuguese colonialism and after the downfall of Haile Selassie and especially because of the considerable extension of the Soviet's military role in Angola and Ethiopia.

The United States reacted swiftly to the Soviet/Cuban intervention in Angola—which, incidentally, had been facilitated by NATO's policy in having supported the Lisbon régime to the bitter end. A change in United States policy was announced by Dr. Henry Kissinger, in his speech in Lusaka on April 25, 1976. Reversing previous American policy, he announced full support for majority black rule throughout Southern Africa.[8] Kissinger at the same time initiated a new diplomatic approach by seeking to bring Amercian and Western policy into closer line with OAU aspirations in the sub-continent. This initiative opened a remarkable period of diplomacy between the United States and the United Kingdom with the so-called Front-line African States (Tanzania, Zambia, Mozambique, Angola and Botswana); this culminated in the Anglo-American initiative on Rhodesia and the initiative taken by the five Western members of the United Nations Security Council (the United States, the United Kingdom, France, West Germany and Canada) on Namibia. An important aspect of these two initiatives was the response it received from the OAU, which not only endorsed, but actively co-operated with, the Western diplomatic involvement in the continent's most serious crisis area. Even the two Marxist-Leninist presidents of the Front-line African States (Samora Machel of Mozambique and Dr. Agostinho Neto of Angola) collaborated in these Western initiatives.

The Western Powers, however, failed to produce any effective response to the Soviet/Cuban intervention in the Horn of Africa. Although the United States and the United Kingdom warned Moscow that their military role in and around the Red Sea area could jeopardise détente, they refused to go beyond issuing these warnings, and they refused to become militarily involved by, for example, responding to Somalia's appeal that the West should replace the Soviet Union as its source of arms after it had renounced its Treaty of Friendship with the Soviet Union in 1977. The West chose to

[8] See C. Legum, *The Year of the Whirlwind* (1977).

leave the defence of the Red Sea region to the anti-Russian local Powers: Saudi Arabia, Sudan, Egypt and Iran.

IV—THE SOVIET INTEREST IN AFRICA

Official Soviet policy towards Africa was restated in a government statement in June, 1978.[9] It expresses "great sympathy and support for the great political and social socio-economic changes taking place in the liberated countries of Africa." It welcomes the development of "a number of African countries" (which) have made their "choice in favour of a socialist orientation." It asserts that the "forces of imperialism, racialism and reaction" are opposed to these progressive changes, and still seek to continue "exploiting the African peoples and the continent's national wealth," and "to think in colonialist categories of zones of influence." It warns against the "dangerous and cynical character . . . of imperialist inter-ference." It blames the growth of tension in Africa on "the aggres-sive actions of a group of leading NATO countries headed by the United States." The Peking leadership is described as having linked forces with "the imperialists . . . in accordance with their chauvinis-tic, hegemonistic and selfish interests." Soviet policy, on the other hand, is described as supporting "the forces upholding the cause of national independence, social progress and democracy. It treats them as comrades in the struggle . . . the Soviet Union seeks no advantage for itself; it is not after concessions, nor does it press for political domination or solicit military bases. The USSR is entirely on the side of the African peoples struggling against the retention, in any form, of the vestiges of colonialism and racialism in Africa, and against necolonialism."

From this broad statement of official policy towards Africa it is possible to extrapolate a number of the Soviet's overt aims: (1) support for the national liberation movements in their struggle to overthrow the minority régimes in South Africa, Rhodesia and Namibia; (2) encouragement and support for the growth of "social-ist—oriented" African governments and movements; (3) support for all efforts to eradicate capitalist exploitation (*i.e.*, Western economic interests); (4) opposition to any Western military links, described as "NATO aggressive designs"; (5) opposition to China's policies in the continent.

As is characteristic of all the major Powers, the Soviets are more reticent when it comes to discussing their covert aims. For these one needs to turn to the work of Soviet Africanists and, especially, of

[9] *Tass*, June 24, 1978.

Soviet military strategists and to look at their actual practices. From these sources it is clear that the Soviet Union has four major aims, all of which derive quite naturally from their role as a super-Power. The first aim (and this is quite understandable from Moscow's view-point) is to diminish Western economic, military and political inter-ests and influence. A second aim is not only to encourage the growth of "socialist" (*i.e.* Marxist) régimes, but to strengthen them through direct military and economic aid and to involve them in a network of alliances with the Soviet bloc. A third aim is to strengthen the Soviet Union's strategic position *vis-à-vis* NATO in the continuing struggle over a new balance of world power. A fourth aim is to oppose all attempts by China to expand its sphere of influence and friendship in the continent and, indeed, in any other part of the Third World—a crucial element of policy in the context of Sino-Soviet rivalry. These two latter aims appear to be the crucial determinants of Soviet policy in Africa.

Having become a world naval power for the first time in Russian history, the Soviets have a natural interest in acquiring the kind of facilities traditionally enjoyed by Western navies around the world's oceans. The need for friendly "blue water" ports is especially strong because of the unavailability of most of Russia's ports during the long winter months. This Soviet interest in acquiring—not naval "bases"—but reliable harbour facilities has been amply described in the published work of Admiral of the Fleet, Sergei Gorshkov, the creator of the modern Red Fleet.[10] This interest is clearly shown by the avidity with which the Soviet Union has utilised every opportun-ity opened up by its familiar Treaties of Friendship with Third World countries to acquire naval facilities: Alexandria in the days of Nasser; Berbera, for so long as its treaty lasted with Somalia; Benghazi and Tobruk in Libya; Aden in South Yemen, Conakry in Guinea (until the recent cooling off of its relations with President Sékou Touré). Such a strategic interest dictates a foreign policy aimed largely, though not exclusively, at developing intimate rela-tions with ocean-bordering nations. Apart from other strategic advantages, Ethiopia stands out as a prime target in the context of Moscow's "ocean politics."

While the Soviets clearly believe that it is possible to develop détente with the West, they appear to have no such faith about China. Both nations are obviously obsessed by their fears of each other's world hegemonistic designs. Until China recently opened up its avenues to the West, its main challenge to the Soviets was in the Third World. It is in this crucial area that Sino-Soviet rivalry can be

---

[10] Admiral of the Fleet S. Gorshkov, *Sea Power of the State* (Moscow 1973).

seen at its most raw—with Africa and South-East Asia as the two primary cockpits. Soviet propaganda and diplomacy against China's policies and activities in Africa are pursued with deadly venom, energy and ruthlessness.

V—THE CUBAN INTEREST IN AFRICA

Although Cuba is widely regarded, especially by the Chinese, as being simply the satraps of Moscow—or, in the language of Peking, as "the Russians' mercenaries"—there are good grounds for suggesting that this is too facile a way of describing Castro's role. The Cubans have cast themselves in the role of being "the vanguard of Tricontinental Revolution." Such an ideological commitment would appear to express a sense of revolt by a small and poor Caribbean nation against the continental role of the United States, as well as an attempt to assert themselves against being treated simply as a dependancy of the Soviet Union.

What Che Guevara failed to achieve through his attempts to "export" Cuba's revolution to Latin America, Castro has achieved, to some extent, though different methods in Africa—the continent of the Cubans' "blood brothers." It was the Cubans who brought the Soviets into Angola, not the other way around.[11] In the Horn of Africa, the Cubans have tried, but with only limited success, to take initiatives independent of the Soviets: first when Castro tried to persuade Somalia to embrace the idea of a Federation of Marxist–Leninist States in the Horn of Africa; later, by trying to force an alternative Marxist leadership on the Dergue in Addis Ababa; and, subsequently, by refusing to allow Cubans to be used in a combatant role against the Eritreans. The Cubans have shown in Angola and Ethiopia that they are more acceptable than the Soviets, possibly because they are not a "white people" and, certainly, because they come from a small country. Their spectacular role in Angola and Ethiopia has unquestionably made a deep impact on Africa.[12]

VI—CHINA'S INTEREST IN AFRICA

Whatever the original idea of Mao Zedong in wishing to make Peking the revolutionary capital of the Third World, there can be little doubt that after his break with Moscow in the late 1950s the Chinese have pursued a strong national interest in seeking to turn the non-aligned nations against both super-Powers—but especially

[11] See Legum and Hodges, *op. cit.*, in note 6, above.
[12] See Z. Cervenka and C. Legum, "Cuba—the Most Important Communist Power in Africa", XI *Africa Contemporary Record* (1977/78).

against "the Russian hegemonists." In their bitter rivalries, both the Soviets and Chinese have found themselves in strange African company: the Soviet, for example, as the main suppliers of arms to Uganda's tyrant, General Idi Amin, and to the fiercely anti-communist, Islamic revolutionary Colonel Ghadaffy; and the Chinese as staunch supporters of Zaire's President Mobutu Sese Seko. These sets of relationships, alone, cast doubt on their respective claims to be just the defenders of "true progressive revolutionaries."

Chinese aid in Africa has been exemplary, with not a singular important failure. If any nation (other, perhaps, than the Swedes and Norwegians) can lay proper claim to giving "disinterested aid," it is the Chinese. This does not suggest that there has been no economic advantage to themselves; but Soviet charges that the Chinese aid programmes are exploitative is certainly untrue. (By contrast, the Soviet barter deals and, especially, their fishing treaties with African countries have often been unashamedly exploitative.)

China's policies in Africa display three notable characteristics. The first is its scrupulous avoidance of becoming involved in the internal affairs of African States—quite different from either the Soviets or the Western nations. The second is its total refusal to use its friendship with African governments to influence them in any overt way to follow the Peking line on any particular issue; for example, in the Angolan conflict, opposite sides were taken by China and Tanzania, despite the latter's strong ties with Peking and the fact that it has benefited far more than any other African country from Chinese aid. Peking's line is to proclaim its own view on any issue, but to leave it to others to make up their own minds. Although it is hard to believe in the "purity" of such a policy, in practice it is impossible to discover any case in which China has deviated from this approach since the end of the period of the "Red Guards." A third characteristic, probably closely linked to the second, is the long-term view which the Chinese take in judging the ultimate success of their policies. The many setbacks they have had in Africa in recent years are dismissed as unimportant events in the evolution of their relations with the Third World.

VII—CONCLUSIONS

Foreign intervention, military and otherwise, has become an increasingly important factor in political developments in Africa. All the major Powers, as well as some of the smaller ones (*e.g.* Cuba, Yugoslavia and Romania), have been drawn more deeply into the affairs of the continent. The role of the Western Powers is largely "defensive," while that of the Communist Powers is expansive, *i.e.* seeking to increase their role and to widen their influence. A major feature of this greater foreign intervention is the rapid growth of military aid to the continent, as well as of actual military intervention—with the volume of Soviet military aid now greater than that of the NATO Powers.

The two major areas of foreign involvement are Southern Africa and the Horn of Africa, with the Mediterranean region becoming increasingly more important. "Ocean politics" appear to be the most crucial aspect of the policies pursued by the foreign Powers, particularly by the Soviets.

African leaders have become seriously concerned about the growth of foreign intervention in their continent. Many of them accept that Africans have only themselves to blame for the opportunities they offer to the foreign Powers to pursue their own interests. Because of the military and economic needs (and weaknesses) of the continent, its leaders offer no clear answer to the threats they perceive as coming from foreign intervention. There is also an element of ambiguity in their attitudes to the role of foreign Powers; this derives largely from their willingness to accept the importance to themselves of certain types of foreign involvement. The problem they face is how to ensure that the "right kind" of foreign involvement (*e.g.* aid for the liberation movements in Southern Africa, or military support for sovereign States) does not turn into being the "wrong kind" of foreign intervention through the major Powers exploiting Africa's political divisions and economic weakness to their own advantage—and thus turning the continent into an arena for the power struggle among the world's major Powers.

EEC-CMEA RELATIONS

By

ROBERT W. CLAWSON

CREATED in January 1949, the Soviet-sponsored Council for Mutual Economic Assistance (CMEA) has been widely interpreted as Stalin's answer to the establishment of the Organisation for European Economic Co-operation (OEEC).[1] The OEEC had been formed in April 1948 to administer Marshall Plan aid in Western Europe; the EEC may be regarded figuratively as one of its organisational descendants.[2] As if to underscore the haste with which the CMEA was created, no founding document was produced for public view aside from the short communiqué announcing the Council's creation.[3] Once they had forced Eastern Europe to reject participation in the Marshall Plan and to join the CMEA, the Soviets appear to have lost interest in the new organisation.

Following Stalin's death, the CMEA was revived by his successors as part of their effort to maintain stability and Soviet dominance in Eastern Europe; in 1954 a Secretariat was finally created and the Council began to show modest signs of organisational animation.[4] The CMEA was not designed as a vehicle for integration as there did not appear to be compelling economic reasons for it to be so. The Council was also not intended to act as a political institution and there is no real juridical basis for supranational authority in the

---

[1] F. G. Ransom, "Obstacles to the Liberalization of Relations Between the EEC and Comecon," *Studies in Comparative Communism* (July–Ocotber 1969), pp. 61–78. In the present essay the Council of Mutual Economic Assistance will be abbreviated CMEA in preference to other short forms. The term "East Europe" will refer to the European members of the CMEA excluding the Soviet Union. Cuba, Mongolia, and Vietnam, though full members of CMEA, present unique problems for the analyst and will not be included in the central focus of this work.

The literature on the CMEA is extensive. The two best known book-length studies in the West are M. Kaser, *Comecon: Integration Problems of the Planned Economies* (1967) and R. Szawlowski, *The System of the International Organizations of the Communist Countries* (1976). Both volumes contain good collections of basic CMEA documents. Recent Soviet literature includes: B. G. Dyakin and B. G. Pankov, *SEV: problemy integratsii* [CMEA: Problems of Integration] (Moscow 1978). V. E. Rybalkin, *Mezhdunarodnyi rynok SEV: perspektivy razvitiya v usloviyakh ekonomicheskoy integratsii* [The International Markets of the CMEA: Perspectives for Growth in the Conditions of Economic Integration] (Moscow, 1978), and the Academy of Science's Institute of State and Law's *Pravovye voprosy deyatelnosti SEV* [Legal Questions of CMEA Activity] (Moscow, 1977).

[2] F. A. M. Alting von Geusau, *Beyond the European Community* (1969), pp. 33–34.

[3] Szawlowski, *op. cit.* in note 1, above, on pp. 48–49. A copy of the communiqué is included in the text. A short, never published CMEA founding document may have been signed at the time.

[4] Ransom, *op. cit.* in note 1, above.

95

international agreements establishing the organisation. It was set up as the economic executive agency of an already established set of international political relationships dominated by the Soviet Union.[5]

In contrast, the Treaty of Rome, signed in March 1957, visualised eventual political unity as the end result of ever closer economic co-operation among West European States under the organisational direction of the supranational European Economic Community (EEC).[6] Its architects hoped that the EEC could create a single integrated market, develop a workable system for the formulation of common internal and external economic policies, and unite formerly hostile States of Western Europe into a harmonious community.[7]

From its very beginnings, CMEA members, and especially the Soviet Union, viewed the EEC with distrust, hostility, scepticism, and derision.[8] Faithful to the pre-revolutionary, tsarist tradition of opposition to European political unity, Soviet antagonism also reflected the basic enmity of both Lenin and Stalin to such dangerous co-operation.[9] East European members of the CMEA were perhaps less concerned with politics, but saw a more immediate economic threat to their exports in the creation of a customs union in Western Europe.[10] Despite continued distrust and hostility, in the mid-1960s, Eastern derision and scepticism began to give way to a more realistic appreciation of the growing and increasingly institutionalised strength and vitality of the Common Market.[11] By the early 1970s the Soviets were proposing a comprehensive deal between the two economic organisations.[12] At the end of the second decade of its existence the European Economic Community had received *de facto* recognition from the Soviet Union as well as from most other members of the Eastern bloc, and was negotiating

[5] J. Pinder, "EEC and Comecon," 58 *Survey* (1966), pp. 101–117.
[6] W. Wallace, "Walking Backwards Toward Unity," in Helen Wallace, William Wallace, and Carole Webb, *Policy Making in the European Communities* (1977), pp. 301–323.
[7] *Op. cit.* in note 5, above.
[8] Z. Brzezinski, "Russia and Europe," 3 *Foreign Affairs* (April 1964), pp. 428–444; G. Ginsburgs, "The Kremlin and the Common Market: A Conspectus," 37 *Social Research* (Summer 1970), pp. 296–305; H. Schaefer, *Communist "Westpolitik" and the EEC*, RFE Research-East Europe (December 21, 1970).
[9] J. Lukaszewski, "The European Community and Eastern Eruope," 249 *Roundtable* (January 1973), pp. 41–49. Also see V. I. Lenin, "On the Slogan for a United States of Europe," *Collected Works*, Vol. 21 (Moscow, 1964), pp. 339–343.
[10] A. Zauberman, "The Soviet Bloc and the Common Market," 1 *The World Today* (1963), pp. 30–36.
[11] M. Shulman, "Communist Views of Western Integration," 3 *International Organization* (1963), pp. 649–662.
[12] *The Economist*, August 30, 1975.

agreements with the CMEA and its member States.[13]

The process by which these two organisations have evolved to their present situation has been characterised by a range of interactions and attitudes that might best be described as reluctant. Contacts between the two organisations have been marked by a degree of crudeness and indecision on the part of the CMEA, and by a certain woolliness and haughty disdain from Brussels. But now the time has nearly arrived for serious negotiations to begin between the two in spite of fundamental questions that have yet to be resolved. Before taking a closer look at those thorny issues, however, it is important to review the development of relations between them; to discover how these two fundamentally unfriendly bloc organisations have come to the point of making a comprehensive mutual accommodation.

I—Twenty Years of Unenthusiastic Encounter

When the EEC and Euratom were created in March 1957 the Soviets angrily reacted as if they had been taken completely by surprise despite the months and even years of public preparation for the event.[14] The Moscow Institute of World Economy published a document containing 17 theses in which the new organisations were greeted with derision, animosity, and the prediction that the "so-called" European Economic Community would meet the same fate as the abortive European Defence Community (EDC).[15]

(a) *1957—72: Years of Apprehensive Appraisal*

Soviet and East European commentators at first saw the "integration" effort as an American scheme to ensure United States domination of Europe and to augment the aggressive capabilities of the North Atlantic Treaty Organisation (NATO).[16] They remained convinced, however, that the effort was not of great consequence because it would soon collapse. They argued that temporary accommodations were totally inadequate to overcome the fundamental contradictions and tensions that haunt capitalist systems, although some short-term relief might result from taking advantage of certain "technical" improvements related to "integration."[17] Thus, while continuing to attack the Common Market in the Press

---

[13] See *e.g.* Yu. Zhuravlyov, "The International Ties of the Council for Mutual Economic Assistance," 1 *Foreign Trade* (Moscow, 1978), pp. 2–9.

[14] Brzezinski, *op. cit.* in note 8, above.

[15] Lukaszewski, *op. cit.* in note 9, above; *op cit.* in note 11, above. The Soviets invariably supplied quotation marks around the term "integration" and usually referred to the "so-called" European Economic Community.

[16] Brzezinski, *op. cit.* in note 8, above.

[17] Ginsburgs, *op. cit.* in note 8, above.

and through international propaganda, no serious Eastern policy was developed in the 1950s other than to try to take advantage of short-term opportunities to disrupt Western unity.[18] At the same time, the very real possibility that the Federal Republic of Germany might end up as the dominant economic and political force in the EEC did bother the Soviets.[19]

During 1958 and 1959, the CMEA's image was augmented as part of the Soviet response to the emergence of the EEC. However, the Soviet Union tried to make it clear to their East European junior partners that the new CMEA initiatives were not aimed at creating any kind of alternative common market because objective economic conditions did not justify such a step.[20] The CMEA Charter along with its Convention were signed in December 1959 in Sofia, some 10 years after the organisation's establishment.[21] In June 1962 the CMEA published a supplementary document correcting a gap in the Charter by providing for consultation on national plans at an early stage.[22]

During the summer of 1962 changes began to emerge in both Soviet and East European attitudes towards the EEC. In an August article prepared for the Soviet Party journal, *Kommunist*, Khrushchev proposed a pragmatic policy towards the EEC, going so far as to intimate that the two economic unions might find it mutually advantageous to enter into some form of co-operation.[23] Khrushchev also recommended a unified supranational CMEA planning organ, suggesting that the idea had emerged from the EEC's initial successes. An authoritative *Pravda* article of August 26, 1962, noted that while continuous international contradictions still threatened the Common Market, and it did continue to serve NATO's aggressive interests, it was also possible that the EEC was actually creating a *new* power centre of its own, perhaps one that would rival even the United States.[24]

In December 1962 amendments to the CMEA Charter created an Executive Committee and a Bureau for Integrated Planning Problems, but (on Romanian insistence) stopped short of creating a supranational planning agency as had been proposed by Khrushchev.[25] That reinforcement, as well as various bilateral probing

---

[18] Schaefer, *op. cit.* in note 8, above.

[19] Brzezinski, *op. cit.* in note 8, above.

[20] Ginsburgs, *op cit.* in note 8, above. Ginsburgs suggests that the Soviets did not want to put themselves in the position of having to bail out any East European economy that might fail.

[21] Szawlowski, *op. cit.* in note 1, above, on p. 50.

[22] *Ibid.*

[23] *Op. cit.* in note 5, above.

[24] Lucaszewski, *op. cit.* in note 9, above.

[25] M. Kaser, "Comecon and the New Multilateralism," 4 *The world Today* (1972), pp. 162–169.

actions taken by CMEA members, was a clear recognition that the EEC was likely to endure. The Soviet Institute of World Economy and International Relations published a revised set of theses—32 this time—reflecting a fundamental reassessment of the Common Market and its likely future.[26]

East European countries perceived a sharper economic threat from the EEC than did the Soviet Union. East Europe's share of trade with the EEC countries was considerably larger; its traditional exports, foodstuffs, would be at the mercy of a common agricultural policy, while its energy exports would be subject to a community quota if the then pervasive energy glut persisted. Thus, most East European leaders were less inclined than the Soviets to ignore the existence of the EEC either diplomatically or commercially. They needed West European technology and could not be helped much by the Soviet policy of strengthening the CMEA while increasing intra-bloc trade.[27]

Apparently, a number of CMEA States made confidential bilateral approaches to the EEC during late 1962 and 1963. The Soviets themselves suggested an informal agreement concerning tariff reductions, and Brussels tried to tempt the Soviet Union into extending diplomatic recognition to the EEC in return for lower tariffs on Soviet export items such as caviar, crab meat, and vodka. The Soviet Union seems not to have responded.[28]

Though it appeared in early 1963 as if some accommodation might be evolving between the EEC and the Soviet bloc, the deepening crises in the West, highlighted by de Gaulle's inclination to violate both the spirit and the letter of the Treaty of Rome, appeared to reconfirm old assumptions that the EEC could not long survive with its inherent contradictions. No East European leader wanted to be in the position of strengthening the EEC against the forces of history. The French Gaullist capacity to prevent European consolidation and hence German hegemony, won a special place for France in Soviet foreign policy during the mid-1960s.[29]

Following Khrushchev's dismissal in late 1964, the Soviets ceased all bilateral initiatives and lapsed back into their hostility and antagonism toward the EEC, accusing it of being " ... [a] harmful relic of the cold war, incompatible with the spirit of peaceful

---

[26] Lukaszewski, *op. cit.* in note 9, above.

[27] *Op. cit.* in note 10, above. The East Europeans have not been reluctant to criticise the EEC but their irritation has usually been directed against what they felt were EEC discriminatory practices and other business-related issues.

[28] *Op. cit.* in note 5, above.

[29] Lukaszewski, *op. cit.* in note 9, above.

coexistence, guilty of the cleavage of Europe, undermined by internal tensions and doomed to failure."[30]

But some East European States continued quietly to seek accommodation. In 1965 an agreement governing Polish agricultural exports to the EEC was concluded as a "technical" arrangement, in which the Poles promised not to sell their agricultural exports for prices below the EEC minimum.[31]

As the Soviets began to press for a European Security Conference, they saw *rapprochement* with West Germany as an important first step in the achievement of a general settlement.[32] By 1966 they seem to have concluded that the EEC did represent a potentially permanent and troublesome economic reality, but that a German-led United States of Europe was unlikely.[33] That made Soviet *rapprochement* with the Federal Republic less complicated, while at the same time removed the political pressure to make long-term policy towards the EEC.

But for the East Europeans, the evolving restrictive trade policies of the Common Market threatened their commercial plans in a fundamental way. EEC customs barriers to their exports, scheduled to be fixed in 1968, would make East European payments for equipment and technology much more difficult than they already were. In 1966, the Hungarians suggested that "horizontal" contacts between the EEC, CMEA, and EFTA might ripen rather quickly. The Soviets apparently argued that any such co-operation with the West would weaken the bloc; no major contacts followed the Hungarian initiative.[34]

Most East European countries continued to pay lip service to the Soviet line while seeking private accommodation where it would most help them. The Soviet Union's snarling reaction to Yugoslav diplomatic recognition of the EEC, and the Warsaw Pact's invasion of Czechoslovakia in the summer of 1968, illustrated how little tolerance Brezhnev's Russia had for East European involvement with the West. Nevertheless, by the end of 1969 the Bulgarians, Hungarians, and Romanians had followed the Polish example in concluding "technical" agreements on agricultural price minimums, to avoid having their produce excluded from the Common Market.

The EEC, however, not much concerned with pleasing either the Soviet Union or Eastern Europe, was proceeding with its timetable. During 1968 the EEC membership gave final approval to the aboli-

---

[30] Quoted in *ibid.*
[31] *Op. cit.* in note 12, above.
[32] Lukaszewski, *op. cit.* in note 9, above.
[33] Schaefer, *op, cit.* in note 8, above.
[34] *Ibid.*

tion of all customs duties and quantitative restrictions on industrial-goods commerce within the EEC. A common tariff system was established for foreign trade and it was agreed that after January 1, 1969, all members would limit their individual right to introduce import quotas. However, following vigorous argument within the Community, it was decided that East Europe would not be included in the tariff or quota schemes; individual members of the Community could continue to make their own separate trade policies with the CMEA countries.[35] This relieved both the Soviets and the East Europeans from having to recognise and deal with the EEC across the board. The Soviets quickly concluded a series of bilateral agreements with individual Community States.

With reference to EEC expansion, the Soviets developed a fairly consistent policy of general opposition and greeted new membership requests from other West European States with extensive and immoderate polemic. The United Kingdom's application was the subject of intense criticism and de Gaulle was applauded for rejecting it. Her continued quest for membership was the subject of additional Soviet invective. [36] When it appeared that Austria might be considering some form of association with the Common Market, the Soviets published thinly-veiled threats, forcing Austria to back away.[37] They also expressed opposition to the formation of a Nordic Economic Community (NORDEC), probably fearing that the Scandinavian countries, so organised, would eventually enter the Common Market as a group.[38]

By the spring of 1969 the Soviets had come to a number of conclusions. First, France had lost the economic race with West Germany, and the Federal Republic was in a potent position within the EEC. Secondly, EEC economic strength was beginning to look like a real threat, not only to Eastern Europe, but also to the Soviet Union. Thirdly, Soviet policy could no longer afford to be based only on short-term opportunism and on the promotion of French delinquency.[39]

Beginning in the autumn of 1969, the Soviets took the initiative by arguing for a Pan-European conference on economic problems,

---

[35] Ransom, *op. cit.* in note 1, above. Also see F. Hartman, *The Relations of Nations* (1973), p. 143.

[36] *Pravda*, January 5, 1970. The Soviets, especially, continue to delight in Britain's various disputes with the EEC. See *Pravda*, June 26, 1976.

[37] *Pravda*, November 29, 1969, and October 26, 1970.

[38] *Pravda*, June 3, 1970.

[39] Y. Rzhevsky, "The FRG in the System of Western Alliance," 12 *International Affairs* (1968), pp. 24–29. D. Andreyev and M. Makov, "The Common Market After Eleven Years," 1 *International Affairs* (1969), pp. 43–49. O. Orestov, "Britain's European Illusions," 2 *International Affairs* (1969), pp. 14–19. V. Kravchenko, "Italy's European Concepts," 3 *International Affairs* (1969), pp. 27–32.

while castigating the EEC as a barrier to Soviet-sponsored détente in Europe.[40] At the same time, the Soviets were working hard to meet Brandt's *Ostpolitik* half-way, and they continued to press for a general settlement through a European Security Conference.

By the end of the decade, it was becoming obvious to East and West alike that however much both blocs preferred to ignore one another, it was not likely to be as easy to do so in the future as it had been in the past. Between 1958 and 1970, CMEA exports to the EEC had risen some 300 per cent. while Common Market exports to CMEA had expanded about 385 per cent. Clearly the two economic blocs were on their way to deeper mutual involvement.[41]

In the early 1970s the Soviets began to push for a stronger, more unified bloc. At its Bucharest meeting, in July 1971, the CMEA announced that after more than two years of preparation and negotiation, it had completed the "Comprehensive Programme for the Further Deepening and Perfecting of Co-operation and Development of Socialist Economic Integration of Member Countries of CMEA."[42] The new undertaking called for greatly increased co-operation among CMEA members at the level of individual firms and industries, but stopped short of creating any new supranational bodies. It was designed to help modernise the CMEA members' economies, envisaging the expansion of intra-bloc "production associations" and other measures to take advantage of economies of scale as well as special regional resources and capabilities.[43] A new CMEA-sponsored International Investment Bank (IIB) began operations in 1971 to provide funding for the envisaged multilateral intra-bloc industrial projects.[44]

(b) *1972—78: Cautious Involvement*

On March 20, 1972, Soviet Communist Party General Secretary Brezhnev made a long speech before the Fifteenth Soviet Trade Unions Congress in Moscow. Although the major portion of his presentation was devoted to other topics, he did find time to include

[40] *Pravda*, September 15, 1969.

[41] S Milligan, "What do the Soviets Want in Brussels?" *European Community* (July, August, 1977), pp. 3–6.

[42] *Pravda*, August 1, 1971. Full text. For a recent Soviet summary of the complex programme see Dyakin and Pankov, *op. cit.* in note 1 above, on pp. 24–33. A detailed review of operations is provided in V. Meshcheryakov, G. Pohlad, E. Shchevchenko, *SEV: Printsipy, problemy, perspektivy* [CMEA: Principles, Problems, Perspectives](Moscow, 1975).

[43] M. Kaser, "Comecon's Commerce," 2 *Problems of Communism* (1973), pp. 1–15. Kaser notes that these provisions were largely antithetical to the firm-centred reforms that had swept through the CMEA countries in the second half of the 1960s.

[44] Yu. Konstantinov, "Promotion of Economic Integration with the Aid of CMEA Countries' International Monetary and Financial System," 12 *Foreign Trade* (Moscow, 1977), pp. 2–8.

two paragraphs on the topic of the European Economic Community. The first denied that Soviet foreign policy was designed to undermine the EEC. The second of the two is the more important: "The Soviet Union by no means ignores the actual situation in Western Europe, including the existence of such an economic grouping of capitalist countries as the Common Market. We are carefully watching the activity of the Common Market and its evolution. Our relations with the members of this grouping will, it is understood, depend on the extent to which they recognise the realities obtaining in the socialist part of Europe, in particular the interests of the countries that are members of the Council of Mutual Economic Assistance. We are for equality in economic relations and against discrimination."[45]

Some Western European observers, noting those few words among the mass of trade union formula rhetoric, assumed that Brezhnev's remarks suggested a firm Soviet intention to begin serious negotiations based on mutual recognition.[46] In April, a Community spokesman, Sicco Mansholt, acknowledged Brezhnev's points and affirmed the EEC's willingness to discuss possibilities. Subsequently, in October 1972, the EEC Conference of the Heads of State indicated its dedication to the cause of co-operation between the Community and the "countries of Eastern Europe."[47] Less publicly, Brussels let it be known that the EEC rejected the idea of mutual recognition because it implied a degree of equality in the natures and legal capacities of the two organisations which obviously did not exist. Additionally, there was perhaps a feeling that what Brezhnev had in mind might augment Soviet domination of Eastern Europe.[48]

Perhaps Brezhnev's remarks had been motivated by anticipation of the EEC's deadline of January 1973 for the inauguration of a joint trade policy towards the "state-trading" countries of Eastern Europe. If so, he could afford to relax; after much internal debate the EEC once again postponed the event, this time until January 1975.[49]

Eastern European nations, noting the West's lack of enthusiasm for any kind of deal with the CMEA and aware of Moscow's hostility towards major bilateral agreements between East European countries and the EEC, took what steps they could to safeguard their

---

[45] *Pravda*, March 21, 1972. Full text.

[46] *Op. cit.* in note 25, above.

[47] Bureau of East West Trade, "EEC-Comecon Commercial Relations," unpublished chronology of EEC-Comecon initiatives, no date.

[48] *Op. cit.* in note 41, above.

[49] *The Economist*, October 5, 1974.

commercial positions. Before the end of 1972 Romania had entered the IMF, and Hungary had joined Czechoslovakia, Poland, and Romania in GATT.[50] In June 1973 Romania was quietly accepted into the EEC's general preference scheme for developing countries.[51] In addition, an agreement was signed in 1973 between the EEC and Finland.[52]

Events in Western Europe during 1973 must have been somewhat confusing for the Soviets. On the one hand the EEC was seemingly strengthened by the accession of the United Kingdom, Ireland, and Denmark at the beginning of the year.[53] On the other hand, the devastating results of the OPEC oil embargo may have led Moscow to assume that the post-boycott Common Market would be forced to deal with the CMEA in order to assure a steady supply of raw materials, and especially fuels.[54]

While on a visit to Moscow in July 1973, Luxembourg Premier and Foreign Minister Gaston Thorn was told by Soviet officials that the CMEA wanted direct talks with the EEC.[55] In August, Nikolai Faddeyev, the CMEA's Secretary-General, passed a message to Danish Foreign Minister Nørgaard who was then President of the EEC's Council of Ministers. Faddeyev proposed an agreement between the two organisations and invited an EEC delegation to visit CMEA headquarters in Moscow. The EEC Council of Ministers, irritated by what was felt to be a Soviet breach of protocol, waited a month and then replied that any such approach would have to be made to the EEC Commission.[56] The CMEA seems to have lost interest for some months following the EEC's reply.

At the same time, the EEC was trying to bolster its supranational authority. During those portions of the Conference on European Security and Co-operation (CESC) concerning items covered by EEC rules, the Community acted as an autonomous agent. This at first was loudly opposed by the Soviets and especially the Romanians, but was subsequently accepted. The Soviets emphasised, however, that their acquiescence did not in any way constitute "recognition" of the EEC.[57]

---

[50] Robin Edmonds, *Soviet Foreign Policy 1962—1973* (1975), p. 131.

[51] *Op. cit.* in note 43, above.

[52] F. Singleton, "Finland, Comecon, and the EEC," 2 *The World Today* (1974), pp. 64–72. Though not a member of CMEA, Finland nonetheless was subject to anti-EEC pressure exerted by the Soviets. The pact left plenty of safeguards for Finland's neutrality, and the Soviet Union finally gave its approval.

[53] *Op. cit.* in note 50, above, on p. 130.

[54] *Op. cit.* in note 12, above.

[55] *The Economist*, August 4, 1973.

[56] Commission of the European Communities, "The European Community and East European Countries," *Information: External Relations series* 347/x/75-F (E) (1975).

[57] *The Economist*, October 20, 1973.

By the end of 1973, trade statistics indicated that an ever greater economic interdependence was continuing to grow between the countries of the EEC and the CMEA. Over the period 1958–73 EEC exports to CMEA markets rose in total value by more than 600 per cent. In 1973 the EEC's total trade value with Eastern Europe and the Soviet Union had increased some 33 per cent. over the previous year. The annual rate of growth for the five-year period between 1968 and the end of 1973 was between 10 and 15 per cent. However, total trade figures for 1973 show that only about 4 per cent. of Community exports went to CMEA countries, while 25 per cent. of all CMEA exports went to the EEC.[58] It was also clear that the East Europeans still needed the EEC more than did the Soviets. But by 1973, the Soviet Union was well aware of its own increasing dependence on the EEC countries for high technology purchases.[59]

At the same time the pattern of exports had shifted. By the end of 1973 the Soviet Union was the principal CMEA exporter to the Community, accounting for about 39 per cent. of EEC imports from the East. Poland, at 19 per cent., was the second largest exporter, followed by Czechoslovakia at just above 11 per cent. and Romania and Hungary both at about 11 per cent. However, despite these changes the principal EEC imports from the CMEA countries remained agricultural products, raw materials, and semi-manufactured goods. Exports from the EEC to the East were still made up primarily of capital goods and consumer products.[60]

In May 1974 the West German Ambassador in Moscow reminded Faddeyev that suggestions for talks should be submitted to the EEC Commission.[61] In September, Faddayev finally responded by sending a message to Commission President, Francois-Xavier Ortoli, inviting him to visit CMEA headquarters in Moscow for preliminary discussions.[62] It was decided that a small preparatory group would precede Ortoli to work out a detailed agenda.[63]

In November 1974 having declared its willingness to negotiate trade agreements with the individual countries of the CMEA, the EEC prepared a model pact and sent it to those CMEA members whose various bilateral agreements and understandings were set to expire at the end of 1974.[64] The model document included provi-

---

[58] *Op. cit.* in note 56, above, and *op. cit.* in note 41, above.
[59] *Op. cit.* in note 12, above.
[60] *Op. cit.* in note 56, above.
[61] *Ibid.*
[62] *Op. cit.* in note 49, above.
[63] *Op. cit.* in note 12, above.
[64] *Op. cit.* in note 56, above.

sions for significant trade concessions without major compensatory demands.[65]

During 1974 the British and the Dutch successfully led a fight once again to postpone the operational date for a common EEC trade policy towards the East. However, in November 1974 it was finally decided that as of January 1, 1976, responsibility for concluding trade agreements would rest with the Community.[66] Additionally, and in spite of Dutch, British, and intermittent French opposition, it had been decided in July that bilateral international economic "co-operation" agreements—which traditionally were exempted from the common trade policy—would nevertheless have to be submitted to an EEC clearinghouse and made available for inspection by the Commission.[67]

Early in February 1975, Commission Director-General for External Relations Edmond Wellenstein and the preparatory delegation spent three days at the CMEA's Moscow headquarters. They had anticipated serious agenda preparations, but reportedly found the conversations largely confined to planning Ortoli's sightseeing itinerary. They saw no Soviet official of any importance and went away irritated and puzzled. They did convey an invitation for a CMEA group to visit Brussels, but received no immediate response.[68] The affair appears to have been a part of a rude Soviet attempt to humble the EEC Commission in the face of what appeared to be an inappropriately negative Western attitude toward CMEA's legal capacity.

On February 18, 1975, Sir Christopher Soames, Commission Vice-President responsible for External Relations, speaking before the European Parliament, reaffirmed the Commission's feeling that no comprehensive trade agreement was possible between the EEC and the CMEA because CMEA rules prohibited it from negotiating for the whole bloc. The EEC would be willing to hold periodic conferences and to sign an information exchange agreement, but still insisted on bilateral trade agreements with each CMEA nation.[69]

On February 16, 1976, CMEA Executive Committee Chairman Gerhard Weiss unexpectedly handed the draft of a proposed trade agreement to the current president of the EEC Council of Ministers, Gaston Thorn.[70] On February 20, Nikolai Faddeyev held a press

---

[65] *Ibid.*
[66] *The Economist*, June 1, 1974.
[67] *Op. cit.* in note 56, above.
[68] *Op. cit.* in note 12, above.
[69] *Op. cit.* in note 56, above.
[70] *Pravda*, February 20, 1976.

conference at CMEA headquarters in Moscow to discuss the nature of the document. It contained provisions for reciprocal most-favoured nation status (MFN), extension of credits, non-discrimination, and co-operation on problems of standardisation, environmental protection, statistics, and economic forecasting. The proposed document also provided for the regular exchange of economic data and for a joint committee to help implement the agreement.[71] Faddeyev made it clear, however, that neither the CMEA nor member countries intended to recognise the EEC, but rather would treat it as having only those powers held by the CMEA Secretariat. In addition, separate agreements would have to be made between the CMEA and member countries of the EEC, and between the EEC and member countries of the CMEA. Brussels would also be expected to extend the system of preferences to Bulgaria and the non-European CMEA countries, Cuba and Mongolia.[72]

The EEC Ministers, perhaps in shock, did not even bother to admonish the CMEA for once again trying to deal with the wrong body. Fumbling for a response to the proposals, they finally replied that the package would "... take a long time to study."[73]

The Soviets had apparently once again convinced themselves that "Little Europe" was facing insurmountable financial and commercial problems from which neither capitalist miracle nor CMEA agreement could save it.[74] Surely now, they seemed to be thinking, the EEC must see the inevitability of a general accommodation between the two organisations. But the EEC did not see it that way at all. Thorn was quoted in an interview of April 21, 1976, with the Soviet newspaper *Literaturnaya gazeta,* as stressing the EEC's long-held view that the CMEA still did not have even the legal competence to sign a comprehensive agreement.[75]

Although in 1976 the trade trend reversed itself—with CMEA exports to the EEC increasing rapidly while imports from Western Europe dropped off—the EEC remained convinced that there was little to gain from a general agreement with the CMEA.[76] Nine months after receipt of the perplexing Soviet-sponsored draft agreement, the EEC replied that while they could discuss such items as standards, pollution, and similar topics, there was no possibility of

---

[71] V. Zoloyev, "An Important CMEA Initiative," 5 *Foreign Trade* (Moscow, 1976), p. 9.

[72] *The Economist,* May 22, 1977.

[73] *Op. cit.* in note 41, above.

[74] A. Bykov, "Two Systems of Integration and Economic Ties in Europe," 2 *International Affairs* (Moscow, 1978), pp. 12-21.

[75] V. I. Kuznetsov, "SEV-EES: Vozmozhnosti sotrudnichestva" [CMEA-EEC: Possibilities for Co-operation], 4 *Sovetskoe gosudarstvo i pravo* (1978), pp. 69–77.

[76] *Ibid.*

a major trade agreement between the two organisations.[77] Neither side had changed its basic position.

Following Brussels' unyielding answer to the CMEA initiative, the Soviets published a number of authoritative essays featuring sarcastic criticism of the EEC reminiscent of the tone so common during the 1960s.[78] "Little Europe..." could not, they argued, "...pass the test of time"; however, it still continues to "...preach the dogma of collective protectionism..." against the interests of the people of Europe and the world.[79]

By 1977, the CMEA was showing signs of evolving a common foreign trade policy. It had already concluded international trade agreements with Mexico, Finland, and Iran.[80] At the same time, East European resistance to increased integration and a common CMEA foreign trade policy had weakened. Continued opposition had become relatively less appropriate with the emergence of a common EEC trade policy towards the East. In addition the oil crisis and subsequent energy-related events forced the East Europeans to realise just how dependent they were on Soviet fuel resources; the ensuing recession in the West may also have convinced some East European countries that the Soviet Union was a valuable and probably vital alternative market for their manufactured goods. Thus the Soviets gained a good deal of effective leverage within the CMEA.[81]

On February 16, 1977, the Soviets, after ignoring the EEC fishing limit for some time, were forced to conclude a short-term agreement limiting their catches.[82] Their arrival in Brussels to sign the document heralded *de facto* recognition of the EEC, but the Soviets continued to deny that it meant real or juridical acceptance of the Community.

In April 1977 while visiting Warsaw, Dr. David Owen—then taking his turn as President of the EEC Council of Ministers—was

---

[77] J. Pinder, "The Community and Comecon: What Could Negotiations Achieve?", 5 *The World Today* (1977), pp. 176–185.

[78] For instance, see Y. Shishkov, "Little Europe in an Impasse," 3 *International Affairs* (Moscow, 1977), pp. 53–61. Although it had been used before, the term "Little Europe" was now an almost obligatory reference when Soviet authors wrote about political economy in the EEC.

[79] Y. Shiryaev and A. Sokolov, "East-West Business Relations: Possibilities and Realities," 2 *International Affairs* (Moscow, 1977), pp. 37–45. An attempt to re-link the EEC with NATO and United States policy is made in A. Rusin, "The Rough Edges of the West European Triangle," 11 *International Affairs* (Moscow, 1977), pp. 106–115.

[80] *Izvestia*, August 16, 1975; *Pravda*, Ocotber 19, 1976.

[81] G. Golnick, "Integration in Eastern Europe: Comecon," unpublished monograph, Brussels, December 1977, Drew University Program.

[82] *Op. cit.* in note 41, above. Evidently the EEC's apparent willingness to arrest Soviet boats caught violating the EEC rules within their economic zone convinced the Soviet Union to come to Brussels.

handed a note by K. Olszewski, current Chairman of the CMEA Executive Committee, proposing further talks. The EEC subsequently invited a CMEA delegation to visit Brussels in the Autumn.[83]

The meeting took place on September 21, 1977, at the EEC headquarters. The CMEA delegation included Mihai Marinescu, Chairman of the CMEA Executive Committee, and Asen Velkov, CMEA Deputy Secretary. The EEC group was headed by Henri Simonet, EEC Commission Chairman, and Wilhelm Haferkamp, Commission Vice President.[84] Marinescu urged that future negotiations should be conducted with member-State representatives present to expedite multiple agreements. In addition, he called for formal negotiations to begin in the first part of 1978, with draft proposals submitted ahead of time by both sides. When the EEC demurred, Marinescu is reported to have suggested that a joint report be written specifying the measures necessary for the negotiations to move ahead.[85]

In early June 1978 an EEC group headed by Wilhelm Haferkamp visited CMEA headquarters.[86] Both sides seem to have stuck to their earlier positions and the best they could do was to agree that a Brussels meeting of "experts" should come next, in the near future. In late July, Asen Velkov brought a CMEA delegation to Belgium, accompanied by representatives from CMEA member countries.[87] They met with a group under the direction of Roy Denman, current EEC Commission Director-General of External Relations. The three-day conference once again resulted in little progress. The EEC was still willing to conclude only an agreement on administrative co-operation; the CMEA still insisted on a comprehensive trade agreement.[88]

During the Spring of 1978, essays in several authoritative Soviet journals suggested that Soviet policy toward the EEC might be on the verge of significant reformulation. In an article in the January issue of *Foreign Trade*, economic analyst Yuri Zhuravlyov concluded that many of the member countries of the two organisations were now engaged in major international trade relationships, and that a comprehensive agreement would be an important step

---

[83] Yu. Zhuravlyov, "The International Ties of the Council for Mutual Economic Assistance," 1 *Foreign Trade* (Moscow, 1978), pp. 2–9.
[84] *Pravda*, September 22, 1977. Also see *The Wall Street Journal*, September 22, 1977
[85] *Izvestia*, October 4, 1977.
[86] *Izvestia*, June 3, 1978.
[86] *Izvestia*, June 3, 1978.
[87] *Izvestia*, August, 9, 1978.
[88] *Ibid.*

towards further co-operation.[89] As of the end of 1977, EEC member countries accounted for some 60 per cent. of all CMEA trade with the capitalist industrial nations. Zhuravlyov also made the somewhat dubious claim that because of that trade, 2 million West European workers were employed in EEC member States.[90]

In the February issue of the Soviet journal, *International Affairs*, Y. Ivanov wrote an article in much the same vein as that of Zhuravlyov, and in a manner that seemed to indicate a shift towards a somewhat less propagandistic approach, as well as a more accurate assessment of EEC realities.[91] However, the tone of much Soviet commentary seemed to be changing from ridicule of the EEC to anger at being rejected by it.

Although the Soviets had continuously claimed that the CMEA had the legal capacity to sign a comprehensive agreement, it was not until the April issue of the legal journal *Sovetskoe gosudarstvo i pravo* that a definitive statement was made.[92] Legal analyst V. I. Kuznetsov wrote with heavy irony that, in fact, none of the EEC's supranational bodies had sufficient legal status to sign a truly comprehensive agreement such as that proposed by the CMEA. Hence, member nations of both organisations would have to sign. He also claimed that the CMEA had as much legal capacity to sign international trade documents as did the EEC.[93]

By the end of 1978, the Soviets and East Europeans had negotiated a set of "co-operative" relationships with West European countries and nations which had, to some extent, lessened the

---

[89] *Op. cit.* in note 83, above.

[90] *Ibid.* Soviet thought with regard to the EEC may also have been affected by the culmination of discussions between China and the EEC. On April 3, 1978, the Chinese signed a Five-year trade agreement with the Community. Having established an embassy to the EEC back in 1975, the Chinese had attracted some Soviet attention. The Soviets had earlier accused the two parties to the agreement of trying to arrange a Chinese flanking movement, using NATO as one of the strategic pincers. I. Alexeyev, "Peking's European Policy," 1 *International Affairs* (Moscow) (1976), pp. 56–65. The EEC-Chinese pact was not a particular surprise to the Soviets, nor is it likely to have created too much stir in the CMEA. nevertheless, it must have triggered some additional anger toward the Nine. See S. Milligan, "EC-China Trade Pact; The Gang of Nine Gets Communist Recognition," *European Community* (May–June 1978), pp. 6–7. Also see *Pravda*, December 2, 1977, April 4, 1978.

[91] Y. Ivanov, "The CMEA Countries and World Economic Relations," 2 *International Affairs* (Moscow, 1978), pp. 30–39. A critical problem for the Soviets and East Europeans appears to lie in making a balanced appraisal of events in Western Europe. They seem continually to be misled by the Doomsday hyperbole that inevitably appears in either news or conversation when the topic of European integration comes up among West Europeans. The fact that the EEC muddles through in spite of it all seems slowly but surely to be dawning on Soviet and East European observers. B Mayorov, "Common Market Economic and Monetary Alliance: Plans and Reality," 12 *Foreign Trade* (Moscow, 1976), pp. 32–42. G. Shakhnazarov, "The Labyrinths of Capitalist Integration," 9 *International Affairs* (Moscow, 1978), pp. 31–39.

[92] *Op. cit.* in note 75, above.

[93] *Ibid.*

pressure to conclude a comprehensive bloc-to-bloc trade agreement.[94] Co-operation pacts fall essentially outside of the Community's common trade policy and thus can be concluded without the direct participation of EEC institutions. They include, for example, such bilateral undertakings as licences, turnkey installations on a compensatory basis, joint construction, and joint production.[95] The pay-off from co-operation agreements and conventional trade deals, as well as from the Soviet shift out of the United States market following the hardening of United States policy, have caused Soviet commerce with the EEC countries to increase significantly. Between winter 1976 and summer 1978 Soviet trade with the United Kingdom expanded more than 40 per cent., and with France by some 25 per cent.[96] Nevertheless, contemporary Soviet and East European analyses of relations between the CMEA and EEC highlighted a central theme: the inevitability of a comprehensive trade agreement between the two economic organisations.[97]

However, significant unresolved issues persist. Actually—as illustrated above—there has been little change in the basic positions of either side since the possibility of a deal was first mentioned by Brezhnev in 1972. The following section is devoted to an analysis of the major problems that still remain to be solved before a comprehensive trade agreement can be signed.

II—EEC-CMEA NEGOTIATIONS: THE PRINCIPAL PROBLEMS

It has been argued that the level of mutual economic involvement has reached the point where neither organisation can afford to ignore the other. However, the parties involved do not at this time

---

[94] These were based in some degree on their intra-CMEA experiences. For descriptive material on international deals within the CMEA see G. Velyaminov and V. Parkhito, "The Legal Status of International Economic Associations," 5 *Foreign Trade* (Moscow, 1978), pp. 12–16. Also see the interview with L. I. Zorin, "A New Form of CMEA Nations' Co-operation," 7 *Foreign Trade* (Moscow, 1978), pp. 2–9. With reference to agreements with West European countries and businesses see Yu. M. Krasnov, *Ot confrontatsia k sotrudnichestvu* [From Confrontation to Cooperation], (Moscow: "Mezhdunarodnye otnosheniya," 1976). Also see the round-table discussion reported as "In the Interest of Mutually Beneficial Co-operation and Mutual Trust," 10 *Foreign Trade* (Moscow, 1978), pp. 16–25.

[95] I. Savyolova, "East-West Industrial Cooperation," 4 *Foreign Trade* (Moscow, 1977), pp. 20–30. Co-operation deals had simply not been considered or foreseen by the framers of the Treaty of Rome.

[96] *Pravda*, August 16, 1978.

[97] See, for example, G. P. Rozanov, *Politika sotrudnichestva – velenie vremeni* [A Policy of Co-operation, An Imperative of our Times], (Moscow: "Mezhdunarodnye otnosheniya," 1977), pp. 155–158. Also see Michael Dobroczynski, *Europejska współpraca gospodarcza* [European Economic Cooperation] (Warsaw: Panstowowe Wydawnictwo Ekonomiczne, 1976). A recent statement of this assumption can be found in Dyakin and Pankov, *op. cit.* in note 1, above, pp. 133–135.

agree on what would constitute adequate "recognition." In any discussion of the problems on which the EEC and CMEA must concur before any agreement can emerge, the recognition question must be considered first.

(a) *The Problem of Mutual Recognition*

The European Economic Community has held the position that *any* bloc-to-bloc arrangement was contingent upon diplomatic recognition of the EEC by the Soviet Union and the East European members of the CMEA.[98] Recognition is traditionally sought to establish legitimacy and to enhance prestige, or for a host of more tangible motives. It has been widely acknowledged that there are virtually no persuasive, tangible reasons why the EEC should insist on diplomatic recognition as a pre-condition to the conclusion of a major trade agreement with the CMEA. Thus, Community motives are most likely based on a felt need for added legitimacy, prestige, and, in some measure, revenge.

The EEC has long been the recipient of the Soviet Union's ridicule, hostility, and sceptical treatment in its domestic and international propaganda; and despite substantial changes in Soviet and East European Press treatment, a degree of sarcasm and invective still remains. Recognition would perhaps imply a certain atonement for misdeeds, and conceivably even make it a bit more difficult for the Soviets to continue in that vein. In addition, the EEC has been well aware of Soviet efforts to encourage disharmony within the Community by playing off individual members against each other. Recognition would undoubtedly include some understanding to curtail that kind of interference.

The EEC Commission members feel that there are sound practical reasons why they need ask for nothing less than full diplomatic recognition. They continue to be either indifferent or opposed to a bloc-to-bloc agreement, certain that trade will go on without it.[99] They know that for the West, trade agreements are largely public relations exercises while for the CMEA countries, foreign trade pacts help to regulate the planning process.[1] As long as the EEC's trade position is still favourable—and they feel it should remain so unless perhaps a major new oil discovery is made in, say, Byelorussia or Poland—the EEC will continue to assume that the CMEA

---

[98] *Op. cit.* in note 43, above.

[99] Interview with Mr. Louis Kawan, Commission of the European Communities, Brussels, Belgium, June 29, 1978.

[1] J. Pinder, "Trade Agreements with Communist Countries: The Shadow and the Substance," 14 *Trialogue* (1977), pp. 15–18.

needs West European markets more than the EEC needs the East. The EEC can thus afford to continue in its "lofty indifference."[2]

But, of course, neither the Soviets nor the East Europeans agree. For the Soviets, the EEC had historically been considered to be in the process of collapse; recognition of the Community would only help prop it up.[3] For a long time the Soviets had advocated an "all-European" solution under an alternative organisational framework (perhaps the United Nations Economic Commission for Europe). Recognition of the EEC would have meant abandoning their own version of the European economic future.[4] Although the Soviet Union has since seemed to move away from those positions, it has hinted that it would recognise the EEC only if the Community would legitimise and increase the prestige of the CMEA by in turn recognising it.[5] The EEC has made it clear repeatedly that it has not the slightest intention of extending diplomatic recognition to the CMEA. Likewise the Soviet draft agreement of February 1976 makes no provisions for recognition, mutual or otherwise.[6]

The East Europeans, for their part, have generally been wary of the whole recognition issue. There is some evidence to suggest that they feel the EEC's demands for recognition have given the Soviets added leverage to push the CMEA towards a Soviet-dominated common foreign trade policy in order to bargain more effectively on a bloc-to-bloc basis.[7] The EEC generally has not responded sympathetically to arguments based on the need to preserve East European economic independence. As far as Brussels is concerned, East European foreign trade automony is, in the final analysis, virtually non-existent where Soviet interest is concerned.[8]

As long as both sides maintain their present positions on mutual recognition, and as long as both the EEC and the Soviets continue to feel no urgent need actually to conclude a bloc-to-bloc agreement, the delegation traffic between Moscow and Brussels would appear to be a waste of time. As things stand, the Soviet and East Europeans can continue to make increasingly complex "arrangements" with the EEC, and when necessary—as in the fishing deal— to make formal agreements, while declaring their continued policy of non-recognition.

---

[2] *Op. cit.* in note 12, above.

[3] Ransom, *op. cit.* in note 1, above.

[4] *Ibid.*

[5] *Op. cit.* in note 43, above.

[6] *The Economist*, May 22, 1976, In an interview with *Le Monde* in June 1977, Mr. Brezhnev reaffirmed his sentiments of March 1972 that mutual recognition was an essential first step.

[7] M. Simai, "Changing Views in Hungary on the European Community" in Frans A. M. Alting von Geusau, *The External Relations of the European Community* (1974), pp. 85–91.

[8] *Op. cit.* in note 99, above.

In the event that the problem of mutual recognition were to be solved, the concerned parties would immediately be faced with a second fundamental difference; the legal competence of both organisations to conclude a comprehensive agreement is the subject of significant disagreement between the parties.

(b) *Legal Competence*

Since the idea of an EEC-CMEA agreement was first raised in the late 1960s, the Common Market has maintained that the CMEA was an altogether different type of organisation from the EEC. The CMEA was not designed as a supranational political institution, its council has no major decision-making powers, it has no legislative assembly or court of justice, members may decide for themselves whether or not to participate in CMEA programmes, major decisions must be made unanimously, and finally, the CMEA rules and procedures do not provide for joint negotiation of international trade agreements.[9] The CMEA was judged by the EEC to be simply a middle-level co-ordinating agency with virtually no major decision-making powers, managed by a group of (mainly) Soviet, lower-level bureaucrats who had to consult their superiors in the government and party on almost any question imaginable.[10] Although the truth of this image was acknowledged in much of Eastern Europe, the Soviets were infuriated at the EEC's "inflexible" stand.[11]

For some time the Soviets seem to have thought that Mr. Brezhnev's implied offer of mutual recognition would be sufficient to change the EEC's position. However, along with the CMEA draft proposal of February 1976 the Soviets appear to have offered to push through whatever changes might be necessary to give the CMEA proper legal credentials to make the deal.[12]

In V. I. Kuznetsov's *Sovetskoe gosudarstvo i pravo* article of April 1978, it was announced that rule changes made "...in response to the needs of the Comprehensive Programme" had given the CMEA specific powers to conclude international agreements between council members and international organisations.[13] The changes, along with Kuznetsov's assertion of "implied competence" and the rather novel argument that CMEA must be legally competent otherwise it could not have proposed the agreement in the first place, seemed to be about as far as the Soviets felt they needed to go

---

[9] Ransom, *op. cit.* in note 1, above, and *op. cit.* in note 35, above.
[10] *Op. cit.* in note 55, above.
[11] *Op. cit.* in note 6, above, on p. 90.
[12] *Op. cit.* in note 74, above.
[13] *Op. cit.* in note 75, above.

to upgrade the CMEA's juridical image.[14] But, in addition, Kuznet-sov charged that the CMEA draft of February 1976 contained points which were outside the legal competence of the EEC itself, especially in the field of co-operative programmes.[15]

This attack on the international legal strength of the EEC in a sense played into the hands of the Community. Brussels had all along held that it did not, in fact, have the power to enter into anything more complex than bilateral agreements with individual States and so indeed would be negotiating only those points raised in the EEC's own model agreement for bilateral relations given in 1974 to the individual governments of the "State trading" nations.[16]

The legal competence argument seems to have a great many facets, and shows no major signs of resolution. Suffice it to say that the question is a somewhat technical one, not unrelated to the recognition problem, but rather more dependent on the question of what form any agreement or set of agreements should take.

(c) *The Form of Relationship*

From the time of the first concrete CMEA initiatives, the Common Market has indicated its willingness to meet periodically for that purpose, but not to conclude a trade agreement.[17] The EEC did state that the Community would be willing to establish relations in those areas where its functions were similar, as well as to conclude agreements with CMEA member States.[18] In response to the draft agreement of February 1976, the EEC said that it would only agree to establish working relationships with the CMEA on topics such as economic forecasting, statistics, environmental protection, and standardisation.[19]

The 1976 agreement proposed by the CMEA included a rather complex scheme for a series of conventions to be concluded between the EEC and CMEA and between each organisation and constituent members.[20] The Soviets have made it clear that other members of the CMEA may not conclude formal trade agreements with the EEC until a bloc-to-bloc agreement has been signed.

---

[14] That the Soviets cannot always push whatever they wish through the CMEA was once again illustrated by Romanian veto of a June 1978 Soviet proposal to substitute majority rule for the current unanimity principle. The Romanians are not alone in their resistance to Soviet efforts. *The Wall Street Journal*, June 30, 1978.

[15] *Op. cit.* in note 75, above.

[16] *Op. cit.* in note 56, above.

[17] *Op. cit.* in note 49, above.

[18] *Op. cit.* in note 77, above.

[19] *Izvestia*, June 3, 1978.

[20] See *ibid.*, and W. Iskra, "CMEA and EEC: Opportunities for Co-operation," 6 *World Marxist Review* (1976), pp. 64–71.

Some East Europeans, on the other hand, still argue for an all-European pact, in which the nations of East and West would agree to mutual MFN, non-discrimination, promotion of technical co-operation projects, and other Pan-European practices that many evidently had hoped to achieve through the ECSS. The EEC, CMEA, EFTA and other such organisations would continue to enjoy their intra-group powers.[21] However, it seems that most East Europeans would rather settle for the EEC model than the Soviet one, if pressed to make such a decision, because it might help to spare them from a strong, Soviet-dominated, supranational CMEA.

Slow movement towards some kind of compromise on the issue of form does seem to be taking place in the final days of 1978. However, this question is certainly not the toughest which remains to be solved on the road to a general accommodation between the two economic organisations. By far the most difficult is the problem of what economic concessions might be made by each side in order to make a general agreement mutually attractive.

(d) *Trade Concessions*

In the various exchanges of draft documents and delegation visits since 1972, the CMEA has made major economic demands on the EEC, but has shown no inclination to give much in return. Yet the EEC has itself failed to demand significant trade concessions, even in its model bilateral agreement of 1974; it did specify "reciprocal advantage" but that is largely meaningless in trade with planned economies.

CMEA, and the Soviets speaking for it, have demanded most-favoured-nation status (MFN), and the extension of credits on liberal terms. They have also called for an end to trade discrimination; especially tariffs, quotas, quality standards, and varying dues on foodstuffs.[22]

The 1974 EEC model agreement, sent to the individual States of the CMEA, offered long-term preferential trade, MFN, and an agricultural understanding.[23] The Community has since unilaterally extended MFN to most of the CMEA States. The Commission has pointed out that tariffs should not really be a point of concern since CMEA exports to the EEC are largely raw materials which are in any case not subject to tariff. What finished products it does export to the EEC are taxed at a very low rate. Quotas and other non-tariff

[21] *Op. cit.* in note 7, above.

[22] N. Shmelov, "Ekonomicheskie svyazi vostok-zapad" [East-West Economic Ties], 12 *Voprosy ekonomiki* (1976). See also *op. cit.* in note 79, above, and *op. cit.* in note 43, above.

[23] *Op. cit.* in note 56, above. It also called for the establishment of bilateral committees to monitor implementation and solve problems that might arise.

restrictions constitute a more difficult problem, but one which has already been solved to a substantial extent.[24]

The availability of Common Market credit also constitutes a problem. The EEC has found it somewhat difficult to make the Soviets and East Europeans understand that the Community not only has no common credit facility like the Eximbank, but that it also does not even have a common credit policy, nor is it likely to create one.[25]

The EEC argues that, in fact, the CMEA countries remain both unwilling and unable to grant meaningful concessions. Such traditionally mentioned items as better access to real business policy-makers, higher quality market and planning information, and better on-site facilities for EEC businessmen are not significant in the current context.[26] Naturally, the Community has demanded some form of anti-dumping provision, but this can hardly be seen as a CMEA concession.[27]

Thus with both sides rather far apart on major trade questions it is difficult to see how even bilateral agreements could be negotiated. After clearing such formidable obstacles as recognition, legal competence, and the eventual form of any trade relationship, the two sides would still find themselves in a very unsymmetrical bargaining configuration. Perhaps part of the solution may be found in the possible indirect mutual benefits that might accrue to the signatories of a CMEA-EEC trade agreement.

(e) *Indirect Benefits*

For many years the Soviets viewed any kind of co-operation with the Common Market as leading to a strengthening of the Community and a weakening of Soviet power.[28] As the Soviet Union realised that the EEC was a long-term reality which it could little affect, it recognised that direct bloc-to-bloc negotiations could help to push the East Europeans into accepting increased CMEA supranationality due to their eagerness to protect and augment their West European markets. That supranationality, if properly designed, could greatly enhance Soviet control of the organisation and its European

---

[24] *Op. cit.* in note 12, above. EEC observers doubt that under present circumstances quotas will be reduced any further.

[25] *Op. cit.* in note 77, above. On the other hand, the Community has publicised its interest in stopping what the Commission feels has been over-bidding in CMEA State-export credits from within the Common Market banking community. *Op. cit.* in note 56, above.

[26] *Op. cit.* in note 99, above. There is also a widely-held feeling that although CMEA countries might agree to such undertakings, they would not be very conscientious in carrying them out.

[27] *Op. cit.* in note 77, above.

[28] Schaefer, *op. cit.* in note 8, above.

member States.[29] Thus, for the Soviet Union, whose direct trade interests have not been critically engaged, the immediate political and eventual economic pay-off of long bloc-to-bloc negotiations might be substantial.[30]

For the Community's part, it is fair to say that it has traditionally shown at least a mild reluctance to do anything that would contribute directly to an increased Soviet dominance within the CMEA. However, the Commission has also not been much interested in using trade as an instrument of foreign policy in the East.[31]

In short, the East Europeans have been caught between Soviet policy, designed—at least in part—to strengthen the Soviet Union's influence within the CMEA, and the EEC's relative weakness and indifference. Where it might have been able to affect Soviet behaviour, the EEC either cannot act (credits), has already given up the option (MFN), or has no taste for it (withholding technology).

Having reviewed the chronology of the evolving relationship between the EEC and the CMEA as well as the principal issues that confront the two organisations, it is appropriate to ask a concluding question. When are the two groups likely to reach a major accommodation, and what will be its likely substance?

III—Conclusions

The final 1978 meeting between the EEC and CMEA representatives ended on November 25, after several days of largely fruitless discussion. Wilhelm Haferkamp announced that once again little progress had been made. He felt the Community had made all the concessions that it could, and that the next move was up to the CMEA.[32]

After considering the record of contacts and initiatives, as well as the nature of the major problems, there does indeed seem to be little likelihood of, or reason for, a full trade agreement. But that, assuredly, does not mean there will not be one. For one thing, in spite of all of the concrete problems facing them, at least some of the people involved seem to feel that a major agreement is inevitable. For another thing, momentum has been built up so that perhaps, with the increasing frequency of talks, the representatives of the two

---

[29] *Op. cit.* in note 55, above.

[30] *Ibid.* Also see *op. cit.* in note 77, above.

[31] *Op. cit.* in note 12, above. See also *op. cit.* in note 99, above. The EEC has viewed with some scepticism attempts to link trade with Soviet political and military behaviour. In addition it should be recalled that the Commission seems to hold the opinion that the East Europeans now hold very little economic or political freedom that can be protected.

[32] BBC World Service, News, November 25, 1978.

organisations will find themselves propelled on to a common ground where critical compromises can be made. Because the issues of recognition, legal competency, form of relationship, and indirect benefits are essentially perceptual problems, they may be amenable to solution by personal interaction through the building of mutual trust. The other major snag, trade concessions, will be less easy to work out. The EEC member countries, having already unilaterally liberalised their trade policies with the East, may decide—as many Western analysts seem to think—that trade agreements are merely indicative rather than contractual. If so, and if the CMEA is willing to do without major quota changes in EEC and other non-tariff restrictions, an agreement is indeed possible, and even perhaps likely.

EQUALITY AND DISCRIMINATION
IN INTERNATIONAL ECONOMIC LAW (IX):

THE COUNCIL
FOR MUTUAL ECONOMIC ASSISTANCE

By

B. G. RAMCHARAN

This is the ninth contribution to the series on *Equality and Discrimination in International Economic Law*, initiated by Professor Schwarzenberger's paper under this title in the 1971 Volume of this Annual, and continued in the 1972 Volume by G. G. Kaplan on *The UNCTAD Scheme for Generalised Preferences* and B. G. Ramcharan on *The Commonwealth Preferential System*, in the 1974 and 1975 Volumes by P. Goldsmith and F. Sonderkötter on *The European Communities* and *The European Communities in the Wider World*, in the 1977 Volume by A. Sutton on *Trends in the Regulation of International Trade in Textiles* and C. Stoiber on *The Multinational Enterprise*, and in the 1978 Volume by B. G. Ramcharan on *The United Nations Economic Commissions—Managing Editor*, Y.B.W.A.

THE continuing relevance and increasing importance of questions of equality and discrimination in international economic law are amply indicated by the Declaration of the Conference of Ministers for Foreign Affairs of Non-Aligned Countries held at Belgrade from July 25 to 30, 1978. The Foreign Ministers warned that "one of the gravest and most obvious manifestations of the crisis in the international economic system is the increasing recourse to the policies of protectionism and discrimination against the developing countries by the developed countries. Developing countries have been adversely affected as the protectionist measures were introduced precisely for products that are of special export interest to the developing countries...."[1]

"The Foreign Ministers accorded great importance to the successful completion of the Multilateral Trade Negotiations now under way in the General Agreement on Tariffs and Trade to further liberalise international trade and reform the international trade

---

[1] The Declaration is contained in Annex I to United Nations document A/33/206, p. 72. See also on this issue, the Report of the International Law Commission on the work of its 30th session (A/33/10), chap. II, "The Most-Favoured Nation Clause, " especially p. 173, "New Rules of International Law in favour of developing countries."

system. Above all, they expect differentiated and more favourable treatment in trade to be granted to the developing countries, thereby at least partially correcting the prevailing inequalities between the developed and the developing countries in international trade which cause profound disparities in their levels of economic development. For the developing countries, changes in the General Agreement on Tariff's and Trade rules, in the sense of introducing a permanent legal basis for preferential treatment to developing countries, is an essential prerequisite to changing their position in international trade relations and attaining the objectives of the New International Economic Order. At the same time, this preferential treatment should include the developing countries' inherent rights to institute and apply particular protective trade measures and subsidies which are essential to their development needs. Of special significance in the Multilateral Trade Negotiations is recognition of the principle of non-reciprocity of concessions in trade relations between the developed and developing countries, which would establish a more equitable foundation for the developing countries' participation in these negotiations."[2] The Foreign Ministers therefore urged that necessary preparatory work for the implementation of a global system of trade preferences among developing countries should be undertaken as early as possible.[3]

In the present paper we shall look at issues of equality and discrimination in the practice of the Council for Mutual Economic Assistance (CMEA). In a review article in *International Affairs*, published in 1976, R. Alexeyev pointed out that "economic co-operation between the countries of the socialist community is of two kinds: bilateral, based on bilateral agreements and treaties, and that based on multilateral agreements within the framework of CMEA and its associated organisations." In this connection, he felt that "Lenin's statement that 'the part must conform to the whole, and not vice versa,' ... was directly relevant."[4] It is important to bear in

---

[2] *Ibid.* p. 81.

[3] *Ibid.* p. 109.

[4] R. Alexeyev, "CMEA—A Community of Equals," *International Affairs* (Moscow, 1976), Nr. 5, pp. 114–116. On the CMEA see generally: S. Ausch, *Bilateralism and Multilateralism in the CMEA* (1969); S. Ausch, *Theory and Practice of CMEA Co-operation* (1972); M. Cismarescu, "Romania and Legal Integration within Comecon," 2 *Review of Socialist Law* (1976), pp. 103–110; CMEA Secretariat, *CMEA:Principles, Problems and Prospects* (1975); CMEA Secretariat, *Survey of CMEA Activities in 1977* (Moscow, 1978); East-West Research and Advisory Publications, *Prospects of Economic Integration in Comecon* (1971); B. Gribov, "The Most-Favoured Nation Principle in Trade," *International Affairs* (Moscow), Nr. 4, April 1974, p. 102. K. Grzybowski, *The Socialist Commonwealth of Nations* (1964); E. A. Hewitt, *Foreign Trade Prices in CMEA* (1974); F. D. Holzman, "Soviet Foreign Trade Pricing and the Question of Discrimination: A 'Customs Union' Approach," XLIV *The Review of Economics and Statistics* (1962); T. W. Hoya, "The Comecon General Conditions—A Socialist Unification of International Trade Law," *Columbia Law Review* (1970), p. 253; T. W. Hoya and

mind this admixture of bilateral and multilateral economic relations because it is a feature found not only in relations among members of the CMEA, but in their relations with outside countries as well. Issues of equality and discrimination may arise at both levels. Thus, Czechoslovakia, Hungary, Poland and Romania, while members of the CMEA, are also members of the General Agreement on Tariffs and Trade (GATT) as are Yugoslavia and Cuba. In this paper we will focus principally on relations at the multilateral level within the framework of the CMEA.[5]

I—THE FOREIGN TRADE SYSTEM OF CMEA MEMBERS

Mutual foreign trade of the CMEA members is conducted on the basis of five-year long-term commercial agreements, linked to the countries' economic development plans. The system of inter-governmental long-term agreements forms an important part in regulating foreign trade among the CMEA members.[6] These agreements are signed on the basis of the results of co-ordinating national economic plans of the CMEA members and are tightly interwoven with the development plans of the separate countries. They are designed to ensure the planned deliveries of raw materials and manufactured goods required for the development of the economies of the member States to ensure a stable market for all types of products.

The Comprehensive Programme for the Further Extension and Improvement of Co-operation and the Development of Socialist Integration (1971) envisaged a further improvement of long-term

---

J. B. Quigley, "Comecon 1968 General Conditions for the Delivery of Goods," 31 *Ohio State Law Journal* (1971), pp. 1–51; M. Kaser, *Comecon: Integration Problems of the Planned Economies* (1967); H. Kelsen, *Communist Theory of Law* (1955); H. Kohler, *Economic Integration in the Soviet Bloc* (1965); A. Korbonski, "Comecon," *International Conciliation*, Nr. 549 (1964); V. I. Kuznetsov, *Economic Integration: Two Approaches* (1976); F. L. Pryor, *The Communist Foreign Trade System* (1963); K. Rabcewicz-Zubowski, *East European Rules on the Validity of International Commercial Arbitration* (1970); P. Ramundo, *The Socialist Theory of International Law* (1964); H. Schaefer, *Comecon and the Politics of Integration* (1972); M. Senin, *Socialist Integration* (1973); R. Starr, "A New Legal Framework for Trade between the United States and the Soviet Union: The 1972 Trade Agreement," 67 *American Journal of International Law* (1973), pp. 63–83; R. Szawlowski, *The System of the International Organizations of the Communist Countries* (1976); *The Multilateral Economic Co-operation of Socialist States: A Collection of Documents* (1977); V. Vassilev, *Policy in the Soviet Bloc on Aid to Developing Countries* (1975); A. Wasilkowski, "Legal Regulation of Economic Relations within the CMEA: Trends of Development," V *Polish Yearbook of International Law* (1972–73), pp. 7–27; P. J. D. Wiles, *Communist International Economics* (1967).

[5] *Cf.* Mr. Perpegel, Observer for the CMEA, A/C.2/32/SR.4, para. 4.

[6] CMEA Secretariat, *Information on Economic Co-operation of the CMEA Member Countries* (1976), pp. 9–14.

trade agreements in order to stabilise and develop exchange of goods, to ensure a high technological level of delivered goods, mutual acceptance of terms concerning quantities, quality, delivery time and other conditions pertaining to trade.

Basing their activities on the principle of State monopoly in foreign trade, the CMEA members have created a legal system to regulate the functioning of their mutual foreign trade, of its planned and stable development, comprising: (i) legal stipulations regarding trade turnover, based on long-term trade agreements; (ii) general conditions of deliveries of goods; general conditions of technical servicing and equipment assembly; general principles on deliveries of spare parts; (iii) general principles of pricing; (iv) an agreed system of trade balancing and of payments for delivered goods, including multilateral settlements carried out through the International Bank for Economic Co-operation.

Long-term trade agreements help to create on a planned basis the required proportions in the development of the national economies of the CMEA members, and contribute to a stable development of their economies and of their trade relations.

Prices in the mutual foreign trade of the CMEA members are established on the basis of principles, worked out in bilateral negotiations, preceding the signing by foreign trade organisations of delivery of contracts for goods. The basis for these prices are the jointly formulated principles utilised within the framework of the CMEA.[7]

Monetary and financial co-operation of the CMEA members constitutes one of the conditions for fruitful development of their economic and foreign trade relations. This was aided by the establishment in 1964 of the International Bank for Economic Co-operation (IBEC) and in 1971 of the International Investment Bank (IIB). Multilateral settlements and crediting within the framework of CMEA members' monetary and financial relations are effected through the use of a collective currency—the transferable rouble.

II—EQUALITY AS A BASIC PRINCIPLE OF THE CMEA

The CMEA is an organisation which is formally committed to the principles of respect for sovereignty, equality, mutual interest and advantage, voluntariness and comradely assistance. The commitment to equality features in Article 1 of the Charter of the CMEA, which provides that "The CMEA is based on the principle of sovereign equality of all the member countries of the Council." Another illustrative example is Article IV of the Agreement concerning Multilateral Settlement of Accounts in Transferable

---

[7] See below, IV—The Pricing System.

Roubles and the Organisation of the International Bank for Economic Co-operation, which provides that "Activities of the International Bank for Economic Co-operation shall be performed on the basis of full equality..." and "Members of the Bank shall enjoy equal rights." Article XI of the Articles of Agreement of the Establishment of the International Investment Bank similarly states: "The Bank may on terms of equality contact and establish business relations with international financial and credit institutions as well as other banks."

The Final Act of the Conference on Security and Co-operation in Europe, to which CMEA countries subscribed, recognised that co-operation in the field of economics with due regard for the different levels of economic development, "can be developed, on the basis of equality and mutual satisfaction of the partners, and of reciprocity permitting, as a whole, an equitable distribution of advantages and obligations of comparable scale, with respect for bilateral and multilateral agreements."[8] The participating States also recognised "the beneficial effects which can result for the development of trade from the application of the most-favoured-nation treatment," and pledged to "endeavour to reduce or progressively eliminate all kinds of obstacles to the development of trade."

In the field of business contacts and facilities the participating States undertook to encourage "the provision, on conditions as favourable as possible and equal for all representatives" of foreign organisations, enterprises, firms and banks concerned with external trade, of hotel accommodation, means of communication, and of other facilities normally required by them, as well as of suitable business and residential premises for purposes of permanent representation.[9]

---

[8] At its meeting in October 1975, the CMEA Executive Committee welcomed the results of the Conference on Security and Co-operation in Europe and noted that the principles proclaimed at the Conference and the agreements achieved, which were formalised in the Final Act of the Conference, created a favourable basis for further expansion of co-operation among the European States in various fields of economy, science, technology and environmental protection. The communiqué on this meeting emphasised that "proceeding from the interest and willingness of the CMEA member countries to pursue the policy of broad international co-operation, the Council for Mutual Economic Assistance is determined to make within its competence its contribution to the realisation of the relevant principles and provisions laid down in the section entitled 'Co-operation in the Field of Economies, of Science and Technology and of the Environment' of the Final Act of the Conference, making use for this purpose of the active co-operation of CMEA with the UNECE, UNESCO and other international organisations."

[9] The co-operation agreements concluded between the CMEA and Finland, Iraq and Mexico also refer to the readiness of CMEA member countries to develop economic relations with other countries on the principles of equality, mutual benefit and non-interference in domestic affairs.

The attachment of the CMEA to the principle of equality is further indicated, for example, by the communiqué issued after the summit meeting of the CMEA in Prague in June, 1973, which stated that "CMEA member countries... confirm their willingness to develop economic relations with other countries regardless of their social and State systems, on the basis of equality, mutual advantage and non-interference in internal affairs." Similarly, in a statement made at the 130th plenary meeting of the fourth session of the United Nations Conference on Trade and Development (UNCTAD) on May 11, 1976, A. Velkov, Deputy Secretary of the CMEA, stated that "CMEA countries were striving to develop their economic, scientific and technological relations with other countries, irrespective of their social system, in line with the principles set forth in the Charter of Economic Rights and Duties of States, the Declaration and the Programme of Action on the Establishment of a New International Economic Order and the Final Act of the Conference on Security and Co-operation in Europe." He informed the meeting that the CMEA "had established official relations with EEC and had proposed to sign the agreement providing for the creation of favourable conditions for co-operation, on a basis of equality, between the two organisations and their member countries." As regards CMEA policy towards developing countries, he said that, "The co-operation of CMEA member countries was aimed primarily at developing the most important branches of the developing countries' economy and their State sector, so as to widen the range and step up the pace of their production with the object of strengthening their economic independence."[10]

It has been pointed out by one source that "CMEA integration efforts have so far mainly been focused on the technical aspects of intertwining certain branches of the production apparatus. The foreign trade sector, however, apart from the co-ordination of the five-year plans between the CMEA Member States, has remained the exclusive prerogative of the sovereign national State." The same author has noted that the CMEA "does not even possess the rudiments of a common commercial policy."[11]

---

[10] Proceedings of UNCTAD, Fourth Session, Nairobi, Vol. II, United Nations Publication, Sales Nr. E.76.II.D.11, p. 154. In the Final Act of the Conference on Security and Co-operation in Europe the participating States pledged to take into account "the interests of the developing countries throughout the world, including those among the participating countries as long as they are developing from the economic point of view"; and reaffirmed "their will to co-operate for the achievement of the aims and objectives established by the appropriate bodies of the United Nations in the pertinent documents concerning development, it being understood that each participating State maintains the positions it has taken on them." The principle of giving special attention to the least-developed countries was also recognised.

[11] B. R. Bot, "EEC-CMEA: Is a Meaningful Relationship Possible?" 13 *Common Market Law Review* (1976), pp. 335–366 at pp. 352–353. J. M. van Brabant, *A Reconstruction of the*

According to another source, "In general...the CMEA community as a whole has not been isolated from the world economy by a common economic boundary based on specific international agreements. The economic contacts of particular CMEA countries with third States are made in an independent way, mainly in virtue of bilateral agreements. But in practice sometimes important differences appear as to the scope of these relations or forms of co-operation.

"It seems that this traditional caution of the CMEA countries, as far as co-ordination of economic policy towards third States is concerned, resulted in a high degree from the reluctance to take actions which from the point of view of third States could have been interpreted as an indirect impediment of access to the CMEA market, for instance, by creating legal preferences stimulating the development of mutual turnover within the CMEA.[12] Lack of co-ordination, however, hindered the defence of interests of the CMEA countries against discriminatory trends which appeared in the practice of some States or economic groupings. That was the reason why the Comprehensive Programme of 1971 proclaimed certain changes in the domain under discussion.

"The Programme confirmed the hitherto existing standpoint of the CMEA countries as far as relations with other countries are concerned by stating: 'In accordance with their policy of peaceful co-existence and in the interest of social progress, as well as assuming that international socialist division of labour is taking place with regard to world division of labour, the CMEA member States will continue to develop economic, scientific, and technological links with other countries irrespectively of their social and State systems, basing themselves on the principles of equality, mutual benefits, and respect of their sovereignty.'

Composition of Intra-CMEA Trade Relations (1974), states at pp. 2–3 that "With few exceptions the centrally planned economies (CPEs) of Eastern Europe do not routinely publish detailed trade data. For this reason, an independent assessment of the place and importance of foreign trade in the individual CPEs and in the region as a whole cannot be undertaken without substantial work. Moreover, the published data are in general not suitable to draw comprehensive conclusions from intertemporal and international comparisons of their commercial relations. So far the raw information one may hope to attain from official statistical releases is confined to the level, commodity composition and geographical distribution of overall imports and exports on the one hand, and more or less detailed, but by no means exhaustive data on the commodity composition of overall trade and by individual partners on the other hand. Data on the composition of bilateral trade or of a CPEs trade with separate economic regions are available for some countries, but then usually in a very aggregate breakdown of absolute data or very detailed quantity data."

[12] Author's note: "Some time ago Z. Kamecki suggested that the instruments of customs policy of the CMEA countries should be used to create appropriate preferences for the development of mutual turnover. These suggestions, however, have not been put into practice. See Z. Kamecki, "Problemy integracji gospodarczej krajów RWPG" [Economic Integration Problems of the CMEA Countries], *Gospodarka Planowa*, Nr. 10 (1968), pp. 12–13.

"At the same time the Comprehensive Programme—and this is a new factor—announced that the CMEA countries 'will co-ordinate their foreign economic policy in the interest of normalisation of international trade and economic relations and, above all, with the view of eliminating discriminations in this domain.'

"Thus the further development of legal regulation with regard to the process of socialist economic integration will comprise in a much larger scale than before the co-ordination of particular economic policy instruments of the CMEA States in relation to third countries, but on the understanding that the defence of justified interests of the CMEA States against discrimination, and not the establishment of barriers against the development of international trade relations, will be the aim of this co-ordination."[13]

III—EQUALISATION OF DEVELOPMENT LEVEL

The Charter of the CMEA recognises that there are differences in the levels of development of the various CMEA countries. Thus, Article 1 of the revised CMEA Charter recognises the need for "the approximation and gradual equalisation of levels of development" of members of the CMEA.[14]

Article II of the Articles of Agreement of the Establishment of the International Investment Bank provides that "[t]he Bank's activities must be organically linked to ... measures which promote ... the gradual elimination of disparities between levels of economic development among member countries" although it goes on to add that "at the same time the principle that the Bank credits must be put to efficient use must remain in force."

This problem is recognised to be a continuing one. This may be seen, for example, in the *Survey of CMEA Activities in 1975* which reported that "research was underway on the ... equalisation of economic levels of the socialist countries."[15]

The official communiqué on the 32nd meeting of the session of the CMEA "stressed the need to take due account, when realising ... programmes, of the tasks designed to ensure a gradual approximation and equalisation of the development levels of CMEA countries and the need to give the Republic of Cuba and the Mongolian

---

[13] A. Wasilkowski, "Legal Regulation of Economic Relations within the Council for Mutual Economic Assistance: Trends of Development," V *Polish Yearbook of International Law* (1972–73), pp. 7–27 at pp. 15–16.

[14] See F. Kozma, *Some theoretical problems regarding socialist integration and the levelling of economic development*, Budapest (1971).

[15] See p.89. See, similarly, the statement by Mr. Perpegel, Observer, CMEA, A/C.2/32/SR.4, para. 2; where he referred to "measures aimed at the approximation and equalisation of economic development levels of the CMEA member countries."

People's Republic assistance and support in speeding up their economic growth rates and in enhancing the efficiency of their economies."[16]

The Comprehensive Programme indicates that the task of approximation and equalisation of the economic development levels of the CMEA member countries becomes particularly pressing in view of the needs of the scientific and technical revolution.

Among the main ways for the gradual approximation and equalisation of the economic development levels of the CMEA member countries utilised are, first and foremost, the mobilisation and utilisation of the efforts and resources of the countries concerned, and the utilisation of the advantages offered by the international socialist division of labour.

Towards this end, in the field of scientific and technical co-operation the Comprehensive Programme envisages in particular the enlistment of the industrially less developed countries in research and design work, the transfer of samples, licences and other results of research and design work on mutually beneficial terms, technical assistance in designing, mounting and commissioning projects, the transfer of professional and production experience, etc.

Preferential conditions of co-operation are also envisaged as an additional means of the development of the national economies of the industrially less developed countries.

As was underlined in the decision of the 30th Session of CMEA held in Berlin in July 1976, CMEA member countries are willing to continue implementing special measures to accelerate the development and raise the efficiency of the economies of countries such as the Mongolian People's Republic and the Republic of Cuba, taking the specific conditions of building socialism in these countries into account.

IV—THE PRICING SYSTEM

Prior to 1975, prices in trade among member countries of the CMEA used to be established for the duration of a five-year plan and based on the average price on the world market over a reference period—usually five years. Under a new system introduced in 1975 prices are fixed each year on the basis of the previous five-year world average. This change was introduced on account of inflationary movements on the world market. World price rises had led to wide differences between the price levels CMEA countries applied in trade among themselves, and those they applied in dealings with

---

[16] The communiqué is reproduced in the Annex to United Nations document A/33/274. See p. 4 of the Annex.

other countries. With higher prices offering on the world market, CMEA exporters had become less interested in supplying their partners; CMEA importers, nevertheless assured of goods at low prices from other CMEA countries, were becoming less keen to embark on joint investment projects to improve the supply of essential products.[17]

According to the *Economic Survey of Europe*, by 1977, the third year of the new system of price adjustment in intra-CMEA trade, the advantages and disadvantages of the system began to show up. An article in a Polish economic journal[18] found the system to be good with respect to the price of fuels, some raw materials and agricultural products. The cost and the quality of these products did not change in the short run, but their prices in the world market fluctuated a great deal which hampered planning. On the other hand, the article found that five-year moving averages were not suitable for the adjustment of prices of manufactures, because the period was too long. The quality of this type of product changed frequently. Fixed prices created disincentives to modernisation and technical progress. Prices within intra-CMEA trade were often below world market prices, which discouraged mutual trade. The article advocated the shortening of the moving average for machinery to two or, at most, three years and the use of current world market prices for consumer goods.[19]

V—CMEA COUNTRIES AND GATT

As was pointed out earlier, Cuba, Czechoslovakia, Poland, Romania, and Yugoslavia are also members of GATT. This means that they commit themselves to, and receive the benefits of most-favoured-nation (MFN) treatment under the GATT rules. This may lead, theoretically, to inequality at two levels: they may grant to GATT members preferences which they do not grant to CMEA members. This type of inequality does not appear to be very prevalent in practice, however. Secondly, they do receive advantages from GATT members which other CMEA members may not receive.

When Romania, for example, became a party to the GATT on November 14, 1971, it was agreed that since Romania had no customs tariff, Romania should express its firm intention to increase its imports from the contracting parties to GATT at a rate not slower

---

[17] ECE, Press Release ECE/GEN/N/97, November 19, 1975. *Cf.* "Soviets raise COMECON oil price," *The Guardian*, January, 21, 1977.

[18] *Gospodarka Planova*, Nr. 11, 1976.

[19] ECE, *Economic Survey of Europe in 1976*, Pt. I, p. 125.

than the rate of growth of total imports laid down in Romania's five-year plans.

In conformity with Article XXXIII of GATT, Romania enjoyed the benefit of all tariff concessions negotiated prior to its accession. Under the terms of the protocol of accession, contracting parties which still maintained prohibitions or discriminatory quantitative restrictions agreed not to increase the discriminatory element in these restrictions, undertook to remove them progressively and accepted as an objective their elimination before the end of 1974.[20]

According to the *Economic Survey of Europe* in 1976, with Romania's accession to GATT, EEC discriminatory quantitative restrictions were gradually reduced from 206 full and 271 partial tariff headings to 113 full and 80 partial headings. In 1976 only five per cent. of EEC imports from Romania were subject to such restrictions. Romania has also been admitted to the United States generalised system of preferences, and enjoys expanding benefits in the EEC's preference scheme.[21]

VI—EAST–WEST TRADE

In an article published in Volume 32 of this *Year Book*, the present writer drew attention to a long-standing issue between the centrally-planned-economy countries of Eastern Europe (in effect, the membership of the CMEA) and the Western market-economy countries involving complaints by the former that discriminatory trade and export licensing policies are practised against them by the latter.[22] It was pointed out that a Committee on the Development of Trade had been established in the Economic Commission for Europe in 1949 which had discussed this question for many years. Complaints against discriminatory trade and export licensing policies continue to be made by the members of the CMEA. The CMEA as an organisation strives along with its members for the elimination of these perceived discriminatory policies. Thus the CMEA has proposed a draft agreement concerning co-operation with the EEC suggesting, *inter alia*, the elimination of quantitative exchange controls and the normalisation of agricultural trade on a most-favoured-nation basis. In an address to the Economic Commission for Europe in 1977, Mr. Ion Perpegel, Observer for the CMEA, disclosed that CMEA had written to EEC on April 18,

---

[20] GATT/1091—October 18, 1971.

[21] *Op. cit.* in note 19, above, p. 129.

[22] B. G. Ramcharan, "Equality and Discrimination in International Economic Law (VIII): The United Nations Regional Economic Commissions" in this *Year Book*, Vol. 32 (1978), pp. 268–285 at pp. 277–285.

1977, with a view to the broadening and strengthening of equality and mutually beneficial relations, both multilateral and bilateral.[23]

The Communiqué on the 31st meeting of the session of the CMEA held in June 1977 referred to the "conclusion of an agreement between the CMEA and the CMEA Member countries, on the one hand and the EEC and the EEC Member countries, on the other hand, on basic principles of mutual relations with the aim of creating favourable conditions for equally and mutually advantageous economic co-operation between them."[24] As CMEA-EEC relations is the subject of a separate paper in the *Year Book*, the reader is requested to refer to that paper on this issue.

According to the *Economic Survey of Europe*, "A number of improvements have recently been made in the legislation of East European countries with the aim of stimulating East-West industrial co-operation. The major development here is an increasingly favourable treatment for the trade arising from co-operation agreements. In Czechoslovakia, for instance, enterprises are granted preferential price advantages, tax discounts of up to 30 per cent., and import subsidies of up to 50 per cent. for their deals arising from co-operation agreements. Poland permits (as from May 14, 1976) foreign individuals and corporations to engage in economic activities such as handicrafts, domestic trade, gastronomy, the hotel trade and services. Hungary is shifting the emphasis of its co-operation programme from consumer products to machinery, with the aim of improving industrial technology and reaping scale economies."[25]

VII—PREFERENTIAL TREATMENT FOR DEVELOPING COUNTRIES

According to a publication of the CMEA Secretariat, "to expand imports from the developing countries, a number of CMEA member countries have adopted tariff and non-tariff measures to ensure a preferential access to their markets of goods from the developing countries."[26]

CMEA members participate in UNCTAD and its Generalised Scheme of Preferences. CMEA members grant as well as receive preferential treatment under this scheme. Thus, according to an UNCTAD study, "Bulgaria and Czechoslovakia grant, respectively, a 30 per cent. and 50 per cent. reduction of MFN rates.

---

[23] UN Press Release, ECE/GEN/16, p. 4.

[24] CMEA Secretariat, *Survey of CMEA Activities in 1977* (1978), p. 74.

[25] *Op. cit.* in note 19, above, p. 130.

[26] *Information on Economic Co-operation of the CMEA Member countries* (1976), pp. 12–13; see generally, L. Zivine, "The CMEA and Developing Countries," *Development Forum*, June-July (1975).

Hungary applies tariff reductions ranging from 50 per cent. to 90 per cent. of the MFN rates on most products, including duty-free treatment on a large number of products; the average reduction can be estimated at more than 50 per cent. of the MFN rates. The Soviet Union grants duty-free treatment on all products."[27] Some non-tariff preferential measures are also granted by countries such as Poland, Bulgaria, Czechoslovakia, and the Soviet Union. Some CMEA members such as Romania also receive preferential treatment under the preference schemes of more developed States.

A joint statement by socialist countries (Bulgaria, Byelorussia, Cuba, Czechoslovakia, German Democratic republic, Hungary, Mongolia, Poland, Ukraine and Soviet Union) at the fourth session of UNCTAD in Nairobi stated that "the socialist countries which are not responsible for the . . . sources and causes of the difficulties of developing countries, uphold the just claims of those countries . . . concerning the need for measures to increase their exports and in particular, to perfect the Generalised Scheme of preferences."[28]

A joint statement by the delegations of Bulgaria, Byelorussia, Czechoslovakia, the German Democratic Republic, Hungary, Mongolia, Poland, Ukraine and the Soviet Union at the resumed 31st session of the General Assembly stated that "the socialist countries base their economic relations with developing countries on strict observance of equality, mutual advantage and non-interference in the internal affairs of others."[29]

However, it added, "We cannot agree with attempts to distort reality and, without any foundation, to involve the socialist community in the scheme of dividing countries into rich and poor and thereby place the socialist countries on a par with the imperialist Powers as regards the historical responsibility for the economic backwardness of the developing countries, the consequences of colonialist oppression, and the continuing neo-colonialist exploitation of those countries. There are, and can be, no grounds for holding the socialist countries responsible either for the consequences of colonialism or for the harmful effects on the developing

---

[27] UNCTAD doc. TD/B/C.5/15: *Operation and effects of the generalised scheme of preferences (1974), pp. 13—17, at p. 15.*

[28] TD/211, p. 14. See on this UN doc. A/33/15: Report of the UNCTAD Trade and Development Board on its 18th session, Vol. II paras. 352-370: *The generalised scheme of preferences.* UNCTAD doc. TD/B/C.5/52/Rev. 1, *The Generalised Scheme of Preferences and the multilateral trade negotiations.*

[29] *Cf.* the communiqué on the 32nd meeting of the session of CMEA, cited in note 16, above: "The Session stressed the CMEA countries' determination to broaden equal and mutually beneficial co-operation with the developing States, thus helping the latter to carry out measures for social, economic and cultural development in line with their national interests, to strengthen their positions in the world economy, to gain freedom from oppression by imperialist monopolies and to eliminate colonialism in all its forms."

countries of the inequality which still exists in economic relations, or for the heavy burden resulting from the crisis of the capitalist economy."[30]

In the UNCTAD Trade and Development Board in 1977, the representatives of several socialist countries of Eastern Europe noted the importance of preferential treatment their countries offered to developing countries which made it easier for the latter to expand their exports to the markets of the socialist countries of Eastern Europe. However, they also stated that their trade evolution with developing countries was not without problems and they urged the developing countries to make appropriate efforts in implementing the provisions of the Charter of Economic Rights and Duties of States, in particular by granting to the socialist countries of Eastern Europe trade conditions no less favourable than those which the developing countries granted to the developed market-economy countries and by refraining from introducing any other kind of discrimination.[31]

A few observations may be made on the preferences granted by CMEA members: (i) The CMEA as an organisation supports the principles of preferential treatment for developing countries and special treatment for less-developed countries. (ii) However, there is no CMEA preference scheme as such; there are arrangements by individual CMEA members which vary from country to country. (iii) CMEA members include both grantors and recipients of preferences.

VIII—Conclusions

The conclusions reached in this paper may be summarised as follows: (1) The CMEA as an organisation is basically committed to the principle of equality in international economic relations, which is advocated both in relations among CMEA members as well as in their relations with outside countries. (2) However, responsibility for foreign trade and economic relations among CMEA members as well as between them and third States is largely in the hands of individual States and treated as a question of sovereignty. It is influenced by the CMEA only inasmuch as they are affected by the co-ordination of plans among CMEA members. The CMEA, as such, does not determine tariff or trade policies. (3) As regards relations with outside countries, the attachment of the CMEA to the principles of equality and most-favoured-nation treatment is influenced by the fact that CMEA members perceive themselves to be

---

[30] A/31/483, Annex, paras. 3–4.
[31] UN doc. A/32/15, paras. 71, 73.

the victims of discriminatory policies by Western countries. The CMEA therefore strives for equal treatment through the most-favoured-nation clause in relations with the Western countries. (4) In the field of intra-CMEA relations, instances of *de facto* inequality, *e.g.*, as a result of the pricing system, appear to be more a result of the usual give and take of economic relations than the result of deliberate policies tending towards inequality. (5) In order to equalise the level of development of CMEA members, preferential treatment is given to those members which are at a lower level of material development. (6) Preferential treatment is also given to non-member developing countries in order to assist in their economic and social advancement.

CHINESE FOREIGN POLICY:

OPTIONS FOR THE 1980s

By

ROBERT BOARDMAN

CHINA was a much more visible actor in world politics in the late 1970s. Hua Kuofeng broke the pattern set by the more reclusive Mao to undertake a major trip to Yugoslavia, Romania and Iran in 1978. Deng Xiaping followed with landmark visits to Tokyo later in the year, and to the United States in early 1979. Peking appeared to be entering a new phase of more assertive diplomacy in its pro-longed slow-motion confrontation with Soviet power. Domestically as well as externally, the broad outlines of Chinese policy became more sharply focused. With the ending of the United States military presence in Indo-china in 1975, a final irritant dissolved to allow precipitation of a different package of goals. Though present to some extent before the death of Mao in 1976, these were obscured by the continued factional conflict which surrounded his last months of life and the initial period of the succession. The package has centred on the joint objectives of counter-Soviet manoeuvring, and modernisation and industrialisation. Resistance to Soviet pressure by accommodation with Western Powers, combined with the prag-matic foreign-policy implications of modernisation along Zhouist lines, are twin paths suggestive of an appealing symmetry. But each is subject to inherent limitations. China's options are in practice circumscribed by a mixture of internal and external constraints. Taking the period 1976–79 as a baseline, we will try to sift out those factors which seem likely to be more enduring influences during the coming decade.

I—DEFENCE AND MODERNISATION

China, unlike the Soviet Union, from the time of Mao's death in September 1976 until early in 1977, has not relaxed the vigour of its denunciations of its enemy. Partly in the light of moves to secure the 1978 Treaty with Japan on its own terms, attacks on "super-Power hegemonism" persisted undiluted in Chinese pronouncements.[1] The United States and the Soviet Union were tarred alike with the same brush as "locked in frenzied contention for hegemony on a

---

[1] See Li Xiannian's comments, *Xinhua News Agency*, June 7, 1977.

world-wide scale."[2] It was clear, however, that Moscow was the real target. Soviet social imperialism, the *People's Daily* argued, was "assuming an even more ambitious posture of offensive" while "flaunting the signboard of 'natural ally' of the Third World." Further, it had not given up its scheme to subjugate China, and was "trying by hook or by crook to cause splits among [Chinese] nationalities to undermine unification."[3] In November 1977 the Party's newspaper devoted a lengthy analysis to the subject. The Soviet Union was "the more ferocious, the more reckless, the more treacherous, and the most dangerous source of world war," not because it occupied Chinese territory: so did the United States (in Taiwan). Rather, danger arose from four sources. (1) The Soviet Union was a late-comer as a Great Power, a situation, as Lenin had demonstrated, fraught with risk. (2) The Soviet Union was relatively inferior in economic strength to the United States. It had to rely more, therefore, on military capability and threats of war. (3) Internally, the Soviet leadership had transformed the already highly centralised Soviet economy into a "State-monopoly capitalist economy without equal." It was thus easier for Soviet leaders to put the entire economy on a military footing. (4) Finally, the Soviet threat arose from the degeneration of the first socialist country. Soviet propaganda could thus exploit Lenin's prestige in dealings with other countries. "These objective historical features of the Soviet Union," it concluded, "undoubtedly make it more dangerous than the United States as a source of world war."[4]

The centrality of the Soviet problem lay at the root of statements and debate on two more formal themes. Speaking in the United Nations in the autumn of 1977, Huang Hua suggested that given conditions of unity of the people of all countries, it might be possible to "put off the war."[5] Other statements on the doctrine of the inevitability of war, however, were still more ambiguous[6]; and the subject remained an important potential point of contention within China. In practice, it was evident that the war being envisaged by policy planners and theoreticians alike in Peking was one between China and the Soviet Union. The prospect nestled uneasily in traditional doctrinal frameworks, which could themselves provide few clues as to the likely reactions to such hostilities of the United States.

---

[2] *People's Daily*, July 21, 1977.

[3] *People's Daily*, July 31, 1977.

[4] *People's Daily*, November 1, 1977. At the 11th Party Congress in August 1977 Hua noted simply that social imperialism was growing, while the other imperialist super-Power was in a state of decline. This contrasts with the 1960s when, in the context of the Vietnam war, dying imperial Powers were, after Lenin, seen as those that might lash out in dangerous fashion.

[5] *Sunday Telegraph*, October 2, 1977.

[6] See for example Deng's interview quoted in *Le Monde*, October 23, 1977.

Secondly, Mao's delineation of the international system into "three worlds" was given renewed attention, support and clarification by Hua, for example at the Eleventh Party Congress of August 1977 and by Deng, who had formerly articulated the model in 1974.[7] Expressions of the doctrine played due part in the Chinese split with Albania in 1977–78, and provided rationales of overtures by Peking to Western Europe and Japan: with Canada (and, less unambiguously, Eastern Europe) the main constituent parts, according to Mao in 1974, of the "second world."

The Soviet threat indicated the need for modernisation of the armed forces (though in the Chinese context the step involved more than elementary logic), which presupposed in turn a flourishing industrial sector. A commitment to industrial growth was not simply a means towards a military end. It arose also from the re-emergence, of which Deng's second rehabilitation was both symptom and cause, of Zhou Enlai's line of 1975 on the future development of China through the "four modernisations." Zhou's own writings and speeches, not to mention the anniversaries of his death, were accorded fresh prominence.[8] "Pushing the economy forward" was one of the four tasks set for the coming year by Hua in his first major policy speech at the end of 1976. The setting of target dates, particularly 2,000, reappeared in Chinese visions of the future. Mao's theoretical work on economic development was projected through different prisms to reveal support for pragmatism in economic policy and other hidden colours. In his visit to Yugoslavia in 1978, Hua went out of his way to express interest in self-management schemes; and Tito's criticisms of "excessive" egalitarianism found ready echoes in Chinese comments. Ravages inflicted on the economy by ultra-leftist groups gave impetus to modernising zeal. Sabotage by the "gang of four" was held at one stage to have "brought the national economy to the brink of collapse," which "enlarged the gap between China's level of production technology and the advanced world level."[9] Improving the quality of Chinese industrial products was the subject of a campaign of late 1978. The key, though, was science and technology. "The proletariat must have its own experts," it was declared: Marxism-Leninism held that to consolidate its political power, the leading class must train its own contingent of intellectuals and experts of all

---

[7] "Chairman Mao's Theory of the Differentiation of the Three Worlds is a Major Contribution to Marxism-Leninism," *People's Daily*, November 1, 1977. See further M. Yahuda, "The Chinese View of a New World Order," 7 *Millennium*, Nr. 1 (1978), pp. 1–19.

[8] See, *e.g.* the excerpts from Zhou's report to a 1949 youth congress republished in the 21 *Peking Review*, Nr. 43, October 27, 1978, pp. 7–15; and "Opposition to Premier Zhou by 'Gang of Four' outrages Decent People," *People's Daily*, January 7, 1977.

[9] 21 *Peking Review*, Nr. 41 October 13, 1978, p. 11.

kinds.[10] Educational and research institutions recommenced functioning at impressive speed. Scientists and engineers were promised more funds, facilities and freedoms; and Einstein's theory of relativity was officially reinstated.

The push to modernisation required some squaring with earlier ideological stands. It was readily, even enthusiastically, admitted that China's scientific and technological prowess fell below that of Japan or the United States. Chinese scientists have demonstrated major achievements in some areas, notably in particle physics and some fields of the biological sciences. But this background was clearly inadequate for solving what the *People's Daily* saw as the "urgent question" of "how to push forward basic sciences and the relevant new branches in the quickest possible time."[11] Memories in educational and research institutions of the impact of leftist ideas helped to ensure acceptance of the implied sweeping away of Mao's disparagement of mere technique. More difficult was reconciliation of the need to learn from other countries, and to import capital equipment from them, with the concept of self-reliance—a keystone of China's foreign policy vocabulary since the early years of the Sino-Soviet split. The slogan of "learning from other countries" was right, Mao had written in *On the Ten Major Relationships*, a text dating from 1956 but taken as one for detailed study in 1977–78. "It must be admitted that every nation has its strong points.... Our policy is to learn from the strong points of all nations and all countries, learn all that is genuinely good in the political, economic, scientific and techonological fields and in literature and art."[12] An article of 1978 emphasised that "Science and technology have no class nature." It was not paradoxical to import high technology from Western countries while "maintaining independence and keeping the initiative in our own hands and relying on our own efforts."[13]

The goals of modernisation and defence converged in the special problems of the armed forces. One of the targets mentioned in 1977 was to beat the advanced world level in science and technology in the field of missiles and weaponry by the end of the century.[14] A wide range of scientific and technical work in China now has implications for defence. When in 1978 a Chinese mathematician won a major British scientific prize, Chinese commentators were quick to

---

[10] *People's Daily*, July 6, 1977.

[11] *People's Daily*, November 4, 1977.

[12] Mao Zedong, "On the Ten Major Relationships," 20 *Peking Review*, Nr. 1, January 1, 1977, pp. 10–25. Distribution of Volume V of the *Selected Works* was accompanied by similar calls from the improving of professional skills.

[13] "Why China imports Technology and Equipment," 21 *Peking Review*, Nr. 41, October 13, 1978, p. 11.

[14] *Japan Times*, July 8, 1977.

point out the practical application of his work in a variety of fields including missile technology.[15] The People's Liberation Army, Hua said in an important speech of October 1977 were "redoubling their efforts to revolutionise and modernise the army and stepping up preparations for war . . . new and important successes have also been scored in our work to build up the national defence and the militia."[16] A few months earlier, China's Defence Minister observed that the country was in a race against time and had decided to step up the manufacture of modern weapons. But as in previous years, progress on this front was hampered by a backlog of low-quality weapons and by residual ambivalence on the question of the ideological propriety of technological innovation in the military field. The implications for foreign policy will be discussed in a moment.

II—INTERNAL CONSTRAINTS

The capacity of any Chinese leadership to achieve declared goals is, however, limited. The state of the Chinese economy in the late 1970s was a familiar mix of high population, population growth, limited resources, inadequate resource development, sporadic disaster, and regional imbalance.[17] Ironically the drive to modernisation of 1976–77 met quickly with traditional restraints. Natural disasters, including earthquakes, led to an economic recession affecting in particular the heavy industry sector. Despite expansions of industrial production during 1977, output still lagged behind 1975 levels. In addition, drought hard on the heels of frost in the spring and summer of 1977 brought setbacks to agriculture. Chinese grain procurement from abroad reached the unprecedented figure of more than eight million tons during the first nine months of 1977, an especially serious problem for the new leadership in the light of significant reductions of foreign wheat imports during previous years.[18] On the other hand, there were indications that population growth was being brought under more successful restraint towards the goal of less than one per cent.; but the inexorable approach to the one billion mark[19] put the achievement in a sobering perspective. Viewed in this light, China's oil resource is a timely asset.

---

[15] 21 *Peking Review*, Nr. 43, October 27, 1978, pp. 29–30.

[16] *New China News Agency*, October 1, 1977.

[17] For a recent assessment, see J. S. Prybyla, *The Chinese Economy: Problems and Policies* (1978).

[18] J. Domes, "China in 1977," xviii *Asian Survey*, Nr. 1, January 1978, pp. 9–10.

[19] One recent United States estimate is 934·6 million. See Department of State, *The Planetary Product in 1975* (Washington, D.C.: Department of State, Special Report Nr. 33, May 1977), p. 12. The one billion mark was probably passed in mid-1978.

Western analysts have forecast production figures of 200 million tons or more during the early 1980s, with a related export capacity of 30–50 million tons.[20] But whether exploited primarily with the aid of Western capital, or in conjunction with a Japanese deal, considerable problems remain of gearing the rest of the economy to match growth in oil production, of competition with rival claimants for funding such as agriculture and defence, and the high capital and foreign exchange costs of development of the petrochemical sector.[21]

The foreign policy consequences are in one sense clear enough: China needs Western technology, and acknowledges the fact. But we should be wary of drawing too many conclusions from this. The mistake was sometimes made in Western analyses in 1949 of China's economic needs. China has remained, and will remain, wary of any relationship that smacks of dependence, the pursuit of trade and development through credit from United States banks notwithstanding. Pragmatic and ideological decision-making are not, for the Chinese, mutually exclusive categories. The potential for external leverage is minimal.

This factor might, however, be eroded a little by the high urgency attached to military procurements. In strategic nuclear terms, the Chinese lag far—between 10 and 20 years, depending on the Western estimate used—behind the Soviet Union, both qualitatively and quantitatively. Even in the hypothetical event of Soviet capability resting at a 1980 plateau, the goal of equivalance by 2,000 is not one that could be achieved, probably, by China. And this leaves out the more exotic areas likely to be mastered by the Soviet Union during the 1980s. By the middle of the decade, Soviet nuclear forces may have reached critical levels of accuracy in terminal guidance systems of 200 yards, with prospects of this being lowered to a few feet within a few years.[22] On the other hand, China as early as 1976 had a regional nuclear force operational with a range deep into Soviet territory and large parts of Asia.[23] Development of the long-range missiles used originally as satellite launchers for use with warheads would significantly enhance this capability. Yet extrapolation from developments in United States-Soviet relations in the early or middle 1960s is a dubious venture. The Chinese have continued to view nuclear forces as an adjunct to conventional strength. Future Sino-Soviet conflict is still pictured in the conservative and defensive

[20] W. Klatt, "China's Food and Fuel under New Management," 54 *International Affairs*, Nr. 1, January 1978, p. 72.
[21] *Ibid.* p. 73.
[22] "Has Russia's Lead been Checked?" *The Economist*, September 9, 1978, p. 75.
[23] International Institute for Strategic Studies, *The Military Balance 1977–8*, pp. 84–85.

terms of protracted war, in which the People's Liberation Army (PLA) would utilise Chinese people's war experiences and doctrines and take advantage of local preponderance to bog down Soviet units. It was this factor, Li Xiannian seemed to be saying in a 1977 interview, that constituted the real deterrent to Soviet attack.[24] In the middle 1970s, China outstripped Soviet rates of expansion of numbers of men in the armed forces, ending in 1977 with higher absolute levels.[25] Expectations of future stability brought about by technological advances on the part of the Chinese, and by consequent importation and acceptance of Western notions of deterrence, are not, then, likely to be realised during the 1980s.

The military imbalance between China and the Soviet Union was instrumental in the late 1970s in encouraging Peking's interest, aroused earlier in the decade, in Western arms supplies. Sale of the British Harrier VTOL "jump-jet" fighter was discussed in Anglo-Chinese talks at senior levels in 1977–79 in a renewed burst of activity. The very short range of the fighter fits neatly with Chinese military doctrine on the course of any future hostilities with the Soviet Union; and is symptomatic of the lack of Chinese interest in developing any significant capability for carrying out operations outside Chinese territory, or, for that matter, in giving priority to the countering of the Soviet Far Eastern naval build-up from Vladivostok. During 1978 the White House, and then the State Department, indicated withdrawal of objections in the NATO strategic trade machinery to arms sales of certain types by Western countries to China. Sustained arms deliveries of a kind and level that can be construed to Soviet critics as defensive (without that implying Soviet aggressive intent) seems likely to become a pattern of the early 1980s. Soviet sensitivity on this point could develop into a brake. Objection to deals with China made bedfellows of Washington "SALTists" and pro-Nationalist conservatives in 1978. On the broader question, the Soviet press was quick to draw attention to an apparent United States responsiveness to Chinese inquiries concerning technological assistance for its oil industry; this was contrasted sharply with restrictions imposed by Washington on deliveries of drilling equipment to the Soviet Union.[26]

---

[24] "The Russians know the way we would fight. We would mobilise the masses of the civilian people and get them bogged down in China .... Even if Russia occupied half of China we would go on fighting" (*Sunday Times*, March 27, 1977). See further R. G. Boyd, *China's Military Power* (Ottawa: Department of National Defence, ORAE Memorandum Mr. M 69, January 1977).

[25] *Loc. cit.* in note 23, above.

[26] *Pravda*, August 6, 1978; cited in *Current Digest of the Soviet Press*, August 30, 1978, p. 3. Washington announced the lifting of restrictions on export of petroleum technology items to the Soviet Union in December 1978.

A third set of actors is less tangible than economic and military considerations. The "liberalisation"—to use a Western term with no real equivalent in the Chinese political vocabulary—of Chinese debate in the late 1970s can to some extent be viewed as a means towards the overriding goal of modernisation, with Party leaders manipulating reference points, texts for study, historical analogies, agendas and the course of argument, while keeping in reserve the option of a return at a later date to conservative orthodoxy should current strategies fail, or should entanglements with Western capitalism prove too compromising for individuals sensitive to the possibility of harsh treatment by future Chinese historians. Cultivation of Western classical composers such as Beethoven, writers such as Shakespeare, and political figures such as Churchill, serves to consolidate the assault on residual leftism, create an atmosphere of interest in learning from Western countries, counter the appeal of Soviet high culture, and promote receptivity of a heroic style of leadership should this become tactically appropriate in the future.

It is more realistic, however, to view 1977–79 as a period when "moderate" factions were able to gain the ascendance. The corollary, that is, is that radicalism, while dormant, is not dead. "Five lost years" in education, science and technology is seen as the heritage of the dominance of ideologically-blinkered leftist factions before Mao's death. There is a new vibrance in educational life, exemplified in the posthumous rehabilitation of former education minister Zhou Rongxin in 1977. Mao continues to be cut down to size. Former errors are either courteously excused by reference to his old age, or else used as a springboard for more fundamental criticism. But how enduring is this Tang-like openness to foreign ideas and the flourishing of argument likely to be? Use of Mao's "hundred flowers" slogan in the defence of potentially sensitive areas of social science research in 1978 is a useful reminder that political debate in China always has its parameters.[27] Elements antipathetic to the revisionism espoused by Deng, and at least acquiesced in by Hua, have persisted in the Party.[28] A number of circumstances could bring to the surface a more radical critique of present policies: political blockage by Western countries of high technology exports combined with failures in agricultural or industrial performance, or simple revulsion at Chinese dalliance with German and Japanese industrialists and militarists and, earlier, the Shah of Iran. These limits are not likely to be encountered in the early 1980s: the appeal to anti-Soviet necessity is a powerful one. But just as the Chinese

---

[27] 21 *Peking Review*, Nr. 43, October 27, 1978, p. 29.
[28] For development of this argument, see *op. cit.* in note 18, above, p. 15.

sense of balance and probity fed anti-leftism in the late 1970s, so it is likely to ward off China's falling prey to the more unacceptable face of Tengism in the 1980s.

A simple radical-moderate polarisation is, however, increasingly an inadequate guide to Chinese politics. It was arguably a product of the Cultural Revolution.[29] If, taking the longer view, we view this upheaval as an aberration intensified by the combined external threats of war in Vietnam and, more importantly, the Soviet Asian presence, then the kinds of cross-cutting factionalism and group conflict that preceded it—particularly in 1965–66—may emerge again as a characteristic feature of the Chinese policy process. As Chinese society and the economy become more complex under the impact of industrialisation and modernisation, it becomes more improbable that disputes generated by issues of regional balance, energy, distribution, allocation of priorities among sectors, education or defence, are realistically containable within the simpler boxes of the early and middle 1970s.

III—External Constraints

While internal Chinese debate has traditionally had a foreign policy component, usually the question of relations with the Soviet Union, the policy consequences of such arguments have tended to be less clear. Even during the Cultural Revolution and the anti-rightist campaign of the early 1970s, Chinese officials insisted in private exchanges with Westerners that China's problems were internal ones that should not be interpreted as having deleterious effects on its international economic dealings. Zhou Enlai on occasion observed to foreign visitors that they should not take Chinese propaganda too seriously. Over a longer term, China's approach to world politics reveals significant continuities. The two decades of the slowly-unfolding Sino-Soviet conflict now represent twice the length of time taken up with co-operation in the 1950s. In retrospect, the 1950 Treaty, formally abrogated by the Chinese in March 1979 (with sufficient advance warning to get maximum Western attention), looks more like a blip in a pattern of mutual Sino-Soviet wariness dating back several decades, and at least to Stalin's reluctance in the 1940s to extend much support to China's Communists, and the hesitation of some members of the Communist Party of China (CPC) in 1949 to go along with Mao's wholehearted denunciation of "third road" possibilities. Over a still longer term, Chinese

---

[29] On the emergence of two discrete groupings in the early 1970s, see K. Lieberthal, "The Foreign Policy Debate in Peking as seen through Allegorical Articles, 1973–76," *China Quarterly*, Nr. 71, September 1977, pp. 528–554.

responses to developments in States on its borders, and to interference by third parties in those countries, constitute another level of continuity between imperial and modern China.

The pivotal nature of the perceived Soviet threat, then, has grown steadily during the 1970s. It has entailed a parallel paring down of Chinese options. By 1980 indeed, some of China's actions abroad have taken on an appearance almost of automaticity. Actual or potential pro- or anti-Sovietism in a foreign country or group stimulates the appropriate reflex. The clash of the Asian giants has accordingly revived interest on the part of some Western observers in Mackinder's geopolitical theories. Mongolia, from this perspective, becomes a critical zone: the "coveted strategic jewel," according to one geographical analysis, "over which the two major Powers would contend."[30] Further, it has been argued that the facts of geography restrict China's options much more tightly than they do those of the Soviet Union, since China's frame of reference points unavoidably north-west whereas those of the Soviet Union stretch out in at least two major directions; but, on the other hand, that China holds a superior strategic position by virtue of such factors as the location of the inner-Asian region, proximity of each national core to the area of contention, or population size.[31] Thus far, however, the incidents that have occurred have been mostly to the east, though the Chinese have reported intrusions on the Xinjiang border to the west; and competition has been sharpest in South-East Asia. Border tension has been kept to a low level. A Soviet complaint of September 1978 was that China was exterminating the salmon population of the Ussuri river, scene of the 1969 skirmishes.

There are barriers both to accommodation and the outbreak of hostilities. At one point in 1978, Moscow officially apologised for its forces having entered Chinese territory by mistake in this region, and in general seemed to be taking care to avoid provocations that could spark fresh hostilities. Neither side has been prepared, in the final analysis, to appear as the obstacle to lasting settlement, nor ready to foreclose even distant options. Following Mao's death in September 1976 the Soviet Union lifted its propaganda attack on Peking and, on China's National Day, called for normalisation of relations based on the "five principles." Not surprisingly the moves were rejected. The Chinese explained to visitors that the border talks were being used by the Soviet Union simply for propaganda purposes and in order to win concessions from the United States in SALT talks by raising the spectre of renewed Sino-Soviet solidarity.

---

[30] C. C. Carpenter, "The Inner Asian Frontier: A Cradle of Conflict," V *Strategic Review*, Nr. 1, Winter 1977, pp. 95, 98.

[31] *Ibid*.

Such "soft and hard" tactics were dismissed scornfully. Deng is reported to have said "with passionate conviction" to a visiting high-level West German team of defence experts in 1977 that there would be no drawing together with the Soviet Union.[32] Other Chinese officials have been even more outspoken in conversation with foreigners about the likelihood of further deterioration of Sino-Soviet relations.

Yet the constraints against war seem equally overwhelming. The flaw in this argument arises more on the Soviet than on the Chinese side: not because it is an "imperial" Power, but because the magnitude and intensity of its perception of external threat are that much greater. Moscow is faced, at a critical internal time, with what is seen as a growing fusion of the dual security threat posed by Chinese and NATO forces. China, for its part, is not equipped, with either intent or capability, to launch an assault on Soviet Asian territory. Aiding the Chinese, moreover, is the strategic advantage denied the Soviets of not having to plan a future war with serious dangers of a second major theatre opening up. America's force is increasingly unusable (more so from a Chinese than from a Soviet perspective); Japan, from 1978, could be in tandem or at least benevolently neutral; and the threat from the Nationalists in Taiwan is negligible (though Soviet overtures in the event of closer ties between Peking and Tokyo could have more effect than in the past). The danger is that the Soviet leadership might see its options narrowing at such a rate that some form of strike against China could appear the only way to clear the air. The option of a nuclear strike existed before the 1969 clashes, and was taken more seriously by the Soviets than by the United States. It could be presented as a feasible option again in the mid-1980s, given the accuracy available then to a Soviet MIRVed strike force, and the growing vulnerability of Siberian economic development to Chinese missiles. The constraints in such an event would be partly military and partly political. China was expanding its nuclear force in the late 1970s at a rate surprising to Western analysts. The Soviet Union can also be counted on to be wary of involvement in a protracted war, a contingency foreseen as much in Soviet military doctrine on war and occupation as in Chinese thinking. Even a limited occupation of parts of north China, the most that would be possible in the circumstances, would be a military venture carrying an extremely high probability of ultimate failure; though whether the Soviets would be capable of thinking rationally at such a time is a moot point. The

---

[32] Colina MacDougall, "A World Power in the Making," *Financial Times*, October 11, 1977.

1983 completion date of the Baikal-Amur (BAM) Railway would relieve some pressure for them, but this second land route to the Far East would itself be vulnerable. More important in the late 1960s were political constraints, the obligations inherent in Soviet roles in the world communist movement and the Third World, together with a desire for détente with a United States known to be opposed to a first strike against China. With economic uncertainties, difficulties in Eastern Europe, and succession problems, these could, depending on the outcome of a post-Brezhnev conflict between pro- and anti-détente forces, be less effective in the 1980s. Even the new factor of a Soviet operation bringing about related destruction of defence systems supplied to the Chinese by Western countries could count for little in such a balance at a time of high stress.

IV—COMPETITION AND CONFLICT

If in 1980 the prospects for Sino-Soviet accommodation appear dim, this is in part because more than two parties are involved. In 1978–79 Chinese officials lost no opportunity in exchanges with West Europeans of identifying common bonds of interest in containing Soviet imperialism. "For the moment," Li noted in 1977, "the strategic emphasis is on Europe and the Middle East."[33] The same year, Deng said in discussions with West German defence experts that their two countries had "common defence interests"; while references in 1978 to "the common enemy" made by Sir Neil Cameron, head of the British defence staff, during a visit to Peking, echoed later by the Conservative M.P. Winston Churchill, highlighted to the extent to which West European conservatives were prepared to play the Chinese game. At a more substantive level, the EEC's trade agreement with China came into force in June 1978. Progressive liberalisation of Chinese imports in the period until 1983 was begun with an expansion of the list of Chinese exports granted free access to the Community, a development which put China in a privileged position compared with other Communist countries' relations with the Nine.[34]

The symbolic importance of this kind of differentiation was not lost on Moscow. Particularly in view of continued Chinese, French and British interest in arms sales in 1978–79, Soviet criticism mounted of the "dangerous identity of views" developing between China and the NATO Powers, and the "building of an anti-Soviet axis between the leaders in Peking and militaristic circles in Western

[33] *Sunday Times*, March 27, 1977.
[34] *The Times*, September 25, 1978. Among large purchases from Western corporations is a projected quadrupling of Sino-British trade by 1985.

Europe."[35] China's leaders, declared *Pravda*, had "embarked on a path leading to the formation of a bloc with the most aggressive forces of imperialism and reaction."[36] The United Kingdom in particular was eager to sell arms to Peking out of motives no higher than simple profit, anti-Sovietism, and euphoria at being able to exploit the "China card" in East-West relations.[37] While there were some signs of the United States in 1977–79 holding back on China policy out of deference to legitimate Soviet anxieties (and to Congressional pressure against deratification of the defence treaty with the Nationalist Chinese),[38] there were fewer in Western Europe of Soviet concerns being treated with great seriousness.

Chinese probing in 1978 nearer to the heart of the Warsaw Pact tweaked an acutely sensitive Soviet nerve. Yugoslavia and Romania were both reproached by the Soviet Union during Hua's visits of 1978 for failing to dissociate themselves from the anti-Soviet comments of their guest. The Yugoslav answer, that Belgrade never allowed feuds between individual countries to affect its relations with them, was hardly a satisfactory one for Moscow. At the same time, the Chinese showed adroit appreciation of the complexities of Balkan politics in Hua's refraining, while in Macedonia, from explicitly taking Yugoslavia's side in its dispute with Bulgaria, even though the Soviet Union had earlier budged off the fence to praise Zhivkov for having offered to meet with Tito to discuss outstanding issues. Similarly, in the Middle East, Li's second area of strategic emphasis, China moved cautiously in tentative steps towards conservative Arab régimes and Israel. These provoked a strong attack from Ethiopia in 1978 and the accusation by Colonel Mengistu that China was supporting claims by a few reactionary Arab States that the Red Sea was an Arab lake; and further, that China was one of 13 countries which directly or indirectly had worked against the Ethiopian revolution by supporting, or supplying arms to, Somalia.[39] The Horn itself can be expected to become a growing area of Chinese interest, in view particularly of its strategic importance to the Soviet Union. The repercussions could be many. If, for example, the Chinese meet with greater Somali responsiveness, it is a reasonable speculation that Soviet cultivation of Nairobi could expand beyond the low level of trade missions of the late Kenyatta period. This kind

---

[35] Cited in *Daily Telegraph*, November 29, 1977; and *Christian Science Monitor*, January 30, 1978. See also the analysis by V. Zorza, *International Herald Tribune*, December 21, 1977.

[36] "In a Militarist Frenzy," *Pravda*, August 5, 1978; cited in *Current Digest of the Soviet Press*, August 30, 1978, p. 1.

[37] V. Kobysh, "Londonskie Kommersanty," *Literaturnaya Gazeta*, September 13, 1978.

[38] T. L. Hughes, "Carter and the Management of Contradiction," 31 *Foreign Policy*, Summer 1978, pp. 34–55.

[39] *The Times*, September 13, 1978.

of ripple effect had earlier produced the military technical assistance agreement between China and Zaire.

But in the zero-sum accounting terms apparently inseparable from cold wars, Asia remained the central priority for the Chinese. And here, China's "win" of Japan in 1978 far outweighed smaller "losses" such as the *coup* in Afghanistan, or even Vietnam's full membership of Comecon and its signature, in November, 1978, of a 25 year treaty with the Soviet Union. Heading off a possible Soviet-Japanese axis erected on the twin foundations of Japanese capital and Soviet development needs in its Far Eastern territories, was a crucial step for Peking to attempt. The China-Japan Treaty of Peace and Friendship included—or hinged around, according to the jubilant Chinese—the crucial "anti-hegemony clause" fought for patiently by Peking, and which had at one time seemed fated to disappear amidst the complex factionalism of domestic Japanese politics. The language used by Deng in Tokyo in October, 1978, is some measure of the importance attached to the document. The Chinese, he said, sympathised with the "masses of Japanese people for what they went through during the Second World War and fully comprehend their strong desire for peace." He also referred in glowing terms to the "friendly contacts" dating back 2,000 years between the two countries.[40] The "Japanese model" was rapidly incorporated into Chinese commentary on industrialisation and modernisation, and the Japanese praised for their ability to learn from abroad while keeping control of their own economic development.[41] Closer commercial and technological ties with Japan have in many ways more to recommend them for Peking than relations with Western Europe, though the geographical proximity and cultural affinity of the former cannot yet compete with the armaments potential and strategic diversionary value of the latter.

Rivalry with the Soviet Union also prompted major changes in China's approaches to South-East Asian questions in the late 1970s. Given Soviet interference in the region, older historical imperatives edged out more recent ideological preferences. Praise for economic co-operation among South-East Asian States, and support for a neutralised zone in the area, was voiced in Chinese statements in 1975. The line was developed during the first summit conference of Heads of State and Government of the members of the Association of South-East Asian Nations (ASEAN) in Bali early in 1976.[42]

---

[40] 21 *Peking Review*, Nr. 44, November 3, 1978, p. 14.
[41] 21 *Peking Review*, Nr. 41 October 13, 1978.
[42] See further Khaw Guat Hoon, *An Analysis of China's Attitudes towards ASEAN, 1967–76* (Singapore: Institute of South-east Asian Studies, Occasional Paper Nr. 48, 1977), pp. 44–47.

Chinese courting of the group as a bulwark against Soviet imperial-ism persisted even when ASEAN members in the later 1970s showed greater interest in co-operation on security (and therefore potentially in taking up more explicitly anti-communist and anti-Chinese positions) as well as economic matters. Overtures con-tinued also despite slow or negligible progress at times in some areas, for example, in China's patient wooing of Indonesia from early 1977.[43] Rapid deterioration of China's relations with Vietnam during 1978, and of Vietnam's relations with Democratic Kam-puchea, then heightened the competitive atmosphere still further as leaders from both China and Vietnam engaged in a vigorous round of more direct attempts to befriend ASEAN members. The speed with which both sets of tensions developed was a particular blow to the Chinese, whose diplomatic activity the previous year had been beginnirg to show fruit. Vietnam's overthrow of the Cambodian régime early in 1979 then seemed to vindicate Peking's growing preoccupation with Soviet presence in South-East Asia. The emergence of this threat to China's ally, combined with Vietnam's interest in securing checks to the tightening embrace of Moscow through a United States rather than a Chinese connection, was probably a decisive factor earlier in accelerating China's pursuit of diplomatic normalisation with Washington.

V—CHINA IN THE 1980s

Chinese goals in the 1980s, then, show few signs of departing significantly from older ones: economic development, national integration, and the ousting of external influences (United States, Soviet, perhaps one day Japanese) from those neighbouring States formerly owing allegiance to the Chinese Emperor. Appeals to harder efforts to achieve targets set for 2,000 have replaced appeals to harder efforts to combat imperialism. Instruments have been changed, rather, and detailed priorities shuffled.

This "grand level" of analysis, though, while giving a useful perspective on day-to-day change in China, particularly with regard to political conflict, gets us little nearer the more immediate issues. Much will depend on the central questions of growth and distribu-tion in the Chinese economy. These are dependent in turn on the capacity of economic policy-makers to tackle the perennial Chinese economic questions of imbalance between population and resources; and the availability of capital and high technology from Western countries or Japan. There is every indication that either or

---

[43] S. Nozaki, in *Japan Times*, October 29, 1977. For the background to the shift by China, see D. Mozingo, *Chinese Policy towards Indonesia, 1949–67* (1976).

both these sources will be productive ones. Even so—and the Chinese capacity for learning, application and determination notwithstanding—the outlook for the end of the century is for steady and incremental development, with sporadic setbacks, rather than for dramatic breakthroughs. As *The Economist* has argued, "even on the kindliest assumptions, including a fair amount of western aid, the realistic prospect for China by the year 2,000 is not a Britain-times-25, or even a Poland-times-40, but a still unwieldy and largely rural country of far too many people which has nevertheless managed to build up a reasonably competent, if neither huge nor hyper-efficient, industrial sector."[44] There is no new Asian economic super-Power in the offing to rival Japan by the end of the century, let alone the end of the present decade. This fact, with its implications for China's future development of its military capability, constrains and overshadows the range of choice in many policy areas in 1980. Further, while a head-on radical challenge to prevailing approaches in economic, foreign or defence policy is not likely, China's path to modernisation may well encompass an increase in the number and intensity of internal political conflicts. Modernisation carries with it the spectre of superpowerhood, a hitherto despised status progress towards which could reopen a number of contradictions within Chinese society and in the ranks of the Communist Party held in check in the late 1970s by the unifying force of anti-leftist fervour.

Three external factors are of increasing importance in this context: the capacity and willingness of the United States to continue pursuit both of strategic détente with the Soviet Union and of relations with China, including toleration of European arms sales to China, in the face of both Chinese and more especially Soviet criticism; the readiness of Japan to effect a significant break with past policies following the 1978 Treaty and embark on a new era of Sino-Japanese co-operation; and, thirdly, the ability of the Soviet leadership in the 1980s to cope cool-headedly with the increasingly threatening character of its external environment.

On the last point, it is a Western interest that the Soviet Union does not see itself as irrevocably surrounded by a string of hostile countries. Cross-cutting of interests between China, the United States and the Soviet Union is one positive feature here. In 1977–78, China and the United States were moving slowly in similar directions to re-establish more normal relations with India[45]; while in relation to Vietnam, Chinese hostility—brought to a head in the military invasion of February 1979—was in marked contrast to

[44] *The Economist*, August 19, 1978.
[45] See reports on Sino-Indian developments in *The Hindu*, January 28 and 31, 1978.

moves towards United States-Vietnamese normalisation, following Hanoi's relinquishing of its former demands for sizeable reconstruction aid as a precondition. However, Sino-Western accommodation in 1978–79 coincided with uncertainties and tensions in Moscow's relations with the East European party-States, particularly with Romania and in the light of evaluations of the post-Tito situation; economic problems of a serious nature, despite impressive progress in agriculture; the problem of the succession; uncertainty about the fate of détente policy after the departure of Brezhnev; and evidence of growing anti-Sovietism in Western countries centering on "human rights" demands. Stress and uncertainty are not ideal conditions for rational policy-making. West Europeans in the late 1970s gave the impression of casually neglecting the point, while pursuing good and profitable relations with a former adversary now evidently only too eager to pitch in and fight with relish their battles of the 1950s. Judging by Western reactions to Soviet expressions of alarm in 1978–79, a Soviet attempt to secure elimination of the China option from the Western strategic calculus—for example in the context of moves to negotiate renewal of the SALT treaty in 1985—would be likely to fail.

This would undoubtedly give comfort to the Chinese. But over the longer term, an angry and hemmed-in bear is not in their interests either.

Appreciation of this is likely to grow during the 1980s. First, a more restrained United States policy, including caution on arms sales to China, should be able to hold its own against sniping from what might be called the Deng-Kissinger line of deepening Sino-American alliance.[46] United States opinion may also be cooled by any hard line towards Taiwan that Peking's Westernists feel obliged to support as the price of their success; Deng has hinted that the use of force cannot be ruled out. Secondly, foreign policy making in China stems from and stimulates factional conflict and group competition.[47] Overtures to the Soviet Union in 1979 had their traditional propaganda value, and may have represented a preliminary attempt to try to use a "Soviet card" in dealings with Washington. More significantly, internal Party criticism of the pace of pro-Westernism may lend greater respectability over time to talking seriously with the Soviet Union. (If so, learning from foreign countries is a slogan that could with little difficulty be applied to the Soviet case, especially as Soviet learning from capitalists, unlike that

---

[46] See Kissinger's interview in *The Economist*, February 10, 1979, p. 36.

[47] R. Boardman, "Ideology, Organisation and Environment: Sources of Chinese Foreign Policy Making," in H. Adomeit and R. Boardman (eds.), *Foreign Policy Making in Communist Countries: A Comparative Approach* (1979).

of Japan, has not led to importation of undesirable Western inventions like strip-tease.)[48] Thirdly, the Vietnam-Cambodia-China clashes of 1979 may eventually act to promote the slow process of learning from crises that the present author suggested in this *Year Book* in 1971 might have to be a preliminary to greater stability in inter-super-Power relations.[49] A return of Sino-Soviet friendship is out of the question; and fear of Soviet intentions is likely to remain for some time the key to Chinese foreign policy. Approaches to the West, however, are not likely to fulfil the high expectations invested in them by the Chinese.

---

[48] See the complaint of Wang Roshui of *Renmin Ribao*, in 22 *Beijing Review*, Nr. 4, January 26, 1979, p. 17.

[49] "China's Rise as a Nuclear Power," in this *Year Book*, Vol. 25 (1971), p. 71.

THE CARTER ADMINISTRATION AND THE ARAB-ISRAELI DISPUTE

By

STEVEN L. SPIEGEL

THE Arab-Israeli dispute has constituted a drama of fascination and intrigue to Americans for decades. Woodrow Wilson approved the Balfour Declaration before it was published; Franklin D. Roosevelt thought he could convince the Saudis to back an Arab-Jewish settlement in Palestine; Harry Truman's solicitude for surviving Jewish victims of Hitler's oppression brought him into frequent dispute with British policy. Only with the Suez crisis, however, did the United States begin to play a major role in the area and even then only sporadically. The Eisenhower Doctrine of 1957 constituted a first initiative with the 1958 intervention into Lebanon its consummation. Prime United States attention soon turned elsewhere; even after the Six-Day War of 1967 American preoccupation was still riveted on Vietnam. Only with the onset of the Nixon Administration did the Middle East rise to an arena considered worthy of prolonged concern, but Vietnam, détente with the Soviet Union, and rapprochement with China still received higher priority.

The October 1973 War revolutionised traditional patterns. By now American troops had been withdrawn from Vietnam, a détente process seemed to have been established with Moscow, the Nixon trip to Peking had occurred. The Administration could consider new foreign-policy challenges and the Egyptian-Syrian surprise attack on Israel presented an enormous one. In 18 days of fighting a host of assumptions previously accepted by Nixon and Kissinger were shattered: (1) the superiority of Israeli intelligence and deterrence; (2) the disunity and poor fighting ability of the Arabs; (3) the willingness of the Soviets to keep their commitment to warn the United States in case of an impending local conflict; (4) the unwillingness of the conservative Arab oil producers—and especially Saudi Arabia—to use the oil weapon for political purposes.

The Nixon-Kissinger team chose to view the War and its aftermath as a diplomatic opportunity to lessen Soviet influence in the area and to begin the process of Arab-Israeli settlement. They were assisted in these objectives by their ability to manipulate aid and pressure to Israel at varying points during the crisis and by President Sadat's public and private overtures to the United States. Nixon and Kissinger were at first less directly concerned about the energy crisis that the war both generated and accelerated, except insofar as it contributed to an enhanced perception of Arab power. Elegant

153

diplomatic successes were the major objective of their approach. It was thought these accomplishments would serve to end the oil embargo, begin a process of momentum towards greater diplomatic achievements, and convince the Arabs that only the United States (and not the Soviet Union) possessed the means to facilitate the regaining of the territory they had lost in 1967. Successes might also enhance Nixon's prestige in a period of growing controversy at home over Watergate. This enterprise involved dividing the diplomatic problem into manageable steps which could produce frequent positive results. It is the basis of the three disengagement accords Kissinger achieved—two between Egypt and Israel in January 1974 and September 1975, and one between Israel and Syria in May 1974.

This approach did place the United States squarely in the middle of the diplomatic process, with Kissinger's "Lone-Ranger" style shuttle serving in place of direct contacts between the two sides. Only the United States, which in this period usually meant Kissinger, was in contact with both the Arabs and Israelis which meant in turn that he had more information about the predispositions of both sides than any other involved party. The Soviets were demoted to observer status in the diplomacy of the area and the embargo suspended in March, 1974, but Nixon was not saved by diplomatic extravaganzas and the diplomatic momentum gradually began to grind to a halt. Kissinger's step-by-step philosophy was running out of steps. In October, 1974, the Arab League, meeting at Rabat, designated the Palestine Liberation Organisation (PLO) as the sole negotiating party able to deal for the future of the West Bank with its approval. Given Jordanian acquiescence in the decision, the possibility of a Jordanian-Israeli disengagement accord was effectively terminated. Syria's fierce criticism of Sadat's second agreement with Israel the following autumn ended the possibility of another Syrian-Israeli arrangement. By the end of 1975, American relations with Egypt and Saudi Arabia had been dramatically strengthened but Israel was becoming progressively suspicious of American motives and actions and uncomfortable with its growing dependence on Washington. In 1976, the Lebanese civil war and the American elections brought the Middle East peace process to a halt. Kissinger himself spent a good deal of time on the question of reorienting American policy in Africa.

I—Basic Conceptions of the Carter Administration

Most of the key figures associated with the new Carter Administration agreed with Kissinger's basic assumptions about the Middle East, but there were fundamental differences over tactics and in the overall approach to United States foreign policy. On the one hand, there was general agreement with Kissinger's conclusion that time was on the Arab side and that Israel should settle for the best terms it could get in the present situation since Jerusalem was likely to be weaker in the future. As in the case of Kissinger, Arab influence in the Organisation of Petroleum Exporting Countries (OPEC) and the growing billions added to Arab coffers created respect instead of resentment and a desire to improve American relations with the Arab States—especially the Saudis. Linked to these attitudes were beliefs that a unified Arab world would be more likely to reach a settlement, that Syria could play a positive role in the pursuit of Arab-Israeli peace as well as serving as a stabilising force in Lebanon, and that, above all, the Arabs were indeed ready for accommodation if only Israel could be brought to realise it. Underlying the sense of urgency of Kissinger as well as of his successors was a fear that a breakdown of the settlement process would lead to another Arab-Israeli war which would in turn lead to another oil embargo with disastrous political and economic consequences at home and among the allies.

This set of ideas does constitute a considerable range of agreement, but there was a significant sphere of difference as well, both in terms of global concepts and of specific tactics. Kissinger, like his two Presidents (Nixon and Ford) had been committed most centrally in foreign policy to balancing off the Soviet Union. In the Middle East the manifestation of this approach was a fascination with weaning Egypt, the most populous and important Arab State, away from the Soviets and of using this opening to reduce the Kremlin role in the region generally. In this sense Kissinger retained at least part of his pre-October 1973 perception that the Israelis, as a stable bastion of anti-communism in the area, were an asset to American interests.

Many of the figures who came to power with Carter, however, were determined to orient their policies away from East-West problems (*i.e.* the Soviet Union) and towards issues of economic interdependence among the industrialised States and in terms of North-South relations (*i.e.* the haves v. have-nots). As President Carter himself stated in an early major foreign policy address in May 1977: "The unifying threat of a conflict with the Soviet Union has become less intensive, even though the competition has become more extensive.... We can no longer separate the traditional issues of war and peace from the new global questions of justice, equity, and human rights."[1]

---

[1] "Text of President's Commencement Address at Notre Dame on Foreign Policy," *The New York Times*, May 23, 1977, p. 12.

This new orientation of foreign policy required a stress on economic and "moral" rather than military tools of statecraft. It was accompanied by much talk of arms limitation, restraint in conventional arms sales, the need to limit the possibility of nuclear proliferation as well as much emphasis on human rights, international economic co-operation, and sympathy for régimes seeking greater areas of international economic equality.

In the Middle East the policy implications of this new approach were profound, because a de-emphasis on the Soviet factor and a concern with international economic problems led directly to the energy question. In practical terms that led to a greater conceptual reliance on Saudi Arabia by comparison with both Egypt *and* Israel. In the opinion of key Democratic-Party thinkers the Arab-Israeli and energy questions were themselves linked. As Brzezinski himself had once written: "It is impossible to seek a resolution to the energy problem without tackling head-on—and doing so in an urgent fashion—the Arab-Israeli conflict. Without a settlement of that issue in the near future, any stable arrangement in the energy area is simply not possible."[2]

This linkage of the Arab-Israeli and energy questions continually reinforced the emphasis on Saudi Arabia. Were the Saudi kingdom to fall to a Qaddafi, the economic future of the West could be severely jeopardised. But if the current Saudi leaders were to turn against the United States by raising prices and/or lowering production in the years ahead, the consequences could also be lethal for the West. Therefore, America must not act in a manner which would lead the Saudis and their allies to question their trust in the United States or lead other Arabs to question Saudi policies. An Arab-Israeli settlement was stressed in order to gain the confidence of the Saudis in United States leadership and to maintain, by extension, Arab confidence in what Washington perceived as a growing primary Saudi role in the Arab world. For example, American officials drew lessons from the Lebanese Civil War which were distinct from the conclusion of many of Israel's American supporters. The latter now stressed that the PLO was on the wane, but the Administration emphasised that Saudi Arabia's key function in bringing the major conflicting Arab parties together in October 1976 demonstrated that Riyadh was capable of exercising leadership and constituting a stabilising influence. The Saudi role in moving Somalia away from the Soviets reinforced this stabilising image. But the crucial significance of this most conservative of Arab monarchies was increased manifold by its perceived function as international banker, oil price regulator, and the world's most critical oil producer.

[2] Z. Brzezinski, "Recognizing the Crisis," *Foreign Policy*, Winter, 1974–75, p. 67.

The Saudi orientation further raised the salience of the Palestinian issue, for the Saudis repeatedly cited the problem in their own dealings with the Administration and Palestinian radicalism was clearly a potential threat to the régime. Moreover, the Administration's Third-World orientation predisposed it in the direction of solicitousness towards the Palestinian issue given Third-World emphasis on the matter in international organisations and intellectual writings. The very urgency with which the Administration regarded the Arab-Israeli conflict meant that it would have to deal directly with every aspect of the problem in order to avoid leaving outstanding questions untended, which meant that the Palestinian issue could not be ignored. Kissinger had handled the Palestinian question timidly and cautiously—promising the Israelis in September 1975, for example, that the United States would not deal with the PLO unless it recognised the United Nations Security Council Resolution 242 and Israel's right to exist. By contrast, his successors were more prepared to deal directly with the Palestinian question as a whole and in addition with the PLO as a specific and separable part of it.

In keeping with this Administration's stress on the Third World, it was bound to pay greater attention to the radical Arabs generally, in addition to the PLO, and to assume that they possess the capacity to ruin the structure of American economic and political power in the area. This premise leads to the origins of the Administration's comprehensive approach to the politics of the region. If the web of diplomacy could ensnare the major radicals deemed amenable and relevant (*i.e.* Syria, the PLO and even the Soviet Union), then Saudi Arabia could be protected from attacks against her by any major Arab faction and even the Kremlin would have to refrain from insinuations against Riyadh because it would become a party to the process. Here lies the rationale for the major tactical differences between the Kissinger approach and that of his successors. He viewed a gradualistic diplomacy as more likely to prevent Soviet encroachments and to divide the problem into manageable proportions. They, however, were prepared to embrace both the Soviets and comprehensiveness because they were anxious to solve the issue in order to move on to matters of international economy involved in questions of finance and energy without interference from the Arab-Israeli theatre. Neither the containment of Soviet influence nor the resolution of a major local conflict were ends in and of themselves, but both were viewed as leading to issues related to problems in a differing arena—*i.e.* they sought to dispose of regional political disputes in order to resolve economic difficulties. Therefore, American policy evolved in an intriguing and imaginative fashion, often distinct from its predecessors. The results were not always successful, but great attention (both public and bureaucratic) was paid to the area. According to the President's chief political aide, Hamilton Jordan, by the autumn of 1978 President Carter had paid more attention to the Arab-Israeli issue than to any other single problem confronting his Administration—public or private.[3] The reasons are not difficult to understand: if the economic future of the Western world depended on resolving the Arab-Israeli conflict, the President would have been unwise not to make a maximum effort.

II—Carter Actions on the Arab-Israeli Dispute

When it entered office, the Carter Administration wasted no time in addressing the Arab-Israeli issue directly. In the early months of the Administration the Secretary of State travelled to the area and the President himself met with key Arab and Israeli leaders. In a series of statements at news conferences and town meetings, the President also identified the key items in dispute and hinted at possible solutions.

First, he dealt with the necessity for Israeli territorial withdrawals; in the tradition of previous Administrations, but more clearly, he stressed that Israel would have to make substantial withdrawals from the territories captured during the Six-Day War and that there should be only "minor adjustments to the pre-1967 borders." Secondly, Jimmy Carter became the first American President to indicate that the United States favoured complete Arab-Israeli normalisation as a viable objective. He suggested that Israel's borders with each of her four neighbours "must be opened up to travel, to tourism, to cultural exchange, to trade, so that no matter who the leaders might be in those countries, the people themselves will have formed a mutual understanding and comprehension and a sense of a common purpose to avoid the repetitious wars and deaths that have afflicted that region so long." Thirdly, President Carter also became the first American President to endorse the idea of a Palestinian homeland, not surprising in the light of the fascination with the subject prevalent within the Administration.[4]

In an effort to bring the parties together to achieve an Arab-Israeli settlement and in keeping with its aim of comprehensiveness, the Administration at first sought to reconvene a Geneva Confer-

---

[3] Interview with H. Jordan, "Face the Nation," Columbia Broadcasting System, November 12, 1978.
[4] The Carter statement is printed in *Presidential Documents* (Washington: U.S. Govt. Printing Office) Vol. XIII, Nr. 13, March 16, 1977, p. 361. See also *The New York Times*, March 11, 1977.

ence attended by every key regional party and co-chaired by the United States and the Soviet Union. As part of this enterprise, Syria in particular was wooed as a State with contacts in both the radical and conservative Arab camps. President Assad was the only Arab leader who the President met out of Washington (in Geneva in May 1977) and he was repeatedly labelled by Carter himself as a "strong supporter in the search for peace." The PLO was also romanced; in September 1977 the President and Secretary of State Vance practically implored the PLO to join in the peace process—lowering the price of American-PLO contacts to an acceptance of Resolution 242 without including an explicit recognition of Israel's right to exist as stipulated in the American commitment to Israel of September 1975. The PLO did not accept the American overture and the initiative failed.

Then, Carter proceeded further. He agreed to a joint communiqué with Moscow released on October 1, 1977 in which the United States for the first time accepted the phrase "legitimate rights of the Palestinians"—until then viewed as code in Arab diplomatic parlance for displacing Israel with a Palestinian State. The Administration took a more restrained definition of the wording. The communiqué also indicated that representatives of the "Palestinian people" should participate in a Geneva Conference; it advocated "normal peaceful relations on the basis of mutual recognition of the principles of sovereignty, territorial integrity, and political independence"; it also suggested a role for Soviet and American guarantees as part of any settlement.

The controversial idea of involving the Soviets in the peace process was much criticised in Congress and the Press. Though it officially remained Administration policy, it was displaced in public discussion by President Sadat's astonishing visit to Jerusalem in November 1977 and the diplomatic efforts which revolved around Egyptian-Israeli contacts. The Administration did not react as swiftly to this initiative as might have been anticipated, for the Carter entourage was still fascinated with Geneva and comprehensiveness. It feared radical reaction and their threats to conservatives, moderates, and American supporters in the Arab world as a consequence of the Sadat visit. American diplomacy hesitated and temporised during the crucial weeks after the Jerusalem visit as the Administration continued to be preoccupied with Syria, Saudi Arabia and Palestinian rights; worried about potential retribution at home and abroad against Sadat for his initiative; miffed at his failure to consult Washington and Riyadh. In the end, the radicals turned out to be weaker and more divided than expected, and Sadat did reject a separate peace in favour of a broader concern for the

Palestinians. About the time in early 1978 that the Administration was becoming more supportive, Sadat was becoming disillusioned with his efforts and broke off the Jerusalem political talks in January.

There followed a series of United States efforts for several months which brought Washington more and more closely entwined in the Cairo-Jerusalem discussions and closer to failures. It became clear that the Sadat initiative was the only available avenue likely to lead to success in the Middle East peace process. No other Arab State, especially Jordan, joined the talks. At a Carter-Sadat meeting at the end of January 1978, the Egyptian President encouraged greater United States involvement. Meanwhile, the Israelis were becoming progressively more disillusioned with both Washington and Cairo. By June, the Carterites were pressing them for answers to specific clarifications about a Begin Plan for Palestinian autonomy over the West Bank and Gaza Strip. On the heels of an arms package and lack of progress *vis-à-vis* Sadat, and with Prime Minister Begin ailing, not surprisingly the answers from Jerusalem were vague and disappointing.

One failure led to another and the range of conceivable alternatives declined as the weeks progressed. With American encouragement, Sadat produced his own peace plan which the Israelis promptly rejected. Meanwhile, the Egyptian President made a point of meeting Israeli leaders other than the Prime Minister as the peace process seemed to grind to a halt. Despite these negative signs, the United States did manage to arrange a Foreign Ministers' Conference at Leeds Castle in July, but Sadat quickly torpedoed the idea of future meetings.

There had been some Egyptian warnings of an October deadline to the peace initiative—the three-year anniversary of the September 1975 Egyptian-Israeli accords with an accompanying indication that failure might lead to war. Sadat had instructed his generals to prepare a plan for a limited attack in the Sinai, but the possibility of war seemed low indeed. Yet, both Israeli pessimists and United States leaders took it seriously. With the Carter Administration team fearing the worst—a breakdown of the peace initiative followed by a war, followed by an oil embargo and the end of its close relations with Saudi Arabia—the desperate gamble of the summit was conceived.

Few observers anticipated major gains from the meetings and indeed on the eve of the summit held for 13 days in September 1978, prospects appeared bleak. However, in terms of a calculus of personal and national interests each side had much to gain from agreement. Carter feared a Middle East war if failure resulted and his low standing in the public opinion polls could be potentially improved with success. Begin was much more popular at home than Carter, but he had long favoured a strategy of making peace with Egypt as a means of lessening his country's crushing defence burden and thereby dramatically reducing the likelihood of another major war with the Arabs. A success might also facilitate retention of the West Bank and Gaza Strip under the framework of autonomy for local residents and would enhance the image of his Likud coalition which had gained power in 1977 after 29 years of Labour Party rule in Israel. As for Sadat, he had risked his politcal career and reputation and even his life to travel to Jerusalem in November 1977; he seemed loath to admit error and return to the Arab fold and to confrontation with Israel—a course of action he was being urged to follow by many other Arab States. His armed forces were ill-prepared for war; the majority of his populace was clearly tired of the conflict with Israel and bitter over the wealth of the oil-rich Arab States by comparison with the poverty of their own. The Egyptians resented dying for other Arabs' gains. Sadat was anxious to resurrect the country's shattered economy and infrastructure, while the average Egyptian had high and probably exaggerated hopes of the practical benefits peace would bring.

Despite this calculus of benefits to each of the three parties from success, the nature of the problems at hand and a distrust generated by 30 years of conflict led to several near-breakdowns during the talks. Through most of the discussions, Carter and his aides shuttled between the two sides raising potential compromises and conveying suggestions from one side to the other. In the end two documents were agreed on and signed at a dramatic White House ceremony. The first consisted of a framework for the conclusion of a peace treaty between Egypt and Israel; the two countries agreed to complete the detailed negotiations necessary before a treaty could be signed within three months. The basic compromise was shortly approved by the Israeli Knesset after a soul-searching and gruelling 17-hour debate. It included a phased Israeli withdrawal from all parts of the Sinai (including Israeli settlements and airbases) to be completed within three years of the conclusion of the treaty in return for diplomatic and commercial normalisation of relations between Jerusalem and Cairo. In addition, United Nations forces and limited force zones would separate the armies of the two States.

The second agreement was more complex and bound to cause greater controversy later. It dealt primarily with the rubric for settling the West Bank/Gaza issue. Under the terms of the agreement a five-year transition administration would be established by a committee consisting of Egypt, Jordan, and Israel; West Bank and

Gaza Palestinians might participate on the Egyptian and Jordanian delegations. This committee would arrange for full autonomy in these two territories by an administrative council to be "freely elected by the inhabitants of these areas to replace the existing [Israeli] military government." Under the accords security during the transition period would be provided in three ways: (1) the Israeli armed forces in both the West Bank and Gaza would withdraw to "specified security locations"; (2) "a strong local police force" would be established, which might include Jordanians; (3) the borders were to be patrolled by joint Israeli and Jordanian units.

By the third year of the five-year transition period negotiations would begin among the four parties (*i.e.* the Israelis, Egyptians, Jordanians, and representatives of the West Bank/Gaza administrative council) to determine the final disposition of the West Bank and Gaza. Meanwhile, the Israelis, Jordanians, and administrative council representatives would conduct negotiations on a final Jordanian-Israeli peace treaty. At the end of the process, the arrangements for the West Bank and Gaza would be submitted for approval to a vote of the elected representatives of the inhabitants of the two areas.

These arrangements presented substantial compromises by both sides. While Israel had already offered the Palestinians autonomy under the "Begin Plan" presented months earlier to President Sadat, the Camp David agreement was more specific in detail concerning Israeli commitments and the exercise of future Arab authority and it did not provide Israel with as many safeguards in implementing the plan. Moreover, Israel now accepted the goals of resolving "the Palestinian problem in all its aspects," of providing "full" autonomy to the residents of the West Bank and Gaza Strip, and recognised "the legitimate rights of the Palestinian people and their just requirements"—all phrases which could later be used against her in future negotiations. Indeed, many Israeli critics of the plan argued that Begin had authorised a process that was bound to end in the establishment of an independent Palestinian State on the West Bank and Gaza Strip which could in their view threaten Israeli security. However, the Israelis retained the right to maintain military forces in both areas and did not necessarily agree that either the forces or Jewish settlements would be withdrawn from the territories after the five-year transition. They had not committed themselves to complete withdrawals at that time and the delicate Jerusalem question was sidestepped when letters were later exchanged indicating the differing positions of each of the three governments which participated at Camp David. Of particular importance, the five-year transition itself was not slated to begin until the administrative council was established and inaugurated. If serious delays were to occur in arranging for elections, the portion of the accords applying to the Gaza Strip and the West Bank might become academic.

President Sadat had agreed to a document in which the PLO was not even mentioned by name and in which the Israelis had not committed themselves as preconditions to accept basic Arab demands. However, he could reasonably argue that the second document provided a framework which, if accepted, offered opportunities for the satisfaction of Arab objectives which he himself had achieved over the Sinai in the context of his own dealings with Israel.

The risks of Camp David were thus asymmetrical. For Israel the agreements involved potentially severe security and economic problems in the long-term by relinquishing the considerable military advantages of holding the Sinai; by giving up promising oilfields; by enduring the painful economic dislocations involved in moving people, expensive equipment and *matériel* back to pre-1967 Israel (estimated to cost several billion dollars); and by possibly destabilising the West Bank and Gaza Strip. But for President Sadat the political and economic risks of isolation in the Arab world were immediately critical. This danger came to fruition when the involved Arab moderates—Jordan, the West Bankers and Saudi Arabia —joined the radicals in rejecting the Camp David accords. When the "Washington Talks" at Blair House convened to negotiate the precise details and wording of an Egyptian-Israeli peace treaty, the hostile attitude of many key Arab States and the growing isolation of Sadat delayed the successful completion of the negotiations. The Egyptians sought to "link" the peace treaty to progress on establishing an autonomous entity in the West Bank and Gaza while the Israelis sought as weak a connection as possible in the fear that if they committed themselves to a timetable for completing the arrangements for autonomy, the West Bank Arabs would be granted veto power over the Egyptian-Israeli peace process. In other words, if autonomy could not be instituted on schedule the Egyptians might delay or even terminate normalisation with Israel.

As a consequence, the favourable completion of the peace-treaty negotiations required the drama of President Carter's sudden trip to Cairo and Jerusalem in March, 1979. The United States now agreed to participate as a "full partner" in talks with Egypt and Israel over the future of the West Bank and the Gaza Strip. These talks had a "target date" of one year from their inception in late May to prepare the "modalities for establishing the self-governing authority."

III—EVALUATION

The Administration's handling of the Arab-Israeli dispute had resulted in one major achievement, the Camp David accords—with the ultimate arrangement of an Egyptian-Israeli peace treaty. But its premises and approach to the conflict raised a variety of questions, which were frequently cited in the domestic debate.

(1) The first controversy involves the problem of whether the Arab-Israeli dispute and the energy crisis are as closely connected as many observers and government officials believe. As Elie Kedourie argues, "it is unsafe to link the two issues in a manner such as to lead to a belief that the supply of oil can be made secure by a settlement of the Arab-Israeli conflict."[5] Many ignore the nature of the distinction between the two problems. If the energy crisis were to be resolved, the Arab-Israeli issue would still exist. Similarly, if the Arab-Israeli dispute were settled, the energy crisis would continue. "... It by no means follows that a settlement—even a pro-Arab settlement—of the Arab-Israeli conflict will necessarily safeguard American interests in Saudi Arabia. Such a settlement will not do away with radicalism and instability in the Arab world, and will thus by no means lessen the threat to the present Saudi régime. It may even, conceivably, increase it.... The Saudi régime needs the friendship and protection of the USA just as much as, or perhaps more than, the USA needs Saudi friendship and good will."[6]

The two problems interact on one major axis: in the case of an Arab-Israeli war, oil supplies could be disrupted. This contingency could arise either by retaliatory acts by frustrated Arab oil producers (*e.g.* embargoes or price hikes), or by an Israeli raid on Saudi oil fields, especially if Saudi Arabia were to become involved in a military confrontation with Israel. However, even if the West Bank/ Gaza issue—the major focus of the Administration after Camp David—is somehow resolved, the energy problem will remain to plague the economies of the major Western Powers and to serve as source of a host of dilemmas for Washington policy makers. Had the Administration over-emphasised the beneficial results of "tackling head on and in an urgent fashion" the Arab-Israeli dispute at the expense of facing the implications of the energy problem more soberly and in a more enlightened fashion? Might the President have been more effective in his dealings with Congress and the public if he had not implicitly offered Middle East diplomatic magic as a panacea for resolving the fundamentals of the energy problem?

---

[5] E. Kedourie, "How to (and How Not to) Seek Peace in the Middle East," 50 *Encounter*, May 1978, Nr. 5, p. 47,

[6] *Ibid*. p. 48.

(2) Similarly, many observers wondered whether the Administration had not overdone the Palestinian-Saudi-energy connection at the expense of fundamental geopolitical concerns. Even if the West Bank entity envisioned in the Camp David accords were to come to fruition, the problems would remain of Iran, the future of the Persian Gulf, a growing Soviet presence among countries peripheral to the area, and the fragility of oil-rich pro-American régimes. These analysts fundamentally were questioning the fashionable current tendency among United States policy-makers to stress economics and North-South relations at the expense of the more traditional foci of Soviet expansion, military strength, and the fabric of society—factors on which world power has traditionally been judged. In other words, have American policy-makers become so fascinated with the new role of petrodollars that they have failed to measure power adequately?

In the perspective of analysts with these concerns, perhaps American officials have spent insufficient time and taken inadequate account of the real dangers posed to United States interests by the growth of Soviet strength on the peripheries of the area because of their ideological preoccupation with "progressivism," economics, and the Palestinian question. They particularly stress that moves towards the Soviet Union in Ethiopia, Afghanistan, and South Yemen—plus the turmoil in Iran—have cast a shadow over the politics of the Persian Gulf. They worry that political instability and radicalism may rise in the Gulf due to forces only marginally related to the Palestinian and Arab-Israeli questions. In that case pressures on the Saudis would increase as would the possibilities of oil-supply disruptions. These analysts suggest that by creating in such areas as Iran a false dichotomy between all-out military intervention on the one hand and occasional verbal outbursts by the President in favour of the Shah on the other, the Carter Administration has perhaps contributed to a negative atmosphere of fatalism and defeatism in the area itself.

(3) The specific tactics of influence used by the Administration in the area have likewise served as a source of discussion and controversy. Given the Administration's basic premises, it is not surprising that its pattern of operating in the area has been to provide assistance to Arab States where considered useful as a confidence-building measure while maintaining assistance to Israel within limits defined by past commitments, domestic politics, and the minimum necessities of on-going security requirements. Almost immediately after entering office, the Carter team was engaged in disputes with the Israelis over a host of issues such as its cancellation of the sale of concussion bombs, its delay of the sale of the latest FLIR night-

vision equipment, its veto of the sale of Israeli-built Kfir jets to Ecuador, and its failure to approve several co-production agreements with Israel. On the other hand, the sale of Hawk and Maverick missiles to Saudi Arabia, which the President had criticised during the Presidential election campaign, was allowed to go forward and American participation in the rebuilding of Egyptian MIG-21 jet engines and airframes was approved.

The most debated aspect of Administration aid policy in its first 18 months was the package sale in 1978 of 15 F-15 and 75 F-16 fighter aircraft to Israel; 60 F-15 jets to Saudi Arabia, and 50 F-5E jets to Egypt. After a bitter fight the Administration succeeded in preventing a Congressional veto of the sales. The arms package was reflective of the pattern of influence which the Administration had assumed upon itself. The number of fighter planes to Israel was cut and they were tied to arms for the Arabs. On the other hand, the opposite approach was employed with Saudi Arabia and Egypt, which received arms as an incentive respectively to resist raising oil prices and to continue the peace process.

A similar pattern was expressed after Camp David when the Administration was at first reluctant to support Israeli claims for large increases in assistance to finance the moving of sophisticated equipment and *matériel* from the Sinai to the Negev. Meanwhile, the White House pressured a reluctant Congress to approve economic aid for Syria despite President Assad's opposition to the Camp David accords and continuing clashes in Lebanon between Syrian peacekeeping forces and Christian militiamen.

These tactics raised specific questions. Was the Administration accurately and effectively exercising influence or was it unnecessarily raising Israeli fears and Arab expectations? Those who took the latter view claimed that the Carter team was jeopardising Israeli security and the prospects for the success of its Middle East diplomacy by its obvious exercise of leverage against Jerusalem. These analysts argued that pressure on the Israelis was likely to reduce domestic support for the President's programme and Jerusalem's trust in United States leadership, thereby decreasing its incentive for new concessions. Those who supported Administration policies pointed to Camp David as an example of the beneficial results of finely-tuned diplomatic efforts. If public displays of acrimony between Jerusalem and Washington were the price of success, these analysts were prepared to accept the inherent risks in the resulting policies and the domestic political costs as well. They also believed this approach was important for preserving Arab-American ties, while the critics argued that the limited value of pressure on Israel was only likely to lead to false Arab expectations while also reducing

Arab incentives for compromise on the grounds that the United States would elicit concessions from Jerusalem. These critics pointed to the Jordanian-West Banker-Saudi rejection of the Camp David accords to bolster their arguments.

In the end a successful conclusion of the treaty required the Carter Administration to request and receive approval from Congress for $5 billion in supplemental economic and military assistance to Egypt and Israel—of which $1·2 billion was in the form of actual grants rather than loans. Nevertheless, as the trilateral discussions between the United States, Israel and Egypt developed over the future of the West Bank and Gaza Strip, the controversy over tactics of influence (*e.g.* over how to handle Israeli settlements on occupied territory) was bound to continue.

(4) Perhaps the most controversial of all Administration approaches was its reliance on the most comprehensive version of any diplomatic process available. Before Sadat visited Jerusalem, it flirted with the PLO and in the opinion of critics it gave Syria—the most radical of the Arab States on Israel's borders—a virtual veto over preparations for Geneva. In involving the Soviets in the peace process critics argue it similarily strengthened the hand of the radicals in the Arab world at the expense of the moderates. The detractors claim that these efforts were never likely to succeed because they forced the Arabs to unite around the least conciliatory consensus available.

These analysts suggest that the Administration was laggard in its response to the Sadat initiative because of its continuing preoccupation with gaining the involvement of as many Arab parties as possible and because it feared the isolation of the Egyptians within the Arab world. In any case, after Camp David the Administration had to settle for a more limited comprehensiveness focusing on Jordan, the West Bankers, and Saudi Arabia because the Soviets, the Syrians, and the PLO would not even consider approval of the United States-sponsored Middle East peace framework. The critics point out that even if a settlement occurs along the lines of Camp David, the PLO and its Arab allies will likely still oppose it. Therefore, terrorist attacks against Israel and radical threats to such countries as Saudi Arabia might actually increase if both frameworks concluded at Camp David succeed.

These observers argue that the Administration has difficulty facing up to this possibility because its strategy is now out of focus. A global strategy conceived in Third-World "progressive" terms has been applied with a regional strategy centring around Egypt and Israel. Put another way, there was a fundamental tactical inconsistency in concluding a framework among three States which applied to non-participants (*i.e.* Jordan and the West Bankers). Only if the Administration had been prepared to present the other moderates with a "take it or leave it" approach could it have accepted the implications of its own strategy. That it could not was reflective of its desire to sponsor a peace between Israel and Egypt and also assuage Saudi Arabia and Jordan.

Administration spokesmen reject this general approach. They argue that Egypt always intended to maintain an explicit linkage between its moves with Israel and other Arab controversies with the Jewish State—especially over the West Bank. They also claim that only by involving other Arab countries can Israel hope for a stable peace process which will continue in the period after Israel has withdrawn from the Sinai. Otherwise, they believe that the Israelis will confront a situation wherein Cairo could abrogate the peace treaty under Arab pressure from outside because progress had not been made on other fronts. This type of argument is an analogue to the comprehensive position itself—that for both Israel and Arab peacemakers security can only be found in numbers. As for the analysis that comprehensiveness has become more limited, Administration spokesmen have taken the position (like Brzezinski himself after Sadat's visit to Jerusalem), that the Arab-Israeli issue is similar to a series of concentric circles with each stage leading to a further arena for involving the parties of the area. Thus, to Brzezinski the first circle consists of Israel and Egypt plus the United States; the second circle involves moderate Palestinians and Jordanians; the third circle encompasses Soviet and Syrian participation.[7] Whatever form comprehensiveness takes, however, it must logically centre on the creation of some type of Palestinian entity, and it is the Administration's argument that no stability in the area and progress on other issues is possible without that accomplishment.

IV—CONCLUSIONS

The Carter Administration has been typical of its predecessors in its concern for the Arab role in the area, in its determination to uphold Israeli security, and in its willingness to work for an Arab-Israeli settlement. But an unprecedented sense of urgency has keynoted Carter's approach. Like Eisenhower, but unlike most Presidents, Carter has been prepared to confront Israel and her supporters. He has gone further than his predecessors in publicly etching out the contours of a possible peace settlement. While he has placed less stress on the question of communism in the Middle East than any

---

[7] Interview with Z. Brzezinski, "Issues and Answers," American Broadcasting Company, December 10, 1977.

President since Roosevelt, he has stressed the energy issue in his conception of the United States role in the area most prominently of any Oval Office occupant.

Perhaps, President Carter has differed most distinctly in his willingness and determination to pursue a comprehensive Arab-Israeli peace as a central goal of his Administration. This objective is a crucial but perilous endeavour which could confront failures on a variety of fronts at home and abroad. The future of the area, of the Arab-Israeli dispute, and perhaps of the Carter Administration itself will be determined by the skill and talent which the Administration brings to bear on the subject and by the degree of success which it ultimately achieves. Though the early record of the Administration was not always encouraging, the successful completion of the Egyptian-Israeli peace treaty was a major achievement. As new challenges are faced in American policy towards the area, observers can only hope that Administration aims will in the end be accomplished.

U.S. LEGISLATORS AND STATESMEN

By

WILLIAM C. OLSON

THAT the Congress of the United States has become an integral factor in world politics was demonstrated in an extraordinary interview given by Chancellor Helmut Schmidt, following his Hamburg conversations with President Carter of May 1978.[1] "We have to deal with Congress directly," he averred, because of the difficulty of discerning through normal channels its "long-term political lines," adding that "Members of our Parliament go over to Washington more and more to talk to the new generation in American politics who have neither emotional ties toward Europe nor specific experience in American-European co-operation. Thus the whole process of inter-allied decision-making becomes far more complex than in the past."

It is not easy for those outside the United States (and not always altogether clear to those inside either) to grasp that Congress does have a legitimate, essential and potentially constructive role to play in the policy process. Basic to current practice concerning American foreign policy is the emergence of Congressional insistence on taking a more direct and active part in its determination and even its conduct as well as its authorisation and eventual judgment. While certain factors peculiar to the immediate past have largely contributed to this phenomenon, in particular the divisions wrought by the Vietnam War, the contradictory outcome of the 1972 elections, and the unprecedented Watergate crisis, the change appears likely to remain for some time to come. New legislation, notably the War Powers Act of 1973 and to a lesser extent (because it is less binding) the National Commitments Resolution of 1969, has served to alter the very nature of the traditional relationship between the executive and the legislative branches so far as international issues are concerned. Neither the Presidential elections of 1976 nor the Congressional mid-term contests of 1978 produced a strong executive mandate. With overwhelming majorities in both Houses and few if any Members owing their election to the campaign efforts of Mr. Carter, an already independent Congress can be expected to maintain its recently acquired habit of flexing its muscles in international matters. Just as the President encountered great difficulty in getting his

---

[1] A. de Borchgrave, "Schmidt: After You," *Newsweek*, May 29, 1978, p. 20.

Panama Canal Treaty through the 95th Congress, the 96th promises to prove reluctant to approve whatever SALT II agreements are placed before the Senate Foreign Relations Committee.

The implementation of policy, even if it is initiated by the President and carried out by his diplomats and generals, can only be put into effect with the co-operation of Congress, if for no other reason than its cost in dollars which only the legislators are in a position to provide. Although it is likely in the long run, it is no longer certain that the appropriations, armed services and foreign policy committees of the two houses can be counted on more or less automatically to support policies and programmes. This is true especially if their members have not been consulted at every stage of the way, and perhaps even more true whenever they find themselves in the least uncertain, first, of what the Administration wants and, secondly, how to explain effectively to their constituencies why they should be taxed to make it all possible. Underlying all this lies a new political characteristic of these times, which is that developments in the outside world have intruded so persistently and often painfully into the lives of the general citizenry. Public opinion must henceforth be taken into account in the determination of long-term objectives, if not the immediate aims, of foreign policy, at least in the United States so long as it remains a democracy active in world affairs.

II—THE CONSTITUTIONAL SOURCES
OF CONGRESSIONAL POWER

Legislative influence and independence derive from two well-known features of the American governmental system.[2] One fundamentally distinguishes it from other democratic régimes: the separation of powers. The other is less unique: federalism. The States of the new Republic, whence the Founding Fathers came to the Constitutional Convention, had not long before ceased being colonies of the British Crown. In Philadelphia, they created a Constitutional order of balance and interdependence between a national President, a Senate representing States which were referred to as, and in some respects actually were considered to be, sovereign, and a House of Representatives whose members were limited to smaller districts and shorter terms. Both of these elementary principles, without their consciously having been established towards that end,

---

[2] The indispensable source is now L. Henkin, *Foreign Affairs and the Constitution* (1972), a definitive and judicious legalistic but readable analysis; see especially Chap. III on Congress and IV on the Separation of Powers. See also F. O. Wilcox and R. A. Frank (eds.) *The Constitution and the Conduct of Foreign Affairs* (1976), which is especially useful as an executive-oriented, policy makers' treatment.

were to possess important implications and consequences for the determination of foreign policy. The separation of powers gave Congress its independence of the President, whereas the Federal system gave its Members independence of the head of their political parties by making the district or State their primary power-base rather than the national party machine.

The first three Articles of the Constitution defined the powers and responsibilities of the Congress, the President, and the Judiciary respectively. They were intended to be co-equal but in the fulness of time the legislative partner (with a notable and significant lapse following the First Word War) came routinely to give its support to the executive in international matters, whereas the justices almost never became involved at all. Foreign policy was the President's concern. More recently, commitments were made by two Presidents, one from each party, the consequences of which the country, speaking through its voice in Congress, could not condone. The legislative branch thereupon asserted or, as many of its leaders preferred to express it, *re*asserted its powers in foreign affairs, just as it always had in the past in other dimensions of national policy, particularly its war powers.[3]

Born of Vietnam but bound to extend beyond it, a crescendo of demand for reform of the policy relationship between the executive and legislative branches should be seen less as a demonstration of what the Philadelphia convention had in mind nearly two centuries ago than as a manifestation of a modern phenomenon of legislative assertiveness combined with—or indeed based on—public alarm. If Congress never had, or was never intended to have, some of the authority now being sought, it would be more a question of acquiring it than of getting it back. Presently, however, the prevailing argument in the halls of Congress is that it has been there from the beginning. Impressive legal interpretation can be brought to bear on both sides of this question. No doubt some of the Senators now so insistent on curbing the President's international powers would be just as insistent on their restoration should "the lightning strike" and they were to find themselves in the White House; like Shakespeare and the Bible, the Constitution can be utilised to serve either side of the argument. In the process of defining the functions of each of the branches, that venerable document leaves many questions unanswered and, except in the opinion of judges and other constitutional authorities, unanswerable. Much more is said about foreign

---

[3] For what is still one of the better expressions of Executive opinion on this vital subject see Secretary W. Rogers' statement before the Senate Committee on Foreign Relations on May 14, 1971 in *Dept. of State Bulletin*, Nr. 1667, June 7, 1971, pp. 721–733.

affairs in Article I than in Article II, where the treaty-making process is defined as a shared power between President and Senate. Nowhere is the term "foreign policy" mentioned, nor is responsibility for its conduct clearly stated save where in section 3 the President is enjoined to "take care that the Laws be faithfully executed." The issue of "who's in charge" perforce becomes more a political and traditional than a definably legal or constitutional matter. Were this not the case, there would be no power contradictions, for the document would have defined the relationship. On the other hand, one of the most explicit features of the Constitution, that giving to the House of Representatives the power to originate money bills, turns out to have unintended foreign-policy implications now that its implementation has become burdensome. Not only does this bring the Appropriations Committee—and particularly its sub-committee on foreign aid—into the picture as yet another element in the process, but it is quite often at odds with other House Committees and with the Senate, to say nothing of the White House itself.

The hitherto apparently clear distinction between foreign and domestic affairs has become so blurred, and the conduct of foreign affairs so costly, that the fundamental direction of American society is affected just as much by the manner in which the President endeavours to achieve his *international* objectives as it is by his purely internal programme. From this point of view, it is not merely Congressional prerogative that needs to be reasserted or rediscovered, it is the place the American people intend to have their country occupy amongst the Powers. Even more important, as de Tocqueville warned or promised in his prophetic book in 1835[4] and Theodore Roosevelt reiterated as the twentieth century opened, is the way in which they intend to do it. America was destined to become a powerful force, of that there was no doubt, but would it be for good or ill? What better forum for the great, continuing debates which would determine that question than the halls of Congress? As nearly every pressing national problem reveals its dual nature, the only way Congress could be kept out of international relations would be to deny it the right to debate the issues of the day.

As the United States has reduced its commitments, particularly in the Western Pacific, to a point more commensurate with its resources and its will, the Presidency may come to reflect more faithfully than it has in recent years the actual consensus of public thinking on international issues than Congress. Should Camp David prove to have been a turning point in this direction, the legislative branch might once again become quiescent. Indeed, it was widely

---

[4] A. de Tocqueville, *De la Démocratie en Amérique* (1835).

expected that with the election of a Democratic President along with a two-thirds majority in both Houses of Congress, this more normal party alignment could be counted on to give him the traditional support denied Nixon and Ford. Yet Congressional disagreement and even attack, particularly from Senators, continued to come as fervently from certain members of the Chief Executive's own party as from the opposition, just as his support came from Republicans on such key votes as the Panama Canal Treaty. One of the most sanguine and co-operative periods in recent times in fact occurred when President Eisenhower and Senator Lyndon Johnson mastered the art of governing together despite their party differences, just as President Truman and Senator Vandenberg had as the post-war era entered its formative phase. They learned how to make foreign policy more or less together, and there was no talk of "reassertion" on Capitol Hill.

Even if such a bipartisan consensus should recur in the years to come, Congress will have made its point. Future Chief Executives (at least those who are as historically-minded as a Truman) are unlikely to countermand it. Though prediction in politics is perhaps the counsel of fools, one needs to recognise that, because fundamental constitutional and political adjustments have taken place in the process by which foreign policy is determined, Congress cannot be expected again to play a subordinate role. Certain obvious executive prerogatives must and will usually be acknowledged, if only in the interest of a clear expression of the national will. As someone has observed, "you cannot have 535 Secretaries of State."

II—The Differentation of Roles and the Problem of Knowledge

At this level of discourse on the direction which national policy-determination may take in future years, it serves no useful purpose to argue that, after all, Congress cannot actually conduct or carry out the policies it has debated, authorised and appropriated funds for. Only diplomats and soldiers can do that. Just as war is too important to be left to the Generals, foreign policy is too important to be left exclusively to the President or indeed to the Secretary of State, even one who knows his way around legislative hearing rooms as well as does Mr. Vance. This is not merely a matter of trust, for one would hope that that particular quality never need be questioned, but one of checks and balances. In other words, Presidents and their Cabinet members need to be checked, and the American method provides a uniquely effective way of doing that, even though it has taken

Congress nearly two centuries to discover how to do it without being much more than nagging and obstructive.[5] A practical balance has been struck.

Nor does it contribute much to intelligent consideration of the broad issues involved to stress that only the President can, in times of emergency, act with speedy efficiency to defend the nation's interest or its very existence, that he must be free to sign the orders and, if need be, to "push the button." Indeed he must. What he should not be able to do is to determine, alone and in advance, what the nation's policy should be nor how he might react to given hypothetical contingencies. Nor should he, after the event, be empowered to act as the sole judge of the legitimacy or the wisdom of what he himself has undertaken. What is at issue here, therefore, is not whether there is a legislative role. There is no doubt about that. It is rather how to delineate what that role is and when and in what way it should be played. In that determination Congress has as much, if indeed not more, to say than the head of the other branch. It does not follow, needless to say, that Congress can, even if in the unlikely event that it would try to, take over the functions of the President in the foreign-policy process. For one thing, Congress almost never speaks with one voice whereas, in its relation with other States, the State must always speak with one voice. For another, Congress is by definition a deliberative body, and many actions growing out of urgent policy decisions—of which the Cuba Missile Crisis and the nuclear alert during the Yom Kippur war represent but two of the most striking examples—must be taken with dispatch, not after excessive deliberation. Even contingency planning, so basic an executive function, is not the sort of approach congenial to the legislative process, especially when immediate implementation of option "A" as against options "B" and "C" is required of a decision-maker.

During the dark days of McCarthyism, a venerable American publicist wrote that the "executive is the active power in the State, the asking and the proposing power. The representative assembly is the consenting power, the petitioning, the approving and the criticizing, the accepting and the refusing power. The two powers are necessary if there is to be order and freedom. But each must be true

---

[5] In his statement reporting the National Commitments Resolution, Senator Fulbright argued, "Foreign policy is not an end in itself.... The means of a democracy *are* its ends; when we set aside democratic procedures in making our foreign policy, we are undermining the purpose of that policy...the committee believes that the restoration of a constitutional balance in the making of foreign commitments is not only compatible with the requirements of efficiency but essential to the purposes of democracy." United States, 91st Congress, 1st Session, "National Commitments," *Report*, Nr. 91–129, April 16, 1969, p. 9.

to its own nature, each limiting and complementing the other."[6] The dualism thus expressed a generation ago still presents a particular danger when it comes to the issue of the role Congress should play, which is that the legislative branch may prove unable to resolve a dilemma whose one horn is the abdication of any role in making foreign policy, and whose other horn is the temptation to play too great a role, to compete with the executive in the formulation and implementation of foreign policy, thereby being untrue "to its own nature."

Applying this to what it knows or can learn, Congress must constantly guard against being submerged in a sea of data so overwhelmingly in support of the policy preferences of the Administration that its ability to challenge or even to criticise is drowned. Inadvertently to turn over to the other branch total control of nation's foreign affairs would be just as great an abdication of responsibility as a voluntary joint resolution granting the President undiluted authority. But to endeavour to match the Executive's massive machinery for the gathering and ordering of intelligence from every corner of the globe would be an exercise in futility if ever there was one, the recently enhanced quality of Committee and Members' staffs notwithstanding. What is required is the wisdom and insight to perceive the *nature* of critical data—timely in its applicability, discreet in its availability, and certain in its relevance.

The American Congress may be regarded as the opposite of the Bourbons, who learned nothing and forgot nothing. While Congress learns everything, it often seems to forget, if not everything, than almost everything. The reasons for this contradiction are not difficult to identify.

On the one hand, the capacity of Congressmen to keep themselves informed is exceptional among the Parliaments in the world. Through an elaborate system of committees and sub-committees, a great many of which are now explicitly concerned with some aspect or other of international affairs, they possess numerous means for ascertaining and checking facts, testing ideas, judging policies, and garnering secrets. Their staffs not only grow in size, but in stature and competence as well, to say nothing of assertiveness. In a more objective manner, the Congressional Research Service experts are continually preparing in-depth studies of any feature or problem in international relations of which a Member or Committee of Congress requests an analysis. The General Accounting Office, which is

---

[6] W. Lippmann, *Essays in the Public Philosophy* (1955), p. 30: this timely and influential book was a plea against "legislative tyranny," just as A. M. Schlesinger Jr.'s critique of the "imperial Presidency" a decade and half later was a pleas against executive tyranny, which is all part of the balancing process in American polity.

responsible to Congress but not the Executive branch, is similarly engaged, but often on its own initiative. Now that the Freedom of Information Act is in full operation, the ability of the President (through the exercise of "executive privilege") to withhold facts from legitimately-inquisitive lawmakers has greatly diminished. The media show Congressmen (and everyone else) more and more about what is going on throughout the world, not only in detail but often at the very moment it happens. Senators and Congressmen develop extensive private or personal sources of information from constituents, newspaper reporters, lobbies, and overseas travellers from all corners of the earth. The opportunity to learn is limited only by the Congressman's ability to absorb, as well as his capacity for discernment; the Chairman of the Senate Foreign Relations Committee once told the present writer that over the years he had come to rely more on reports from newspapermen than he did on the State Department and especially the Pentagon on Vietnamese matters.[7]

Sifting through all this and remembering it may be another matter. With some notable exceptions, knowledge slips away. Members lose elections and are replaced by new legislators who must learn it all for themselves. Members die. Their parties decline. They are "gerrymandered" out of their districts. Those who remain shift their interests in response to new domestic and foreign crises. They adapt, if they are to survive, to changing constituent demands as old voter concerns give way to more urgent new ones. National values may even change, so that what was relevant yesterday has become crucial today and is simply outdated tomorrow. A kind of "generation gap" appears when the formerly unquestioned Atlantic principle of national security underlying the American commitment to Europe is threatened 30 years later when Congress questions defence appropriations for new construction at NATO bases in Europe. Congress does seem to forget the lessons of the past (illustrating the wisdom of the old adage, "History teaches that history does not teach").

Yet that judgment is too severe. There are individual Members of brilliance or of phenomenal memory. As a body, one thing Congress has learnt lately is unlikely to be forgotten, and that is what the constitution says about foreign affairs, which is considerably more than their predecessors realised that it did. There may be continual debate and doubt about the Constitutional *authority* of Congress. Experts on the policy-making process may argue about the actual *functions* to be performed on international matters. On one point,

---

[7] Interview of J. W. Fulbright, June 25, 1967, in the Foreign Relations Committee meeting room.

however, there is no debate, and that is the ability and right of the Representatives and Senators to determine for themselves how they should *organise* themselves for learning and deciding about these vital questions.

This does not mean that in this realm there is no connection with the Executive branch. Quite the contrary. The connection takes the form primarily of what has traditionally been called "oversight." Many, if indeed not all, committees and sub-committees have been established and operate as they do precisely because of the nature of the responsibilities assumed by the Administration's burgeoning civil and military activities overseas. Though the Executive sets the pace and the focus of attention on particular international concerns. Congress pursues the hounds in any way it chooses. That is why several legislative hunters seem to be after the same prey at the same time. Certain other potential objects of the hunt appear to be left unattended, neglected or overlooked. In fact, practically nothing is overlooked in this task of strictly overseeing the Administration.

The oversight function represents yet another source of contradiction. Far from being concentrated in the two obvious committees. Foreign Relations in the Senate and International Relations (formerly Foreign Affairs) in the House, the 94th Congress saw almost 80 committees and sub-committees examining some aspect or other of the country's external responsibility, and the vaunted reforms of the 95th only managed to reduce this number to about 65. One must be prudent not to attach too much *overall* importance to this multiplicity of internationally-involved committees, for still only a handful have responsibility for overseeing the whole panoply. In addition to the obvious pair cited above, only Appropriations and Government Operations can be said to have even comparable breadth of jurisdiction.

While tradition is of tremendous importance, not only in terms of jurisdiction, but in terms of the influence committees have in legislative life, what we are seeing today is a *challenge* to tradition. Newly-elected liberal Congressmen and Senators, bent on reform, recently brought about changes in such venerable practices as seniority as the sole basis for determining powerful committee chairmanships and rigid cloture rules, which have for decades allowed filibusters to block legislation. Conceivably, these key changes might have occurred even without the combined disillusionments of Vietnam and Watergate, but at all events they are probably here to stay now that they have been brought about. Representing a truly revolutionary development, they have already had a discernible impact upon the formulation and execution of foreign policy, and the trend to the right in the 1978 off-term elections is not likely to reverse this.

III—The Recent History of Legislative Involvement

The first time a cleavage came about between the two branches on a foreign policy issue bearing grave historic consequences was as a result of the First World War. With the Versailles Treaty failing to muster a two-thirds' majority of the Senate, the United States declined to become one of the founding members of the new League of Nations. To Europeans who had reluctantly gone along with President Wilson on the new institution, this historic failure was a source of confusion and doubt, matched by even a feeling of guilt on the part of many internationally-minded people in the United States throughout the inter-war years. From the point of view of political sociology, however, there can now be little doubt that Senator Henry Cabot Lodge and his Senate colleagues in their opposition reflected the reluctance of the public at large, whereas Woodrow Wilson and his devotees did not. This was fundamental. But that particular episode was only the first of many during the 1920s as successive Republican Administrations, endeavouring to get the United States involved in the World Court and other institutions, found Congress, itself dominated by Republicans of the midwest until the end of the decade, unwilling to enact legislation which would have made the country an active, integral part of what was hoped would be a new international order. In the following decade the same reluctance took on a different form in the face of the Axis threat to peace: neutrality legislation. The dominant figure throughout all this was the proudly isolationist Senator William E. Borah of Idaho, Chairman of the Senate Foreign Relations Committee from 1924 until his death shortly after war broke out in Europe.

By contrast, two figures one thinks about in the period immediately following the Second World War are Senator Arthur Vandenberg (the father of bipartisanship) and Representative Christian Herter who, as Chairman of the Foreign Affairs Committee of the House of Representatives, headed the famous Herter Mission to Europe.[8] That Congressional body painstakingly studied the proposals made by the Europeans which resulted in the Marshall Plan, one of the several fundamental changes in American foreign policy. It forged a consensus between two of the three branches of government (the Judiciary is rarely concerned with foreign affairs) which had the support of what Almond calls "the attentive public"[9] from

---

[8] On the significance of this mission, and the earlier debate on Lend-Lease in 1941, for development of the Unites States foreign-policy-making process see this writer's "The American Congress and Foreign Policy: a Functional Adaptation of the Constitution," *Jahrbuch des Öffentlichen Rechts der Gegenwart*, Band 21 (1972), pp. 591–602.

[9] G. Almond, *The American People and Foreign Policy* (1948), *passim*.

1947 or 1948 right up until the early 1960s. To use Roger Hilsman's term, the "foreign policy consensus"[10] broke down only in face of the frustrations of the Vietnam War with disaffection, first on the part of the people, and then on the part of Congress. The revolution in American foreign policy was not reversed, but the post-war basis for executive-legislative co-operation, as something one could take for granted as a solid feature of world politics, began to crumble.

The final manifestation of that post-war consensus took the form of the Gulf of Tonkin Resolution in 1964. Lyndon Johnson sought support (some say unnecessarily) for whatever he, as Commander-in-Chief, regarded as essential to protect American security in South-East Asia. He asked his old colleague from the days when Johnson was an exceptionally effective Majority Leader of the Senate, Senator William Fulbright, Chairman of the Foreign Relations Committee, to shepherd this piece of legislation through Congress. From that point forward, whenever the President was challenged on Vietnam it is said that he would extract a copy of the Tonkin Resolution from his pocket with some such observation as, "Well, I am doing just what the Senators authorised me to do. If you want to change it, go to the Senate." What he was really saying was that he possessed full support of Congress on this issue and therefore whatever he chose to do in South-East Asia constituted national policy.

IV—THE POLITICS OF RELUCTANT COLLABORATION

The Senators soon began to have second thoughts. With Nixon in the White House in 1969, Fulbright himself, working with Senator Jacob Javits, Republican of New York, successfully sponsored new legislation called the "National Commitments Resolution."[11] No fundamental change in American policy should henceforth be undertaken without Congressional collaboration. It was merely a statement of principle, with no binding effect on the Chief Executive. Indeed the President did not regard himself as being bound by it and made a number of commitments which did not in fact carry Congressional approval. Consequently, by 1973 the War Powers Act[12] was passed, which markedly restricted the President's power

---

[10] "Congressional-Executive Relations and the Foreign Policy Consensus," 52 *American Political Science Review*, September 1958, pp. 725–745.

[11] United States, 91st Congress, 1st Session, *Senate Resolution 85*, agreed to June 25, 1969; this was a "sense of the Senate" type of legislation, the sense being "that a national commitment by the United States results *only* from affirmative action taken by the executive *and* legislative branches..." [italics added].

[12] United States, 93rd Congress, 1st Session, H.J. 542, *Joint Resolution concerning the war powers of the Congress and the President*, November 7, 1973.

to deploy American forces throughout the world. On Constitutional grounds, Nixon vetoed it. When Congress overrode the veto (an exceedingly rare event in foreign policy), the consensus was gone, threatening a fundamental division in the conduct of foreign policy. Congress had become the active, no longer the passive, partner. Coming down almost to the present moment, a day seldom passes when one does not find reference, not only in the national but also in the world press, to Congressional action.

As everyone is aware, there is a growing emphasis on human rights as a basic world goal of United States foreign policy. The greatest thrust to this new departure has come from Carter himself and Zbigniew Brzezinski, his National Security Adviser, who regards human rights as one of America's greatest advantages in its competition with a Soviet power dependent in part on the denial of such rights. Some time before this initiative, the Congress required the President or the State Department to submit to it reports on any country receiving American economic assistance in which there were "gross violations of human rights." The State Department, understandably reluctant to comply, nevertheless did make such a report, at first identifying six countries in particular. The list could have been longer than that. Congress has not ruled that the President cannot provide assistance to these countries; it is simply going on record as saying that the Members have some reservations about it. As this is consistent with the President's own passionate beliefs, something new has emerged in American foreign policy, although a moralistic urge does seem to express itself from time to time in American history. Since this particular initiative can really be said to have come from Congress even before Mr. Carter made human rights part of his election campaign and later a cornerstone of his foreign policy, it represents the ideal form of legislative-executive co-operation at the highest level. Both branches have exercised the same basic policy initiative, demonstrating that independence and collaboration can go together.

In a related context, however, legislative independence has recently taken quite a different form: the so-called Helsinki monitoring group.[13] Many Members of Congress harboured doubts about the validity of the 1975 Helsinki Declaration which, as it did not constitute a treaty, was not submitted to the Senate for ratification. To the annoyance of President Ford, they set up a special select group to venture on its own to Europe to see whether or not the declaration was being carried out, particularly on the part of the

---

[13] The full title of this bipartisan, two-House group is "Commission on Security and Co-operation in Europe"; in addition to the 12 Members of Congress, there are three executive branch commissioners as well. United States, 94th Congress, *Public Law 94–304.*

Soviet Union, finding in some cases that it was not. This activity of Congress abroad remains a source of some embarrassment to the Administration, even though it appears to comply with its own stress on the human rights issue, because of possible linkage to other issues. Indeed, in a subsequent dialogue in Moscow between Brezhnev and a group of twelve Senators led by Abraham Ribicoff, it was made clear to the Soviet leader that this was precisely the Senate's intention, in this case with reference to a possible SALT II treaty.[14]

One of the most statesmanlike shifts in Congressional opinion has emerged from a conference committee considering Rhodesian chrome imports. In 1971, when the United Nations voted for restriction of all imports from Rhodesia, Congress made an exception of this particular product, allowing the import of Rhodesian chrome mainly in response to the motor lobby. Later, there was a reversal towards consensus on this point, with a conference committee voting to go along with the ban until all-party democratic elections in Rhodesia took place.

The Middle East provides another example of Congressional involvement, though certainly not initiative, not dissimilar to "the politics of reluctant collaboration" exhibited by the State Department on the "gross violation of human rights" issue. A proposal made by the Ford Administration in connection with the Sinai disengagement agreement of 1975 contained a provision for the stationing of 200 American civilians in the buffer zone between the Egyptian and the Israeli lines. Israel initialled the proposal, on which the entering into force of the entire agreement depended, but declined to sign until Congress explicitly approved the placement of the monitors in the Sinai. These were to report at once on any violations of the accord by either side. Despite serious reservations, the lawmakers agreed to this proposal in order to preserve the delicate balance which had been so painstakingly achieved by Secretary of State Kissinger's "shuttle diplomacy." One would have to search for a long time in the archives of diplomatic history before finding another instrument between two States contingent upon the action of a *legislature* of a third State, not party to the agreement itself, for its implementation. Here was an extraordinary demonstration of outside recognition of the growing significance of the United States Congress in international politics.[15]

---

[14] At a meeting with Brezhnev in Moscow on November 17, 1978, Senator Ribicoff, a senior member of the Foreign Relations Committee, is reported to have "warned that Soviet policies on Africa, the Middle East; human rights and reported sales of MiG-23 jets to Cuba could complicate Senate ratification of a new SALT pact, once one is reached." *International Herald Tribune,* November 18, 1978, p. 2.

[15] The United States was not a party to the disengagement agreement as such despite its Secretary of State's crucial role in bringing it about; Congress carefully delimited the authority

While this incident showed response rather than initiative, the well-publicised cutting-off of military supplies to Turkey after intervention in Cyprus by Turkish forces actually originated in the House of Representatives. It took the form of an amendment to a military aid bill which banned further United States arms shipments to Turkey until its troops were withdrawn, the technical reason being that the Turkish forces had used United States weapons provided under NATO with Congressional authorisation. But as the amendment was about to be voted on by the lower House, the then Deputy Whip of the Democratic Party is reported to have stood at the door of the Chamber and as the loyal Democrats filed in he advised them to "Vote yes for Greece." He is a leading member of the so-called "Greek lobby" in Congress. His colleagues followed his advice, cut off aid to Turkey, and created a crisis which was resolved only after the Carter administration persuaded Congress to change its mind several years later.

V—THE POLITICS OF CO-EQUALITY

In his final address to Congress, president Ford, who had himself been a Congressman for 25 years, made an urgent plea to his former colleagues to stop intruding in foreign affairs, arguing that there "can be only one Commander-in-Chief."[16] This was his way of saying that the Congress should let the Executive do its job, restricting itself to what it is proper for lawmakers to do. Presidents traditionally have regarded this as being to support the White House whenever there is an international crisis or even a serious issue of policy at stake. In recent years, they no longer do so without question.

Ford went out of office, Carter came in, and the assumption was sometimes made that, with a Democratic Congress and a Democratic President, the tension and conflict between the two branches on international issues might all but disappear. However, that just did not happen; even before he was inaugurated, the new Chief Executive ran into serious difficulty with the Senate when it failed to approve one of his major appointments and dragged its heels on yet another. Theodore Sorensen's withdrawal as potential CIA Director was followed shortly after the new President was sworn in by wearisome hearings before Paul Warnke was confirmed as the head of the Arms Control and Disarmament Agency on a very small majority, prompting Carter to assert that the dispute represented a

---

contained in an Annex based on the proposal of Kissinger. Eleanor C. McDowell, *Digest of United States Practice in International Law*, Dept. of State Publication 8865, September 1976, pp. 829–830.

[16] State of the Union Message, *International Herald Tribune* (Paris), January 14, 1977, p. 2.

serious challenge to his knowledge and his authority as President.[17]
Right at the outset of his Administration a portent of foreign policy
crisis was in the air, showing that the theory that division on foreign
affairs only occurs when parties of different persuasion control the
respective branches is not necessarily sound.

Though Congress appears to be determined to be an independent
force, regardless of party, it does not follow from this that it now
intends to oppose the Chief Executive on crucial policy issues. This
seems to be born out by the fact that it is in the foreign policy field
that the President has enjoyed most of his few successes. Whereas at
one point only 27 Senators were prepared to go on record in favour
of the controversial Panama Canal Treaty, in the end 68 cast their
votes for it—one more than the necessary two-thirds majority.
Patient and quiet diplomacy on "the Hill" finally produced a lifting
of the ban on military aid to Turkey. The Rhodesian chrome issue is
being resolved in a statesmanlike way. Much to everyone's surprise,
Congress went along on Middle East arms sales, to Arab States as
well as to Israel. Though the White House cannot command the Hill
to do its bidding on domestic issues, as the long debate on the
Energy Bill so forcibly demonstrated, it has shown capability in
gaining its co-operation on most of his overseas efforts, the refusal of
Chairman Zablocki of the International Relations on Korean troop
withdrawal being one of the few significant exceptions. A major part
of the credit for this certainly must go to Secretary of State Cyrus
Vance, who in addition to having had considerable negotiating
experience in Cyprus and elsewhere, performed as Counsel for the
Preparedness Sub-committee of the Senate Armed Services Committee during the Johnson Administration. He knows Capitol Hill.

A searching and not always automatic partnership seems to be
replacing the old reliable principle of simply supporting the President, "no matter what." It is the only formula which can now truly
serve the American national interest in international as well as in
domestic affairs; Congress has become co-equal. Until another
strong President appears on the scene, this stance will not change.
For the time being, whatever his moral stature and courage in taking
on the most basic issues such as energy, or peace in the Middle East,
rather than merely treating their symptoms, Carter has yet to
become such a leader. He ran "behind the ticket,"[18] as the expres-

[17] Mr. Warnke subsequently, some say due to Senatorial displeasure, resigned effective at
the end of the SALT talks in Moscow in the autumn of 1978: see *International Herald Tribune*,
October 11, 1978, p. 1.
[18] It may be worth noting for future reference that in the Nebraska primary preceding the
Democatic National Convention in 1976, Senator F. Church led the contenders, ahead of
Governor Carter. By virtue of the retirement of Senator Sparkman, Senator Church emerged
as the new Chairman of the Foreign Relations Committee.

sion goes in American party parlance, in narrowly winning the Presidency in 1976, and in the elections of 1978 no trend of dependence on his persuasiveness by successful Democratic Congressmen and Senators was discernible. Though overall foreign-policy consequences of the mid-term elections were minimal, James Reston saw as its "single most important result"[19] the defeat (in two cases quite unexpected) of five pro-SALT agreement Senators, all of whom had the President's support. As Chancellor Schmidt remarked, "Presidents are not as successful with Congress as before",[20] and thereby hangs the tale of a significant new development in international politics.

Despite its sporadic and earnest efforts to do so, Congress still cannot *make* foreign policy,[21] however much it may affect its course. However, its influence is not, as some persistently contend, principally negative. The traditional functions of Congress—providing funds, scrutinising the conduct of public agencies, representing the views of constituents back home, and in the end strengthening the hand of the President in his dealings with other States—still pertain. What has changed is that in the process its behaviour is now more critical, better informed, and in the aggregate, more responsible.

---

[19] In an article entitled "SALT, Moscow and the U.S. Elections," Reston went on to suggest that in fact SALT's prospects might be improved because the more conservative Senators might favour "a major reduction in the defense budgets of both countries." *International Herald Tribune*, November 13, 1978, p. 8.

[20] *Loc. cit.* in note 1, above.

[21] At an unprecedented meeting with the Foreign Relations Committee requested by President-elect Carter, Senator Church stated his own position as follows: "I have often said that the Foreign Relations Committee of the Senate – and we function for the Senate – cannot make foreign policy. As I construe the Constitution, that authority, and not only the authority but the responsibility, is given to the President of the United States; but we can help shape that foreign policy," United States, 94th Congress, Transition Period, *Meeting with President-Elect Carter*, November 23, 1976, p. 6.

THE UNITED STATES IN (AND OUT OF) VIETNAM

By

JAMES N. ROSENAU
and
OLE R. HOLSTI

YEARS have elapsed since the end of United States military involvement in Vietnam and yet the consequences of the episode resist coming into focus.* Notwithstanding a burgeoning literature, what the commitment in Vietnam and its abrupt ending meant for the United States, its prevailing policies and its approaches to future situations, remains elusive. At one extreme are those who argue that Vietnam was not an ordinary foreign-policy situation, that it constituted some kind of major turning point for American society, its internal dynamics and its external orientations. At the other extreme are analysts who are disinclined to treat Vietnam as a watershed experience and, instead, view it as merely one other episode—a ghastly and regrettable mistake—in the sometimes erratic course of American foreign policy. Within each of these approaches, moreover, a variety of contradictions, emphases and interpretations can be found. In effect, there is little agreement on exactly what the prime consequences, if any, of the decade-long (or was it decades-long?) episode have been and may continue to be.

How, then, can we put Vietnam in perspective? What kind of theories should we employ in order to assess whether the Vietnam experience can better enable us to comprehend the United States in the world today?

I—SOME POSSIBLE AVENUES OF INQUIRY

The literature offers several options. One is a conventional power analysis that posits the United States as a super-Power, acting to enhance its national interests through the performance of its global responsibilities. Analysts employing this option compare the relative power of the United States and other parties to situations of

* Part of the first draft of this paper was written while one of the authors was a Visiting Fellow in the Department of International Relations at the Australian National University and we are pleased to record our gratitude to that institution for its assistance. We also gratefully acknowledge the continued support of our project from the Duke University Research Council, the Duke Computation Center, and the Institute for Transnational Studies of the University of Southern California.

186

conflict in the post-Vietnam era, and identify the best alternatives thereby available to the United States and the likelihood of these being achieved. To proceed from this analytic base is to play down the long-run significance of episodes such as Vietnam. Time moves on in the balance of relative power and the configuration of conflicts, with the result that the relevance of earlier situations lessens as new issues arise. Thus, while American policy makers may be somewhat more cautious and their policies a bit more circumscribed since Vietnam, these modifications may not be enduring as new challenges and problems come to dominate the international scene. The United States may have suffered a setback in Vietnam, but any analysis founded on the comparison of relative power is likely to see it as having since recovered its super-Power status and to be formulating its strategies and policies accordingly—sometimes skilfully and often egregiously, but always in response to current rather than prior situations. As a result, any modifications induced by Vietnam are not likely to loom as major departures from what have long been the central tendencies of the country's post-War orientations towards the external world.[1]

A second option to be found in the literature involves a preoccupation with the domestic scene and how Vietnam served to alter some basic institutions and patterns of American life. Those who follow this option are not concerned so much with how policy is conducted abroad as they are with the ways in which Vietnam may have changed the dynamics of life at home. And, having found profound impacts within the society, they inferentially assume that these can be traced to the direction and quality of its conduct in Vietnam. One analyst, for example, posits Vietnam as having fostered the emergence of a new élite—the intellectual-industrial complex—that competes over domestic issues but has begun to converge around foreign-policy questions.[2] Another analyst stresses the large extent to which the basic value system of the society underwent transformation with, presumably, major consequences for the conduct of its foreign policy: "In Vietnam we lost not only a war and a subcontinent; we also lost our pervasive confidence that American arms and American aims were linked somehow to justice and morality, not merely to the quest for power. America was defeated militarily but the idea of America, the cherished myth of America, received an even more shattering blow."[3] There are many other

---

[1] For a cogent example of this line of reasoning, see J. Siracusa, "Lessons of Viet-Nam and the Future of American Foreign Policy," 30 *Australian Outlook* (August 1976), pp. 227–237.

[2] L. Berger, "The Greening of American Foreign Policy," *Commentary* (March 1976), reproduced in Berger, *Facing Up to Modernity* (1977). We offer some data relevant to this thesis in note 16, below.

[3] M. Dickstein, *Gates of Eden: American Culture in the Sixties* (1977), p. 271.

domestic variables that have been subjected to probing inquiry and yielded the conclusion that Vietnam was, profoundly and irrevocably, a major turning-point in American history.

A third option suggested by the literature is to treat policy makers as endowed with memories and an ever-active readiness to learn, qualities which make it impossible for them to approach each new situation solely on its own terms. Rather, cognitive processes lead them to recognise, assess, and respond to emerging situations at least partly on the basis of their experiences in previous situations. Their recollections and applications of the past may or may not be appropriate, but their decisions and actions in the present derive from prior learning as well as current stimuli. This cognitive process option allows for the possibility that Vietnam did serve as a turning point in the conduct of American foreign policy. If policy makers and publics rely on what they perceive to have been the "lessons" of Vietnam as they react to new developments abroad, then that episode can be viewed as a continuing source of behaviour. We have focused on this option in our research on Vietnam and uncovered enough evidence to indicate that memories of Vietnam may long linger as sources of future actions.[4]

II—THE CONCEPT OF NATIONAL ADAPTATION

While the several options have yielded valuable insights into Vietnam as a possible historical watershed, none of them seems sufficient to the task of achieving an overall perspective. If the entrance into and exit from Vietnam was a major turning-point for the United States, each of the three approaches is too narrow in scope to account for the full array of internal and external consequences that may be relevant. Relative power is only part of any political story and, as indicated, this kind of analysis tends to preclude the attribution of continuing influence to prior experience. Likewise, not only are the lessons of history too variable and too subject to idiosyncratic interpretation to be theoretically reliable, but they are also limited in the sense that the cognitive factors from which they spring do not necessarily encompass the societal forces at work in any

---

[4] For detailed analyses of some of the early findings of our Vietnam project, see the sources cited in note 16 and also our papers entitled "Vietnam Revisited: Beliefs of Foreign Service and Military Officers about the Sources of Failure, Consequences, and 'Lessons' of the War," paper presented to the 10th Congress of the International Political Science Association, Edinburgh, 1976; "Vietnam, Consensus, and the Belief Systems of American Leaders," paper presented to the Hendricks Symposium on American Politics and World Order, University of Nebraska, Lincoln, 1977; and "America's Foreign Policy Agenda: The Post-Vietnam Beliefs of American Leaders," in C. W. Kegley, Jr. and P. J. McGowan (eds.), *Challenges to America: United States Foreign Policy in the 1980's* (1979).

major socio-political transformation. The domestic option does embrace these forces, but it suffers from too haphazard a treatment of the ways in which trends and events abroad may contribute to the transforming processes.

What is needed, in short, is a theoretical perspective that spans the cognitive, domestic, and international levels of analysis and that does so in such a way as to highlight the variables that must undergo significant change if a conclusion is to be reached that a society has passed through a major historical turning point. Stated differently, a theory of watersheds, of societal transformation, needs to be outlined, one which focuses on the inter-action among cognitive, domestic, and international processes.

Elsewhere one of us has developed a theoretical framework that may meet this criterion. Founded on the concept of national adaptation, this framework focuses precisely on the interactions of domestic and foreign variables as they shape or sustain any nation-State's capacity to keep its essential structures within acceptable limits (the theory's definition of national adaptation).[5] Cognitive processes are central to the framework in that the acceptability of the essential structures derives from certain basic orientations—cognitive as well as affective—held by those who comprise the nation-State. As is the case with any other human group, the more these adaptive orientations are shared by the élites and publics of a national society, the more will it be able to maintain acceptable essential structures and move towards its goals.

Four basic and mutually exclusive adaptive orientations are conceived to exist and, if one of these is widely shared, to underlie successful adaptation and survival as a national society. All four sets of orientations involve the way in which the present self (*i.e.* domestic needs and wants in the case of the State as an entity) and the present environment (*i.e.* demands, constraints, and opportunities originating abroad) are brought into balance: citizens and/or élites can seek to adjust their present selves to their present environment (an orientation called *acquiescent adaptation*); they can be ready to shape their present environment to their present selves (*intransigent adaptation*); they can be oriented towards creating a new equilibrium between their present selves and their present environment (*promotive adaptation*); or they can be ready to accept the existing equilibrium between their present selves and their present environment (*preservative adaptation*).[6]

---

[5] J. N. Rosenau, *The Adaptation of National Societies: A Theory of Political System Behaviour and Transformation* (1970).

[6] Present-day Czechoslovakia, South Africa, the People's Republic of China, and the United Kingdom are, respectively, illustrative of these four types of adaptive orientations. For a full analysis of each type, see *op. cit.* in note 5, above.

Each of the four sets of orientations is conceived to be a basic posture from which policy decisions spring, and as stable and enduring as long as the relative strength of the demands emanating from within the society and those arising in its present environment do not change. If such changes do take place to the extent of significantly altering the balance perceived to be desirable between the self and the environment, the national society either undergoes a transformation to one of the other adaptive orientations or it enters a period of maladaptive disarray in which a clear-cut configuration of new self-environment orientations fails to emerge. A period of disarray is not necessarily a prelude to societal extinction. It may be merely transitional if the widespread consensus supporting the new adaptive orientation is slow to form. Or, in those instances when the disarray persists inordinately and becomes stable in the absence of widely-shared self-environment orientations among various segments of the society, it may result in stalemated government and the avoidance of decision, a form of maladaptation that leads to stagnation rather than extinction.[7]

This is not to imply that the widely-shared consensuses on which adaptive orientations and transformations rest are to be highly prized. From a value perspective maladaptive disarray may be desirable if it involves, say, a transition away from internal tyranny or external domination. Our adaptation framework, in other words, contains no hidden biases favouring social order or governmental decisiveness. Rather it is an empirical framework, designed to allow for assessments of how societies do or do not cope with dynamic changes at home and abroad.

It must be stressed that adaptive transformations do not occur readily. Most changes at home and abroad are not so significant as to alter perceptions of the appropriate self-environment relationships. To repeat, the four types of adaptation rest on orientations that are so deep-seated as to easily absorb the day-to-day perturbations of domestic and international life. The severing of a diplomatic relationship, the worsening of a recession, the flare-up of a border

---

[7] It is, possible that significant changes at home or abroad are so great as to overwhelm and destroy, through fragmentation from within or external conquest from without, a society's essential structures. Such an outcome would indicate, in effect, a failure either to adapt or to manage maladaptive disarray, with the eventual result that the disarray culminates in extinction (*i.e.* the disappearance of the society as a viable social unit). While there are instances of national societies being conquered, voluntarily absorbed into a larger entity, or otherwise losing their essential structures, modern history records that they are usually able to survive and that adaptive transformation and/or maladaptive disarray rather than extinction is the typical response to profound social and technological change. For this reason, and because our focus is on a society (the United States) that seems unlikely to go under (however poorly it may adapt to change), no further note will be taken of the non-survival response to change in the ensuing analysis.

conflict, the advent of a crippling strike, the introduction of a new weapon, the outbreak of race riots—such events may have important short-run consequences, but none of them is normally so far-reaching as to precipitate new orientations towards the self relative to the environment in order to cope with the change involved. This being so, and with habitual thinking lying at the heart of cognitive processes, most citizens and élites of most countries are unlikely to revise their view of what constitutes an appropriate national adaptation under most circumstances.

In short, adaptive transformations are rare. The currents of history seldom converge in a watershed where the causal flow undergoes sharp redirection. What, then, are the circumstances under which the exceptional occurs? Under what conditions are transformations most likely to take place?

Here one peels off several layers of causality, each of which is dependent on the operation of the others. First, there must be change at home and/or abroad that is so profound as to jolt habitual thinking. Secondly, it must be perceived and commonly interpreted by élites. Thirdly, the structures or circumstances of domestic politics must be such as to enable the élites to perceive the changes and form a consensus as to the bases for new self-environment relationships. Each of these layers and the interactions among them will involve different dynamics for each of the four types of adaptation to undergo transformation to the other three. In many instances an electoral or violent ouster of political leaderships may be necessary if the changes that allow for a new self-environment balance are to be perceived. In other instances major societal upheaval may be required for the new élites to come to power and upgrade or play down the self in relation to the environment. In still other cases the changes abroad may be so jolting as to permit new adaptive orientations without corresponding disruptions at home.[8] On the other hand, profound changes in the environment are not always recognised in time to prevent internal disruption, just as some (perhaps even most) electoral ousters do not alter the course or conduct of societal life and just as violent ousters are not always followed by changes of watershed magnitude.

In short, adequate criteria for discussing watersheds and applying them to a particular society depends on an initial assessment of what kind of adaptation it may be undergoing and an anlysis of its political institutions and processes and their capacity to facilitate redefinition of historic (and habitual) self-environment orientations. In the case

---

[8] For an initial analysis of the differences among the 12 types of transformations, see *op. cit.* in note 5, above, at pp. 16–20.

of the United States and the consequences of its Vietnam involvement such an assessment is not difficult to make, though determining whether it has in fact undergone an adaptive transformation involves an empirical problem of monumental proportions which we have only partially solved.[9]

III—The United States as an Adaptive Society

The likelihood of super-Powers undergoing adaptive transformations is even less than for most nations. Having enormous wealth and self-perceived global responsibilities, they possess enough control over their external environments and the stability of their internal processes as to be especially capable of absorbing change without altering their self-environment orientations. Lesser Powers, constrained by limited resources, plagued by border problems, and locked into trade dependencies are much more susceptible to the dynamics whereby the self gets redefined relative to the environment.

Yet super-Powers are not immune to change. Their capabilities may lessen the probability of new self-environment orientations emerging, but this does not mean that their leaders and publics are free of the need to adjust to the profound and long-term structural alterations fostered by the imperatives of industrialisation and the dynamics of technology. Indeed, the United States can be said to have undergone a transformation from intransigent to promotive adaptation during the Second World War. Perhaps its first in the twentieth century, if not of its entire history, this transformation involved a heightened awareness that super-Power status and super-Power responsibilities had been acquired as a consequence of the changes wrought by the war. Prior to that conflict the United States, its leaders and its publics, were inwardly oriented and tended to attach much less priority to developments abroad. There were exceptions, to be sure, as continental expansion passed beyond the shores and an American presence was extended into the Caribbean, the Philippines, and elsewhere in the Pacific. And concern over deterioration in the environment led to the sending of troops to Europe in 1917. Such involvements abroad as occurred prior to the Second World War, however, were limited in scope and did not rest on broadly-shared perceptions of what the basic structures of the environment should be. The preoccupation was with growth at

---

[9] As will be seen, our data were gathered at only one point in time and thus we are not in a position to make precise estimates of the extent to which self-environment changes may have occurred across time. We anticipate solving this problem with additional (and comparable) surveys in the near future.

home and the performance of domestic institutions, so much so that the society turned its back on the League of Nations in 1920 and was slow to acknowledge a threat from Hitler's Germany in the late 1930s. Indeed, in 1941 the military draft was extended by a margin of one vote in the House of Representatives, a margin that, given the world situation at the time, suggests the reluctance with which the United States abandoned orientations in which the self was assumed to predominate over the environment.

The destruction and disarray abroad that resulted from the Second World War was so extensive that these intransigent orientations were no longer tenable. Technology, military and otherwise, had made the world smaller even as the war's aftermath had reduced most of the pre-War Great Powers to skeletons of their former selves. Only the Soviet Union was relatively stronger and it and its ideology seemed to threaten the very existence of democratic institutions in Western Europe and the potential of such institutions in the colonial empires that were rapidly breaking up. In short, the world beyond the American shores was in great flux, with longstanding economic, political, and social structures undermined and inviting opportunities for leadership even as their deterioration also seemed threatening.

At home, too, the end of the War brought change, from a baby boom to a surge in the economy to heightened racial sensitivities. The problems were numerous, but so were the opportunities as, again, a dynamic technology enlivened the sense that new forms of social and economic life lay ahead.

The circumstances in the late 1940s, in other words, were conducive to a transformation of the adaptive orientations of publics and élites alike. Now it seemed possible—indeed, necessary—to promote new arrangements at home and new structures abroad. There may have been all kinds of obstacles to such promotive efforts, but they seemed miniscule in comparison to the opportunities they afforded and the necessity of undertaking them. Thus it is hardly surprising that the victorious political party in the first post-War election sought to build a "Fair Deal" at home and a "Free World" abroad. The former was articulated through domestic policies designed to enhance, among others, farmers and their productivity, veterans and their education, workers and their job security, minorities and their rights, and the aged and their comfort, while such foreign policies as the Marshall Plan, the sponsorship of NATO, and the Truman Doctrine were the forerunners of many efforts to fashion new institutions of world order. The sense of having triumphed over evil during the war and having become relatively far more powerful than any other nation, with a currency that underlay the world's economy and a weaponry that seemed to assure military security, led Americans to see their collective selves as capable of bringing about whatever changes seemed desirable. One observer called this orientation "the illusion of omnipotence,"[10] but such criticisms did not deter attempts to build a new self-environment relationship rather than simply preserve the one that prevailed. No longer, in sum, was preservation of the self in relation to the environment the predominant orientation. It can fairly be said that the nation, its public as well as its élites, emerged from the Second World War with transformed orientations.[11] Whether or not these amounted to an illusion of omnipotence, they closely approximated what we conceive to be the dynamics of promotive adaptation.

The foregoing characterisation of the consequences of the Second World War is, admittedly, sketchy and short on documentation. But our task is not to substantiate that an adaptive transformation occurred at that time. Rather we are concerned with whether transformed self-environment orientations attended and followed Vietnam. Thus, the foregoing is set forth merely as a baseline, a premise that promotive orientations prevailed widely throughout the society as the United States entered the 1960s. This is the initial, organising assumption, from which the ensuing, more intensive inquiry proceeds.

IV—Vietnam as a Watershed

If Vietnam was a source of an adaptive transformation, clearly this occurred more through a process whereby the habitual thinking of existing élites was jolted rather than one in which new élites came to power. The 1960s witnessed considerable turmoil on the domestic scene, from racial tensions that led to burning cities to peace demonstrations that led to protest marches and riotous confrontations with the police. While a far cry from the torpor of American life in the 1950s, however, these tumultuous events were not the basis of either a violent or an electoral ouster of the nation's political leadership. The Democrats retained control of the Congress throughout the period and resisted the appeals of the mavericks among them, such as Eugene McCarthy and George McGovern, to downgrade the environment in relation to the self. To be sure, Lyndon Johnson

---

[10] D. Brogan, "The Illusion of American Omnipotence," 205 *Harper's* (December 1952), pp. 21–28.

[11] For evidence that the transformed orientations were the·basis of a widespread consensus among the élites in various walks of life, see J. N. Rosenau, *National Leadership and Foreign Policy: A Case Study in the Mobilization of Public Support* (1963).

apparently perceived the outcome of the 1968 New Hampshire primary as indicating that the country's involvement in Vietnam would prevent his re-election, and it is also the case that the Republicans took over the White House from the Democrats in the 1968 election and began to reverse the process of greater involvement in the Vietnam conflict. On the other hand, Nixon's margin of electoral victory was infinitesimal and his campaign was certainly not founded on the premises or promises of a new self-environment relationship.[12] McGovern's 1972 presidential candidacy did hold forth the prospect of a reconsidered, if not a revised, relationship in which the self was to be substantially upgraded in relation to the environment; but his overwhelming defeat at the polls may be just as easily attributed to the fact that his opponent had already begun the process of winding down the Vietnam involvement as to the difficulty of initiating adaptive transformations through the electoral process in the United States.

Yet, despite the essential continuity of the nation's political leadership, there are indications that many of its élites were so severely jolted by the Vietnam experience and the turmoil on the domestic scene as to question the adequacy of their self-environment orientations. More accurately, our research suggests that the American military entry into and exit from South-East Asia during the 1965–1973 period was, at the very least, a source of profound maladaptive disarray among the élites of the society and, at most, the beginnings of a transformation from promotive to preservative adaptation.

Our research findings derive from a lengthy mail questionnaire carefully completed and returned by élites in various walks of American life. Drawn from *Who's Who* and other leadership compendia, our sample consists of 2,282 persons in 11 occupational clusters whose leadership positions readily accord them élite status. Mailed in February 1976 the questionnaire contained more than 60 items that focused on the failure of United States policies in Vietnam, its sources, consequences, and lessons, as well as several other items that called for more general evaluations of United States foreign and domestic policies. Hence, although no single research instrument is sufficient to justify broad conclusions as to the adaptation of national societies, and while there are definite limits to the instrument we employed, our questionnaire has yielded results that

---

[12] That is, while the commitment to cut back in Vietnam was pledged and the bases of a new "doctrine" for involvement in conflicts abroad were hinted at by Nixon during the campaign, such projected changes were cast as policy shifts and not as fundamental alterations in the balance between self and environment.

cannot be readily dismissed and that allow for cautious speculation.[13]

One indicator that Vietnam was a jolting experience is provided by the responses to a series of items that called for self-assessments of what the conflict meant personally and for the society in general. These are presented in Table 1 and here it can be seen that a preponderance of the respondents were, in each case, deeply affected by Vietnam and anticipated its consequences to be considerable. Perhaps even more revealing are their self-perceptions of how their policy preferences towards the conflict underwent change from its inception to its conclusion. The results of the item tapping these perceptions are set forth in Table 2, which reveals that striking proportions of the élite sample reported having undergone significant reversals in their orientations towards the war. Indeed, combining all the possible shifts together, 62 per cent. reported having changed their positions on the war (see Table 3). Since it may have become unfashionable to admit ever having supported United States foreign policies in Vietnam, moreover, this percentage and the data in Table 2 probably understate the degree to which attitude change occurred.

To be jolted by a single sequence of events, however, is not necessarily to undergo the thoroughgoing reorganisation of attitudes that is necessary for the transformation of self-environment orientations. As conceived here, such orientations are so basic that they extend across the entire range of issues extant at any one time, providing attitudinal structure and coherence for each of them in terms of the relative importance of self to environment. For Vietnam to have been a watershed experience for American élites, therefore, its repercussions ought to be manifest—or at least traceable—in a broad spectrum of foreign and domestic policy questions.

Our data contain some strong hints that the repercussions of Vietnam approached such a magnitude. These were uncovered as a result of creating seven groups of respondents out of the answers to the item presented in Table 2 and then assessing the extent to which the seven groups differed in their reactions to exactly 100 other items in the questionnaire. As can be seen in Table 3, the seven groups ranged from those we called the Supporters of American policy in Vietnam to those we designated the Critics, with the five

---

[13] For discussions of the various methodological aspects of our Vietnam project—the procedures used to compile our sample, administer the questionnaire, and process the results—see O. R. Hosti and J. N. Rosenau, "The Lessons of Vietnam: A Study of American Leadership," paper presented to the 17th Annual Meeting of the International Studies Association, Toronto, 1976.

Table 1

*Personal Assessments of the Vietnam War Recorded by
2,282 American Leaders (in percentages)*

To what extent do you feel that the conduct of United States foreign policy has been affected by the American participation in the Vietnam participation in the Vietnam War?

To a very great extent	38
Quite significantly	53
Somewhat	8
Slightly	1
Not at all	0

In your judgment, how long will the American experience in Vietnam continue to influence the conduct of United States foreign policy?

As long as one can see into the future	14
Perhaps for a generation	40
Perhaps for about a decade	39
Through the next presidential campaign	6
It will have no impact on American policy	1

Which of the following statements describes what your feelings were about the war in Vietnam?

	When the war first became an issue	*Towards the end of U.S. involvement*
The war in Vietnam was one of my major worries and concerns at the time	28	57
I was concerned about the war, but it was not one of my major causes of worry	55	38
I was not very concerned about the war	16	2
Don't know	1	0
[did not answer]	0	3

In retrospect, how would you assess the meaning of Vietnam for you personally?

It was a profoundly important experience that is likely to influence my outlook for a long time	52
It had an important influence on me at the time, but this influence has now waned	30
It had no more effect on me than any other foreign policy issue	14
It did not influence my outlook in any significant way	4

Table 2
Early and Late Positions on the War in Vietnam
(Percentages of 2,282 respondents favouring various policies)

Some people felt that we should have done everything possible to gain a complete military victory in Vietnam. Others felt that we should have withdrawn as soon as possible. Still others had opinions in between these two. Please indicate which position came closest to your own feelings—both when the war first became an issue and later towards the end of United States involvement.

	When the war first became an issue	Towards the end of U.S. involvement
I tended to favour a complete military victory	51	22
I tended to favour a complete withdrawal	22	57
I tended to feel in between these two	22	18
Not sure	5	3
	100	100

intermediate groups representing varying degrees of change and/or ambivalence in their positions on Vietnam. The 100 other items to which the reactions of the seven groups were compared spanned a diverse array of considerations, from foreign-policy goals to the performance of policy-making institutions, from military-strategic calculations to assessments of Third-World situations, from domestic policy problems to the role of the Press and public as a source of policy outcomes. On 93 of these items the differences among the seven groups were found to be statistically significant.[14]

The importance of these findings as an indicator that Vietnam may have been a watershed experience can hardly be understated. The likelihood of a single questionnaire item yielding differences that so fully organise the rest of the data is extraordinarily small. And, even more important, this one item allowed us to classify the respondents into seven groups *solely* on the basis of their overall policy preferences towards the Vietnam conflict. This is, admittedly, a simple classification scheme, but it serves well the purpose of assessing the magnitude of the attitudinal shock waves produced by Vietnam because its isolates views on the conflict from other variables such as age, education, occupation, ideology, and party iden-

[14] At the 0·001 level of significance.

Table 3

The 2,282 Respondents Classified into Seven Groups by Positions on Vietnam During Early and Late Stages of the War*

Some people felt that we should have done everything possible to gain a complete military victory in Vietnam. Others felt that we should have withdrawn as soon as possible. Still others had opinions in between these two. Please indicate which position came closest to your own feelings—both when the war first became an issue and later toward the end of United States involvement.

When the War first became an issue	*Towards the end of United States Involvement*			
	I tended to favour a complete military victory	I tended to feel in between these two	Not sure	I tended to favour a complete withdrawal
I tended to favour a complete military victory	SUPPORTERS (n=363)	AMBIVALENT SUPPORTERS (n=346)		CONVERTED CRITICS (n=867)
I tended to feel in between these two	CONVERTED SUPPORTERS (n=128)	AMBIVALENTS (n=128)		
Not sure				
I tended to favour a complete withdrawal		AMBIVALENT CRITICS (n=63)		CRITICS (n=378)

*Nine respondents did not indicate their position on Vietnam in either the early or late stages of war.

tification.[15] Indeed, it is precisely because the classification scheme described in Table 3 is so simple and based purely on the Vietnam issue that the 93 out of 100 significant differences are such striking indicators that the magnitude of the shock waves approaches that of a watershed.

V—MALADAPTIVE DISARRAY OR ADAPTIVE TRANSFORMATION?

It will be recalled that while habitual thinking must be jolted for new self-environment orientations to develop, such a process is not in itself sufficient to induce an adaptive transformation. Widespread agreement among élites as to the meaning of the changes that are so jolting must also evolve, else the society will enter a period of maladaptive disarray as tensions mount over the most appropriate way to relate the self to the environment. To be sure, adaptive transformations do not occur instantaneously, and there is bound to be some disarray while the agreement on a proper self-environment orientation forms and spreads widely throughout the society; but if the changes at home and abroad jolt different élite groups in different ways, consensus among them may never become deeply embedded and prolonged disarray may ensue, greatly inhibiting the society's capacity to cope with challenges abroad and conflicts at home.

Since our research thus far has tapped élite orientations at only a single moment in time (1976), one that was not so far removed from the end of United States military involvement in Vietnam as to allow for the formation of a widespread consensus, we are in no position to offer definitive observations on whether the United States is in the process of an adaptive transformation or whether it is headed for a long era of maladaptive disarray. But some of our data are suggestive in this regard and worthy of notation. Anticipating our conclusions, they most clearly suggest that a transformation to preservative adaptation may be under way, but that considerable disarray lies ahead which, indeed, may never yield to clear-cut and widely-shared self-environment orientations.

Several findings indicate that if an adaptive transformation is under way, it is headed in a preservative direction, *i.e.* towards an

---

[15] This is not to imply, however, that these and other background attributes are irrelevant to the transformation of self-environment orientations. We have already found, for example, that occupational differences also help explain (although to a lesser extent) the different responses to the 100 other items (in "Cold War Axioms in the Post Vietnam Era," cited in note 16). The age generation variable, on the other hand, appears to have been of negligible importance (see O. R. Holsti and J. N. Rosenau, "Does Where You Stand Depend on When You Were Born? The Impact of Generation on Post-Vietnam Foreign Policy Beliefs," University of Southern California (Los Angeles: Institute for Transnational Studies, Monograph Nr. ITS 78–01, 1978).

acceptance of the equilibrium between the limits of United States influence abroad that were highlighted by Vietnam and those inherent in the domestic problems that became manifest at the same time. First, a closer look at Tables 2 and 3 reveals that the predominant attitudinal change from the beginning to the end of the Vietnam conflict involved scaled-down expectations and reduced commitments in South-East Asia. Nearly three-fifths of the respondents favoured "complete withdrawal" from Vietnam at the war's end and, of these, 69 per cent. reported converting to such a position during the course of the conflict. Indeed, the Converted Critics were more than twice as numerous than any of the other six groups listed in Table 3.

Secondly, the responses to three other items bearing directly on the self-environment relationship point up the prevalence of the tendency towards a more even balance between internal and external demands: (a) 71 per cent. agreed (either "strongly" or "somewhat") that "the real long-term threats to national security—energy shortages, the environment, *etc.*—have been neglected as a result of our preoccupation with Vietnam"; (b) 56 per cent. agreed that "America's conception of its leadership role in the world must be scaled down"; and (c) 64 per cent. agreed that "the best way to encourage democratic development in the Third World is for the United States to solve its own problems." A majority of the responses to still another item, on the other hand, indicate a reluctance on the part of a sizeable majority to redress the self-environment relationship to the point where the balance is tipped in favour of the self: 61 per cent. disagreed (either "strongly" or "somewhat") that "we shouldn't think so much in international terms but concentrate more on our own national problems."

Notwithstanding these indicators of a transformation from promotive to preservative adaptation, other aspects of our data hint even more strongly at the possibility that the transforming process may never fully unfold, that a broadly-based consensus around preservative orientations may not evolve beyond the proportions cited above, and that therefore a lengthy period of maladaptive disarray may be part of the American future. In part, such a conclusion derives from the obverse of the foregoing findings. The latter describe central tendencies, but the deviations from these tendencies are not insubstantial. As can be seen in Table 2, for example, nearly one-quarter of the respondents still favoured an extensive United States involvement in Vietnam towards the end of the conflict and two-fifths did not favour a complete withdrawal from it. Likewise, although Table 3 reveals that 62 per cent. changed their basic posture towards the conflict while it ensued, not all of these

shifted in the direction of a greatly reduced United States commitment: eight per cent. (the Converted Supporters and the Ambivalent Critics) moved either towards greater involvement or away from
complete withdrawal and another 15 per cent. (the Ambivalent
Supporters) moved away from greater involvement but did not go so
far as to favour complete withdrawal. Similarly, proportions ranging
from 29 to 44 per cent. disagreed (either "strongly" or "somewhat") with the four propositions in the previous paragraph calling
for a more even balance between internal and external demands.

It could be that such deviations from the central tendency towards
preservative adaptation are transitory, that they depict leaders
whose attitudes change at a slower rate, and that subsequent surveys
will thus yield even larger majorities in the central direction. Other
aspects of our findings, however, give pause in this regard. Most
notably, the pattern of responses to the 64 questionnaire items
focusing on Vietnam recorded by the Supporters and Critics proved
to be so internally consistent within each group and so divergent
between them as virtually to constitute two mutually-exclusive
belief systems. The discrepancies between the two groups can be
incisively depicted: using only a moderately stringent criterion for
identifying the 64 items that received the strongest support on the
part of each group, 24 items qualified for the Supporters and 17 for
the Critics, but *only one item appears on both lists*. That such
differences can be viewed as mutually-exclusive belief systems can
be inferred from Table 4, which summarily outlines some of the
major dimensions of the responses of the two groups, both with
respect of Vietnam and United States policy in general. Here can be
seen not only the extent of the strong cleavages between the Supporters and Critics, but also—and more significantly—the various ways
in which each dimension for each group tends to reinforce the
others, thereby forming a coherent and systematic set of beliefs.

Such coherence within each group is among our more important
findings because it suggests that, in the absence of dramatic (or
traumatic) new international developments, further attitude change
in the direction of a more widespread leadership consensus is highly
unlikely. In contrast to opinions about a particular issue, which can
fluctuate considerably as its dynamics unfold, belief systems tend to
be so structured and encompassing that they do not readily shift in
response to new developments. Indeed, it is the very nature of a
belief system that it can absorb unexpected events: one or another
of its elements serves to explain the surprising event so that the
entire structure of the system is preserved. Viewed in this way, our
data summarised in Table 4 suggest that those American leaders
who have thus far resisted the central tendency towards preservative

adaptation are likely to continue to adhere to promotive orientations. Vietnam may have jolted a goodly proportion into restructuring their belief systems and revising their self-environment orientations, but a substantial minority appear destined to remain unaffected by the dynamics of adaptive transformation.[16] Maladaptive disarray, and the contentious, oft-times paralysing politics to which it gives rise, may therefore mark the American scene for a long time into the future.

In short, the United States has come out of Vietnam differently than it went in. Its people, as measured by our sample of leaders in 1976, have accorded more significance to the environment in relation to the self and, in so doing, have passed through a watershed, a profound transformation of their basic orientations towards the several conflicting worlds in which they live at home and abroad. Despite the greater balance between self and environment, however, the prospects of its serving as the basis for wise policies in the future are questionable. The leadership consensus on which it rests is not so widespread as to permit decisive action or reaction in response to the many novel situations that are bound to arise in the decades ahead.

Table 4
Supporters and Critics of the United States in Vietnam:
An Outline of Their Belief Systems

Beliefs about the Vietnam War

	Supporters	*Critics*
Position on the War	greater support for:	greater support for:
	complete military victory in the early stages of the war	complete withdrawal in the early stages of the war
	complete military victory in the late stages of the war	complete withdrawal in the late stages of the war

---

[16] In the context of this apparent limit to the shift to preservative adaptation, it is interesting to note that our data do not support the interpretation (cited earlier) that Vietnam fostered a new élite—the intellectual-industrial complex—who converge consensually around foreign policy issues even as they continue to compete on domestic matters. Whereas 45 and 51 per cent. of the 294 "business executives" in our sample, for example, were classified, respectively, among the three Supporter and three Critic groups, the comparable figures for the 565 "educators" were 21 and 73 per cent. (the remainder in each occupation were classified as Ambivalents). For more elaborate data on this point, as well as on eight other occupational groups, see O. R. Holsti and J. N. Rosenau, "The Meaning of Vietnam: Belief Systems of American Leaders," XXXII *International Journal* (Summer 1977), pp. 452–474, and O. R. Holsti and J. N. Rosenau, "Cold War Axioms in the Post-Vietnam Era," a paper presented to the Annual Meeting of the International Studies Association, Washington D.C., February 1978.

Table 4—continued

Diagnosis: sources of failure	greater emphasis on impact of: domestic constraints American decision-making self-imposed constraints on the conduct of the war Soviet and Chinese aid to North Vietnam	greater emphasis on impact of: lack of knowledge and understanding about the Third World and South-East Asia unrealistic American goals lack of popular support for the régime in Saigon
Prescription: lessons of Vietnam	greater emphasis on: the bipolar structure of the international system the threatening nature of communist adversaries more effective management of military power	greater emphasis on: limiting the U.S. role in the international system the multipolar structure of the international system limitations on the effectiveness of military power

Beliefs about United States policy in general

	stress on international/ military issues	stress on issues such as arms control, inflation, hunger, resources, and living standards in under-developed countries
	maintaining the balance of power is essential, as is containment of expanionist régimes	maintaining a global balance of power and containing communism a lower set priorities
	force and subversion have considerable utility as instruments of foreign policy	highly sceptical about use of force, but foreign economic assistance has considerable utility as an instrument of foreign policy
	stable government with pro-American, or at least neutral, foreign policies should be supported	governments that protect civil liberties, live at peace with neighbours, and capable of achieving rapid economic growth should be supported
	strengthen American institutions, and the U.S. economy in particular, to cope with military threats from abroad	place coping with urgent domestic issues at top of the agenda and scale down expectations about what the U.S. can achieve abroad

THE PANAMA CANAL
AND FUTURE UNITED STATES
HEMISPHERIC POLICY

By

M. F. C. BERNER

On April 18, 1978, after 38 days of intense debate, the United States Senate ratified the Panama Canal Treaty by a vote of 68 to 32—one more than the required two-thirds vote—after earlier approving the Neutrality Treaty by the same vote on March 16, 1978. Ratification of the two treaties after 14 years of often acrimonious negotiations heralded the end of what many Latin American countries considered an era of Yankee Imperialism and marked a significant political and diplomatic victory for President Carter over an independent Congress. Victory for the President was considered crucial for success in his pursuit of other foreign-policy objectives, especially a SALT II agreement. Moreover, the Panama Treaties marked, in Carter's words, "... the beginning of a new era in our relations not only with Panama but with the rest of the world.... They symbolize our determination to deal with the developing nations of the world on the basis of mutual respect and partnership."[1] The forging of a new relationship with Latin America may be Carter's intention; whether it is likely, or even feasible, is another matter.

It is appropriate at this juncture in the development of Pan-American relations to review the final treaty provisions and to analyse the forces which contributed to the ratification of the treaties. These forces transcend the particularities of the bilateral issue and promise to shape United States-Latin American relations for at least the next decade. The questions which this paper will address are: (1) What pressures led to the ratification of the treaties in Panama and the United States? (2) What do they tell us about the changing shape of United States-Latin American relations? (3) Is Carter's promise of a "new era" likely, even if pragmatically desirable?

I—THE 1978 PANAMA CANAL TREATIES

The Panama Canal Treaty and the Neutrality Treaty replace the original "Hay-Bunau-Varilla" Treaty of 1903, which granted the

---

[1] 36 *Congressional Quarterly*, Nr. 16, April 22, 1978, p. 1006.

United States the Canal and its contiguous Zone "in perpetuity" together with the right to exercise control over the Zone "as if it were sovereign."[2] Under "The Panama Canal Treaty"—which was considered secondly by the Senate because it was the more controversial of the two treaties—the United States will retain operating control of the Canal and the right to defend it until December 31, 1999, after which Panama will assume complete sovereignty. Once the Treaty goes into effect, pending the necessary Congressional implementing legislation, Panama will assume general territorial jurisdiction over the present Canal Zone, though the United States will retain control over 40 per cent. of the Zone needed for the continued operation of the Canal. In exchange for certain defence concessions from Panama, the United States guaranteed Panama powerful economic inducements in the form of toll surcharges and annuities amounting to from $50 million to $70 million per year until the year 2000, at which time Panama will both collect and control all revenues. The annuity alone will jump from $2·3 million to between $40 and $50 million. In addition, the United States will give Panama $295 million in economic loans and guarantees, as opposed to outright grants, over a period of five years, together with an additional $50 million in military assistance during a 10-year period.[3] These economic guarantees are frequently overlooked in the discussion of the Canal treaties but are particularly important because of their implications for future United States-Latin American relations.

The issue of the Canal's neutrality was so sensitive that the negotiators wrote a second and separate treaty. Under "The Treaty Concerning the Permanent Neutrality and Operation of the Panama Canal," the United States will not only have the primary responsibility for defending the Canal until the year 2000 but will also retain the permanent right to intervene to maintain the Canal's neutrality. This provision authorised the use of force to ensure the passage of United States merchant vessels and warships in the event of an emergency.[4] This crucial provision marked Panama's major concession in the negotiations, a concession considered necessary for Senate passage. Yet debate over ratification proved difficult for Treaty proponents, and victory was assured only after the Senate

---

[2] S. B. Liss, *The Canal: Aspects of United States—Panamanian Relations* (1967), pp. 450–460, which contains excerpts of treaties governing United States-Panamanian relations from 1903 to 1967.

[3] *Op. cit.* in note 1, above, at pp. 995–1003, which contain a full text of "The Panama Canal Treaty" with conditions and reservations.

[4] *Op. cit.* in note 1, above, at pp. 1003–1006, which contain a full text of the Neutrality Treaty with amendments.

adopted a series of two amendments, two conditions, two reservations, and five understandings that clarified United States defence
interests.[5] The most important additions provided each country with
the permanent right to defend the Canal and the right of "head of
the line passage" in emergencies. The first and most controversial
addition, the "DeConcini Condition" (named after its sponsor,
Senator Dennis DeConcini), permits the United States to "use
military force in Panama" to reopen the Canal. The Senate considered stipulation of this prerogative necessary, even though it was
implicit in the original Treaty language, because it felt that in the
future Panama might adopt a strict construction of the Treaty
barring United States defence rights. This Condition was particularly embarrassing to the Panamanian government of General
Omar Torrijos, which already faced growing domestic opposition to
treaties perceived as a challenge to Panama's dignity, if not its
sovereignty. In an attempt to mollify Panamanian criticism and
diffuse mounting opposition to the Torrijos government—and by
association to the Treaties themselves—the Carter Administration
added a reservation to the second Treaty ("The Panama Canal
Treaty") when it was considered a month later.[6] This reservation
guarantees the sovereign right of Panama by stipulating that any
action the United States might take to keep the Canal open and
neutral does not confer on it the right to intervene in Panama's
internal affairs.

Shortly after the Senate vote, Torrijos said in a nationwide speech
that the various amendments, conditions, reservations, and understandings were within the spirit of the Treaties, thereby avoiding the
necessity of a second plebiscite. A vote of approval in a second
plebiscite, the Panamanian method of ratification, was considered
doubtful. Torrijos's statement therefore cleared the way for formal
ratification of the two pacts on October 1, 1979, pending final
implementing legislation by the United States Congress.

II—Pressures Leading to the Final Settlement

(a) *Panama*

Omar Torrijos Herrera assumed power in an October 1969 *coup*.
He replaced an inefficient and corrupt civilian oligarchy which ruled
a nation with deep racial antagonisms, an inequitable system of
income distribution, and, as its primary resource, an inter-oceanic
canal owned by a foreign Power. Torrijos quickly moved to consolidate his power by solidifying his support within the National Guard

---

[5] *Congressional Record*, March 16, 1978, pp. S3857–S3858.
[6] *Congressional Record*, April 18, 1978, pp. S5796–S5797.

(Panama's army) and by developing a populist style of government based on extensive use of the mass media, "anti-imperialist" rhetoric, and a programme of urban growth.[7] By building his power base on a coalition of urban and rural sectors, Torrijos attempted to rest his authority on more than personal charisma and a strong army. Resting power on such a volatile coalition required not only guns but an ability to distribute considerable amounts of largesse. To sustain this coalition, Torrijos had to create sizeable new internal wealth or secure control of the ultimate source of economic power in Panama—the Canal.

Torrijos embarked on a series of major reforms designed to consolidate his urban and rural support. These included both the construction of urban housing and office complexes financed by increased taxes and a series of labour law reforms passed in 1972 regulating job conditions, establishing a minimum wage, and imposing compulsory collective bargaining. His top priority, however, was a programme of rural development involving massive land redistribution and the formation of 270 farm collectives. By extending his power base to the rural poor, Torrijos also hoped to strengthen his influence with the National Guard, which recruited heavily from the countryside.

By 1976 Torrijos's reform programme was in disarray, his coalition was splintering, and his country was on the verge of insolvency. Serious structural weaknesses began to surface within the Panamanian economy, especially a severe and sustained capital shortage. To finance his reform programmes, Torrijos had stimulated the economy in 1969 with $45 million in public investment, one-half of it borrowed from international banks, along with another $50 million from Swiss banks. As a result, debt service in 1972 absorbed one-quarter of the government's revenues, the highest rate of any country in Latin America. Only a $115 million loan from a North American banking consortium in 1973 rescued Panama from insolvency. These structural problems, combined with a series of uncontrollable external factors, such as drought, falling sugar prices, and international inflation, eventually forced Torrijos into accepting unpopular treaty terms in exchange for desperately needed funds.

However, before turning to the United States for economic relief, Torrijos had sought support from international banks. In 1970 he initiated permissive banking laws in an attempt to make Panama the Switzerland of Latin America. These required no minimum reserve and placed a lid on domestic interest rates while allowing all other lending rates to be determined by the market. These lenient laws,

---

[7] W. LeFeber, *The Panama Canal: The Crisis in Historical Perspective* (1978), pp. 156–167.

along with Panama's strategic location and close ties with the dollar, brought foreign banks to Panama in droves, from five in 1963 to 74 in 1977. By 1976, foreign banks controlled 91 per cent. of the nation's deposits and 77 per cent. of its loans. By eliminating the reserve requirements, however, Torrijos effectively surrendered control over Panama's money supply to the banks, which could withdraw whenever it was to their advantage, thereby sending Panama's economy into chaos. The economy was further weakened, albeit ironically, by its close tie with the United States dollar. Legally dependent on the dollar as the basis of its own currency, Panama found itself caught in an inflationary squeeze: as inflation in the United States sky-rocketed and the dollar value of imports correspondingly spiralled, Panama's currency bought less on the international market. Real economic growth declined from 8 per cent. in the mid-1960s to 4 per cent. in 1974 and 0 per cent. in 1976 as credit lines were rapidly exhausted. By 1976, Panama lost effective control of both its currency and its trade and was desperately in need of a radical solution.[8]

Panama's economic crisis was predictably accompanied by the reappearance of government corruption and a growing restiveness within the National Guard over slow promotions and lagging benefits. An annual population growth of 3·3 per cent. one of the world's highest, and the failure of agricultural reform because of plummeting sugar prices, added to an already severe unemployment problem. Income distribution, the highest *per capita* in Central America ($1,378 in 1976), remained as maldistributed as in the 1960s. Moreover, the 1972 labour code was progressively abrogated in an attempt to influence favourably vital business and banking interests. Left-wing protest was temporarily quieted by Torrijos's public relations junket to Cuba in 1976 only to be renewed later that year in rioting over milk and rice prices prompted by severe drought and inflation. Above all, the fundamental danger to the Torrijos régime was the nagging reality of a 0 per cent. growth rate compounded by a domestic market which was limited and an inflation rate which was too high to attract desperately needed foreign investment. With credit lines exhausted, only large Canal revenues could rescue the government from its debt.[9] By the time the Carter Administration assumed power in early 1977, Panama was ready to negotiate in earnest, prepared for the first time to make

---

[8] H. Johnson, "Panama as a Regional Financial Center: A Preliminary Analysis for Development Contribution," XXIV *Economic Development and Cultural Change*, January 1976, p. 286, noted in *op. cit.* in note 7, above, at p. 175.

[9] R. E. Looney, *The Economic Development of Panama* (1976), p. 5 and *passim*.

major defence concessions in return for immediate access to Canal moneys and United States aid.

(b) *The United States*

Torrijos's weakened negotiating stance coincided with a watershed in United States foreign policy crossed in the early 1970s with the success of détente and the decline of United States economic pre-eminence. Increasingly, the Cold War ceased to be the overwhelming foreign-policy issue. The United States and the Soviet Union were burdened by the escalating costs of nuclear confrontation and with technical advances in weaponry which reduced the need for overseas bases and alliances. The main concern of United States (and Soviet) foreign policy then became the prevention of regional conflicts from escalating into super-Power confrontation. One effect of this change was to decrease the dependence of the Western nations on the United States for security.

The international monetary system simultaneously moved away from fixed exchange and reliance on the American dollar, stimulating a challenge by Western Germany and Japan for economic pre-eminence, especially in the developing world.[10] Inflation gradually replaced unemployment as the single most important economic factor affecting international relations.[11] The United States' ability to control its allies was further undermined by the effects of the oil crisis, commodity shortages, the fragility of the international economic order, and the growing influence of such representative "non-State" actors as multinational corporations, Amnesty International, and the International Monetary Fund.

Economic co-operation and "resource diplomacy" therefore became increasingly important as détente reduced the danger of nuclear confrontation. President-elect Carter recognised this important change in testimony before the Senate Foreign Relations Committee in December, 1976. He said: "The future, I think of foreign policy might be changing, for there is a new emphasis on economic matters."[12] This theme was repeatedly underscored in a subsequent report on United States-Latin American relations issued a month later by a Commission comprised of top Carter aides, including the new Secretary of the Treasury, his Assistant Secretary for International Affairs, and the chief Panama Canal

---

[10] H. Schmidt, "The Struggle for the World Product," *Foreign Affairs*, 1974.

[11] C. F. Bergsten, "U.S.-Latin American Economic Relations to 1980: The International Framework and Some Possible Approaches," in S. M. Linowitz (ed.), *The Americas in a Changing World* (1976), pp. 175 *et seq.*

[12] United States, 94th Congress, Second Session, Senate Committee on Foreign Relations, *President-Elect Jimmy Carter's Views Concerning Foreign Policy* (1976), p. 8.

negotiator.[13] The Commission argued that economic co-operation, not security concerns, was going to be the critical issue in the coming decade, especially the need for stable and equitable terms of exchange, access to commodities and markets, and the transfer of technology. The Commission maintained, moreover, that failure to resolve the Panama dispute would seriously jeopardise future inter-American relations. It argued that while the Canal was useful, it was no longer as vital to United States interests as good relations with Latin America and access to its resources. Since all of Latin America viewed the Canal dispute as a bellweather for its future affairs with the United States,[14] the Commission held that United States interests in the region would be far better served by negotiating the new treaty in terms acceptable to Panama and the rest of Latin America. It might be further argued that with Panama, the United States had an important opportunity to demonstrate its appreciation for changing diplomatic relations with the developing world while still in a strong negotiating position. Moreover, a successful treaty would strengthen United States influence in the region at a time when its hegemony was declining.

Top Carter administration officials, therefore, viewed resolution of the Canal dispute as crucial for their foreign policy. A new treaty would be received as a sign of United States interest in Latin America and the rest of the developing world and would help to secure relations with commodity-rich nations like Venezuela. As C. Fred Bergsten, now Assistant Secretary of the Treasury for International Affairs, commented in the Commission report, "Securing assured access to Latin American raw materials should be the primary objective of United States economic policy toward Latin America."[15]

(c) *The Final Negotiations*

A variety of pressures thus converged and propelled the Canal negotiations into their final stage: the rapidly deteriorating Panamanian economy and Torrijos's increasing dependence on outside private investment, and the United States' need for assured access to Latin American resources and its growing awareness that Panama was vital to such interests. By early 1977 the negotiating advantage shifted to the United States as the Panamanian economic

---

[13] S. M. Linowitz, *The Americas in a Changing World* (1976), *passim*.

[14] *E.g.*, Venezuelan President Carlos Andreas Perez, whose country is the second largest exporter of oil to the United States, remarked that "How can the United States—which is a leader of democracy in the world, take a colonial's stand on the Canal?" Without a quick resolution, he added, "very bad relations will develop between the two Americas, North and South." Quoted in *op. cit.* in note 8, above, p. 183.

[15] *Op. cit.* in note 11, above, at p. 182.

crisis worsened and as the hesitant Ford Administration was replaced by a Carter Administration determined to obtain a treaty that would be politically acceptable both in the Senate and in Latin America. The United States was able to wrest from Panama the concessions it considered necessary because Torrijos was forced to place top priority on immediate access to United States funds. The final treaties, especially as amended by the Senate, were a diplomatic success for the United States. The Treaties were especially successful given the extent of Panama's earlier demands (*e.g.* $1 billion in developmental moneys and reversion of the Canal to Panama in 15 years), the strong pro-Panamanian sentiment in Latin America, and the increasing limitations on United States hegemony in the hemisphere.[16] President Carter had good reason to exult in the Treaties, for they demonstrated to Americans his ability to steer difficult legislation through an independent Congress and to foreign governments his ability to negotiate to mutual advantage. One crucial question remains, however: to what extent do the Treaties anticipate a "new era" of "mutual respect" between the United States and Latin America, as President Carter predicted?

III—THE FUTURE OF UNITED STATES LATIN AMERICAN RELATIONS

Insofar as the Treaties reflect the unique history of the United States-Panamanian relationship they portend very little about future hemispheric relations.[17] The United States possessed negotiating advantages that are unlikely to be repeated elsewhere. It bartered with an extremely small country that it had virtually created, whose major resource it had developed and controlled, whose currency was legally tied to the dollar, and whose economy was controlled by United States banks. However, insofar as the Treaties reflect the deeper economic forces shaping Pan-American affairs, they are reliable indicators of the near future. This is not to say that economic forces are the only factors at work in hemispheric relations; but they will be the most important for the next decade according to senior members of the Carter Administration. While conceding the importance of other factors such as human rights, intra-regional diplomatic competition, law of the sea disputes, and

---

[16] *Op. cit.* in note 8, above, at p. 206.

[17] The best early history of Panama, the United States, and the Canal is D. McCulloch, *The Path Between the Seas* (1976); the best account of United States-Panamanian relations up to the signing of the treaties is W. LeFeber, *The Panama Canal* (1978).

nuclear power competition,[18] the remainder of this paper will analyse the seminal economic issues that will affect hemispheric relations in the next decade.

Since the early 1970s, United States foreign-policy priorities have reflected a growing concern for economic security, especially the availability of natural resources.[19] Therefore, securing access to raw materials at reasonable prices has become a primary objective of United States policy towards Latin America.[20] Such a policy is bound to put constraints on the exercise of United States power in the hemisphere, because it grants Latin America a powerful bargaining advantage at the same time as the United States economy is severely strained by inflation and an oil-related balance of payments deficit. The one-sided economic advantages the United States possessed in its Panama negotiations will remain for a time, but an increasingly insistent Latin America will meet a United States increasingly unwilling to grant its demands. What are those demands and what are the likely United States responses?

(a) *Latin American Priorities*

Latin American concerns reflect the rest of the developing world's priorities in their economic relations with the United States. The five most important are: (1) greater access to the United States market for exports (raw, manufactured, and agricultural); (2) United States co-operation in raising and supporting commodity prices; (3) increasing United States concessional and commercial ties with Latin America; (4) United States assistance in Latin American efforts to maximise gains and minimise costs of United States foreign direct investment, including assurances that diplomatic levers will not be used to support United States investors in commercial disputes with Latin American countries; (5) United States sponsorship of technology transfer on cheaper terms than presently available.

United States-Latin American relations are likely to improve to the extent that these five concerns are resolved. As Roger Hansen, Senior Fellow of the Overseas Development Council, has written regarding Latin America: "This is the agenda for the 1970s beyond; almost all non-economic issues are of marginal importance by com-

---

[18] The best recent studies in this area are G. Pope Atkins, *Latin America in the International Political System*, (1977), J. Cotler and R. Fagen (eds.), *Latin America and the United States* (1974), and R. Chilcote and J. Edelstein *Latin America: The Struggle for Dependency and Beyond* (1974).

[19] R. Hansen, "The Politics of Scarcity," in J. W. Howe (ed.), *The U.S. and the Developing World* (1976), p. 212.

[20] *Op. cit.* in note 11, above, at p. 182 *et seq.*

parison."[21] Latin American judgments concerning the United States commitment to it will be based on United States responsiveness to these five areas. If the United States response is marginal, North-South conflict will intensify. If this happens, then the role of the United States market for Latin American exports and the role of United States multinational companies will lead to major tensions. In order to anticipate the likely United States response, it is necessary first to survey some basic trends in United States-Latin American economic relations.

(b) *Basic Trends in Hemispheric Economic Relations*

Beyond potential constriction of the flow of natural resources, Latin America presents no serious economic security concern for the United States, since it is a dwindling market for United States exports and investments. In 1950, Latin America accounted for 35 per cent. of United States direct foreign investment; now the proportion is 17 per cent. It is also a less significant market for United States exports: 27 per cent. in 1950, 19 per cent. in 1960, and 16 per cent. in 1975. United States sources of supply have similarly diversified, relying on Latin America for 35 per cent. of its imports in 1950, 27 per cent. in 1960, and 15 per cent. in 1975.

Statistics citing United States dependence on Latin America for imports of industrial raw materials fail to note that for many of the products, domestic United States production is relatively high. This is true of iron ore, copper, and lead. More generally, of course, the present pattern of trade is not a good measure of the costs of its disruption. There is no lurking threat from widespread Third-World cartelisation that would itself compel the United States to regard Latin American supplies as indispensable.

What has always been true is that the United States is more important to the economic fortunes of Latin America than the reverse. It is both a larger factor in Latin American trade as well as predominant in capital flows. Yet that too is changing, partly as a consequence of the rapid economic growth of Western Germany and Japan, and partly as a result of deliberate United States policy. In 1950, 46 per cent. of Latin American exports were sold to the United States compared to 38 per cent. in the early 1960s and 32 per cent. in the early 1970s. The corresponding series for imports were 57 per cent. in 1950, 42 per cent. in the early 1960s and 37 per cent. in the early 1970s. While Latin American trade with the United States was decreasing, its reliance on the Euro-currency market for its foreign capital was increasing. This inflow of capital mounted

---

[21] R. Hansen, "U.S.-Latin American Economic Relationships: Bilateral, Regional or Global?" in S. M. Linowitz (ed.), *The Americas in a Changing World* (1976), p. 212.

from less than a quarter of the private gross capital inflow in 1971 to more than three-quarters by 1973.[22]

This diversification does not alter either the considerable absolute magnitudes of trade or the asymmetrical character of regional dependence, which explains why United States economic policy and performance are so important for Latin America. When United States imports declined in 1975, Latin America's trade balance with the United States underwent an adverse shift of $3·6 billion within a single year. Many decisions that are taken without considering Latin America often have a more considerable impact on its economy than deliberate policies. Three trends in the United States and other countries of the Organisation for Economic Co-operation and Development (OECD) are particularly important: (1) the decline in the rate of real economic growth; (2) the reduction in the rate of trade liberalisation; and (3) the slower growth of capital markets.

A slower real economic growth rate in the OECD countries will result in lower relative prices for Latin American primary resources (and perhaps a lower growth rate of primary exports as a response to these lower prices). In any event, traditional exports will not be a leading sector in the non-oil-producing countries. To sustain economic growth, increasing reliance must be placed upon non-traditional exports, particularly manufactured goods. Starting from a very low base, such exports grew rapidly after 1960 as a consequence of trade liberalisation in the OECD countries.[23]

The prospects for economic growth in the United States are not particularly promising. The unemployment generated as a result of the anti-inflationary policies of 1975 exceeds the maximum level reached since the economic recovery from the Second World War. As the United States continues to run periodically into constraints posed by capacity limitations, periods of inflation followed by restrictive monetary and fiscal policies will sustain these relatively high levels of unemployment. The relative large increase in the fraction of the population in the 20–30 age group (a product of the post-war "baby boom") and the continuing influx of females into the labour market has the effect of swelling the labour force in the face of the slackening pace of demand. In such circumstances, continued liberalisation of trading relationships with Latin America will continue to encounter staunch opposition.

---

[22] United States, 94th Congress, First Session, Subcommittee on Inter-American Economic Relationships of the Joint Economic Committee, Statement by S. Weintraub, "The Economic Scene in Latin America and the Caribbean," June 28, 1976, pp. 16–18 and 20.

[23] United States, 94th Congress, First Session, Subcommittee on Inter-American Economic Relationships of the Joint Economic Committee, Statement by Professor T. E. Davis, "The Future of U.S.-Latin American Relations," June 28, 1978, p. 10.

The immediate consequence for Latin America is the prospect of declining rates of growth in the United States and other OECD capital markets. United States direct investment in Latin America consists of two-thirds of its developmental investment, controlling over 50 per cent. of all net financial flows. Increasingly, this is shifting to the manufacturing sector, where it often controls 50 to 100 per cent. ownership.[24] In Wall Street parlance, the United States Banks are no longer creditors of Argentina, Brazil, and Mexico—the major borrowers—but their "partners." Such financial "shotgun marriages" generate friction, especially when the banks have the opportunity to upgrade their portfolios. Not only are some of the far more creditworthy Organisation of Petroleum Exporting Countries (OPEC) countries increasing their borrowing to sustain ambitious development programmes, but the prospective decline in OECD "savings ratio" (resulting from the transfer to OPEC) and the prospective capital shortage (due to present capacity limitation) in the OECD countries will make it unnecessary for the banks to seek out marginal borrowers as they have in the past. Given the declining prospects for trade and aid (the latter due to domestic politics reflecting capital shortages and growing balance of payments deficits), a significant reduction in Latin American indebtedness to United States banks is unlikely; "roll-over" agreements, such as those in Panama, will predominate, but a number of defaults would appear to be inevitable and could prove to be contagious.

(c) *Likely United States Response to Latin American Requests*

On the basis of these trends, the likely United States response to the five issues raised by Latin America will probably be negligible, the good intentions of the Carter Administration notwithstanding.

(1) *Greater access to United States markets for Latin American products*. This is the greatest Latin American concern, and also the least likely to be accomplished. United States labour, business, and agricultural interests are all pushing for a more protectionist policy. This is augmented by "stagflation" (concurrent high rates of inflation and unemployment), which increases the pressure on Congress to restrict access to the United States market wherever imports threaten workers or firms. Dropping trade barriers to Latin American imports might lead to bankruptcy for some United States companies. This could be mitigated by some form of central planning, a highly volatile political issue unlikely to appeal to a Carter Administration known for temporising on economic issues.

---

[24] *Op. cit.* in note 20, above, at p. 215.

(2) *United States support for commodity arrangements*. This area offers more opportunity for co-operation. However, as long as Latin American States feel that short supply is permanent, they will be reluctant to enter into commodity arrangements in return for assured access to supply, since they are more interested in gaining access to markets for their industrial products.

(3) *Greater concessional and commercial financing*. The United States is increasingly less rather than more responsive to this form of support. Official development assistance as a percentage of Gross National Product has fallen steadily since the late 1960s, and is now only 0·2 per cent. Support for resource transfers is also on the wane: *e.g.* the United States has been reluctant to support the efforts of the International Monetary Fund (IMF) to finance the Third World's balance of payments deficits. Furthermore, authoritarian Latin American governments with bad human-rights records, increasing arms budgets and growing interest in nuclear technology are very unlikely to get a sympathetic hearing for their aid requests in Congress. The Congress is especially sensitive to resource policies that "export inflation" to the United States—policies that take from the poor in rich countries and give to the rich in poor countries. Such Congressional attitudes could change dramatically, however, if resource scarcity becomes a major problem. A recent example is United States support in late 1978 for the embattled Shah in oil-rich Iran.

(4) *Revamped relations with multinationals*. Here, too, Latin American governments are unlikely to receive United States support in what may become the major source of conflict in the region. The sheer magnitude of United States direct investment, and its importance for the United State's trade balance, will be set against growing nationalism, Japanese and European competition, and lack of a compensation scale for expropriation.

(5) *Technology transfer*. As understood by Latin Americans, this policy means the transfer from United States parent companies to Latin American subsidiaries, at cheaper prices, of the latest technology adapted for indigenous use. An effective United States policy would require centralised planning and domestic redistribution, which would be immediately challenged by organised labour and by Congress.

IV—IMPLICATIONS AND CONCLUSIONS

The implication of these likely United States policies is that economic relationships will provide the main sources of friction in inter-American relations during the next decade. The market for

Latin American exports in the United States will expand less rapidly than in the past decade both because of a slower growth rate and because of a slower rate of trade liberalisation. As a result of this slower growth, capital markets in the United States will expand less rapidly and will be increasingly dependent for funds on the OPEC countries (that may develop their own capital markets) and will be less capable of supplying Latin American borrowers than they have been in the recent past. The "credit worthiness" of Latin American nations will decline as a consequence of large and increasing balance-of-payments deficits (resulting from the substantially higher cost of food and energy) and existing indebtedness positions that already loom large in relation to export earnings. To avoid default on expiring credit lines, many Latin American countries may well be required to curtail the growth in imports. Such action would reduce domestic consumption, production and employment, particularly in the more industrialised countries. In such circumstances, Latin American governments would be forced to limit political participation and suppress dissent, and the temptation to "blame" the international economic system—and particularly the leadership of the United States—would be very strong. Therefore, tighter exchange controls, restrictions on remittances, debt defaults (or moratoria), and nationalisation of foreign investment are likely responses.

These circumstances will confront virtually all non-oil-exporting countries to a greater or lesser degree; consequently, Latin American governments will tend to negotiate collectively with the United States on economic issues. Many issues have been identified: reform of the international monetary system to increase development assistance, unilateral trade concessions, formation of commodity agreements or cartels, further initiatives towards economic integration and the exclusion of multinationals from any benefits.

Three other issues will also become increasingly important. Illegal immigration of Hispanics into the United States will accelerate markedly, and will become an increasingly significant issue in domestic United States politics.[25] Tension over the proliferation of nuclear technology, already a highly sensitive issue involving France and Germany as well as North and South America, will increase since few Latin American countries have sufficient coal resources to supplement their limited hydro-electric potential. United States human rights policy may also remain a sensitive problem, especially if Latin American countries continue in retaliation to deny defence and development contracts to United States firms.

---

[25] *Time*, October 16, 1978, p. 48, where United States government estimates of illegal Hispanic aliens in the United States at 8·2 million are quoted.

These trends portend a period of antagonism and a strong resurgence of nationalism and protectionism. Such developments may be attenuated if the United States opens its economy to manufactured imports, increases net income transfers as a percentage of GNP, and develops co-operative immigration, nuclear, and human rights policies. However, United States compliance with Latin American demands is unlikely because the policy of détente relegates the common security interests of the West to a secondary level. With the declining United States security interest in Latin America, and its declining ability to satisfy the military, diplomatic, and economic needs of the Southern Hemisphere, the United States' role will become more one of diplomacy and influence than hegemony. Détente, which helped to stimulate Latin American self-interest, also means that Latin America will represent no major challenge to United States' security, without a real or cartel-imposed resource shortage. Neither is likely in the short term. Therefore, no national consensus within the United States will emerge on the subject of United States-Latin American relations. Latin American policy will continue to be determined by the aggregation of pluralistic interests in the United States and is therefore likely to prove inconsistent. Good future relations between the United States and Latin America will require structural changes that go far beyond the relatively minor economic inducements that gave the United States its negotiating advantage over Panama. The "new era" of "mutual respect and partnership" with Latin America heralded by President Carter will therefore be some time in coming.

PLURALIST AMERICA
IN A HIERARCHIC WORLD

By

R. PETTMAN

"PLURALISM," both as a description of the political mechanics of
State affairs and as a prescription for how such affairs might best
proceed, is an essential component of the liberal ideology of the
contemporary Western world.* Deprived, some would say, of the
potency it once possessed, the pluralist doctrine still retains well-
placed advocates, who purvey with vigour the assumptions about
"democratic" government and individual "freedom" that are central to the civil traditions of trans-Atlantic States. American scholars
and foreign-policy makers have played no small part in promoting
these assumptions, and their pluralist premises have become a
fundamental reference point for political practitioners and public
discourse.[1] It is important, then, that we understand these premises
and what they imply for world affairs.

I—PLURALISM AND ITS AMERICAN APPLICATION

Pluralism grants the multitude of groups with which human society
abounds a quite distinctive status. The diverse corporations that
make up any society are seen to be the ultimate and preferred source
of identification, of obedience and command. "Good" government
holds the ring or acts as a referee so that intergroup disputes might
better be resolved. It does not co-opt their primary authority, even
though co-option might well serve, for example, some neo-Hegelian
notion of national majesty, or the "public interest" however construed.[2] The individual is ostensibly rescued, on the one hand from
that sense of personal alienation considered endemic to industrial
society, and on the other from the remote manipulations of total

---

* My thanks to Dr. R. J. Vincent of the University of Keele for his critique of the original
draft.

[1] H. Kariel, "Pluralism," in D. Sills (ed.), 12 *International Encyclopaedia of the Social
Sciences* (1968), p. 168.
[2] In abbreviating my argument I have done violence to the variety of pluralist positions. See
the works of the English pluralists, in particular, J. N. Figgis, F. Maitland, H. Laski, and
G. D. H. Cole, as well as those of the French theorist L. Duguit. Note also K. G. Hsaio,
Political Pluralism: a study in contemporary political theory (1957); H. M. Magid, *English
Political Pluralsim: the problem of freedom and organization* (1941); D. Nichols, *The Pluralist
State* (1975); W. E. Connolly (ed.), *The Bias of Pluralism* (1969).

régimes or the "sovereign State." The conflict of social entities can be regularised; can be conducted in a co-operative *milieu* that maximises personal freedom, while minimising the tyranny of determined men, or the risk of civil war.

Whether the theory really obtains in practice or not, the pluralist faith is a pervasive one, emerging from American foreign policy by two related routes. The first is inherent in the general theory of political democratic reform that Americans have foisted on other countries by conquest or by being able to dictate the terms of their "responsible development." The second is the American view—so far as it may be discerned from the statements of authoritative spokesmen—of the world system as a whole. They generally eschew any notion of this system in terms of "class," favouring the "group" model to describe its social structure and the philosophy of national self-determination and State "freedom" that sustains it. Thus: "The parallel to individual freedom in international society ... [has been] the principle of national independence and self-determination, and the parallel to infringement of individual rights ... [has been] the violation of territorial sovereignty and foreign interference in the internal affairs of a free nation."[3]

It is no surprise that given the "self-evident" character of the pluralist ethic and the universal truths that its adherents have felt it conveys that many influential Americans have sought to reproduce their political system abroad, generating ideal versions of their own way of conducting civic business as a blueprint for the rest of the world. The pluralist ethic as applied to international affairs would seem to suggest toleration for other systems, rather than the imposition of one ideology over all, particularly a pluralistic one. Two world wars and a subsequent period of sustained political confrontation has demonstrated that the process of extension is not likely to be an automatic one however.

The self-help promise of "political association" forms an important article of faith in this regard, one that was early endorsed in its American context by Alexis de Tocqueville. "The most natural privilege of man next to the right of acting for himself," de Tocqueville argued, "is that of combining his exertions with those of his fellow creatures and of acting in common with them .... In no country in the world has the principle of association been more successfully used or applied to a greater multitude of objects than in America."[4]

Whether this is an accurate description of the present-day United States polity or not is unimportant. The nation has certainly seen its

---

[3] S. Rosen and W. Jones, *The Logic of International Relations* (1974), p. 36.
[4] A. de Tocqueville, *Democracy in America* (1953), Vol. 1, pp. 191, 195–196.

share of conspiracy in recent years, and the sustained growth of a military-commercial-administrative conclave at its centre, while necessary to meet the requisites of a large capitalist State perhaps, may have permanently pre-empted any effort by peripheral minorities to establish new equilibria serving interests closer to their own. It is the ideology of the continuing influence of such efforts that is at issue, and this persists.

How does such an ideology bear on the American conception of the world as a whole? Originally, hardly at all. De Tocqueville observed, a century and a half ago, that: "The foreign policy of the United States is eminently expectant; it consists more in abstaining than acting." George Washington in his Farewell Address of September 19, 1796, proclaimed that: "The great rule of conduct for us, in regard to foreign Nations is, in extending our commercial relations, to have with them as little Political connection as possible.... Our detached and distant situation invites and enables us ... to steer clear of permanent alliances, with any portion of the foreign world...."[5] And the attractions of this commercially-engaged but politically-aloof posture were manifest in early American political practice,[6] inspiring an important school of diplomatic thought that is still very influential. The commercial and political aspects of the country's foreign affairs have drawn closer together over the years, however, and Washington's hope that they might be held apart has been frustrated by market imperatives that have grown apace and of which he was unaware, imperatives that radical theorists consider beyond democratic control.

As should be evident by now pluralism is a doctrine which places human groups over and against the "State." It was a specific response to and protest against the idealist philosophy of the "monistic" State, the sort of administration possessing "unitary and absolute sovereign power"[7] that has become so conspicuous in the modern age. The ideal "pluralist" State has no *locus* of authority sufficiently influential to co-opt the "general will." American plural-

---

[5] *Ibid.* pp. 233–234. See George Washington, "Farewell Address," in S. Padover (ed.), *The Washington Papers* (1955), pp. 321–322; also F. Gilbert, *To the Farewell Address: ideas of early American foreign policy* (1961), Chap. 5: "To Hamilton, sovereign States, competition among them, and power politics were necessary factors in social life; successful political action depended on proceeding according to these presuppositions." (pp. 133–134).

[6] This general detachment did not deter the United States from armed intervention in its own hemisphere on at least 84 occasions from 1798–1945. See the "Report of the Committee on Foreign Affairs" (87th Congress, 2nd Session) as published in the United States Congress, Committee on Foreign Relations and the Committee on Armed Services *Situation in Cuba* (1962). Most of these expeditions were made to "protect" American and foreign interests, property, commerce, shipping, and lives, in times of civil or revolutionary strife. They were presidential acts, made without Congressional approval.

[7] K. Hsiao, *op. cit.* in note 2, above, p. 7.

ists have tended to take a much more benign view of government as an "arena" or as an "umpire" for social disputes,[8] since groups can attempt, as they see it, to convince "government" of their particular cause, and "government" can then play a positive and significant role in furthering group affairs. This is in marked contrast to the position of the English pluralists who have remained ever suspicious of the intervention that administrations are able to make in individual affairs. Americans have been less reluctant as a result to articulate a global version of their doctrine that reifies the State. Indeed, they emerge in the international arena as the firm champions of a "statist" ideology of the pluralist sort.

The notion of discrete geographic regions as bounding human groups, serving their members' concerns, bargaining with and balancing their competing claims, is the most commonplace assumption of American foreign policy. Indeed, the proliferation of States feeds back into the pluralist picture, for State boundaries bolstered by exclusivist nationalist sentiments help act as barriers against the extension of hierarchy in cultural, political, social and economic terms. The model was severely strained when it became apparent that many of the new States emerging after the Second World War were not in any sense "individual." For the most part they consisted of rudimentary political machines that had successfully claimed or been reluctantly granted the right to rule, along with a more or less recognised set of boundaries, all of which proved of rather marginal relevance to the mass of the people such borders contained. The world was less troubled by the advent of trans-State commercial corporations, whose self-interests and relentless pursuit of profit more closely approximates the pressure-group thesis that pluralism sustains. Americans, de Tocqueville observed, "almost always manage to combine their own advantage with that of their fellow citizens ... explaining almost all the actions of their lives by the principle of self-interest rightly understood. ...."[9]

America's *laissez-faire*, co-operative anticipation of world affairs has not found much favour with régimes from the majority of poor States, who seem to have arrived at a notion of the global system that, rhetorically at least, feeds upon conflict, not co-operation; a world that seems *structuralist* rather than pluralist in character, hierarchically arranged to the advantage of the rich industrialised ones and the persistent disadvantage of the rest.

---

[8] See W. Connolly, *op. cit.* pp. 8–13. Also R. Dahl, *A Preface to Democratic Theory* (1965); A. Berle, *Power Without Property* (1959).

[9] A. de Tocqueville, *op. cit.* in note 4, above, Vol. II, pp. 121–122.

II—INDUSTRIALISATION AND EQUALITY

In American practice the bargaining of political groups is prompted by a robust sense of personal equality. De Tocqueville found this the most striking condition of the country's population, the basic datum of its political and social life, the New World expression of a protracted historical development of providential power. "... [U]niversal ... lasting ... it constantly eludes all human interference, and all events as well as all men contribute to its progress."[10]

How has America sought to duplicate the conditions of individual equality, so essential to the realisation of pluralistic co-operation, in other societies where the conditions of life are so clearly antipathetic to them? Here they have placed considerable faith in the powers of a socio-technological instrument de Tocqueville did not account for—that of industrialisation. Industrialisation, it is argued, leads to a rise in the material standard of life, a process that in time dissipates socio-economic inequalities not only inside communities but between them, creating new sources of political dissent to be sure but hopefully under conditions sufficiently advantageous to all as to presage political compromise and preclude violence. We might well ask about the progress of this process, about its socio-political effects and the part played by the United States in expediting them.

"America" itself is a prominent feature of the global industrial landscape. Its productive capacity is enormous, and in economic terms it is inherently expansionist: "... there is something fundamental to American corporate capitalism—the capitalism of tightly held technology, uncertain information, large economies of scale, and unstable imperfect competition ..." that leads to "... intense, even frantic pressures to create and preserve an international system that facilitates foreign economic expansion."[11] We might legitimately expect in this light to find the United States playing an important role in the growth of industries in the rest of the world, and practising the kind of politics most appropriate to securing such growth.

Global industrialisation has proceeded apace, not only under the State-directed aegis of the governments of China and the Soviet Union, not only for the countries in Europe and for those outside this "developed" world who have been "invited" to apply,[12] but also among so-called Third World countries too. "Industrialisation" is a

---

[10] *Ibid.* p. 6.

[11] T. Moran, "Foreign Expansion as an 'Institutional Necessity' for U.S. Corporate Capitalism: the search for a radical model," 25 *World Politics* (1973), pp. 14–15.

[12] On the concept of "promotion by invitation" see I. Wallerstein, "Dependence in an interdependent world; the limited possibilities of transformation within the capitalist world economy," 17 *African Studies Review* (1974), pp. 14–15.

composite affair but in the case of a number of poor States evidence of it has been used to argue that, in international terms at least, the links between metropolitan and Third World Powers have been growing weaker, the "distribution of power within the capitalist world . . . less uneven," and the international system more pluralistic as a result.[13]

Without asking what *kind* of industrialisation has occurred, it would seem that many poor countries have shown a significant and consistent degree of growth over the last 30 years, despite the fact that no dramatic events have intervened to throw these States back upon self-reliance and the forcing-house of import substitution. Furthermore, advances in manufacturing capacity have served burgeoning domestic markets, as well as providing cheap goods for rich consumers overseas. What, we may inquire, has been the effect of this process upon the comparative place of global groups and the opportunities open to them? Bill Warren, for one, claims that: ". . . the post-war period has witnessed not merely a change in the character of . . . inegalitarian relationships but a significant and con-tinuing reduction in inequality as well.... The term 'neo-colonialism' . . . is thus misleading in so far as it obscures the new and dynamic elements in the situation, both as to causes (concerning the role played by the achievement of formal sovereignty itself) and as to effects."[14] The winning or granting of "independence," he argues, has effectively severed imperial ties, and allowed industrialisation to proceed on more autonomous terms. Competition between imperialist Powers, and the rivalry of the Cold War, has allowed room for individual States to strike bargains to their own advantage and for their industrial advance to be sustained. An alliance with an erstwhile imperialistic Power, if managed by economic nationalists, can be used to foster national "development" rather than merely inhibiting it as structuralist analyses would suppose.

The progress made so far, Warren adds, is real not apparent. The diversity and range of Third World industries is considerable and the grip of foreign finance has begun to fail. "The historical evidence unambiguously shows," he says, "that since their independence underdeveloped countries are steadily improving their bargaining positions and their ability to control foreign firms operating in their territories."[15] The problems of inappropriate technology, exacer-bated by the fact that rich States and corporations possess a mono-poly of advanced production techniques (a monopoly that must

---

[13] B. Warren, "Imperialism and Capitalist Industrialisation," 81 *New Left Review* (1973), p. 4.

[14] *Ibid.* pp. 10–11.

[15] *Ibid.* p. 20.

inhibit any poor country attempting to extend its industrial reach), is being reduced through a range of judicious incentives and controls. Balance-of-payments reserves seem to be rising; national debts, viewed constructively, appear as credit in disguise; an export of an economic surplus turns out to be no more than "the foreign exchange price paid for the establishment of productive facilities"[16]; the international division of labour is by no means immutable; and the global pattern of resource accumulation reflects not one bipolar hierarchy but a changing and uneven spectrum of them. In economic terms, for Warren at least, global pluralism is a reality, and the political consequences are profound.

The global *milieu* is co-operative, then, not fraught with funda-mental contradictions. The forces compelling industrialisation are "statist" ones, creating the need for machineries of governance that *bourgeois* or military élites are only too eager to fill. They are bolstered in turn by the growing ranks of a petty-*bourgeois* class in Third World cities and towns. And these régimes, mostly repressive at home and bound to large industrialised Powers abroad, are "fully compatible with a real margin of autonomous choice corresponding to specific national interests"[17]; interests advanced by pluralist devices of every kind.[18]

The thesis of a pluralist industrialisation process outlined above, particularly as it pertains to the Third World, is, however, a con-troversial one. That formal independence has allowed of develop-ment of sorts is not in dispute. Nor is the fact that many poorer States, with or without reactionary élites, have on occasion managed to play off foreign forces, whether countries or companies, against each other or against strategic "socialist" rivals. The question that persists is precisely what *sort* of development or growth has occur-red. If one chooses, as Warren has done, not to discuss the "ade-quacy" of "development" in meeting mass needs, nor the problems of uneven development and impoverished agricultures; if one con-templates only "some" of the "implications"[19] of capitalist indus-trialisation as manifest at the level of the international system; then the analysis can be highly misleading when we come to consider its pluralist consequences. Arghiri Emmanuel has demonstrated that capitalist industrialisation is not in and of itself a satisfactory index of development. "Consequently, when Warren speaks of the transfer-ence of active population from 'backward agriculture' to 'modern

---

[16] *Ibid*. p. 30.
[17] *Ibid*. p. 43.
[18] For a list of devices conferred by formal political independence which "must" in the end sustain economic advance (undifferentiated), see *ibid*. p. 12.
[19] *Ibid*., p. 5.

industry,' he is begging the question. Quite simply, he forgets that
there is also 'modern agriculture' and 'backward industry': ... The
superiority of the OECD countries over the Third World does not
consist in the larger share occupied by manufactures in their
national production, but in the fact that both their manufactures *and*
their agriculture are on a far higher level than those of the Third
World."[20]

Even if we do concede that overall development has occurred (a
very significant concession given the diverse forms industrialisation
has taken in the Third World) we must still ask whether it can
proceed any further by capitalist means, or whether that path is one
that soon peters out. If we consider comparative productivity figures
and respective growth rates per head of population[21] the gap between the richer and poorer world blocs has more than doubled this
century, which is not a situation likely to promote equality or global
pluralism. And this can be explained in terms of the logic of the
system itself. If Emmanuel is correct then the key impediment to the
development of the Third (Fourth) World consists "neither in a
peculiarity of ... social structure nor in a deliberate strategy of the
Great Powers or of big capital (although both of these factors may
worsen the situation), but in the free working of market forces. For
in the capitalist world ... the primary problem being not to produce
but to sell, he who dominates is not the biggest producer but the
biggest consumer," which is quite sufficient to place "developed"
countries with affluent domestic markets in an exploitative position
vis-à-vis "underdeveloped" ones.[22]

Again, even if we concede the thesis (not lightly done given the
increasingly integrated character of the world economy) that as
capital is diffused through the global system capitalist economies are
stimulated elsewhere and "imperialism" tends to disappear, the
point remains that capital is not at the moment so diffused and that it
is highly unlikely to be in the future. The burden of servicing debts,
the repatriation of profits and financial principal, corporate ploys
for maximising gains and minimising losses, and clandestine monetary exports of many kinds mostly outweigh any real benefits, such
as there might be, from public aid, private credit and investment.
The calculations are extremely complex, but the balance seems to
move out rather than into poorer States. "Apart from raw materials
and certain agricultural products which have to be sought where
they can be found, the movement of capital is not an increasing but a

---

[20] A. Emmanuel, "Myths of Development versus Myths of Underdevelopment," 85 *New
Left Review* (1974), p. 67.
[21] *Ibid.* p. 71.
[22] *Ibid.* p. 72.

decreasing function of difference in incomes [anyway].... The advanced countries are nowadays too rich not to be able to absorb themselves, without difficulty, all the new capital that is formed in them, and the underdeveloped countries are too poor to offer attractive investment prospects to this same capital, apart from their few import-substitution industries.... All this, in turn, keeps them poor, or makes them even poorer. Imperialism is not self-destructive; it is self-reproducing."[23]

All of this would suggest a hierarchic conception of world affairs rather than a group/State pluralistic one. The imminent paucity of resources alone precludes any attempt to bring a style and standard of life familiar in the global North to all but enclave élites in the impoverished South. The reflex defence of privilege would largely foreclose any prospects for radical change. The dissatisfactions of dispersed and repressed peoples on the global periphery are the fuel, but such peoples are ill-placed to perceive the principal contradictions that reinforce their plight. American foreign policy, in this view, has set itself the task of defusing strategic antagonisms and meeting only such symptomatic injustice as serves American interests. It does not assail the fundamental cause, which is the global system of capitalist industrialisation itself.

One conspicuous result of such a system has been to reinforce the historically-derived structure of it, exacerbating the tendency for economic if not political intervention, and reconstructing in a day-to-day fashion its major features as they presently exist. Warren's thesis looks more and more threadbare the deeper one probes. He largely ignores, for example, the complex social patterns that such a process is apt to produce or sustain. Is the "bargaining" by Third-World régimes a meaningfully pluralist ploy; is it bargaining over the "terms of dependence," the "diversification" of dependence, or over "national development" *per se*?[24] Where lies the line between "national" control over foreign inputs and those instances where State involvement has merely served to secure more successfully the interests of transnational decision-makers in their pursuit of local advantage and global gain? With export sectors still dominated by foreign firms "the expansion and growth of trade is hardly an expression of the dynamism of Third World countries,"[25] and this trade has to a significant extent retained its pre-independence emphasis on oil and other minerals and agricultural products. The offer to service a poor State's debt burden, or provide those funds

---

[23] *Ibid.* p. 77.
[24] P. McMichael, J. Petras and R. Rhodes, "Imperialism and the Contradictions of Development," 85 *New Left Review* (1974), p. 89.
[25] *Ibid.* p. 91.

necessary to maintain its credit worthiness, can conceal an ideological weapon of great power. Poor-State weakness has been used extensively to promote "capitalist" modes of development that lead in the particular case to economic denationalisation, a widespread decline in standards of living and political violence.[26] A meaningfully plural system, under conditions like these, is hardly likely to thrive. The capitalist example is not one to inspire confidence here, serving, as it seems to do, the fractional advance of liaison élites to the absolute and not simply relative impoverishment of majority populations,[27] providing social continuities that bind in common concern those who for pluralist purposes should be prised apart.

III—A STRUCTURALIST VIEW

One might assume then a profound difference between *pluralist* and *structuralist* ideologies. The former, as I have indicated, depicts the world as divided into a multitude of discrete groups—States—of unequal "size" to be sure, but equally dedicated to the pragmatic pursuit of their interests and moral desires. By strategic alliance, weaker groups augment their influence and articulate their demands. World affairs remain relatively fluid as the balance-of-power forms and re-forms, and if it is polarised into blocs by differences too profound to be readily resolved, the pressures of the system work nonetheless towards their domestication, towards understandings and agreements that sustain the co-operative framework of the whole.

As a prescription, pluralism only reluctantly anticipates the fundamental reconstruction of the global system as a whole. The practical force of any radical idea that goes beyond the procedural necessity of preserving "pluralism" itself, is ignored or repressed. It becomes progressively more difficult to visualise in pluralist terms a world that is divided by horizontal hierarchies that run across geographic boundaries, to non-pluralist effect.

In this sense structuralist ideologies, derived ultimately from Marxist theories of imperialism, constitute a direct challenge to the pluralist view. What seems clear in one camp becomes opaque in the other. Talking across the divide becomes a matter of crude political gestures, not made easier by a mutual lack of understanding and a high degree of apprehension and mistrust. As our perspective shifts, we find less mention of "States" in the traditional sense and much more of "class"; less of balance and co-operation and substantially

---

[26] *Ibid*. p. 92.
[27] See I. Adelman and C. T. Morris, *Economic Growth and Social Equity in Developing Countries* (1973).

more of "exploitation" and of the enervating ennui or the revolutionary antagonism that relations of selfish advantage are apt to breed.

Some aspects of a structuralist position have been discussed already. The fundamental premise is a materialist one, outlined in a famous passage by Karl Marx thus. "In the social production of their life, men enter into definite relations that are indispensable and independent of their will, relations of production which correspond to a definite stage of development of their material productive forces. The sum total of these relations of production constitutes the economic structure of society, the real foundation, on which rises a legal and political superstructure and to which corresponds definite forms of social consciousness. The mode of production of material life conditions the social, political and intellectual life process in general. It is not the consciousness of men that determines their being, but on the contrary, their social being that determines their consciousness."[28]

There is considerable ambiguity here, though some but not all of the terminology is given more precise exegesis elsewhere in Marxist writings. As a general proposition it leaves much to be desired, playing down the human capacity for reflection and self-aware acts. Furthermore, it does not accommodate the monopolisation of the means of violence and taxation that accompanied the succession (in European terms at least) from "dynastic" to "nation" States, that was the *precondition* ... [whereby] economic power resources (control of the means of production) [became] crucial for the distribution of power between social classes within state societies."[29] Nevertheless as the "structural" violence implicit in exchange relations has become more visible and more significant as a contemporary cause of human suffering, and this is seen to be manifest on a global scale, Marxist concepts of "dependence" have emerged to explain them. Behind the notion of a global core and a subordinate periphery lies an acute sense of the punitive effects of the contemporary world hierarchy.

The mechanics of dependence are intimately connected, as indicated already, with those of industrialisation.[30] Drawing attention to the contingent character of poor State "development," structuralist

---

[28] K. Marx, Preface to "A Contribution to the Critique of Political Economy," in K. Marx and F. Engels, *Selected Works* (1970), p. 181.

[29] G. V. Benthem v.d. Bergh, "State formation and inter-state competition from pre-industrial to contemporary Europe," Institute of Social Studies, The Hague (mimeo, 1975), p. 26.

[30] For further description see T. Dos Santos, "The Structure of Dependence," 60 *The American Economic Review* (1970), pp. 231–236.

ideologies point up a number of highly-organised, historically-derived devices that condition wide-spread, self-sustaining growth. "Internal" events, institutions and social structures, and the "external" affairs usually considered at least in theory as separable from them, are seen as aspects of one on-going process—in this case, the maintenance and promotion of the capitalist mode of production. If we live, as Immanuel Wallerstein has observed, in a capitalist world economy, the key feature to note is the "production for sale in a market in which the object is to realize the maximum profit,"[31] or at very least, to "optimise profitability."[32] This is only one mode among a putative many, but it is the one that for many reasons arose in Europe in the sixteenth century and co-opted the world in the nineteenth. (Though this is misleading, since "capitalism" was "from the beginning an affair of the world-economy and not of nation-States.... It has never allowed its aspirations to be determined by national boundaries ... and ... the creation of 'national' barriers—generically, mercantilism—has historically been a defensive mechanism of capitalists located in States which are one level below the high point of strength in the system."[33])

The economic power of "developed" States is reproduced within "underdeveloping" ones, repeating a pattern of domestic imperialism that is a preferred if not necessary aspect of an asymmetrical world at large. The economic inequalities that result have military, cultural, social and political concomitants. Given that "developed" sectors will in their own interests remain committed to global stability and the material advantages such stability provides, then one would expect them to employ every means to reinforce class distinctions between "States" and within the poor ones, except when stability is threatened by exaggerated class discrepancies and modest ameliorative measures must be applied. Poor-State élites will actively invite class stability, an invitation that grows more urgent as they take recourse to repression in the face of popular demands and revolt. The observer grows wary of the statements of the representatives of poor-"State" régimes in the United Nations or the periodic conferences of States ostensibly non-aligned, since they will speak in "upper-class" or "middle-class' accents as much as "lower-class" ones. Within a global capitalist system their options are constricted, and mainly involve tinkering with trade concessions or the terms of economic or military aid.

[31] I. Wallerstein, "The Rise and Future Demise of the World Capitalist System: concepts for comparative analysis," 16 *Comparative Studies in Society and History* (1974), p. 398. Compare Wallerstein's account of the evolution of the global capitalist system (pp. 406–412) with that of H. Magdoff "Imperialism: a historical survey," 24 *Monthly Review* (1972), pp. 1–17.

[32] See C. Levinson, *Capital Inflation and the Multinationals* (1971).

[33] Wallerstein, *op. cit.* in note 31, above, p. 401.

The notion of a "core," and a "periphery" beyond the centres of economic, political, military, ideological and cultural might—a core linked by indigenous enclave élites or liaison corporations to a multitude of more or less mendicant fringe "States"—is, however, by no means sufficient to characterise a world "class" structure. It fails, for example, to represent the critical role played by a number of "semi-peripheral" (or "semi-core") countries as a sort of "middle-class," that defuses a polarised and potentially antagonistic socio-political situation. It seems hardly adequate, either, as a description of both core State and peripheral complexities, but it does at least point in that direction.

IV—The Liberal Response

The structuralist/class approach to global politics is a complex one. It must locate human beings in the social interstices of an industrialising world; it sees in human relationships a growing subservience to modern technologies that deny the individual the direct capacity to sustain him or herself; it depicts "State" formation as an integrative process paralleled by the equal if not predominant differentiating force of the capitalist mode of production. How have American analysts responded to such a view of the world? A radical minority has embraced it, while a larger more conservative group has rejected it outright. "Liberal" scholars for their part have revived the "power" theories of world affairs[34]; and "underdevelopment" and the failure to expand or sophisticate industrial, agricultural, educational and medical capacities have been credited once again to "overpopulation" and the lack of capital inflow rather than any more pernicious interplay of global investment or trade. These notions are backed by the cogent and quite practical objection that in making the "implausible assumption that none of their values can be realised under capitalism, the neo-Marxists are indifferent to the range of actual policies likely to be pursued in the foreseeable future."[35]

That "power theories" have been the most durable of the American responses seems hardly surprising given the extent to which notions of *Realpolitik* are compatible with those of pluralist competition, and the enduring belief in a political realm divorced from that of material "production." Global "interdependence," a concept repeatedly emphasised by American policy-makers, is elaborated in terms of its mutual opportunities and the belief in a co-operative

---

[34] See the work of R. Tucker, B. J. Cohen and C. Kindleberger.

[35] J. L. Richardson, "World Society: the 'Structural Dependence Model'," unpublished seminar paper delivered to the Department of International Relations, the Research School of Pacific Studies, Australian National University, August 1975, p. 15.

accommodation to competing interests and needs. The idea of inequalities so entrenched, of historically-derived advantages so readily reproduced as to make them virtually unassailable, is rarely confronted as such.

A notion of comparative "power," while it may produce a description of a pluralist world, has still to account for monopolies. How can a world of super-Powers, where what is most striking is the hierarchic concentration of "strength" rather than its dispersion, be adequately depicted as plural in character? Here the proponents of pluralism point to the growing importance of exclusivist national loyalties. "Pluralism," it is argued, has given rise to a "far more complicated world . . . a safer world. . . . For the triumph of pluralism is, in essence, the triumph of nationalism."[36] A monolithic system propounding "communism" or any other hegemonic creed cannot occur because of the preordinate potency of State boundaries and the fact that the global populace tends to identify itself in terms of States, or is effectively coerced into doing so.

Suitably expanded a "power" theory of world politics can be used to co-opt the bulk of a "class" critique as well. From the fund of historical experience it is seen to be apparent that the "interests of States expand roughly with their power" and that it is "power itself, more than a particular form of power, which prompts expansion."[37] America is a capitalist country and simply because it is "powerful" it has sought to reproduce capitalism and liberal-capitalist values abroad. The mechanism is a "natural" one[38] and we should expect Americans to defend their interests, to secure a sympathetic global environment, and to applaud their own version of life in this way. Any notion of capitalism and its intrinsic "needs" can be dismissed as "dogma," or some exotic "metaphysic" without substance at all.[39] "America's interventionist and counter-revolutionary policy is the expected response of an imperial Power with a vital interest in maintaining an order that, apart from the material benefits this order confers, has become synonymous with the nation's vision of its role in history. In the manner of all imperial visions, it is also solidly rooted in the will to exercise dominion over others."[40]

The tautologous nature of such a theory—that power leads to power—is evident, however, when it is made more specific. Thus, in discussing the American reliance upon foreign sources of supply for many of its strategic raw materials, the author of the quotation

---

[36] R. Tucker, *Nation or Empire? The debate over American foreign policy* (1968), p. 123.
[37] R. Tucker, *The Radical Left and American Foreign Policy* (1971), p. 151.
[38] *Ibid*. p. 69.
[39] *Ibid*. pp. 82, 75.
[40] *Ibid*. p. 111.

above talks in terms of "safe areas" and "secure" producers such as Brazil, India, South Africa, Turkey and the Philippines. Even hostile revolutionary élites would need to sell their products abroad, he observes, to secure foreign capital, and why not to the United States? In what respect, however, are the former areas "safe" and "secure"? In fact, with informative exceptions, the list of States supplied are repeatedly cited as "dependent" or "sub-imperialist" Powers in structuralist parlance. They are repressive, with large poor populations and highly exploitive régimes, far removed from self-reliant socialist policies and most unlikely on the whole to deny the United States whatever resources it requires. Any denial could only be made at considerable economic and political cost. The notion that even anti-American revolutionary régimes would find themselves in the same position is likewise compatible with the structuralist description of global hierarchies, and constitutes a key part, for example, of Emmanuel's argument about the logic of "free" market systems.

"Would a Socialist America pursue a foreign policy fundamentally different from the foreign policy pursued by a Capitalist America?"[41] In the context of a capitalist *world* economy the answer, as structuralist scholars have pointed out, must be negative. Robert Tucker has represented the radical critique as unanimously devoted to the opposite point of view. This is, however, a misrepresentation. Establishing any particular socialist polity does not mean the same thing as establishing a socialist world economy. A socialist government, as strictly defined, would not look "anything like the Soviet Union, or China, or Tanzania of today. Production for use and not for profit, and rational decision on the cost benefits (in the widest sense of the term) of alternative uses is a different mode of production, one that ... [could] only be established within the single division of labour that is the world economy and that ... [would] require a single government."[42] This is not an immediate prospect, and not one that any government seems to envisage today, the United States least of all.

American policy-makers constantly refer to the nation's moral responsibilities and to the difficulties of securing human dignity and self-fulfilment in a world of hardship and deprivation. They do, however, have interests to defend and it would be difficult for any country to ignore the constraints of the contemporary political-economy. "Our trade with East Asia now exceeds our transactions with the European community. American jobs, currency and raw

---

[41] *Ibid*. p. 138.
[42] Wallerstein, *op. cit.* in note 12 above, p. 13.

materials depend upon economic ties with the Pacific Basin," Gerald Ford, then United States President, observed in his reading of the "Pacific Doctrine" in Honolulu in December 1975.[43] Economic interdependence, he declared, has followed the growth of political co-operation between "developed" and "developing" States. One might ask, however, if this equation is not just as accurate with the variables reversed.

As Tucker explicitly admits, American policy is a self-regarding conceit. "... [T]he United States is the world's most powerful economy," Henry Kissinger once said. "Together with our allies among the industrial democracies, we are the engine of global prosperity, technological innovation, and the best hope for widening economic opportunity to millions around the globe."[44] How far such opportunities are likely to extend is highly debatable, even if we view the American model as universally superior to that, for example, of the People's Republic of China, and as "best" for the world as a whole. In discussing America's relations with "developing" States Kissinger was wont to identify the "world interest" directly with that of the United States, positing bloc co-operation rather than radical confrontation as the "realistic" and "responsible" way to proceed. He always decried what he termed the "spoiler's" role and the nationalistic attempt to control the supply of resources, trade and investment opportunities.

It is apparent, though, from the experience of the last two decades in particular that "development" of the kind that will rescue the world's poor is not readily derived from such a political-economic philosophy and the sort of political-economic interests America represents. Kissinger argued that: "Human suffering and human deprivation are not questions of ideology or bloc politics. They touch the elemental needs of mankind and the basic imperatives of universal moral values."[45] President Carter has deliberately endorsed this argument. Yet how does one reconcile even declaratory moralism with the desire to protect and promote domestic employment and the general well-being consistent with its denial? Expanding global wealth, if structuralist analysis is correct, can only deliver benefits to a minority of people—to a handful of States already advantaged, and to rich fractions within poor ones. Extending the global economy and realising global development did not

---

[43] G. R. Ford, "Honolulu: The Pacific Doctrine," *Presidential Documents* (1976), p. 1387.

[44] H. Kissinger, "U.S. Responsibilities in a Changing World Economy," speech to the Senate Committee on Finance, January 30, 1976, Department of State *Bulletin*, February 23, 1976, p. 234.

[45] H. Kissinger, "UNCTAD IV ...," speech before the fourth ministerial meeting of the UN Conference on Trade and Development, Nairobi, May 6, 1976, *ibid*. p. 671.

occur historically at the same time except for those societies favour-
ably placed to reap the original harvest from the industrial mode of
production, and those who later seized strategic chances or were
promoted by "invitation," or adopted, if they had the resources, the
austere course of self-reliance.[46] There is no reason to believe that
growth and development are any more consonant now either, and
the United States has yet to counter the conceptual and empirical
challenge this observation represents.

---

[46] I. Wallerstein, *op. cit.* in note 12 above, p. 9.

DILEMMAS OF DEFENCE
AGAINST NATIONAL LIBERATION

By

DENNIS DUNCANSON

GOVERNMENTS under attack in national-liberation struggles must expect a bad Press. Public opinion in open societies, whether spontaneous or professionally formed, is anti-government *a priori*, and so are national-liberation movements. The latter display the attributes of David; the authorities they attack the futility, by inference, of Goliath; and the conflict rarely appears to outsiders to be a war at all until the authorities' defence measures make it so. Indeed, the Polish delegation to the International Commission for Supervision and Control in Vietnam used to argue, during the second Indochina War, that guerrilla action in secret did not amount to hostilities within the conventions of international law.[1] National liberation and the counter-insurgency it generates may be judged noble or base, always or sometimes; but the struggle has become a feature of international life in our times and has developed such professional technique, independent of any ethical quality, that it merits attention for political study on a par, say, with public administration or psephology. The following paragraphs draw attention to a score of dilemmas over defensive action with which national liberation—for reasons that are summarised first—commonly confronts governments it is directed against.

I—REVOLUTION AND COLD WAR

Throughout his career, Lenin execrated nationalism as "dead chauvinism" irreconcilable with a Marxist socialism calling for abolition of national differences; yet it was he who first proposed the concept of *national liberation* as an instrument of positive statecraft. He relied on Marx's advocacy of *national emancipation* (in the 1848 *Manifesto*) at the expense of the major European Powers—not to benefit the nation liberated, but to weaken its suzerain: Irish nationalism was good as a temporary step favouring revolution in Great Britain, after which Ireland could be reunited with Great Britain.[2] In

---

[1] E.g. in minority statement attached to *Special Report to the Co-Chairmen of the Geneva Conference on Indo-China*, June 1962 (HMSO, Vietnam Nr. 1/1962, Cmnd. 1755).

[2] *Collected Works*, Moscow 1960—XXI, 300.

industrial States, Stage 1 of Lenin's programme for winning power entailed temporary Communist support for a *bourgeois-democratic revolution*, in dependent countries for a *bourgeois-national revolution*; but Communists should shun all "bourgeois" alliances that did not further Stage 2—a violent struggle to set up a proletarian dictatorship exercised by the Communist Party in a universal State transcending national frontiers.[3]

Lenin ignored black Africa and South America: India, China, and Turkey-Persia-Afghanistan bounded his horizon for national liberation. Stalin gave up the universal Communist-Party (CP) State for "socialism in one country" and made defence of the Soviet fatherland the focus of CP activity under Comintern direction.[4] By 1945 the Soviet Union was out of danger, but in a world henceforward of nation-States in which local CP leaders too wanted to have their own States to rule. The Yalta formula for accelerated colonial emancipation committed colonial Powers themselves to gradual fulfilment of Stage 1 of the revolution, but also made it imperative that CPs should upset the orderliness of the process if they were to make sure of Stage 2. Zhdanov's Cold-War doctrine re-instated national liberation as the key to Stage 2 in Asia, with help from the Chinese CP on behalf of the CP of the Soviet Union.[5] Khrushchev extended national liberation to Africa and South America, but the Sino-Soviet dispute and *multipolarity* led to rivalry between the Chinese and Soviets to be patrons of lesser CPs struggling for power; the two factions came to blows in Angola and in Ethiopia. Subsidiary bases for Kremlin-patronised national liberation became available (Congo-Brazzaville, Mozambique, South Yemen), as well as non-Soviet political technical assistants (East Germans, Cubans), but also some new patrons with a will of their own—Libya, Vietnam, Egypt for a time in North Yemen, North Korea, and Zambia. Occasionally, movements have turned their backs on their patrons after victory (Cambodia on Vietnam), and one only became a movement of national liberation by adopting Marxism-Leninism after its triumph—Cuba. Under Soviet or Chinese patronage, national liberation still purports to be anti-nationalist[6] and unconcerned with the national cost: "Only nations which achieve independence [*i.e.* CP rule] by bitter struggle can consider themselves truly liberated,"[7] and "Revolution by violence is the only way of

---

[3] *Ibid*. XXXI, 241–242; XXI, 342.

[4] The Comintern ordered the Indochina CP to drop anti-colonialism from its propaganda: see D. Guérin, *Front Populaire—révolution manquée* (1963), p. 182.

[5] Sources in J. B. Brimmell, *Communism in South-East Asia* (1959), pp. 255–263.

[6] For the CPSU, B. Ponomarev writing in *Kommunist*, Nr. 15, 1971, for the CCP, *Polemic on the General Line of the International Communist Movement* (1965), pp. 206–208.

[7] R. McVey, *The Calcutta Youth Conference* (1958), p. 11 (for the CPSU).

turning bourgeois countries into proletarian States."[8] Nations that
have not been dependent for a long time, like those of South
America, or never at all, like Siam, face the same dilemmas of
defence as ex-colonies[9]; in South-East Asia, wherever CPs do not
rule yet, independence is not reckoned to be a reality—only an
"aspiration of the people," its attainment part of the struggle "to
consolidate the world socialist system."[10]

II—NATIONAL LIBERATION STRATEGY

Lenin did not prescribe a strategy for national liberation, but his
government took steps which set a precedent for one. The Bol-
sheviks proclaimed autonomy in Russian Turkestan as "a
revolutionary beacon" for Chinese Turkestan, Tibet, Afghanistan
and India—in Azerbaijan for Persia, Arabia and Turkey; common
languages, they said, would exert "direct influence" by "stretching a
friendly hand" across frontiers in support of "*class* revolution"
within those nations.[11] The Bolshevik hope did not materialise, but
it had imperial precedents: as fast as Tsardom annexed one "bar-
barous" khanate "in the interests of order," it came into conflict
with another beyond, "and thus the boundary of civilisation was
inevitably extended."[12] The Chinese empire had a similar tradition
of expansion through gradual absorption of client princes in borderlands. In both traditions the horizon was local, but for Lenin and
Mao Zedong the declared purpose has been less the welfare of those
immediately liberated, or even the security of frontiers, than to
weaken "the capitalist Powers" farther off and "conquer the whole
world"[13]; by Marxist-Leninist criteria, the merit of the national
liberation in Indochina is the injury done through it to France and
the United States—eventually in southern Africa and Arabia isolation of America, Europe and Japan from energy sources.

Although national liberation has been promoted, successfully or
unsuccessfully, by industrial unrest, parliamentary participation,
coup d'état, urban terrorism, and military invasion—all of them in
turn in Vietnam—rural-based *people's war* has become the characteristic strategy. Lenin looked on peasants as potential malcontents

---

[8] *People's Daily*, Peking June 12, 1977 (for the CCP).
[9] A joint Lao-Vietnamese statement of February 5, 1976, draws no distinction as to former political status.
[10] Arts. 4 and 5 of Soviet-Vietnamese Treaty of Friendship and Co-operation, November 3, 1978.
[11] X. Eudin and R. North, *Soviet Russia and the East 1920–27*, (1957), p. 96.
[12] Doctrine of Prince Gorchakov, quoted in H. Seton-Watson, *The Russian Empire 1801–1917* (1967), p. 442.
[13] Lenin, *op. cit.* in note 2, above XXXI, 438; for the CCP, Lin Piao, "Long live the victory of people's war" [originally in *Hung Ch'i* (Red Flag), Peking, Nr. 10/1965].

no different from industrial workers,[14] but Stalin appreciated their worth for guerrilla warfare,[15] Mao Zedong put the idea into practice in the Chinese environment,[16] and Ho Chi Minh perfected the diplomatic dimension. The strategy calls for these features: (a) an *external centre* and safe haven on the patron's territory; (b) a target government that commands limited public confidence, either because, as colonial power, it is withdrawing, or because it has recently succeeded to power; (c) military operations planned to avoid presenting targets for counter-attack but to bleed, discredit and dishearten the defence, wringing from it "progressive" concessions, preferably confirmed by international *accord*. Mao envisaged escalation from scattered acts of terrorism to the deployment of a fully-equipped army; in places like Aden and in Africa the escalation has been condensed into shorter time-spans. All exponents of the strategy attach overriding importance to skill in applying, within an indigenous political culture, the strategy and tactics of Lenin, and above all in using the defence's own resources against itself.[17]

III—National Liberation Tactics

Lenin laid down no tactics either: national liberation did not differ in essentials from other roads to power, so that the same secretive and "conspiratorial" precepts from *What is to be Done?*, *Two Tactics of Social Democracy*, and *Left-Wing Communism, an infantile disorder* have held good in armed struggle too. A singleminded, sternly-disciplined, party of intellectuals exploits any and every *contradiction* [*i.e.* social tension], opportunity[18] and *temporary ally*, and forms *united fronts* with misleading *minimum programmes* of appeal especially to the poor and the artless; the CP projects its minority political interest as a majority economic or patriotic interest; it is loud against evils of the present régime but reticent about the post-liberation régime; it isolates and intimidates opponents in order to procure mass compliance in manoeuvres devised to obstruct reform and vilify the whole existing order of society as judged by that society's own, "bourgeois," standards. Lenin condemned pre-revolutionary terror, not as unethical, but because he found it

---

[14] *E.g.* 1917 Manifesto, *op. cit.* in note 2, above, 368–373.

[15] A. Neuberg [Comintern pseudonym], *Armed Insurrection* (Moscow, 1931).

[16] Originally with Stalin's encouragement, according to Hsiao Tso-liang, *Chinese Communism in 1927—city versus countryside* (1970), p. 27.

[17] *E.g. op. cit.* in note 6, above, pp. 260–274, and analyses in *Hoc Tap* (theoretical journal of the Vietnamese CP) for September 1966 and October 1975.

[18] Lenin condemned what *he* called "opportunism," but meant thereby "strategic compromise" of ultimate CP power.

"inexpedient"[19]; yet it has proved expedient, and efficacious, in every CP-led guerrilla movement—at least in preventing betrayal, at most in commanding services from the masses.

Fighting tactics have been transmitted through revolutionary training schools rather than through Marxist-Leninist writings, but the essential ungallantry of guerrilla warfare is already discernible in the romantic penmanship of Marx's contemporary and antagonist, Mazzini.[20] "Guerrilla war is a war of judicious daring, active legs, and espionage.... Guerrilla bands must make friends with the peasants ... and plant spies in every village.... Their principal aim will be constantly to damage and molest the enemy with the least possible danger to themselves, ... systematically observing secrecy ... and making it a rule to try to compromise all large cities. The means are: to attack the enemy as often as possible in the flank or rear; to surprise small detachments; to seize convoys of provisions, ammunition or money; to interrupt communications by lying in wait for couriers, destroying roads and bridges; ... continually to break in on hours of refreshment and sleep and to seize his generals and superior officers and so on." Modern exponents of the subject (Mao, Giap) insist that guerrillas must never attack except when they are momentarily in overwhelming strength, because only thus can a minority prevail over the majority.[21] They have a right, adds Mazzini, to exact "forced contributions" for their subsistence and for the "Centre"; it is that practice which gave rise to claims of "self-reliance" by national-liberation movements in the 1960s, when Soviet and Chinese helping hands had to be circumspect for reasons of *peaceful co-existence*. On the other hand, whereas Mazzini urged guerrillas to draw fire away from the masses, modern *freedom fighters* prefer to put the masses between themselves and their enemy—in a riot, for instance, or where guerrilla bases are deliberately sited in refugee camps (Lebanon, Zambia).

It is commonly supposed that all freedom fighters are zealots, if not for the unspoken maximum programme of national liberation, then for the bourgeois-national revolution or, after Stage 1, for some minimum programme like land reform or the cause of religion; the fedayeen of Palestine fight to regain their homeland, but elsewhere the facts often point to less elevated and less simple motives: the initiative comes from the *armed propagandist* recruiter, drawing on tribal and personal antagonisms, blackmail, and youthful zest for adventure or ambition to cut a figure. Captured children in the Balkans and in Africa, or kidnapped adult conscripts in

---

[19] *Op. cit.* in note 2, above, XXXI, p. 33.
[20] *Life and Writings*, Vol. 1 (1891), pp. 369–378.
[21] *Hoc Tap* for September 1966, quoting Lenin, *op. cit.* in note 2, above, XXXI, pp. 70–71.

South-East Asia, have shown few qualms about coercing their neighbours at home; free or forced, the "volunteer's" commitment to the cause from the role of informant to auxiliary, and thereafter to guerrilla, is mostly gradual—his subversion to the movement precedes his conversion to its cause.[22]

The subtlest field for Leninist tactics is the diplomatic. Abandonment of the ideal of a world State and dissolution of the Comintern did nothing to reduce the necessity of foreign patrons, not only to supply arms but also to procure the movement international recognition. Victorious movements have generally taken care not to outstrip acquiescence in their growing strength by public opinion in the wider world—or at least in countries where public opinion controls public policy. In recent national liberations in Africa, swift military campaigns have been followed by instant and universal international recognition of victory; but in the 1950s and 1960s, victory had to be earned with a wilier statecraft fortified by more arduous modes of combat. The Foreign Minister of the Socialist Republic of Vietnam has claimed that the present, happy, position is due chiefly to the astuteness of *his* CP in the earlier, less fortunate, period.[23] The tactics he alludes to include the piecemeal acquisition of territory—and advance of "domino" bases—by *international accord* (Geneva 1954 and 1962, Paris 1973), moderation of immediate demands in order to accustom both the masses being liberated and international opinion to the idea of the maximum programme by stages, and the Khrushchevian *troyka*—that is, the offer of "provisional" ceasefires on condition that the government under attack gives up one-third of its authority to the freedom fighters and another third to a putative group of *neutrals* (unavowed Marxist-Leninists) who inevitably attract some support away from the defence and, abroad, make the movement's intransigence sound like sweet reasonableness.

The underlying assumption of such tactics is that the target society is open and competitive and opposite in character to its assailant: for example, trade unions can only be a front for a secret Party in a country where they are tolerated free from State control. Armed struggle over national liberation is therefore by nature asymmetrical, so that the two contestants are bound to practise different strategies and tactics; national liberation is a system of outlawry for use against a State constituted on principles of rule of law: as Lenin implied in his two-stage programme, it has little chance against

---

[22] "Compulsion combined with persuasion" is Lenin's precept: see *op. cit.* in note 2, above, XXXI, p. 496; as advocated by Vietnamese theorists, see *Hoc Tap*, April 1976.

[23] Nguyen Duy Trinh in *Hoc Tap*, October 1975.

entrenched despotism. No victorious national liberation has ever set up a parliamentary democracy. Most significant, Leninist methods cannot be put into practice in reverse against a sponsoring communist government because of the latter's totalitarian society. Many of the dilemmas of defence arise from tactical asymmetry.

IV—COUNTERREVOLUTION AND DÉTENTE

The inability of the Comintern between the World Wars, despite a dozen notable attempts, to promote a single, victorious, national liberation had complicated causes, but not the least of them was political control of Asia by a handful of European Powers. In the 1920s, the United Kingdom, France and the Netherlands understood very well what Chicherin was up to in Western, Southern and South-East Asia and in the Far East. But the regaining of unfettered sovereignty by Iraq, Persia and Afghanistan, followed by the rise of fascism in the 1930s, ended international police collaboration against Stalin's agents, grown more discreet anyway; there was détente on both sides. In the 1940s the American-designed United Nations superseded the pre-War concert of Europe, and the Soviet Union's membership of it barred its engagement in defence against national liberation, except (by accident) in Korea. The Truman doctrine seemed to be meant at first for Europe and the near East at most; Mao's triumph in China was no "Moscow plot," and the United States government washed its hands of the refugee Chiang Kai-shek on Formosa. It was the Korean war that alerted Truman to the implications of the Zhdanov line, that extension of CP rule by violent means was a connected process wherever it occurred.

When it came to CP insurrections in dependent territories, however, Truman was inhibited from repeating his mobilisation of the United Nations flag for defence in Korea by the American public conviction that colonial emancipation would obstruct national liberation, whereas Leninists calculated that it furthered it—perhaps the Cold War's greatest irony; the colonial Powers, once the United States had hastened their relinquishment of political control, hesitated to go on shouldering the burdens of their former charges' defence. Under the mini-détente of the 1954 Berlin and Geneva conferences, the United Nations flag continued to protect South Korea, but Moscow and Peking kept the United Nations out of Indochina and rendered the tripartite International Commission ineffectual. The NATO-CENTO-SEATO chain of defence arrangements along the southern flank of the Soviet Union and

People's Republic of China for a time shielded the prime targets for national liberation from Korea-type onslaught and no doubt influenced Khrushchev's choice of subtler methods consonant with peaceful co-existence; but the South-East Asian Treaty Organisation (SEATO) failed to work out any method for collective security against guerrilla warfare, and decolonised governments in Indochina, though challenged by one national-liberation command in Hanoi, preferred each to fight alone. Foreign aid and technical assistance may have reduced the poverty that a humanitarian public opinion in the United States and Europe believed was the source of guerrilla recruitment in "bourgeois-national" States, but it did nothing to the recruitment.

The United States' eagerness, in the 1960s, to hold the line against national liberation singlehanded did not slow but speeded the decline of international collaboration as soon as it became obvious that American public resolve to sustain the burdens, so confidently taken on at first, was brittle. The Vietnamese CP boasts that growing boldness on the Communist side, especially in Africa, as well as expansion of the Afro-Asian (later "non-aligned") movement sponsored by Communist governments—even though attended by rivalry among the latter for "hegemony"—are consequences of American discomfiture in Indochina. President Nixon's rapprochement to China—at the very moment when Mrs. Gandhi was arming national liberation in East Bengal—the inauguration of the Chinese People's Republic's representation in the United Nations with a speech reaffirming dedication to national liberation, and Nixon's acceptance, perforce, of Zhou Enlai's assertion in the joint communiqué in February 1972 of the CCP's right to promote it, were successive signs that even the watered-down Nixon version of the Truman doctrine had become a "paper tiger." The general forward movement of national liberation in Africa and in south Arabia provoked no United States reaction. The present Association of South-East Asian Nations, even though its members all face the threat of national liberation supported from China and Communist Vietnam, has renounced regional collective security against it and bowed to the Chinese doctrine that State-to-State relations need not be impaired by "Party-to-Party" support for national liberation.[24]

---

[24] For discussion of the doctrine, see D. Bonavia in *Far Eastern Economic Review*, November 17, 1978. "The matter is exclusively *bilateral* between [*e.g.*] Thailand and China," according to the Thai Foreign Minister (Radio Bangkok, November 9, 1978). The ideological source of the Chinese Communist Party doctrine is, again, Lenin: "We must proclaim a separation, though fictitious, of our government from the party and especially from the Comintern": see Annankov memorandum in B. Lazitch and M. M. Drachkovitch, *Lenin and the Comintern*, Vol. 1, p. 549 (1972).

V—STRATEGIC DILEMMAS OF DEFENCE

Since national liberation was conceived by Lenin as a conflict of wits, it is in the field of psychological warfare—the contest for public confidence as to which side is likely to win—that the defence encounters its most taxing dilemmas. The prevalent providential view of politics—that those who do not prosper must be wicked unless they prove their innocence up to the hilt—assumes every act of rebellion to be the *cri de coeur* of an underdog against oppression unless its guilty motives can be exposed up to the hilt. It was with this double "bourgeois" standard in mind[25] that Lenin used the word "defence" to mean an *offensive* against the "reactionary" established order.[26] In hope of redeeming itself from the original sin of governments, so to speak, the defence usually gets persuaded—even driven—to tackle its troubles by indirect methods, namely administrative and social adjustments calculated to satisfy the grievances or aspirations of the national liberators; these can afford to go on proclaiming one minimum programme after another, insatiably, for people of goodwill rarely bring themselves to discredit a David with greed or malice. Policies adopted on these grounds are often dogged by the particular dilemmas considered below; but there is also a general one which tends to be overlooked, namely the dilemma resulting from receipt of foreign aid. It is usually sufficient for a national-liberation movement to rely on its implied patriotic pride and a repeated declaration of *self-reliance* in order to allay suspicions about external supplies, as long as these are delivered with discretion; in contrast, supplies received by a government are blatant, and the greater the demands to meet social adjustments or to face an escalating armed struggle, the more they bear out charges that the recipient is the donor's puppet. Worse still, foreign aid is inseparable from a foreign share in the defence strategy, and that in turn makes the recipient answerable to a distant public, not itself under attack; in an extreme case, like that of Vietnam, the defence may actually find itself betrayed by former sympathisers. This eventuality has to be weighed all the time against risk of succumbing directly, for want of preparedness and munitions, to national-liberation tactics at earlier stages.

The dilemmas caused by indirect methods centre on processes of modernisation and of democratisation. It was an essential element in the Zhdanov strategy to confront developing countries, ex-colonial or other, with national liberation before they had completed either of these processes. The dilemmas of their governments

---

[25] See *ibid.*
[26] *Op. cit.* in note 2, above, XXI, p. 300.

have arisen from two directions. In the first place, contrary to widespread belief, neither process is necessarily welcomed by the beneficiaries: the notorious rejection by Indian peasants of improved farming methods makes less surprising traditionalist resistance to modernisation in Afghanistan (1930s) and Iran (1970s). There, without resorting to people's war, Communists have found temporary bourgeois-national allies against the monarchy among the mullahs incurious about their new friends' maximum programme; similarly, in South-East Asia, Muslims, Buddhists and aborigines have all been recruited for people's war because their identity was threatened by modernising governments. It follows that modernisation and democratisation cannot always be pursued together, as was assumed by development experts in the 1950s: the central planning and control over resources for the former may meet hostility instead of co-operation from parliamentary institutions set up under the latter and perversely eager to assert themselves. In such circumstances, a government can but choose which stick to be beaten with.

Whether in order to forestall a national-liberation movement or in order to combat one that has started, a developing government will be obliged to intensify public administration in rural areas and perhaps among minorities who live in the borderlands. A choice lies between extending the arm of central-government departments and entrusting unaccustomed types of work to local authorities—between efficiency and self-determination—and, where there is fighting, between introducing army garrisons and arming local militias for self-defence. It is attractive to argue that men will work and fight best for their own communities, yet local personnel are also more exposed to subversion and more given to reaching accommodations with guerrillas for mutual tolerance. On the other hand, personnel from other localities or the capital—often representing a government that has never administered its provinces with such intensity before or is still trying to find its feet after colonial emancipation—may have difficulty commanding respect and inspiring confidence, even if their arrival does not arouse antagonism on ethnic or historical grounds. There might exist easy ways out, were it not for the haste imposed by the Leninists' readiness to move into every gap in social control.

Land reform has many advocates as an indirect defence against national liberation. Land tenure has been oppressive in the past in many societies and frequently still is at the moment national liberation is launched; it is tempting to link the two, notwithstanding that either is also common without the other. It is in this sphere that the widest discrepancy is to be found between Lenin's minimum and maximum programmes, for *land-to-the-tiller* is regularly the CP slogan before coming to power, suppression of small holdings under collectivisation the policy after. Whatever the old tenure, a reform based on liberal principles of legality and the upholding of individual rights cannot but be a huge administrative task; if it is shirked, a threatened government leaves another stick in the freedom fighters' hand that can be wielded locally—if genuine grievances are prevalent—and certainly abroad even if they are not. Iran and Vietnam are examples of the first category, Laos and Cambodia of the second. Yet diversion of administrative resources to this purpose rarely seems to make any difference to the progress of national liberation[27]; that remained true in Vietnam even after introduction of computers had speeded administration a hundredfold. Rack-rent tenancy is an evil which every government has a duty to eliminate from time to time—for no land reform, short of nationalisation, has yet solved the problem for good—but it is not one from which relief from the threat of national liberation is to be expected.

Having seen a neighbour go under, or perhaps having lost part of its own territory domino-fashion, a threatened government may be tempted to make a pre-emptive attack. For all that the decision was in reality not taken by Syngman Rhee, such was the strategy of the 1950 threat to Mao across the Yalu; from then on, the principle has not been disputed that, once liberated, territory must remain so. The Korean lesson applies to all strategies lying between all-out retaliation and acceptance of *protracted war* (in the original Chinese, *war of endurance*)—the world at large will classify the former as aggressive, the latter as a relatively peaceful mode of struggle. Nor is it a question of opprobrium alone: President Johnson could discover no pattern or intensity of tactical bombing, against a totalitarian society, capable of deterring assaults across the Vietnam demarcation line without risk that the Communist régime might be bombed into collapse—an event that would have violated the principle of invulnerability, besides breaching previous United States promises never to use force to *overthrow* the régime. On the other hand, leaving the initiative to the national-liberation movement at a time of its choosing confronts the defence with all the other dilemmas.

In a people's war, from the very first attacks on its periphery, a government will have to make up its mind whether to dissipate its efforts in endless hot pursuit or to yield territory for the time being and perhaps not protect its citizens against atrocities. The latter

---

[27] There may be an exception in Ethiopia: there, the Marxist-Leninists claim to have been welcomed in the south of the country, where tenure was oppressive, but certainly were bitterly resisted in the north, where land rights were equitable. However, reliable evidence is scanty, and land may have had nothing to do with the different reception in different provinces.

policy may well enable guerrillas to dig themselves in politically so well that they can never be dislodged again, whereas the former exposes the defence to the erosion of resources and of confidence in victory that Mazzini set above all other guerrilla objectives. Paradoxically, it is often those sectors of society with the biggest stake in the status quo whose confidence is shaken first, for all that Marxist-Leninists justify violence in revolution by the anticipated ferocity of their defence of property and privilege by the "capitalist" class: the well-to-do and the technicians will be the first to be dismayed by abandonment of territory and, fearing ultimate defeat, liquidate their assets if they can and prepare to leave the country, as seems to have happened in various parts of Africa (not only Rhodesia), whereas, if the defence holds on to districts hard to make secure, those with a little less to lose who live there will be tempted to appease the Goth at the gate with cash or clandestine services that help him gather strength.

VI—TACTICAL DILEMMAS OF DEFENCE

There is a tactical dimension to this last dilemma. The disheartening effect on soldiers all the time of their no-win situation, aware as they are that their attackers operate from unassailable territory, is rarely appreciated by people who have not experienced national-liberation struggles: a platoon of men may be needed to guard a strategic bridge every night for 20 years, knowing, platoon after platoon, that if they are lax just once damage may be done which will cost immense effort to put right, whereas it takes two guerrillas half an hour to blow it up and, if they bungle the charge, they can try again next week. If the government decides to evacuate territory strategically, it brings the front line of demoralisation nearer the capital; if it holds on, it faces another agonising choice—whether to deploy its forces for mobile defence and risk decimation by ambush, or to spread its garrisons thin and either have them picked off one by one or let them reach their own local accommodations with the freedom fighters. A subsidiary dilemma arises over soldiers' families: men in lonely garrisons will fret without wives and children, yet the presence of non-combatants far from hospitals adds to the horror of casualties, and the women may be even more susceptible than their husbands to guerrilla subversion.

The commonest of all tactical dilemmas is the police officer's nightmare: how much force to use in any incident. All Marxist-Leninists are trained to provoke strong action, if possible against the innocent, and to insist that arrest of a rioter who is a trade unionist or a mullah amounts to government suppression of trade unionism or of Islam. The Communist liberation of Hanoi from its bourgeois-national administration in August 1945 depended on police hesitation to fire on agitators in a crowd; the police forces from Bangkok to Mexico City have learnt prudence and now keep off university campuses, which in consequence make ideal urban bases for national liberation. In many tactical situations, a government has to choose between popularity and security: on the whole, the public caught up in the struggle will understand the imperatives of security, but outsiders rarely do. Rural curfews, issue of identity cards and detention of people without them, sometimes relocation of villages—all of these may be necessary to protect the masses from intimidation, kidnap or murder at the hands of freedom fighters; yet they smack of tyranny and will be so portrayed in the reports of journalists who accompany foreign aid. In Malaya in 1951, the rigours of food denial, which forbade home cooking, were welcomed by many rural folk as a protection against guerrilla intimidation, but not always, and they got the colonial administration a bad name abroad.

Guerrillas victual themselves off the land, whether or not, in addition, like Mazzini's followers, they send some of the money they take from peasants to their "centre." Modernisation programmes mean nothing if not that they will raise the masses' income; without strict (oppressive) controls, the benefit is mulctable to step up the national liberation, and, without intrusive security forces standing by, the freedom fighters can destroy new roads, clinics and welfare services, so that replacement opens a bottomless drain and confidence is lost in the survival of a government so easily made a fool of. A similar dilemma attends belated redress for genuine social grievances such as land reform. And with the whole process of colonial emancipation, demanded on Communist initiative in many countries only after it was published policy of the metropolitan power, so with programmes to forestall recruitment for national liberation, and even relief for flood or drought; wily Leninists will set up an agitation for what is going to be done anyway and make it appear that the authorities are bowing to their pressure.

A tactical dilemma frequently arises over what agencies of public administration meet the crisis of national liberation best. Traditional institutions are naturally unsophisticated in the matter of modernisation and democratisation; the temptation is to appoint a parallel administration of specially-trained staff in districts where programmes are being pushed forward fastest and security problems are the most intractable. The difficulty is to obtain the advantages without creating uncertainty about powers and relationships in the minds of staff and public, or giving play to mutual jealousy and all manner of "contradictions" exploitable by revolutionaries. Where fighting is heavy and unified command vital, the dilemma is whether to put civilians under army or army under civilians—in some places whether to proclaim martial law. (It is a corroboration that, when Mao Zedong tried to "seize power" back through the toy people's war of the Great Proletarian Cultural Revolution, paralysing government and production, his comrades used the Red Army to restore order.) Soldiers are forthright, but also high-handed, and can make the defence look no more law-abiding than the freedom fighters; civilians stick to the rules but hesitate. Civilians cannot direct tactics against guerrillas, but soldiers may neglect other, less familiar and congenial duties; soldiers lack local prejudice but also local knowledge; both are equally open (as in CP States) to corruption.

The dilemma arises acutely over the courts. Protection of witnesses and civilian judges—all the more, juries—against reprisal by freedom fighters thwarts judicial punishment of terrorism; military courts help over judges though not witnesses, but are universally taken to be biased. In any case, punishment of crime is less important for the defence against national liberation than keeping the culprits locked up; there seems no alternative to detention without trial, but the very act of confining a terrorist untried by liberal rules of procedure turns him into a prisoner of conscience. The career of Kerensky in Petrograd highlights the dilemma: a defence lawyer bent on satisfying the liberal aspirations of political malcontents, he became justice minister, then Prime Minister, and lifted all arbitrary tsarist constraints on them; at once the exiles flooded back home and pushed the Russian revolution through Stage 2. In the same order of ideas comes the dilemma over censorship: freedom of fair comment and of information includes freedom of unfair comment and of rumourmongering, but, since there is no censorship in totalitarian States (because all means of communication are in State hands), a government resorting to it incurs, here too, contumely as tyrannical by comparison. Efficient defence measures of governments under attack are regularly denounced in national-liberation propaganda as if the dismantling of them were the sole object of the insurrection—as a minimum programme to mask the maximum one.

Lastly, whenever it features in national-liberation strategy, the *troyka* manoeuvre puts the defence in a dilemma from which no government has ever yet found a way out. Although Marxist-Leninists' willingness to take part in elections can never betoken willingness to submit to an unfavourable result—because that would amount to what Lenin condemned as *opportunism*—a government which does not lend itself to the manoeuvre, aimed at its destruction, will appear to be rejecting decision by ballot box, the adherence to which is the sole justification for resisting national liberation by warlike means. It is then not worthy of the money, still less the spilt blood, of its friends.

VII—Conclusions

It is true that national-liberation movements get into quandaries on their side, but they appear to arise mainly over decisions affecting the exercise of power after victory—for example, strategic disposi-tions of guerrillas affecting their future control of Zimbabwe, or the Chinese Communist Party's problem between 1965 and 1975 of how far to support the Vietnamese high command in Hanoi and risk what has happened since, namely emergence of a client neighbour outgrowing its patron and allying itself with the Soviet Union. In pre-War days, many CPs had to choose between Comintern instruc-tions, the following of which was tactful to qualify for International Red Aid, etc., and their survival on the ground; in 1948 the Malayan CP had to choose between clinging to its declining hold over trade unions as workers' standards of living recovered and embarking on a people's war without an adjacent patron. But, on balance, the scales are weighted in favour of national liberation against the defence.

Would a government under attack be best advised not to defend itself or its people but to surrender power straightaway? Ironically, alas, because of the very secrecy surrounding the beginnings of a national liberation, there is rarely any moment when that is feasible or when it is clear who is the appropriate rebel leader to surrender to: the French government did surrender Tonkin to Ho Chi Minh in 1946, but, once recognised as Head of a State in consequence, he withdrew to the hills to gamble for a much bigger territory: all of Indochina. In both Aden and Angola the colonial authorities backed the wrong one among several national-liberation move-ments, and the post-colonial government of Burma has discovered repeatedly that appeasement of one ambitious movement only draws heavier fire from the others, their common Marxist-Leninist ideology notwithstanding. President Sukarno offered his CP a third of the influence in his government *troyka*-fashion, hoping to satisfy them; but Leninism countenances no half measures, and, with CCP help, they tried to seize a monopoly of power from him. National liberation is, for those it is directed against, like lumbago: whatever posture the patient adopts to alleviate his distress, including prone immobility, it always gets worse.

THE FACTOR OF CULTURE
IN THE GLOBAL INTERNATIONAL ORDER

By

R. J. VINCENT

INDIVIDUAL, group, nation, State, region, globe, system, society: why should "culture" be added to this list of concepts for the interpretation of international politics? There are three reasons: two that would justify more attention to cultural factors in order more accurately to convey the reality of world politics, and a third that might explain the increased attention that cultural approaches to world affairs are already receiving. There is, first, the fact of the plurality of cultures in world politics. It may be that the attempt to understand world politics as they are seen from the various perspectives of the participants in it is as important as the attempt to see the system as a whole: not the principle of the balance of power, but Chinese conceptions of power politics. Secondly, culture is a concept connected with the system as a whole as well as with partial perspectives on it. When Martin Wight writes that "a states-system will not come into being without a degree of cultural unity among its members," or that "a states-system presupposes a common culture,"[1] he puts forward an important theme for empirical investigation of the international system at large. In the third place, it may be that cultural factors are forcing their way on to the agenda of international political concern because they have powerful protagonists interested in that destination. Recognition of a distinct Soviet, or Chinese, or Islamic, or even African, approach to world politics may be more a reflection of the power of these cultures than of new enlightenment in the West. And the extent to which they are now Powers to be reckoned with may be in turn a reflection of the decline of the European system and its American operator—though this is an arguable and complex point which will be raised again below.

Meanwhile, there is the question of definition, and culture is a concept that it is difficult to detach from its neighbours in the field of sociology and anthropology. With "system" it shares the idea of patterned interaction; with "society" the idea of a pattern of a particular kind (conformity to rules, for example) and with civilisa-

---

[1] M. Wight, *Systems of States* (1977), pp. 3 and 46.

tion the idea of refinement, a quality opposed to barbarism.[2] Culture as everything is illustrated in T. S. Eliot's definition: "all the characteristic activities and interests of a people: Derby Day, Henley Regatta, Cowes, the Twelfth of August, a cup final, the dog races, the pin table, the dart board, Wensleydale cheese, boiled cabbage cut into sections, beetroot in vinegar, nineteenth-century Gothic churches and the music of Elgar."[3] That Eliot could refer elsewhere to the decline of culture, and even to a social situation in which no culture obtained indicates his own concern with "high culture." Presumably, a culture might be said to be in decline if it lost Elgar and the Church, but could survive the absence of beetroot and cabbage.

Anthropology, "the science of culture," once took a definition of the Eliot kind as a description of what it was about: "Culture or civilisation, taken in its wide ethnographic sense, is that complex whole which includes knowledge, belief, art, morals, law, custom, and any other capabilities and habits acquired by man as a member of society."[4] Since this description of a century or so ago, definition has so crowded upon definition as to persuade two eminent American cultural anthropologists to attempt, at book-length, to impose some sort of order on the concept of culture.[5] They sorted definitions into six categories: the enumerative-descriptive sort already discussed; historical definitions which took "How it came to be?" as the distinguishing mark of culture; normative definitions which stressed rules of and for behaviour; psychological definitions dealing with culture as learned behaviour, or as the rationalisation of habit; structural definitions concerned with system and pattern; and genetic definitions taking culture as the man-made part of the environment.

The lay inquirer into the place of the factor of culture in world affairs might, then, do well to touch base with each of these varieties of definition. But if this seems too formidable an exercise, there is, closer to home in International Relations, a literature on political culture that might be plundered for guidance on culture in world affairs. This notion of political culture was both to elucidate and

---

[2] This is too simple for all three concepts, but especially so for the third. The literature encompasses the use of civilisation for refinement distinguished from the mere material and technological data of culture; the opposite usage—culture "high" and civilisation "low"; and usage as synonyms—both "high" or both "low." See, in particular, Robert K. Merton, "Civilization and Culture," XXI *Sociology and Social Research* No. 2., November-December, 1936.

[3] T. S. Eliot, *Notes towards the Definition of Culture* (1948), p. 31.

[4] E. B. Tylor, *Primitive Culture* 5th ed. (1913), Vol. 1, p. 1. Tylor called anthropology the science of culture.

[5] A. L. Kroeber and C. Kluckhohn, *Culture: A Critical Review of Concepts and Definitions* (1963).

supersede the idea of national character by studying, in a scientifi-
cally respectable way, the attitudes of individuals to the political
system and to their own roles within it.[6] The gap between the
individual, the domain of the psychologist, and the group, that of the
sociologist, was thus to be bridged.[7] It may be that something called
international political culture similarly connects the State with the
States-system, or with a sub-system within it, and the investigation
of this is something that will be raised again later.

With regard still to the definition of culture, as distinct from the
inquiry into hypotheses about it, the writers on political culture draw
our attention to its cognitive and evaluative aspects: how actors see
the system and what they judge to be their own role within it. Hedley
Bull makes use of this distinction in finding in all historical international societies some element of a common *intellectual* culture—language, philosophical outlook, artistic tradition—and some
element of common *values*.[8] He goes on to distinguish between a
diplomatic culture uniting the official representatives of States, and
an international political culture reaching out into the societies
making up the States-system, a mass culture as opposed to an élite
one on whose successful cosmopolitanisation the future of international society might be said to depend. For the purposes of the
discussion that follows I shall distinguish between an international
political culture of States including in its upper echelons a diplomatic culture, and a world culture, for which cosmopolitan civilisation might be one example, in the definition of which the State has
no place. Thus world culture might denote a way of life that is to be
found around the globe but which does not surface in international
society—as, for example, with peasant culture. Or it might refer to
the extent to which all societies are tending to take the similar shape
required if they are to modernise. Or it might mean the imperialist
mould in which the relationship between global centres and
peripheries is formed.

I—THE IMPORTANCE OF CULTURE
IN WORLD AFFAIRS

The idea that one might borrow the methods of the writers on
political culture to shed light on the place of culture in international

---

[6] See G. A. Almond and S. Velba, *The Civic Culture* (1963).

[7] L. W. Pye, "Culture and Political Science: Problems in the evaluation of the concept of
Political Culture" in L. Schneider and C. M. Bonjean (eds.), *The Idea of Culture in the Social
Sciences* (1973), p. 69.

[8] H. Bull, *The Anarchical Society* (1977), pp. 316-317.

affairs is a formal one about procedure. But there is a pattern of thought, exemplified by Kant's requirement of republican government within States if peace was to prevail among them, which posits a more substantial connection between the domestic and international arenas. If it is true that "a country's conduct and organisation of its foreign relations is an organic aspect of the life style that informs its inner order,"[9] then no account of international relations can afford to neglect the study of domestic political cultures. If, on the other hand, what might be called the London School of Economics (LSE) orthodoxy is true, that the international system, in Professor Northedge's phrase, "doles out" roles to its constituent units whatever their internal structure then culture can be dropped without loss. And there is a third school of Realist thought whose organising concept is neither culture, nor system, but power: no patterns here nor roles, but merely the interests of the strong.

Leaving the Realists aside as people whose shortcomings have been rehearsed elsewhere,[10] the assertion of the importance of cultural factors in international politics must undermine the LSE orthodoxy of system dominance. Each of the marks by which Martin Wight suggests we may recognise a States-system[11] might be said to be visible in contemporary international politics. Thus there are sovereign States that recognise each other; an acceptance of hierarchy in the Security Council of the United Nations and elsewhere; regular communication through the diplomatic network; universal allegiance to international law; and, more problematically, the defence of common interests by a variety of means from the calling of conferences to self-help. Indeed, it might further be argued that the new members of the international system whose differences from the old ones are often rehearsed as a challenge to the existence of that system, are the most enthusiastic members of it; anxious to send their diplomats to the gatherings of the international community at the United Nations, insistent upon fidelity to international law, and quick to point out the obligations of the powerful. The system, it might be said, like the British Civil Service, works, and the bases of its working are not cultural but functional. States engage in the international system for the benefit they derive from it, neither committing nor compromising their cultures, and protesting against its working if their interests are overridden by greater Powers but not their cultures. The preservation of the integrity or authenticity of a local culture might be invoked, but merely for propagandistic

---

[9] This is Adda Bozeman's conclusion in *The Future of Law in a Multicultural World* (1971), p. 168.

[10] See *e.g.* H. Suganami, "Why ought treaties to be kept?" In this *Year Book*, Vol. 33, 1979.

[11] *Op. cit.* in note 1, above, p. 129.

purposes, so that a better bargain might be struck in any negotiations.[12]

But Wight went on to assert, as we have seen, that a States-system
pre-supposes a common culture. He surely intended that this idea
should have a content of its own, and not be the mere summation of
the ingredients of a States-system. It may be that the functional
account of the workings of the system is so superficial as not to
encounter the observation that it holds true only in a context of
broad agreement about fundamentals. And just as the British Civil
Service works not because of any mystic quality in the design of the
system, but because of patterns established at Eton and Oxford, so
the international system might work, to the extent that it does, not in
spite of cultural differences but because it is the produce of one
culture grafted successfully on all others. It is in the context of this
argument that the presupposition of a common culture takes on
meaning. A feature of the European States-system, now made
universal, was its limitation: not a global Leviathan, but a society of
States tolerating each other's existence; not Holy Wars but the
adjustment of frontiers; unity in an agreement about independence
rather than continental solidarity. A doctrine of limitations is a
mature political doctrine which has won a place in a system wise to
the alternatives, and preferring the political drama to take place
elsewhere than in the society of States.

In this sense we may understand the presupposition of a common
culture as a set of attitudes and values produced by the experience of
co-existence. It has its classic statement in Burke: "In the intercourse between nations, we are apt to rely too much on the instrumental part. We lay too much weight on the formality of treaties and
compacts.... Men are not tied to one another by paper and seals.
They are led to associate by resemblances, by conformities, by
sympathies. It is with nations as with individuals. Nothing is so
strong a tie of amity between nation and nation as correspondence
in laws, customs, manners and habits of life. They are obligations
written in the heart. They approximate men to one another without
their knowledge and sometimes against their intentions. The secret,
unseen, but irrefragable bond of habitual intercourse holds them
together even when their perverse and litigious nature sets them
to equivocate, scuffle, and fight about the terms of their written
obligations."[13]

An international political culture characterised by attitudes and
values that are, in the cant word, moderate, stands in constant

---

[12] For an argument along these lines, see W. Levi, "International Law in a Multicultural
World," 18 *International Studies Quarterly*, Nr. 4, December 1974.
[13] *Letters on the Regicide Peace* Vol. I, Pt. III, pp. 78–79 (Payne's edition).

danger of being overwhelmed from the edges of politics. And while the system of States might yet command the centre of the stage from the point of view of the student of international politics, the sources of its stability and persistence might be found, if at all, not within it but in the society beyond its borders. Further, if the State itself is a transitory feature of the international landscape, no lasting order can be based on it, all internationalist schemes to do so are misconceived, and we should look instead to the unity of culture for the real source of world order.[14] In the inspection of this argument we pass from international political culture to world culture.

Uniting Europe culturally, in Dawson's view, was the spiritual bond of the Christian religion. It held society together by providing the reason for obedience to law, and determined the content of the common culture by its pronouncements on how social life was to be lived: the Church created public opinion.[15] In the cosmopolitan civilisation of the contemporary world there is no such religious underpinning, nor yet an ideological one to take its place, but merely a sharing by the whole of mankind of the common predicament of "modernity." The industrial revolutions, together with the advances in science and technology with which they are associated, have created a standardised, mechanised culture of global dimensions. The cities of the world, which are the characteristic artefact of this culture, have not only increased in numbers and size but "the time is approaching when the cities become one city—a Babylon which sets its mark on the mind of every man and woman and imposes the same pattern of behaviour on every human activity."[16]

How substantial is this cosmopolitan culture? Can it be said to have taken root in societies around the globe, or is it more impressive for its breadth than its depth? Margaret Mead says that the spread of thin networks of similar facilities all over the world— money, telephone systems, airplanes, trains and boats, hotels and post offices and banks, food service places and barber shops—means that the traveller or immigrant can make his initial moves with ease, but that the next step to the local intricacy of custom is very great.[17] On this view the global culture may have submerged local cultures, but it has not yet eroded them. Opposed to this view is the one which has the global culture knocking down and rebuilding local cultures in its own image. Science and technology impose a rationality which is universal not culturally specific.[18] There is also a rational-

---

[14] C. Dawson, *The Judgement of the Nations* (1943), pp. 54–58.

[15] *Ibid*. p. 83 and Pt. II, generally.

[16] *Ibid*. p. 1.

[17] "World Culture," in Q. Wright (ed.), *The World Community* (1948), p. 52.

[18] See Jaguaribe, "World Order, Rationality, and Socioeconomic Development," XCV *Daedalus*, Spring 1966.

ity of social management involved in *The Bureaucratization of the World*.[19] Some see evidence that world-wide family patterns are converging on a norm common to urban-industrial societies.[20] Others have spoken of modern "industrial man" who manifests a similar structure of attitudes and values wherever he occurs.[21] And, finally, there is the idea that the centralisation of systems of political and economic control is a process that continues regardless of the ideology of the controlling régime.[22]

However substantial this edifice of modernity appears, it may yet be the reflection of a dominant political order and not of a world that has discovered through science a super-political rationality. Thus it is a commonplace that much of what is meant by "modernisation" can be rendered by "Americanisation," and that this in turn means not merely becoming like America, but also being Americanised: the United States imposing its model as well as just representing one. It has been said that while the form taken by the American "transnational" empire is economic it is nonetheless imperial: upheld by a doctrine of technological superiority just as the European empires were justified by one of racial superiority; achieved by a process of economic penetration to compare with the European acquisition of land; and resulting in an economic dependency as truly "occupied" as the formal colonies of the past.[23]

If there is, in this way, a political structure hidden behind but propping up the social one, then we might expect its impermanence as empires have waned in the past. Indeed, there are those who argue that the retreat of the American empire is not something to be dated from the defeat in Vietnam, but almost from the time that W. T. Stead wrote *The Americanization of the World, or the Trend of the Twentieth Century* in 1902.[24] Lumping the United States together with the Old World, Barraclough thinks the century to be more Mao's and Nehru's than Coolidge's or Baldwin's, the former two being a better guide to contemporary history than the two latter.[25]

The contemporary cosmopolitan civilisation is not then a "given" of international intercourse either in the sense that it has set a standard of modernity from which there is no turning back, or in the

---

[19] H. Jacoby (1973).

[20] W. J. Goode, *World Revolution and Family Patterns* (1963).

[21] A. Inkeles, "Industrial Man: The Relation of Status to Experience, Perception, and Value," 64 *American Journal of Sociology* (1960).

[22] Inkeles, "The Emerging Social Structure of the World," XXVII *World Politics*, Nr. 4, July 1975. The paragraph above borrows Inkeles' indices of cultural convergence.

[23] See S. P. Huntington, "Transnational Organizations in World Politics," XXV *World Politics*, Nr. 3, April 1973.

[24] See G. Barraclough, *An Introduction to Contemporary History* (1967), pp. 25 and 75.

[25] *Ibid*. p. 36.

sense that it exists regardless of its political context. But it is time to return from the question of "whose culture" to the larger theme that this section has addressed—that of the importance of the factor of culture in world politics.

To recap, there is first of all the doctrine of the dominance of the system, the idea that international politics impose a pattern of their own regardless of the cultural differences of the participants. There are two difficulties with this point of view, each of them involving the attempt to separate the international system from its environment. In the first place, an analysis of the system which seeks reasons for its stability within its boundaries might overlook crucial factors beyond them. I take Martin Wight's emphasis on a States-system's presupposition of a common culture to be an underlining of the importance of this point: culture might be, in Parsonian language, a prerequisite and not a mere requisite, and thus fundamental. Secondly, if the modern history of Europe can be written in terms of the defence of the system against revolutionaries who broke its rules, it is as important to pay attention to the attack on the system as to its defence. And if revolutions take place for something as well as against something else, data for the former can only be gathered from beyond the boundaries of the system.

There are difficulties also with the view that places culture, and in particular, domestic culture, in the system's position as the principal guide to the interpretation of international politics. In the first place, when Adda Bozeman decided that the future was not bright for law in a multicultural world, her main source material was the doctrine of the several cultures rather than their practice of co-existence.[26] And just as *The Soviet Design for a World State*[27] seems more alarming when put together from Marxist-Leninist texts than it does when mixed with the historical record, so might a textual approach give a harsher view of the clash of cultures in world politics than is justified by the reality of their mutual recognition. Secondly, while it is true that interaction between cultures might lead as easily to conflict as co-operation, it is hard to render these relations as simply the collision of forces in the void. For social action is by its nature norm-bound, and it is odd to suppose that all pretence to proper behaviour is swept away in the confrontation with strangers. The cults of nativism—predicted as second-generation élites took over in the Third World,[28] or as technology too crudely obliterated local cultures[29]—have not led, to the extent that they have taken hold, to

---

[26] *Op. cit.* in note 9, above, *passim*.
[27] E. R. Goodman (1959).
[28] *Op. cit.* in note 9, above, p. 163.
[29] Mead, *op. cit.* in note 17, above, p. 53.

the wholesale repudiation of the society of States. There is, in short, an international political culture, however rudimentary, whose content is not entirely determined by the cultures that participate in it.

The question of how far this international culture is buoyed up by a more widespread cosmopolitan culture is one that I shall return to in the last section of the paper. Meanwhile, the rather unsatisfactory conclusion is that neither the doctrine of the primacy of the system, which would dismiss cultural approaches to world politics as a kind of picturesque antiquarianism, nor the view which holds that the several cultures with their unique histories cannot be mixed in a transcendent, cosmopolitan world, gives a true account of international politics. But this is a judgment, or a guess, made before extensive empirical inquiry and it is to how this might proceed that I now turn.

II—APPROACHES TO THE STUDY OF CULTURE IN WORLD AFFAIRS

Implicit in the discussion so far has been the idea that "culture" is important for the student of international politics to the extent that it affects the stability of the international system. This disposition is borrowed from anthropology along with the idea of culture itself and the record of certain primitive societies with which international society has been compared.[30] International society apparently breaks the anthropological rules as formulated in a famous work on *African Political Systems*.[31] Professors Fortes and Evans-Pritchard say that "centralized authority and an administrative organization seem to be necessary to accommodate culturally diverse groups within a single political system," while "a centralized form of government is not necessary to enable different groups of closely-related culture to amalgamate."[32] But to the extent that order obtains in contemporary international politics, it is a condition associated neither with central authority nor with cultural homogeneity. There is a question here about the meaning of "political system" and "amalgamation" in the context of international politics, but the Stateless societies studied by anthropologists are a suggestive starting place for thought about them.

The same connection between culture and stability is made by the writers on political culture. Almond and Verba, for example, suggest that "there exists in Britain and the United States a pattern of political attitudes and an underlying set of social attitudes that is

---

[30] See R. D. Masters, "World Politics as a Primitive Political System," XVI *World Politics*, Nr. 4, July 1964.
[31] M. Fortes and E. E. Evans-Pritchard (1940).
[32] *Ibid.* pp. 9–10.

supportive of a stable democratic process."[33] And though it is not quite this pattern that Martin Wight seems to have in mind when writing of international public opinion as a notion coming "closest to the general culture of the society of states,"[34] the recording of that opinion might be advanced by the methods of investigators of political culture, and would then provide important evidence for the assertion of a cosmopolitan culture—one in which coalitions of opinion could be assembled across cultural divides.

A second area of inquiry connects culture not to the values of stability and order, but to those of justice and liberty. It is concerned not with how social life is possible, but with whether it is worth living. Under this heading the idea that the contemporary cosmopolitan culture is a triumph for Western civilisation, its superiority acknowledged by its subordination of all rival cultures, is challenged by the view that culture deteriorates in quality as it increases in quantity.[35] The world-wide extension of Western civilisation by imperial expansion, material progress, and intellectual penetration has led, says Dawson, as is the tendency of all world empires, to its losing touch with its spiritual roots.[36] The place in the making of public opinion once occupied by the rites and festivals of the church in Catholic countries, by the Bible and the preaching of the Word in Protestant ones, is now filled by the mass media, and "the greatest danger that threatens modern civilization is its degeneration into a hedonistic mass civilization of the cinema, the picture paper and the dance hall, where the individual, the family and the nation dissolve into a human herd without personality, or traditions or beliefs."[37] The twin pillars of Western civilisation, its cherishing of liberty and the Christian religion are threatened if not destroyed by the mass organisation and secularisation involved in the standardisation and mechanisation of culture.[38] The barbarism that was once opposed to civilisation is now within the city gates.

The power of this statement of the decline of Western civilisation is diminished if it is considered as a mere manifestation of a fashionable belief in decadence in the twentieth century compared to, and a reaction against, the nineteenth-century belief in progress. E. H. Carr puts Spengler, Toynbee and Butterfield together in this category and invites us to consider the context in which they wrote so that we ourselves can resist the impulse to follow the fashion to

---

[33] *Op. cit.* in note 6, above, p. vii.
[34] *Op. cit.* in note 1, above, pp. 71–72.
[35] *Op. cit.* in note 14, above, p. 23.
[36] *Ibid.* p. 67.
[37] C. Dawson, *Beyond Politics* (1939), pp. 78–79.
[38] This is a theme which Dawson returns to throughout his work.

which they have yielded.[39] Thus, for example, Toynbee's *Study of History* is what it is, but it is also a reflection of the weaknesses and failures of British policy in the 1930s,[40] and might not be a reliable guide beyond that parish. If this is a protest against an orthodoxy from within a culture, the view from without, or at least half-in and half-out is rather different. For the decline of Western civilisation might mean the rise or rebirth of other civilisations, and the Western preoccupation with the decline of "civilisations" would then be parochial and racist: parochial in its ignorance of other civilisations; racist in its assumption that only Western civilisation is civilisation.[41]

There is a lot to be said about the conditioned quality of political judgments. Indeed, a lot has been said in the branch of sociology devoted to it, the sociology of knowledge, and need not be rehearsed here. One striking feature which unites the writers who have stressed the importance of culture, whatever their other disagreements, is the view that it either has taken or should take its place as a building block of world order. Thus Dawson wrote in 1943 that there was not now a single relationship between one nation and the League of Nations, or the State and world society, but a threefold relationship involving a cultural unity which was intermediate between the nation and the world. The new world was a civilisation of civilisations made up of different cultural provinces, each of which in turn was made up of different peoples or nations.[42] This is a theme which Ali Mazrui has made his own in his plea for *A World Federation of Cultures*.[43] And Adda Bozeman, when writing about "political systems and the role of law" chooses cultures—the West, the Islamic Middle East and so forth—rather than States as the dominant political watersheds in world society.[44]

Three themes for the study of culture in world politics have been suggested: the question of the relationship between culture and stability or order; the question of the quality of civilisation—culture as connected to justice or high achievement rather than to order; and the question of cultural engineering—of how the world order is to accommodate cultures as well as States, or regions, or individuals, or classes. Data for the pursuit of the first question might be derived from case studies of particular actors in international politics or of particular interactions. Material for the second question might be gathered by looking at attitudes to some great issue in world politics

---

[39] *The New Society* (1956), pp. 6 and 15.
[40] *Ibid*. p. 12.
[41] See A. A. Mazrui, "In Search of Africa's Past," *The Listener*, August 17, 1978. "Half-in and half-out" describes Mazrui's position: one foot in Africa and the other in the West.
[42] *Op. cit*. in note 14, above, pp. 147–148.
[43] A. Mazrui, *A World Federation of Cultures* (1976).
[44] *Op. cit*. in note 9, above, Pt. II.

such as human rights and judging them against some standard of civilisation: a philosophical as well as an empirical inquiry. There is no readily available data for the third question which is about how something might be done rather than about what is happening in the world, but speculation about it would profit from inquiries conducted under the first two headings.

III—Conclusions

Whatever the context, whatever the cultural conditioning—Western writers attempting to catch a glimpse, Spengler-style, of their civilisation in the moments before its extinction, or Third-World scholars asserting the importance of cultural factors as the last stage of their attack on colonialism and the first in their rediscovery of a pristine pre-colonial integrity—there seems to be a case for more attention to cultural factors in world politics, and not less.

But the definition of culture, theories advanced about it, even its mere description, are contested. Thus, for example, the contemporary cosmopolitan culture might be thought of as primarily European, a manifestation of the imperialism of the past, or as American, a demonstration of present imperialism—"cocacolonisation," or as a post-colonial culture in which the flow of ideas and values is not from Europe or the United States to the Third World, but in the opposite direction: Yoga, communalism, oriental mysticism, etc. It might also be thought of as something separable from the political order, determined not by who governs but by the advance of science and technology. This is crudely formulated, but it serves to show that some distance has to be travelled before the description of a global culture can become as uncontroversial as the definition of a States-system.

There is finally the question to which I promised to return of whether the contemporary cosmopolitan culture can be said to underpin the present international order, as, it is said, Christendom bound together the European order of the past. When "industrial man" is taken as the exemplar of the global culture of today, and the similarity of his habits and values noted, there is no sense of the spiritual commitment of the Christian to a universal society and a pattern of rights and obligations deriving from it. There is merely a role to play, willy-nilly. If something does sustain the international order it is a physical mould not a spiritual bond. It is in this context that we may understand the concern to create a world federation of cultures as a recognition of the shallowness of the global culture of rootless cosmopolitanism, and of the need to devolve the spiritual community to a less inclusive and more organic grouping. Whether this would constitute a step towards civilisation or away from it is another question.

A REALISTIC JURISPRUDENCE
OF INTERNATIONAL LAW

By

J. S. WATSON

"What you cannot enforce, do not command"—Sophocles,
Oedipus at Colunnus.

THAT international law lacks a competent body endowed with the power compulsorily to settle disputes, is a truism in the theory of international law. Likewise, the lack of a central source of authoritative rules, a legislature, is also routinely acknowledged by writers of all persuasions. To the layman, what this means is immediately apparent: international law cannot and does not behave in the same prescriptive manner that one has become accustomed to in dealing with domestic legal systems. There are, however, few theorists in international law who fully appreciate the extent of the problem so created. Rather than seek to discover the technique whereby the system operates, the tendency is clearly towards the suppression of this knowledge, while creating or advocating rules that require, for their successful implementation, the same degree of competence enjoyed by a domestic legislature or appellate judiciary. That international law requires, as a result of its decentralised nature, significantly greater attention to the questions of compliance and efficacy than one is accustomed to in the orderly environment of internal State law, is something that is quickly forgotten in the rush towards more attractive topics.

The result of this is that the norms generated by theorists are frequently not observed even by a majority of States. Consequently these rules do not have a normative function, nor are they descriptive of reality. But this does not seem to concern these writers for, as is so often the case in the social sciences, rather than question the utility or the validity of their theoretical framework, they adopt a posture reminiscent of Canute, to the effect that there is a considerable amount of behaviour that does not conform to their rules, and the sooner it stops the better. But the central question, how this "illegal" behaviour is to be made to stop, is seldom dealt with, beyond the proposal of schemes in treaty form that would work extremely well if only States would sign such treaties, and comply with them.[1] The underlying problem is that enforcement is seen as a

---

[1] See, *e.g.,* G. Clark and L. B. Sohn, *World Peace Through World Law*, 2nd ed. (1960).

separate topic, one that is to be considered only after the content of the substantive rules has been settled. In international law, however, enforcement and the feasibility of rules is part of the process whereby they are created.

The vain insistence that international reality must conform to carefully-deduced norms is due in large part to the extension into international law of the coercive habit of thought acquired by lawyers in domestic legal systems. As a result of this there is a widespread tendency to assume that international law may maintain a prescriptive function to the same degree that a domestic legal system can, despite its acknowledged lack of centralised authority or overall political stability. As a result of this one tends to find that many writers are quite comfortable with, for example, the reiteration of Lauterpacht's argument that Article 55 of the United Nations Charter contains a specific legal obligation for States to observe the human rights of their citizens, despite substantial evidence of contrary State practice. Widespread reports in the world Press and by non-governmental agencies,[2] such as the Red Cross and Amnesty International, of torture and unlawful incarceration of political prisoners in dozens of countries, and the killing of native populations, are, if they are acknowledged at all, regarded as reports of deviant or "illegal" conduct. Despite the clear lack of implementation, Lauterpacht's conclusion remains unaffected in the legal literature. Similarly the impotence of international law in the face of genocide in Burundi,[3] murder by the thousand in Uganda,[4] and by the million in Cambodia,[5] is only emphasised by reference to the verbal history of the General Assembly, or reasoning by analogy from the opinions of the International Court of Justice. The current failure of international law theorists to come to terms with the reality of the system's limitations is likewise clear in regard to the control of the use of force. Under prevailing theory, which has a strong tendency to isolate law from reality, the Kellogg-Briand Pact is still valid law, as are Articles 45 and 46 of the United Nations Charter. But whether it means anything to talk of such provisions as being valid is an elusive, and largely neglected, topic.

---

[2] On the increase in such organisations, see D. Weissbrodt, "The Role of International Nongovernmental Organisations in the Implementation of Human Rights," 12 *Texas International Law Journal* (1977), p. 293.

[3] "Massacre in the Heart of Africa," *The New York Times*, June 4, 1972, p. 2, col. 1; quoted in N. E. Leech, C. T. Oliver and J. M. Sweeney, *The International Legal System* (1973), p. 653.

[4] "Genocide in Uganda," *The Manchester Guardian* (Airmail Edition), Vol. 119, Nr. 18, October 29, 1978, p. 8, col. 3. The death role is put at 300,000.

[5] A United States Senate Report recently put the number of executions and deaths in Cambodia at 2·5 million, *Senate Report*, Nr. 95–1166, 95th Cong., 2nd Sess. (1978).

If law and legal theory are to have any useful function in international law beyond the making of value-judgments on the activities of individual States, it is imperative that more attention be given to the testing of conclusions and propositions of law against the prevailing international social reality. This is particularly true in view of the clear tendency in the literature towards reliance on verbal legal sources, such as General Assembly resolutions and World Court opinions, rather than on actual State practice. Since international law has no centralised institutional structure, validity can only be tested in relation to reality.

I—The Coercive, Centralised Model of Law

In a passage which ultimately formed the theoretical underpinning of his seminal work on human rights, Sir Hersch Lauterpacht stated that international law is superior to State law and has the ability to enforce its norms. He wrote: "The rights of man cannot, in the long run, be effectively secured except by the twin operation of the law of nature and the law of nations—both conceived as a power superior to the supreme power of the State."[6] While many would agree that international law, like natural law, is morally or conceptually superior to State law, that does not mean that it is politically superior. Likewise, the lack of enforcement mechanisms of the hierarchical type cannot be compensated for simply by "conceiving" of the one system as being superior to the other. If all that Lauterpacht was saying was that international law is morally superior, then that would be unobjectionable, but that is obviously not his position for he talks of "effectively" securing the rights of man, and subsequently added that "[i]t is only within the scheme of an overriding international order that we can give reality to the otherwise contradictory notion that the supreme authority of the State is limited and that the rights of man must be based on that limitation."[7] But he gives no evidence to support the contention of a supranational authority. Nor is there any discussion of how such a system might be brought about, or whether, as many believe, the creation of such a system might entail a greater violation of the rights of individuals than might be protected by its eventual implementation. Instead, in this and in his subsequent work on human rights in international law, he assumes the fully prescriptive model of international law, and proceeds to generate a normative structure which, when set against the reality of State behaviour, can only be characterised as

---

[6] H. Lauterpacht, "The Law of Nations, The Law of Nature and The Rights of Man," 29 *Grotius Society Transactions* (1943), p. 1.

[7] *Ibid.* p. 29.

totally inefficacious. Despite this, in the 30 years since Lauterpacht wrote the above passages, a vast literature on the role of general international law in protecting the rights of individuals has appeared. This literature depends, if one examines it closely, on a naturalistic view of international law as a superior force, and hardly ever does one encounter an attempt to demonstrate this superiority in any practical sense.

There clearly continues to be a bias in favour of Lauterpacht's position. A centralised, hierarchical, coercive legal system is seen as the only feasible solution to virtually every international problem, and little or no attention is given to the fact that the creation and implementation of such a system is a meta-legal issue, one which cannot be controlled by academic or judicial effort, no matter how well-intentioned or sincere. In addition, a supranational legal system cannot be built on the foundation of the current system of international law because the latter is an entirely different system. It does not rely on sanctions but on consent, mutual accommodation and reciprocity.

An example of this current bias can be found in the writings of Professor Falk who is representative in many respects of the "new" international lawyers. He does not present a test for legal validity, but rather seems to rely for support on the self-evident improvement to mankind that would result from a centralised system of enforcement. He is of the opinion that what is needed is "some form of central guidance"[8] and that this may be achieved by means of a populist transitional process which will, on the one hand, centralise control and planning and, on the other hand, decentralise political structures.[9] Quite apart from the intriguing question of the extent to which these two processes may be carried on simultaneously, he fails to provide any information not only on the advantages of such a world system, but also on its feasibility. He seems to be of the opinion that no one can seriously doubt that such a system would be better than the current horizontal structure and that there is really no need to explain how it will be brought about. He does, however, indicate that he sees a parallel between the shift, during the Middle Ages, from centralised Papal control to the State system, and a shift at the present time away from the State system to "some form of central guidance." While he uses the concept of central guidance throughout the article he at no time defines it even to the extent of whether it is primarily political, legal or spiritual in nature. We are once more presumed to believe that central guidance is better than

---

[8] R. Falk, "A New Paradigm for International Legal Studies: Prospects and Proposals," 84 *Yale Law Review* (1975), p. 969.
[9] *Ibid.* p. 1014.

horizontal reciprocity and mutual accommodation. Falk is not unaware of the vast difference between horizontal and vertical legal systems, between unilateral and reciprocal norms,[10] so this presumption in favour of the former cannot be attributed to oversight. As is so often the case with the "new" international lawyers a coercive model of international law is chosen without any assessment of the relative merits of international and supranational law. What is most interesting is that, although the more specific aspects of Falk's programme are attacked, this assumption of a prescriptive model as a goal meets little resistance. There is little need to defend it because it is so widely accepted amongst international lawyers as the only type of legal system. If international law is to be law "properly so called" then it must be modelled on its coercive domestic counterpart. That international law might be law "improperly so called" is one of the taboos of the discipline.

While one might be safe in assuming that Falk is not predicting or advocating the return of Papal rule, he gives no help to the curious in his elusive descriptions of what he envisions. Little help is given by his statement, "I believe that a paradigm shift is both necessary and possible in the years ahead, and that such a shift would help to influence the transitional process in the direction of preferred world order options,"[11] but the remark typifies the nature of Falk's overall argument. First, it hinges on his own personal belief that there is a holistic trend afoot. He gives no evidence of this, though evidence to the contrary immediately springs to mind: the widening gap between developed and undeveloped nations; the politicisation of voting in the United Nations resulting in such partisan behaviour as to render worthless much of its product; the paucity of cases before the International Court of Justice; the spread of nuclear and strategic arms throughout the world; the failure to reach agreement at the Law of the Sea conferences; and the lack of effective action taken in response to the massive violations of human rights in many countries. Falk does not show how such facts fit into his scheme. We are left to agree or disagree with his statement. Those who agree with him will feel that their position has been reinforced. Those who disagree will enjoy a similar experience.

A second problem of the "new" international lawyers' philosophy that is brought into focus by the above quotation, is that it is not at all clear whose preferences will be the basis of the "preferred world options." Falk seems to be of the opinion that world populism will produce a homogeneous value structure despite the widening

---

[10] R. Falk, "International Jurisdiction: Horizontal and Vertical Conceptions of Legal Order," 32 *Temple Law Quarterly* (1959), p. 295.

[11] *Op. cit.* in note 8, above, at p. 998.

gaps between rich and poor, developed and undeveloped, nations. While he shows from his perspective that there are weaknesses in the Clark-Sohn approach, the diplomacy of Henry Kissinger, and the Trilateral Commission, he makes no attempt to present the value preferences of his own world populist system. This lack of information is particularly unfortunate in view of the fact that he commences his article by saying that international lawyers have a key role to play in the creation of a central guidance system, "if they give self-conscious support to a set of *explicit* world order goals that structure both the means and the ends of transition."[12]

A final problem in Falk's position that is attributable to the prescriptive habit of thought is that he is clearly of the opinion that theory can affect reality to such an extent that academic advocacy alone may create world order. Again, this is a position that is shared by the "new" international lawyers, either openly, as in Falk's case, or more discreetly, as in those writers, discussed subsequently, who advocate modification of the concept of customary law formation. The idea that a few academic commentators can have a controlling effect on the flow of world events to the extent of substituting one universal *Grundnorm* for another is shown in a passage in which the transition to the State system is attributed to Hugo Grotius[13] as though Grotius' writing was the sole cause of the nation-State's evolution. Bringing this misconception up to date, Falk advocates the active participation of academics and international lawyers in a "paradigm shift" to his proposed system. This is perhaps the most unrealistic aspect of any world order project. While it is true that academics and international lawyers occasionally have access to those in power, their contribution to global policy is a small one indeed. The fact of the matter is that the functions of the academic and the lawyer are such as to preclude the success of their effective involvement. A lawyer canot be expected to put the advocacy of an unrevealed world order before the interests of his client. If he does, he is likely to be replaced by a lawyer with more predictable loyalties, and his brief foray into the realms of monism will have been in vain. As for academic involvement in such a scheme, the academic function is entirely incompatible with the unremitting advocacy of any idealistic order. Since the academic function is a very subjective activity at the best of times, being primarily concerned with the selection and sifting of material in order to present a coherent whole, any academic who is committed to one particular cause, and openly advocates such a cause without empirical data to support his position, immediately calls his or her professional judgment into

---

[12] *Ibid.* at p. 969 (italics added).
[13] *Ibid.* at p. 976.

question. While it is perfectly acceptable for an academic to adopt the role of advocate in private life, it must not, as Max Weber convincingly demonstrated,[14] be allowed to intrude on his professional activities.

For any academic activity to be of value to others, a clear distinction between the descriptive and the prescriptive aspects of one's work must be maintained. Before any normative activity can succeed, a firm descriptive base must first be built. This is particularly applicable to the study of international law where there is increased reliance on the descriptive aspect of the science of law due to the lack of norm-validating institutions. Curiously, it was the continual objective testing of theories against facts that was the theme running through the work on paradigms which Falk used as the basis for his argument. The major point that Kuhn was making was that when a scientific paradigm fails to account for available data then there is a need for a new paradigm. This new paradigm must then be tested by what Kuhn calls "normal science" and the eventual acceptance of the paradigm is dependent on its being "more successful than [its] competitors in solving a few problems that the group of practitioners has come to recognise as acute."[15] Thus, not only is Falk adopting Kuhn's view of scientific thinking and incorporating it into a normative science, against Kuhn's own advice,[16] but he is failing to use the approach properly by insisting on advocating a position where there is little or no empirical evidence to support it and indeed most would agree the vast weight of evidence is against it. The function of a paradigm is not normative, as Falk uses it, but descriptive, subject to subsequent empirical verification. In any event, just as a scientific rule cannot alter reality, a legal system cannot displace the political system on which it is based.

The idea that emerges from this loose mixture of *lex lata* and *lex ferenda*, of the advocate and the scholar, and of normative and scientific rules that is so typical of the "new" international law is that one is justified in reaching a conclusion concerning the existence of an international norm not so much on the basis of valid legal reasoning within the confines of the system's limited capacity, but rather on the basis of the overall desirability of the conclusion, and the goodness of the proponent's intentions. This naturalistic reasoning presupposes a legal system within which such conclusions may be enforced, regardless of their relationship to reality. It is thus, to a large extent, completely circular in that it assumes what it sets out to

---

[14] M. Weber, "On Science as a Vocation," in M. Truzzi (ed.), *Sociology: The Classic Statements* (1971), p. 22.

[15] T. S. Kuhn, *The Structure of Scientific Revolutions* (1964), p. 42.

[16] *Op. cit.* in note 8, above, at pp. 976–977.

prove. Before one can have a supranational legal order, one must have a pre-existing international political stability, for a viable coercive order is completely impossible in an unstable political environment. Historically law always follows, rather than precedes, the attainment of political stability. Its function is to dispense, in an orderly manner, the monopoly of political power and to ensure that this monopoly is not challenged by alternative systems, such as self help, that would be detrimental to the structure as a whole.

The preoccupation with the prescriptive model of international law is often evident in attempts to show that such a system is already in existence. One argument that is often made is that the United Nations is similar to a government in many respects. The multiple citation of resolutions,[17] or the alleged consistency of resolutions[18] are seen as being tantamount to an international common law. In a recent article by Brownlie[19] an attempt was made to show the parallel between the United Nations and a domestic government by means of emphasising the fact that the United Nations shared many flaws with governments. Among the shortcomings listed as being common to both were: budgets being less than is required for effective action; political weakness in the face of special interests; the use of discretion to avoid confrontation; inefficacious norms; and reliance on consensus rather than formal institutional mechanisms. That such similarities exist is undeniable, but the fact that an entity shares some of the commoner symptoms of governmental weakness could just as easily be applied to a tramway preservation society. What is lacking, and what Brownlie apparently would like to see, or would like to convince us exists, is the possession by that organisation of the degree of political power necessary for it to behave like a government, to enforce its directives and decisions. The argument that international law, or in this instance the United Nations, is as inefficient as a domestic legal system can be, ignores the fact that in a domestic legal system enforcement is always possible by a third party as a last resort. The fact that this heavy reliance on force is not clearly visible at all times is the result of other mechanisms such as the "habit of obedience"[20] which appear after

---

[17] An example of this argument may be found in S. A. Bleicher, "The Legal Signficance of Re-citation of General Assembly Resolutions," 63 *American Journal of International Law* (1969), p. 444.

[18] See, *e.g.*, R. Higgins, "The United Nations and Lawmaking: The Political Organs," *Proceedings of the American Society of International Law* (1970), p. 37.

[19] I. Brownlie, "The United Nations as a Form of Government," 13 *Harvard International Law Journal* (1972), p. 421; For a similar argument see J. H. E. Fried, "How Efficient is International Law?" in K. W. Deutsch and S. Hoffman (eds.), *The Relevance of International Law: Essays in Honour of Leo Gross* (1968), p. 63.

[20] H. L. A. Hart, *The Concept of Law* (1961), pp. 49–64.

the passage of time. This does not mean, however, that force is not the ultimate basis of law. No matter how inept a government might be, such power is always latent within the system. This power cannot be created by wishful thinking, or projected into reality by a comparison of symptoms of its absence. It is either there or it is not, and it is on this fact that all efficacious, prescriptive legal systems are built.

Support for this position, which has frequently been put forward by Schwarzenberger,[21] comes, rather surprisingly, from the writings of Hans Kelsen. Kelsen, in trying to remove the non-legal elements from legal theory, rested the validity of individual norms within a legal system on the validity of superior norms in the same hierarchy. Ultimately, the validity of this hierarchy depends on the validity of the *Grundnorm*. As long as one confines one's inquiry to the lower levels of Kelsen's system this theory is indeed potentially pure of meta-legal factors. But, if one addresses the question of the *Grundnorm's* validity, it quickly becomes apparent that the validity of his system depends on social and political facts, on power. The key to this lies in what Kelsen terms "the principle of effectiveness." In discussing this principle Kelsen states: "Every single norm loses its validity when the total legal order to which it belongs loses its efficacy as a whole. The efficacy of the entire legal order is a necessary condition for the validity of every single norm of the order. A *conditio sine qua non* but not a *conditio per quam*."[22] Thus even Kelsen's pure theory ultimately depends on metapositive factors, the efficacy of the system or the power behind the law. According to him a system which is not efficacious is not legally valid, and efficacy is simply a social fact, not unlike the habit of obedience, for "[t]he content of the basic norm is determined by the facts through which an order is created and applied, to which the behaviour of the individuals regulated by this order by and large conforms ... the validity of a legal order is thus dependent upon its agreement with reality, upon its 'efficacy.'"[23]

II—CUSTOM AND MAJORITY RULE

(a) *The Traditional Approach*

The preceding examples of writers dealing directly with the need for, or the desirability of, a supranational system is only the tip of the iceberg. The major areas in which supranational aspirations are

---

[21] G. Schwarzenberger, *International Law and Order* (1971), p. 1; "International *Jus Cogens?*" 43 *Texas Law Review* (1965), pp. 456–457.

[22] H. Kelsen, *General Theory of Law and State* (1945), p. 118.

[23] *Ibid.* at pp. 119–120.

evident are the developing areas of international law, such as the protection of human rights, the calls for a new international economic order, and international environmental law. While the goals are admirable and possibly beyond reproach from a humanistic viewpoint, it is very doubtful whether the approach that is being taken has any significant chance of success. Unlike Lauterpacht, Falk, Brownlie and the many other writers who confront directly the issue of supranational enforcement, the advocates of the "new" international law usually take a more indirect approach. What they do is to make what appear, at first sight, to be innocuous changes in the definition of custom. But on closer examination it becomes readily apparent that they have moved the theoretical basis of obligation from consent to majority rule. The approach is a little more subtle, but the efficacy, and hence the utility, of the result is no greater.

Consent is a crucial element in the overall functioning of effective international law, and any theory that disregards it is certain to experience severe problems in compliance, when looked at from the normative viewpoint, and in accuracy, when looked at from the descriptive viewpoint. This is so because, without organs of magisterial competence, international law must avoid unilateral commands and gain compliance by eliciting the support of States. This is the reason for the heavy reliance on consent in the traditional theory. It springs, not from a desire to maintain or further the prestige of the nation-State, as is so often charged, but rather from a realisation that since nation-States as a matter of fact are the primary wielders of power in the world, their co-operation is essential for the success of the limited normative role of international law. By requiring consent, express or tacit, on the part of States, the effectiveness of international norms is made possible.

The traditional concept of custom requires that two elements be present, the actual practice of States and *opinio juris*, the sense of obligation. When both of these are present then the rule in question is law. But it is not law in the unilaterally-sanctioned sense that one is familiar with in domestic legal systems. International custom receives a limited prescriptive effect in the following manner. The practice of States is the result of a complex, fluid process of mutual accommodation, trade-offs and reciprocity. It is, for each State, the end result of an evaluation of what it considers to be behaviour rightly expected of it by other States and also an indication of how it wishes to be treated in return by those States. Because of the reciprocal element that is inherent in the process, the practice of States tends towards uniformity in space and time. It is this uniformity that is its primary attraction since States, wishing to make the conduct of their international affairs easier, see the benefit to their own individual decision-making in maintaining this practice. This is the *opinio juris* element; States simply feel obligated, in a reciprocal sense based ultimately on self-interest, to behave as they have been behaving in the past. The prescriptive element at the core of international law is thus the norm that, in the main, the current practices ought to continue. Since there is considerable self-interest in this general maintenance of practice, since the system involves a reciprocal element, and especially since States are already behaving in the indicated manner, the system is virtually self-enforcing. Custom, the basis of all international law is thus primarily descriptive. The normative element is dependent on a community perception of the need for stability and the maintenance of expectations based on prior activity.

(b) *The "New" Approach*
The central theme of the new theory of custom is dependent on the view that the political organs of the United Nations must be endowed with legislative competence. Since this position is clearly untenable on the basis of the treaty obligations involved, another basis has to be found. The alternative method is custom, misconstrued. In an address to the American Society of International Law, Rosalyn Higgins, one of the leading advocates of this position, presented her argument.[24] It is that the resolutions of the General Assembly and Security Council can be used to fulfil the practice element of custom. There is, she says, no longer any need for an analysis of individual State practice, one need only refer to the practice of these organs. While she admits that there is a problem with regard to *opinio juris*, since the motivation for voting in a particular way on any resolution is often unconnected with a legal evaluation of its substance, she considers that problem insufficient to prevent the creation of law.

The problem with her approach is that it fails to provide rules that are self-enforcing, a problem that is absent if one limits oneself to the traditional definition. Higgins' approach fails to appreciate the horizontal enforcement mechanism of international custom outlined above. By using the practice of an organ rather than the practice of States, majority rule is obviously being introduced. Furthermore, even if an organ is perfectly consistent over a substantial period of time, the positions taken by its constituent members may have been anything but consistent. In almost every instance of voting in the political organs of the United Nations there is a sizeable minority which votes negatively. Since the factors that go into

---

[24] *Op. cit.* in note 18, above.

determining the vote are primarily political and ad hoc, this minority will not contain the same States in each instance of voting. Thus it is possible for a majority of States to have voted against a proposition at some time during the history of a perfectly cosistent practice by an organ. If a State is required to conform with this "practice" it should be able to point to negative votes cast by it, and characterise those as an objection to the evolving custom. If Higgins wishes to view positive votes as legally significant for custom, then negative votes must be accorded equal treatment. In addition, if a State has consistently voted against a position, has never acted in accordance with the proposed rule and has no intention of ever acting in accordance with it, then one has a very difficult enforcement problem indeed. Under the traditional theory such a State would not be bound, indeed it is unlikely that there would be a binding customary rule at all. Yet under the "democratic" approach currently in vogue such an objecting State would be bound. But bound by what? Since there is no way of requiring compliance, the best that can be said is that the objecting State is morally bound. While a certain amount of leverage can be gained from establishing moral obligation, Higgins' argument is based ostensibly on legal techniques and is thus not a proof of moral obligation. Nor can it be said to be proof of legal obligation since, while she may be correct in asserting that "[t]he interest of the vast majority is a real and legally relevant one,"[25] that does not by itself require the conclusion that valid international law has been created.

Not only is the practice of States dispensed with as a constituent element of custom under the new approach, but *opinio juris* also receives short shrift. Even if States were voting on the basis of purely legal assessments of the general propositions on which the resolutions were based, there would still remain a serious problem. As already indicated, custom is essentially descriptive, the prescriptive, *opinio juris*, element being dependent on the accuracy of the description of State practice. Under the new approach *opinio juris* cannot mean the same as it does in the traditional definition since the element of practice is missing. *Opinio juris* thus becomes oriented towards what the law ought to be rather than what the current practice is. It is *opinio juris de lege ferenda* rather than *opinio juris de lege lata*. This change, which is easy to overlook, makes the question of the efficacy of the rules produced a major problem, even an insoluble one. Since the *opinio juris* element does not relate to a current state of affairs, which would requie virtually no enforcement, but relates instead to a future situation in which reality must

---

[25] *Ibid.* at p. 42.

be made to conform to the law, it would require a supranational authority for this to be successful. But hypothetical legal systems cannot achieve concrete results. The conclusions presented are thus invariably attractive, but cannot be implemented.

Despite such problems, a considerable number of writers have endorsed this position. Akehurst, for example, has rejected the "restrictive" definition[26] of traditional international law in favour of a broader, more dynamic view. The fact that the traditional definition is "restrictive" for very sound reasons received little or no attention. Akehurst does, however, avoid the problems faced by Higgins' acceptance of *opinio juris de lege ferenda* and instead limits the material that may form the basis of custom to the "practice" of the General Assembly where the assertions made concern *lex lata*.[27] This removes part of the problem, but by no means all of it for, by including statements about law within "State practice" rather than insisting on the traditional requirement of actual State activity, the enforcement problem still remains. This is so because there is considerably less commitment to a position that is taken by mere vote at an Assembly meeting than is the case when a State is faced with the decision of whether or not to behave in a particular manner. This inconsistency is not due entirely to a lack of good faith on the part of States. More often than not States fail to live up to such announced standards for a variety of reasons that were not considered or foreseen at the time of the vote. For example, internal political pressure may have built up unpredictably, opposing the position taken. Economic pressures likewise can have a decisive effect on the relationship between verbal and actual behaviour, as has been shown most clearly in the history of the economic sanctions imposed on Rhodesia. That there was a gap between announced standards and subsequent practice on the part of many States is all the more relevant here in view of the mandatory nature of the Security Council's actions. To sum up, a State that is actually involved in an international activity has a higher commitment to that activity than it does in a mere vote because the activity involves the entire filtering process of reciprocity and mutual accommodation that is the very core of international law. A State must assess whether the position it takes is not only one which it is willing to advocate for itself but is also one which it is willing to tolerate when adversely applied to it by other States. This is a far cry from voting for or against a non-binding resolution in New York City.

---

[26] M. Akehurst, "Custom as a Source of International Law," XLVII *British Year Book of International Law* (1974–75), p. 1.

[27] *Ibid.* at p. 6.

III—THE ROLE OF THE INTERNATIONAL
COURT OF JUSTICE

(a) *Academic Commentary*

Another symptom of the presumption in favour of too great a prescriptive role for international law is to be found in the use of the opinions of the International Court of Justice as sources of law. Brownlie, for example, in discussing the General Assembly's tendency to act *ultra vires* stated that this had been "legitimated by the advisory opinion of the International Court in the Namibia case."[28] This statement is indicative of the extent to which the juridical positivism of a common law system tends to be transferred into the international arena. The Court is treated as though it were a fully competent domestic court, the opinions of which may be analysed in order to find generally-binding law. But the use of this technique assumes yet again the existence of a supranational authority where none exists. *Stare decisis* does not, and cannot, apply in the present international system. The International Court of Justice, consistent with the traditional theory of international law, bases its jurisdiction firmly on State consent.[29] This acknowledgment of the importance of State consent has the effect of substantially increasing the compliance rate of the Court's judgments since, in deciding whether to appear before the Court, a State can assess its own willingness to comply with an adverse decision. A State that is not willing to comply with such a decision will simply not appear before the Court. This system is clearly unsatisfactory to those who think in terms of coercive legal orders, but it is the prevailing system nonetheless. The Court, on the basis of the terms of its Statute and as a matter of political reality, cannot create a legal rule adverse to a State that is not a party to the proceedings, which is the essence of the *stare decisis* philosophy. To assume that it can is to lose oneself in a world of unenforceable norms.

Indeed, even when State consent is taken into account, there is no guarantee that compliance will result. The continuing lack of implementation of the Corfu Channel Judgment, to mention only one example, is indicative of this. If there are problems under the traditional system then, it is submitted, there will be a significant increase in non-compliance if the theoretical base of international law is allowed to shift towards any presumption of magisterial competence on the part of the Court.

The juridical positivism of the "new" international lawyers is categorically dismissed by Article 59 of the Court's Statute which

---

[28] Brownlie, *op. cit.* in note 19, above, pp. 422–423.
[29] Art. 36, Statute of the International Court of Justice.

quite clearly states that the opinions of the Court are not law-creating in any general sense, but only affect the specific case submitted to the Court.[30] While it may be true that the opinions of the Court are of great persuasive value they are not sources of law and thus, along with the writings of academic commentators, are relegated to the position of "subsidiary means for the determination of rules of law" in Article 38 of the Statute.[31] Thus, in order to reach the conclusion that the Court has "legitimated" any historical activity of the General Assembly, one must ignore completely three valid treaty provisions of the Statue of the International Court of Justice. If the aim is to establish a system of supranational law by such dexterity, one might consider that in doing so the prevailing legal norms of the present system are being ignored. It is curious to disregard law, however "restrictive" it may be, in order to attempt to create a higher order which, it is safe to assume, is worthy of our attention because it is based on the rule of law. *Ex injuria jus non oritur.*

Another question that merits attention is the relationship between custom and the Court as sources of law. Akehurst, for example, relies very heavily on the Court's opinions in putting forward his broader theory of custom, citing in the process passages from about a dozen cases. But he does not discuss the legal significance of these cases as they relate to the creation of law. In view of Article 38 of the Court's Statute, there is reason to doubt that the Court's opinions can ever have any effect on the definition of what constitutes custom. It would appear that, as a primary source of law, custom is of a much higher priority than the "subsidiary means" of judicial decisions. Clearly, since custom is a source of law and the Court is not, the Court does not have the power, as it is presently constituted, to alter the definition of custom in any significant way. Akehurst, Higgins *et al.* must demonstrate on what basis the Court is empowered authoritatively to alter a primary source of law to the extent they advocate. Perhaps there is a convincing argument. If so, it needs clearly to be made.

A final point merits attention on the question of the academic treatment of the Court's role as lawmaker. If the Court cannot, under Article 59, create generally binding norms in contentious cases, precisely what is the legal significance of an advisory opinion? Brownlie's statement, quoted above, clearly envisions an advisory

---

[30] *Ibid.* Art. 59 which states, "The decision of the Court has no binding force except between the parties and in respect of that particular case."

[31] *Ibid.* Art. 38 which states, "The Court ... shall apply ... subject to the provisions of Article 59, judicial decisions and the teachings of the most highly qualified publicists of the various nations, as subsidiary means for the determination of rules of law."

opinion "legitimating" *ultra vires* United Nations activity. Yet an advisory opinion is not even binding on the organisation that requested it. This extremely liberal use of juridical positivism is increasingly common in articles purporting to generate rules in the developing areas of international law. The 1971 opinion on South-West Africa is a particular favourite since there are many passages in it which indicate, as one writer put it, "an extended role for the Court and for international law and organisation."[32] The quoted writer is thus not only assuming that the Court has law-making power and the power to modify the basic principles of international law, but also that it may do so on the basis of an advisory opinion. Unfortunately, no indication is given of the extent to which this position is accepted in the practice of States. Schwelb, long an advocate of the protection of human rights in international law, and a writer to whom the discipline owes a great deal, also fell prey to the temptation. He cited the 1971 Opinion[33] and concluded therefrom that there was an obligation on South Africa flowing from it. He was reinforced somewhat in his conclusion by being able to point to the fact that the decision was in agreement with the writings of Hersch Lauterpacht, but with respect to all concerned, the fact that two "subsidiary means" agree, especially when one of those means is only an advisory opinion, is not a particularly strong indication of valid law. Schwelb's perception of the court in common law terms is further evidenced by his use of the distinction between *ratio decidendi* and *obiter dictum* in his analysis,[34] a technique also used by Akehurst.[35]

(b) *Judicial Activism*

For some time, the view that the International Court of Justice could adopt a law-creating role was confined largely to academic circles. While there were writers whose theories assumed, explicitly or implicitly, the superiority of international law in terms of power, this philosophy did not appear significantly in the Court's opinions. There was always a minority on the Court that felt that it should take a more dynamic role, but it was only recently that this position came to the fore. Attention became focused on Judge Tanaka's Dissenting Opinion in the 1966 decision on South-West Africa[36] which,

---

[32] N. K. Hevener, "The 1971 South-West African Opinion, A New International Juridical Philosophy," 24 *International and Comparative Law Quarterly* (1975), p. 807.

[33] E. Schwelb, "The International Court of Justice and The Human Rights Clauses of the Charter," 66 *American Journal of International Law* (1972), p. 346.

[34] *Ibid.* at p. 350.

[35] *Op. cit.* in note 26, above, at p. 33.

[36] *South-West Africa, Second Phase*, I.C.J. Reports 1966, p. 248.

despite its being a dissent,[37] was cited and discussed frequently as support for the evolution of a dynamic theory. His statements concerning the development of international law by consensus rather than by consent were obviously welcome to the "new" international lawyers. For example, without explaining the source of authority or competence of the political organs, he stated, "the accumulation of *authoritative* pronouncements such as resolutions, declarations, decisions, etc., concerning the interpretation of the Charter by the *competent* organs of the international community can be characterised as evidence of the international custom referred to in Article 38 (1) (*b*)."[38] What Judge Tanaka did, as Lauterpacht had suggested, was to place international law on a par with natural law and attempt to create, particularly in the context of human rights, an area of *jus cogens*. The attempt fails to take account of the fact that State practice has not yet achieved the standards of behaviour that are advanced, nor does it suggest any means of implementation. Central to this dynamic view of international law is a disregard for State sovereignty, evidenced by unsuccessful attempts to show that Article 2 (7) of the Charter is now invalid, either on a legal or on a practical basis.[39] That this disregard should produce little in the way of concrete results should serve as a warning to the Court that it is reaching the limits of its usefulness to international law, and the limits of tolerance of nation-States.

By 1971, the dynamic philosophy of the Court's function had spread, and it was on this basis that the Court could conclude that South Africa was under an obligation to terminate its administration and occupation of the territory of Namibia. The efficacy problem of the new philosophy is indicated by the fact that, seven years after the decision, South Africa still occupies and administers the territory. The issue is thus much more crucial to the future of a viable international law than whether some academic theories are more valid than others. The issue now involves the Court's own credibility. Since the Court has to rely on an amalgam of non-coercive techniques for its effectiveness, its credibility is perhaps its greatest asset. Further, even if one were willing to discard the role of third-party adjudication as being irrelevant to a horizontal legal order, the fact

---

[37] In line with the cavalier treatment of legal materials it is not unusual to see a dissenting opinion analysed in much the same way as the Court's majority opinion. In view of Art. 59 of the Court's statute, this practice is, however, probably defensible. For other examples see, *op. cit.* in note 17, above, at p. 448; and in note 18, above, at pp. 39 and 47.

[38] *Op. cit.* in note 36, above, at p. 292 (italics added).

[39] For an assessment of the various arguments that have been presented in an attempt to undermine the authority of Art. 2 (7) see J. S. Watson, "Autointerpretation, Competence and the Continuing Validity of Article 2 (7) of the United Nations Charter," 71 *American Journal of International Law* (1977), p. 60.

remains that there is a symbiotic relationship between the Court's credibility and that of the entire legal order.

Those who are concerned with the viability of the international legal order, as well as those who are concerned with the role of the Court, should assess whether the modest gains that accrue from the attempt at a dynamic role is really worth the risk. A cavalier treatment of the realities of the international legal system by the Court can very quickly call into question the efficacy and the validity of the entire system. If this is done without any concrete results being achieved to compensate for it, then one has paid very dearly indeed for the luxury of adding the phrase "international law" to what might otherwise be a perfectly defensible position.

The gap of seven years since the Court's decision indicates that even if South Africa were to withdraw from Namibia in the near future, it will be more the result of political pressure from African and Western countries than the result of a supranational legal order. Even those who insist on a very loose definition of law must see the need for a reasonably close causal connection between the announcement of a norm and its subsequent implementation. The *ad hoc* and relatively unpredictable processes of international politics must be kept separate from international law if the latter is to have any meaning of its own.

What the Court must bear in mind is that, relying as it does on consent, the adoption of a dynamic, teleological reasoning process is likely to be counterproductive. Rather than causing States to behave in conformity with its "common law" directives, the effect will be to discourage States from ever appearing before the court. If States cannot be sure of the rules which will be applied by the Court, and cannot predict the approach that will be taken, there is little likelihood that even the historically sparse use of the Court will continue. This would seem to be supported by the slimness of the last three volumes of the reports, following two further instances of dynamic legal reasoning. In both the Fisheries Jurisdiction Case[40] and the Nuclear Tests Case[41] interim measures of protection were ignored by Iceland and France respectively. One author, in a detailed and sympathetic analysis of these two cases noted the liberalisation of the circumstances in which such relief may be granted, and stated: "The expansionist tendency inevitably conflicts with the fundamental rule that the jurisdiction of an international tribunal depends upon consent ... the Court cannot afford to reach decisions ...

---

[40] *Fisheries Jurisdiction (United Kingdom* v. *Iceland), Interim Protection,* I.C.J. Reports 1972, p. 12.
[41] *Nuclear Tests (Australia* v. *France), Interim Protection,* I.C.L. Reports 1073, p. 99.

which suggest support for rules which are too far advanced for community acceptance."[42]

IV—The Legality of a Coercive System

In the previous discussion of the process whereby custom, the effective basis of international law, creates a limited prescriptive effect due to the shared self-interest of States in the maintenance of predictable behaviour patterns, the emphasis was placed on the internal aspect of reciprocity and no mention was made of the external (coercive) methods of inducing compliance. The external methods comprise the varying degrees of force that can be used by other interested States either to force the deviant State into immediate compliance, or else to intimidate that and other States to such an extent that they will be deterred from future noncompliance. This technique, self-help, is often seen as forming an integral part of the international legal system[43] and it obviously has great attraction for those who insist on a coercive element in the definition of law.

There are however, two problems with this attempt at indirect enforceability in international law. The first is that the use of even a modicum of force is an unlikely and an inappropriate response to a violation of the typical international norm. It is highly unlikely, for example, that it would follow the violation of treaty provisions on topics such as import quotas, the exchange of technical information or maritime safety. In these and the vast majority of cases the motivation for compliance is still the internal one of keeping one's word for the general benefit, *pacta sunt servanda*. The typical response to a violation of an international norm falls well short of coercion in even the loosest sense of the word, and usually takes the form of protest, or the withdrawal of benefits of approximately the same level in a related or unrelated area. This process of trading one minor violation for another is well within the reciprocal, self-adjusting model of international law. In all but the most highly-charged issues coercion is an unlikely and an inefficient response to norm violation, and thus may be discounted as a viable enforcement mechanism.

The second reason for rejecting the use of force in this connection is that it is illegal.[44] Articles 2 (3) and 2 (4) of the Charter prohibit

---

[42] P. J. Goldsworthy, "Interim Measures of Protection in the International Court of Justice," 68 *American Journal of International Law* (1974), pp. 262–263.

[43] See, *e.g.*, H. Kelsen, *Principles of International Law* (1952), p. 14.

[44] This point is more fully developed by Fitzmaurice in "The Foundations of the Authority of International Law and the Problem of Enforcement," 19 *Modern Law Review* (1956), p. 1.

self-help in very specific terms. The philosophy behind this was to put a monopoly of the legitimate use of force into the hands of the Security Council. In attempting to reach that goal, by oversight or by intention, these articles, and Article 2 (4) in particular, imposed a general ban on the use of force. Even more important for our purposes is that Article 2 (4) also bans the threat of force, for it is the deterrent effect of the threat of force that is at the core of any coercive system.

The instances in which the use of force is permitted the organisation are of little help to those who see this ban as an unwelcome predicament. The Security Council is permitted to use force in obtaining compliance with an individual judgment of the International Court of Justice,[45] but not its "common law." It may also use forceful means to cope with breaches of the peace under Chapter VII[46] but the latter is obviously not addressed to matters of routine enforcement of legal rules. Even if it were, it is not likely that disinterested or unaffected States would be sufficiently motivated to involve themselves in the enforcement of rules affecting only a few States. The history of the collective security system is sufficient proof of that. Finally, Article 51, which permits the use of force to individual States in self-defence, is no less helpful to the advocates of self-help since it only permits the use of force "if an armed attack occurs."

International law has thus outlawed coercion by other States as a means of compliance with its norms. While this might dismay those with a coercive concept of law, it is entirely consistent with the perception of international law as a decentralised, reciprocal system based ultimately on State consent.

V—Conclusions

Most legal theories presuppose the existence of developed legal institutions and their test of legal validity is invariably tied to some such source, be it the sovereign, the legislature or the courts. In international law there are no such institutions and thus the validity of its rules must be founded on some other basis. This other basis, this other "institution," is the practice of sovereign States. This is acknowledged in the traditional concept of custom which has long formed the ultimate basis for legal validity.

International law cannot, by its own terms and as a matter of political reality, prescribe rules of conduct except in a very limited

---

[45] Art. 94 (2) of the UN Charter.
[46] *Ibid*. Art. 39.

sense. Its prescriptive effect is entirely dependent on the accuracy of the codification of State practice. Any attempt at altering or studiously ignoring this basic fact by superimposing a simplistic model of coercive law derived from domestic law is destined to result in inefficacious rules and sterile theory. To do so is to ignore the unique nature of international law, and to emphasise its weaknesses rather than its strengths.

THE INTERNATIONAL CENTRE FOR SETTLEMENT OF INVESTMENT DISPUTES

By

PATRICK J. O'KEEFE

THE Convention on the Settlement of Investment Disputes between States and Nationals of other States came into force on October 14, 1966. It established the International Centre for Settlement of Investment Disputes (ICSID). The Convention thus provided the facilities for conducting a conciliation or arbitration as well as a detailed procedure for resolving such disputes as came within its term of reference. As of June 30, 1978, there were 71 States party to the Convention.

In practical terms conciliation plays a minor role to arbitration in the operation of the scheme established by the Convention. Academic studies of the Convention and the ICSID scarcely refer to it. Material issued by the ICSID makes little mention of it. The ICSID has not publicly recorded any request for institution of conciliation proceedings.

Nine times have the arbitration facilities and procedures been used since 1966:

Registered	Parties	Current status (June 1978)
December 27, 1971	Holiday Inns/Occidental Petroleum v. Government of Morocco	Proceedings continuing
March 6, 1974	Adriano Gardella SpA v. Government of Ivory Coast	Award rendered on August 29, 1977
June 21, 1974	Alcoa Minerals of Jamaica Inc. v. Government of Jamaica	Proceedings discontinued on February 27, 1977, after amicable settlement
June 21, 1974	Kaiser Bauxite Company v. Government of Jamaica	Proceedings discontinued on February 27, 1977, after amicable settlement
June 21, 1974	Reynolds Jamaica Mines Ltd. and Reynolds Metals Company v. Government of Jamaica	Proceedings discontinued on October 12, 1977, after amicable settlement
October 5, 1976	Government of Gabon v. Société SERETE S.A.	Proceedings discontinued on February 27, 1978, after amicable settlement
November 4, 1977	AGIP SpA v. Government of the People's Republic of Congo	Tribunal being constituted

286

Registered	Parties	Current status (June 1978)
December 15, 1977	Société Ltd. Benvenuti & Bonfant srl v. Government of the People's Republic of Congo	Tribunal constituted
March 20, 1978	Gaudalupe Gas Products Corporation v. The Federal Military Government of Nigeria	Tribunal being constituted

In reality the nine instances listed arise from only six incidents. As shown three instances involved the Government of Jamaica and two the Government of the People's Republic of Congo. Thus, just six incidents involving a dispute over investment between a national of one State and the government of another have come for resolution under the Convention in the 12 years of its legal existence. One might say that there has been one incident come forward in each of the past three years but this does not really add much to the record.

The ICSID incurred unrecovered running costs of $US1,349,186 in the years 1966–78. This represents the value of services provided by the International Bank for Reconstruction and Development: services of staff members and consultants plus other administrative services and facilities. It allows for costs recouped by sales of publications and registrations. We thus have a facility costing in the vicinity of $1 million being used in only six incidents of the type it was established to deal with. Could that money have been better spent elsewhere, or is this not a fair assessment of the situation of the ICSID?

I—Basis for Valuing ICSID

In 1976 the Secretary-General of the ICSID made this statement: "In view of the large number of existing ICSID arrangements, the small number of arbitration cases appears to confirm the often expressed belief that the very existence of binding arbitration arrangements acts as a powerful incentive for the amicable settlement of such disputes as may arise."[1]

On this basis, when we examine the value of such a facility as the ICSID we should look, not at the number of times it has been used for arbitration but rather at the impact of its mere existence. Knowing that arbitration will occur if a dispute is not settled induces settlement. This is really an *in terrorem* argument. It is one for which there is considerable support in general arbitration; "... in international commerce clauses on arbitration fulfil principally a

---

[1] ICSID, *Tenth Annual Report 1975/76*, p. 3.

prophylactic, preventive function. . . ."[2] This arises from the notion that the existence of an arbitration clause "compels the disputants to recognize that if they cannot agree on a solution themselves, then, at the instance of any one of them, they may be bound by the decision of a third person. The introduction of such a person involves a significant qualitative change in the nature of the dispute and rather than face such possibility there may be greater readiness to nego- tiate and compromise rather than delay resolution of the dispute or allow it to continue in the hope of wearing the other party down."[3]

The validity of this argument as applied to the role of the ICSID depends on the extent to which provision actually is made in invest- ment contracts for arbitration under ICSID auspices. Here it is impossible to obtain accurate figures. The Secretary-General of the ICSID in 1974 estimated that "the volume of investments covered by ICSID clauses" probably run "into several thousands of millions of dollars."[4] Although large in absolute terms this sum is not particu- larly significant when considered in the light of total world foreign direct investment.

Some argument has been made that provision for ICSID arbitra- tion in investment contracts will increase as the laws of various countries accept ICSID jurisdiction in advance. In other words, that countries will enact laws requiring all, or specified classes of, investment contracts to be entered into on the basis that they contain an ICSID arbitration clause. There was a spate of such laws in the period 1970–74. The ICSID now lists 12 States with provi- sions relating to itself in national investment laws.[5] In only one case is the legislation later than 1974—Sri Lanka, 1978.

The ICSID lists 30 bilateral treaties in force providing for its jurisdiction in the case of disputes arising out of investments covered by the treaty or requiring investors to accept ICSID arbitration clauses.[6] An example is the Agreement of July 22, 1975, between Singapore and the United Kingdom on Promotion and Protection of Investments. Most of the 30 bilateral treaties mentioned came into force during the years 1972–76—23 in all and 15 during 1975 and 1976. There were only five such treaties in 1977 and none in 1978. These figures are not perfectly accurate for the years 1976, 1977 and 1978. Recording of a treaty will depend on when the ICSID is informed or learns of its existence. Nevertheless, a comparison of

---

[2] G. Ginsburgs, "Execution of Foreign Commerical Arbitral Awards in Post-War Soviet Bilateral Treaty Practice," 9 *Canadian Yearbook of International Law* (1971), p. 99.

[3] P. J. O'Keefe, *Arbitration in International Trade* (1975), p. 221.

[4] A. Broches, "Arbitration in Investment Disputes," in C. M. Schmitthoff (ed.), *International Commercial Arbitration* (1974–75), p. 299.

[5] ICSID, *Twelfth Annual Report 1977/78*, p. 30.

[6] *Ibid.* p. 22.

previous Reports reveals that the ICSID keeps a close watch in this regard and figures for immediate years will need only marginal increases at a later date to take account of presently unrecorded treaties. On this basis the number of treaties for each year can be taken as relatively correct. A further interesting point is that only 20 States are party to these treaties; seven being party to only one treaty. France and the Netherlands are party to 10 and nine respectively, *i.e.* two-thirds of all such treaties.

On the basis of the above information there would seem to have been a trend on the part of States to require acceptance of ICSID jurisdiction in investment contracts whether on a unilateral (in municipal legislation) or bilateral (in international treaties) basis. This trend appears to have peaked in the middle of the current decade. Since 1976 it has slowed. Moreover, less than one-third of the States party to the Convention have entered into these bilateral treaties and even then a great proportion of those involve France and the Netherlands in particular.

What is the position in other bodies offering arbitral facilities? Statistics are difficult to establish. There are few of these bodies appropriate for and capable of conducting arbitration of an international investment dispute. One which may be appropriate is the Court of Arbitration of the International Chamber of Commerce (ICC). The function of this institution is to "provide for the settlement by arbitration of business disputes of an international character" in accordance with the Rules of Conciliation and Arbitration of the International Chamber of Commerce.[7] Does this overlap the jurisdiction of the ICSID? The latter has stated with reference to the ICC system of arbitration "... a number of Contracting States, in particular among the developing countries, are reluctant to accept existing facilities for dispute settlement for other than routine commercial cases and would prefer to avail themselves of the services of the Centre."[8] This was said in the context of a discussion concerning borderline cases of "investment" and what might be comprehended by that term as defining the jurisdiction of the ICSID. On the other hand, the ICC states that the average sum involved in arbitrations supervised by its Court "... has risen steadily in recent years, due firstly to disputes concerning very large contracts for public works on industrial projects, often in developing countries. ..."[9] Not all of these contracts would be covered by the term "investment" used in

---

[7] ICC Publication 291.

[8] ICSID Doc. AC/78/8, "Rules Governing the Additional Facility for the Administration of Proceedings by the Secretariat of the International Centre for Settlement of Investment Disputes (Additional Facility Rules)," p. 4.

[9] ICC Publication 301, p. 34.

establishing the jurisdiction of the ICSID. Yet, in view of this observation concerning the developing countries, it is relevant that approximately 27 per cent. of parties to Court-administered arbitrations involve government organisations.[10] In real terms this has been a rising figure.

The American Arbitration Association has administered arbitrations of disputes involving governments but these are rare; rarer yet are those of a nature which would allow them to come to the ICSID. The Japan Commercial Arbitration Association has had no case of the kind we are discussing. The Permanent Court of Arbitration, while competent in this field, has administered only one such arbitration since 1950.[11] Other arbitral institutions would not appear to be relevant. The ICC Court of Arbitration is thus the body of major significance.

Some of the most significant arbitrations involving international investment of recent years have been ad hoc, *i.e.* there has been no arbitral institution appointed with competence to administer and supervise the arbitration proceedings. An example is the Arbitration in the dispute between Texaco Overseas Petroleum Company and California Asiatic Oil Company on the one hand and the Government of the Libyan Arab Republic on the other.[12] The sole arbitrator was appointed by the President of the International Court of Justice; the procedure determined by the parties and arbitrator decided on the basis of international law. A second example is the Arbitration between the British Petroleum Company and the Government of the Libyan Arab Republic.[13] Some of these arbitrations, such as the first mentioned, depend on agreements made before the ICSID was established. However, this should not obscure the fact that it is possible for parties to have recourse to arbitration under ICSID auspices after the dispute has arisen and, if there be mutual agreement, in spite of a previous acceptance of an alternative form. All that is required in terms of the Convention is for the parties, a Contracting State and a national of another Contracting State, to consent in writing to submit to the ICSID. The fact that this has not been done must surely indicate a lack of complete acceptance of the role of the ICSID.

At the present moment we thus have a body which, over a period of 12 years, has been utilised as a result of six incidents. Advance provision for recourse to its facilities is declining in relative terms.

[10] Letter to author from Secretary-General, ICC, September 19, 1978.
[11] *Op. cit.* in note 3, above, at p. 228.
[12] 17 *International Legal Materials* (1978), pp. 1–37.
[13] E. W. Benton, "The Libyan Expropriations: Further Developments on the Remedy of Invalidation of Title," 11 *Houston Law Review* (1974), p. 938.

The use of the ICC Court of Arbitration as an institution providing somewhat equivalent facilities has increased over the same period and recourse to ad hoc arbitration has continued.

Does it mean anything in these circumstances to claim, as does the ICSID, that: "It was recognized from the beginning that the success of the Centre should not be measured by the number of disputes submitted to it, but rather by the degree of willingness of governments and investors to accept conciliation and arbitration under the auspices of the Centre."[14] The above empirical evidence suggests that the degree of willingness displayed by governments is declining with the passage of years.

The statement is highly ambiguous as indicating a measure by which the value of the ICSID may be established. A cynic could say that governments and investors are perfectly willing to adopt an ineffective procedure. By doing this they lose nothing of their freedom to manoeuvre in the event of a dispute and at the same time gain public acclaim for their support of what is conceived of as a worthy project. On the other hand, if the statement is taken on its face value, as a measure of success of the ICSID, it must go back to the *in terrorem* argument. In either case the effectiveness of the facilities and procedures available is of paramount importance. If these are effective the cynical view as stated loses its validity while the *in terrorem* argument gains in importance.

II—Effectiveness of the ICSID

There are factors both external and internal that bear on the question of how effective are the facilities offered by the ICSID and the procedures established by the Convention.

(a) *External Factors*

First among the external factors are the number and spread of States party to the Convention. As indicated there are 71 States with this status. Only States members of the International Bank for Reconstruction and Development may become party to the Convention of their own volition. Others must first receive an invitation to sign approved by two-thirds of the members of the Administrative Council of the ICSID. With the exception of Switzerland, States currently party to the Convention are also members of the Bank, comprising 54 per cent. of its total membership. The major suppliers of foreign direct investment capital and members of Group B in the United Nations political groupings are numbered among the 71.

---

[14] ICSID, *Tenth Annual Report 1975/76*, p. 3.

The most notable omissions from Group B are Canada, Australia and New Zealand. These States have relatively little foreign investment of their own but rather are on the receiving end to a greater extent than others in Group B. The others have obviously become party to the Convention in order to give their nationals the opportunity, if they so wish, of consenting to use of the facilities and procedures available. These become another weapon in the armoury for protection of foreign investment. At the same time, in cases where recourse has been made to the jurisdiction of the ICSID, the State of the national involved cannot invoke the principle of diplomatic protection. In many instances this may be very convenient politically for that State as justifying its refusal to take action on behalf of the national. The Convention states that diplomatic protection "shall not include informal diplomatic exchanges for the sole purpose of facilitating a settlement of the dispute" (Art. 27). One may wonder just how effective the prohibition on State interference beyond this will be in the event of a dispute where the investor or investment are of importance to the State of the national. On the other hand, the fact that most members of Group B are party to the Convention means that, if enforcement of an award becomes necessary, it is easier to find a jurisdiction where assets are available for attachment or satisfaction.

The other notable feature about the geographical spread of States party to the Convention is the virtual complete absence of those from Central and South America—a most important region as a destination for investment funds and one of considerable risk for the investor. The reasons for this boycotting of the Convention are said to rest mainly on arguments derived from the Calvo Doctrine as espoused by those States; namely, the impermissibility of State intervention in the affairs of another State and the necessity for equality of treatment between nationals and foreigners.[15] The Secretary-General of the ICSID has refuted these arguments and commented that "... Latin American opposition to the Convention was essentially based on strongly held political-philosophical views and sovereignty concepts peculiar to that part of the world, which to some outside observers may appear to have outlived both their usefulness and their justification."[16]

The absence of States from the Central and South American region is a substantial defect in the effectiveness of the ICSID. The presence of so many from Group B enhances prospects for the

---

[15] P. C. Szasy, "The Investment Disputes Convention and Latin America," 11 *Virginia Journal of International Law* (1971), pp. 256–265.

[16] A. Broches, "The Convention on the Settlement of Investment Disputes between States and Nationals of Other States," 136 *Hague Recueil* (1972), p. 348.

ICSID playing a significant role, particularly from the point of view of enforcement.

Another external factor which affects the effectiveness of the ICSID is the results to date of arbitrations administered by the ICSID. When considering the utility of resort to such a body as the ICSID, businessmen, governments and their respective legal advisers must be influenced by the standing of the body. This, to a large extent, is established by the conduct and outcome of previous arbitrations. The parties to an arbitration need certainty and justice in resolving the dispute together often with speed of resolution, cheapness, expertise on the part of the tribunal, maintenance of their business relationship, privacy or secrecy and the establishment of a degree of formality. Whether one can expect these needs to be met when resorting to arbitration under the auspices of a particular institution depends on the past history of that institution. The ICSID is thus in a difficult situation. Potential users will hesitate when confronted with the small number of resolved disputes—particularly those going forward to award and compliance—while a record cannot be built but by their having recourse to the system.

In part this problem is related to the low level of awareness among the investing community and, although probably to a lesser degree, among governments, of the ICSID and its facilities and procedures. A study done in the United States has shown that a significant proportion of major companies of that State involved in substantial foreign investment activities have never heard of the ICSID. Others, although aware of the ICSID, have not considered utilising its facilities.[17] The United States is one of the world's largest suppliers of foreign investment funds. It is the State in which the ICSID is located; making for easy access and collection of information. If the above is the situation in the United States of America what is it likely to be in other States? Some 110 legal articles and books have been written on the Convention. Officers of the ICSID have made speeches when invited and attended appropriate seminars. The ICSID is publishing a loose-leaf service *Investment Laws of the World—Developing Countries*. It would seem that these activities are not sufficient to bring knowledge of the ICSID to the appropriate people. Major emphasis has been placed on contacting the business legal adviser. He undoubtedly plays a significant role—particularly in American business operations. Yet in providing for dispute settlement the lawyer does not always play a dominant role. Rather it is the businessman who ultimately decides what, if any, provision there will be—a decision often based on extra-legal con-

---

[17] J. K. Ryans and J. C. Baker, "The International Centre for Settlement of Investment Disputes," 10 *Journal of World Trade Law* (1976), pp. 65–79.

siderations.[18] In confronting its potential audience the ICSID may
have to expand its range of addressees. Ryans and Baker suggest
"... more references and articles on the Convention and ICSID in
accounting/finance journals or general business publications ...
increased attempts to publicize the Convention and the Centre in
public business forums." They do acknowledge "... that the Centre
does not have the staff or funding for extensively employing such
promotional efforts."[19]

Both the above factors bearing on the effectiveness of the ICSID
interact with another entirely beyond its control. Although either
party may initiate proceedings and, jurisdiction being established,
these may proceed independently of the presence of the other party,
the State concerned is in a superior position if it can offer further
investment opportunities. The threat can be made that none of these
will come the way of the national if he persists in pursuing the
arbitration. In the long term it may be more profitable for the
national to accept defeat on one issue in the expectation of future
profits. This is in the nature of business and inherent in the relationship over which the ICSID has jurisdiction.

Finally, the persons of the arbitrators can affect the effectiveness
of the ICSID. It maintains a Panel of Arbitrators and a Panel of
Conciliators. Forty-two States have exercised their right under the
Convention (Art. 13) to appoint up to four persons to the Panel of
Arbitrators and 41 to that of Conciliators. The last contains 145
names while there are 144 arbitrators listed. The Chairman of the
Administrative Council has designated one person out of the 10 to
which he is entitled.[20]

The experience of the ICSID with these Panels to date appears
not to have been entirely happy. The Secretary-General has
emphasised the fact that less than "... two-thirds of the Contracting
States have exercised their right of designation, and several Contracting States have failed to keep their designations current."[21] The
ICSID has exhorted member states to make appointments to the
Panels so that, not only may parties have a pool of talent easily
available but also the Chairman has the widest possible choice if he
is called upon to nominate an arbitrator.[22]

At the same time the ICSID has admonished governments to be
careful in the appointments they make. The Convention requires

---

[18] Lazarus *et al.*, *Resolving Business Disputes: the Potential of Commercial Arbitration*
(1965), Nr. 85 American Management Association Reports.
[19] *Op. cit.* in note 17, above, at p. 79.
[20] This information is at June 30, 1978.
[21] ICSID, *Twelfth Annual Report 1977/78*, p. 4.
[22] *Ibid.*

persons designated to serve to be "... of high moral character and recognized competence in the fields of law, commerce, industry or finance, who may be relied upon to exercise independent judgment" (Art. 14). This is said to indicate an "intention to obtain participation in the Panels of men with a wide range of abilities and experience, so that, for example, if a judgment on an industrial matter is required, or a judgment on a financial matter, the proper arbitrators ... will be available."[23] It is unfortunate that people with these qualifications will usually be elderly or deeply engaged in their normal occupation. Death may intervene or the person may not be available when required. The Secretary-General has expressed the view that "representation on the Panels of outstanding personalities is of practical value only to the extent that these persons are in principle willing to serve on Commissions and Tribunals if invited to do so, and to devote to the proceedings the considerable blocks of time which may be required to deal with complex disputes in an expeditious manner."[24] In fact the ICSID has found that "... [i]n a few cases Panel members have not accepted invitations to serve, and the official functions of many Panel members may impose limitations on their ability to serve."[25]

This last observation ties in with an allegation to the effect that the Panels are " 'top-heavy' with member nations' administrative functionaries."[26] There seems a degree of truth in this. Of the 144 listed arbitrators 36 (25 per cent.) appear to be public servants, 31 (21·5 per cent.) judges, 29 (20 per cent.) lawyers, 27 (18·8 per cent.) academics (often of a legal background), and 16 (11 per cent.) businessmen. On this basis 46·5 per cent. would come within the category "administrative functionaries." The characteristics of competence in "commerce, industry or finance" seem comparatively poorly represented on the Panel.

Two further problems with ultilising arbitrators from the Panel become evident from the following statements: "... it is not helpful if a Panel member turns out to be willing to serve only as president of a Tribunal ..."[27]; "... Contracting States should also keep in mind that because of provisions of the Convention regarding nationality of arbitrators, persons designated by a State would normally only be

---

[23] J. G. Starke, "The Convention of 1965 on the Settlement of Investment Disputes between States and Nationals of Other States," in J. G. Starke (ed.), *The Protection and Encouragement of Private Foreign Investment* (1966), p. 10.

[24] ICSID Doc. AC/76/4 Annex A, p. 1.

[25] ICSID, *Twelfth Annual Report 1977/78*, p. 4.

[26] *Op. cit.* in note 17, above, at p. 72.

[27] *Op. cit.* in note 24, above, at p. 2.

invited to serve in proceedings to which neither that State nor one of its nationals is a party."[28]

In practice the conduct of arbitrations under the auspices of the Centre has suffered considerably from problems affecting arbitrators. In the three cases involving the Government of Jamaica the original arbitrator appointed by the claimants resigned. In the Arbitration *Holidays Inns/Occidental Petroleum* v. *Government of Morocco* the arbitrator appointed by the claimants (Sir John Foster) became a member of the board of the Occidental Petroleum Corporation. The other members of the Tribunal and the Secretary-General of ICSID regarded this as incompatible with his office of arbitrator. Sir John thereupon resigned. The Tribunal withheld consent to his resignation because of the actions of Sir John and Occidental Petroleum leading to the resignation. Consequently, his successor was appointed by the Chairman of the Administrative Council pursuant to Article 56 (3) rather than by the claimant. Two months later the President of the Tribunal died. The death of two arbitrators also occurred in the arbitration *Adriano Gardella SpA* v. *Government of Ivory Coast*. The proceedings in this case "... had lasted about three-and-a-half years in part because of the deaths of the President and one of the arbitrators of the initially designated tribunal."[29] Finally, the case *Société Ltd. Benvenuit & Bonfant srl* v. *Government of the People's Republic of Congo* was registered on December 15, 1977, the Tribunal constituted on May 9, 1978, to be followed by resignation of the President thereof on May 25, for "personal reasons."

(b) *Internal Factors*

The jurisdiction of the ICSID extends "... to any legal dispute arising directly out of an investment, between a Contracting State (or any *constituent subdivision* or agency of a Contracting State designated to the Centre by that State) and a national of another Contracting State, which the parties to the dispute consent in writing to submit to the Centre" (Art. 25). Any institution whose jurisdiction is circumscribed in this way can expect disagreement to arise in borderline cases. Two questions thereupon emerge: (1) How clear are the rules of circumscription? (2) Who, and on what authority and with what power, decides the issue of jurisdiction?

The answer to the first question is that there is a fair degree of consensus on the content of the rules circumscribing the jurisdiction of the ICSID. This does not mean to say that "hard cases" will not arise—just that they will be less frequent than would otherwise be

---

[28] *Op. cit.* in note 25, above.
[29] ICSID Doc. AC/77/7, p. 2.

the case. The following paragraphs illustrate the basic requirements for ICSID jurisdiction and some of the areas where difficulty may arise.

For the ICSID to have jurisdiction, this must be invoked by the parties, preferably by agreement ". . . to submit to the jurisdiction of the International Centre for Settlement of Investment Disputes, for settlement pursuant to the Convention on the Settlement of Investment Disputes between Staes and Nationals of other States."[30] The Secretary-General of the ICSID is required to screen applications and will refuse to register a request for arbitration if ". . . the dispute is manifestly outside the jurisdiction of the Centre" (Art. 36). There is no appeal from his decision but ". . . this official will refuse registration only where the dispute, as the Convention says, is manifestly outside the jurisdiction of the Centre on the basis of information supplied by the applicant himself. In case of the slightest doubt he will register the request and leave the decision as to the Centre's jurisdiction to the . . . arbitral tribunal."[31]

For the ICSID to have jurisdiction there must be a "dispute" which is of a legal nature. Ordinarily the existence or not of a "dispute" will not cause difficulties. As to the nature of the dispute it ". . . must concern the existence or scope of a legal right or obligation, or the nature or extent of the reparation to be made for breach of a legal obligation."[32]

"Investment" is not defined in the Convention. States can notify the ICSID of any class or classes of disputes which they would or would not consider submitting to the ICSID. This was done by Jamaica after entering into the investment agreement with the alumina companies and shortly before passage of the legislation which gave rise to the dispute. The Tribunal in *Alcoa Minerals of Jamaica Inc.* v. *Government of Jamaica* ". . . held the notification ineffective to abrogate Jamaica's prior consent to ICSID arbitration of disputes arising out of the investment agreement with Alcoa . . . ."[33] Furthermore, the Tribunal apparently rejected ". . . the notion that mutual consent to arbitrate can singly satisfy the separate jurisdictional requirement of an investment. It would now seem

---

[30] C. F. Amerasinghe, "Submissions to the Jurisdiction of the International Centre for Settlement of Investment Disputes," 5 *Journal of Maritime Law and Commerce* (1974), p. 215.

[31] *Op. cit.* in note 16, above, at p. 365.

[32] ICSID, *Report of the Executive Directors on the Convention on the Settlement of Investment Disputes between States and Nationals of other States*, Doc. ICSID/2, p. 9.

[33] J. T. Schmidt, "Arbitration Under the Auspices of the International Centre for Settlement of Investment Disputes (ICSID): Implications of the Decision on Jurisdiction in *Alcoa Minerals of Jamaica, Inc.* v. *Government of Jamaica*," 17 *Harvard International Law Journal* (1976), p. 102.

to be firmly established that an analysis of the parties' actual capital relationship is necessary in each ICSID case."[34] In general it may be assumed that the word "investment" will be given a wide meaning by a tribunal faced with the question.

The fact of whether a person is or is not a national of another Contracting State could cause difficulties. There appears to be agreement among commentators that the test need not be as stringent as that applied to diplomatic protection. Most difficulty will arise when the investor is a juridical person. The Convention does pay regard to the realities of control of corporations in that the parties may agree on the nationality of the juridical person for the purposes of the Convention (Art. 25 (2) (b)). There are possibilities of problems arising here but it does give considerable scope for the parties to meet the needs of their particular situation.[35]

Constituent subdivisions or agencies of a Contracting State have not figured largely in the work of the ICSID. So far only the United Kingdom has designated subdivisions as competent to become parties to disputes submitted to the ICSID.

Consent is the cornerstone of the jurisdiction of the ICSID. There is only one formal requirement—that the consent be in writing. The executive directors of the Bank, in their Report, took the view that "... a host State might in its investment promotion legislation offer to submit disputes arising out of certain classes of investments to the jurisdiction of the Centre, and the investor might give his consent by accepting the offer in writing."[36] This has been substantially accepted in practice and comment[37] although there has been disagreement.[38]

It will be obvious that much can be done by the parties themselves providing in advance for these problems and others not mentioned. Success will depend on their knowledge both of the ICSID system and comment on it. A great deal of assistance in this can be gained by perusal and use of the "Model Clauses Recording Consent to the Jurisdiction of the International Centre for Settlement of Investment Disputes."[39]

Finally, on this matter of jurisdiction the Administrative Council of the ICSID on September 27, 1978, approved a proposal authorising the Secretariat to administer proceedings between a State and a

---

[34] *Ibid.* p. 100.
[35] *Op. cit.* in note 30, above, at p. 227.
[36] *Op. cit.* in note 32, above, at p. 8.
[37] *Op. cit.* in note 16, above, at p. 352.
[38] N. S. Rodley, "Some Aspects of the World Bank Convention on the Settlement of Investment Disputes," 4 *Canadian Yearbook of International Law* (1966), p. 50.
[39] ICSID Doc. ICSID/5.

national of another State, falling within the following categories: (a) conciliation and arbitration proceedings for the settlement of legal disputes arising directly out of an investment which are not within the jurisdiction of the Centre because either the State party to the dispute or the State whose national is a party to the dispute is not a Contracting State; (b) conciliation and arbitration proceedings for the settlement of legal disputes which are not within the jurisdiction of the Centre because they do not arise directly out of an investment, provided that either the State party to the dispute or the State whose national is a party to the dispute is a Contracting State; and (c) fact-finding proceedings. These are known as the Additional Facilities. Proceedings thereunder will be based solely on contract and are in no way governed by the Convention.

The second question concerning the jurisdiction of the Centre is who, and on what authority and with what power, decides issues arising in relation to it. This is a perennial problem with arbitration tribunals.[40] It involves an element of their "pulling themselves up by their own boot-straps" if they rule on the matter and has thus been criticised. Article 41 (2) expressly provides that any objections as to jurisdiction of the ICSID or competence of the Tribunal "shall be considered by the Tribunal which shall determine whether to deal with it as a preliminary question or to join it to the merits of the dispute."

Associated with this aspect is the question of what happens if a party to the dispute does not want to take it to arbitration in spite of previous consent. The Convention provides a procedure for this whereby the other party may request institution of arbitration proceedings and, if no tribunal has been constituted within a stated time, the Chairman of the Administrative Council must make the necessary appointments from the Panel (Art. 38 and 40).

To date Jamaica has been the only party to a dispute referred to the ICSID to refuse to appear. In the case *Alcoa Minerals of Jamaica Inc.* v. *Government of Jamaica* the chairman appointed two arbitrators and designated one of them president of the three-man tribunal. The tribunal asserted jurisdiction arising from the agreement to arbitrate despite the host State's failure to attend the proceedings. The chairman has also been required to make appointments of arbitrators in *AGIP SpA* v. *Government of the People's Republic of Congo*, the respondent once again having failed to act.

Proceedings of the arbitration are to be conducted in accordance with section 3 of the Convention and the Arbitration Rules in effect

---

[40] *Op. cit.* in note 3, above, at p. 167.

on the date on which the parties consent to arbitration (Art. 44). Provisional Rules of Procedure were adopted by the Administrative Council at its First Annual Meeting. These were superseded by the adoption of permanent Rules at its Second Annual Meeting.[41] *Lacunae* are to be filled by the tribunal.

The convention has avoided one pitfall in the operations of tribunals established under it; no tribunal may bring in a finding of *non liquet* on the ground of silence or obscurity of the law. A hierarchy of criteria of decision is established: rules of law agreed by the parties; *ex aequo et bono* if the parties agree; otherwise the law of the Contracting State party to the dispute and such rules of international law as may be applicable (Art. 42). Resolving a dispute on the latter basis will not be an easy task. In the Secretary-General's view it will involve application of host State law to the merits of the dispute followed by testing of the results against international law.[42] This would not create difficulty if the content of international law were universally accepted for all situations. This is patently far from the case for a number of types of disputes likely to come within the jurisdiction of the ICSID.

Finally, we come to the matter of enforcement. This factor must bear heavily on the effectiveness of the ICSID. The Convention requires each party to "... abide by and comply with the terms of the award ..." (Art. 53). This is inherent in the very nature of arbitration proceedings. The effectiveness of the ICSID depends rather on the availability of methods to compel compliance or ensure the effect of an award when the losing party refuses or fails to take appropriate action. Any person or State contemplating resorting to this method of dispute settlement must envisage that possibility and examine the methods available.

There is nothing, nor could there be anything, in the Convention itself which would compel observance of an award beyond the general statement quoted above. Pressures for this must come from outside. There are two major avenues in the case of the ICSID. First, refusal to comply with an award can elevate the matter to an interstate dispute. Secondly, public opinion may play a decisive role.

As to the first, if the State party to the contract defaults the State of the national may exercise diplomatic protection under international law. There is not space here to discuss the problems of this, but it must be recognised that such protection in modern conditions is often illusory. In addition, failure on the part of a State to abide by the award is sufficient to ground an action against it before the International Court of Justice (Art. 64). Once again the practicality

---

[41] Presently ICSID Doc. ICSID/4/Rev. 1.
[42] *Op. cit.* in note 16, above, at p. 392.

of this device can be doubted although threat of such action may well be used as a tactic to secure compliance.

Public opinion is often of significance in enforcing observance of an arbitral award. Default involves the breach of an undertaking to observe the award—this in itself carries a considerable stigma in international business. Moreover, default has implications for future activities in the field; whether attraction of future investment by the State or future openings for the national. If the award is not observed the Convention requires each Contracting State to recognise it as binding and enforce its pecuniary aspects. Each Contracting State undertakes to "enforce the pecuniary obligations imposed by that award within its territories and if it were a final judgment of a court in that State" (Art. 54). The formulation here is deficient in that, the presumed intention being that there should be no possibility of judicial review of the award, it refers only to "final judgment of *a* court" (italics added). Academic comment has made a strong argument that this should be interpreted to mean final judgment of the highest court of appeal.[43] On the other hand, there are allegations that some States, in their implementing legislation, have left open the possibility of judicial review. The United States, it has been suggested, is in this category.[44]

Contracting States are required to notify the ICSID of the competent court or other authority to which the party seeking enforcement must present a copy of the award. As of June 30, 1978, 51 States had notified the ICSID of this designation. Failure to do so makes the task of enforcement very difficult. On the other hand, the States which have notified the ICSID include those most prominent in world trade and financial dealings. It is highly likely then that an appropriate jurisdiction may be found where there are sufficient assets of the defaulting party to satisfy the award.

Another difficulty that arises with enforcement is the allowance made in the Convention for continuation of sovereign immunity from execution (Art. 55). If the law of a Contracting State allows such immunity then it or another defaulting State is permitted to hide behind this shield in case of enforcement action in that forum. The only joy for a national here is that there are significant moves to limit the scope of sovereign immunity from execution.[45]

---

[43] *Op. cit.* in note 38, above, at p. 47; W. E. Albrecht, "Some Legal Questions Concerning the Convention on the Settlement of Investment Disputes between States and Nationals of other States," 12 *St. Louis University Law Journal* (1968), pp. 681–682.

[44] R. J. Coll, "United States Enforcement of Arbitral Awards Against Sovereign States: Implications of the ICSID Convention," 17 *Howard International Law Journal* (1976), pp. 410–413.

[45] *E.g.* the Foreign Sovereign Immunities Act 1976 (U.S.A.).

The above shows that there will be problems in enforcing the pecuniary aspects of the award. Primarily these will depend on where assets of the defaulting party are located, the effectiveness of steps taken by that State to implement the requirements of the Convention and its law on sovereign immunity from execution. These can be checked out before the arbitration agreement is entered into so that effectiveness of this aspect in the individual case will depend on the attention paid to it by the parties. It will require time, effort and expense that may not be available.

III—ALTERNATIVES TO ICSID ARBITRATION

What are the available alternatives under the ICSID? For the national, probably the most effective is insurance of his investment under a government-sponsored scheme. These are widespread throughout the major investment-providing countries—OPIC in the United States; ECGD in the United Kingdom; MITI in Japan, EFIC in Australia. Disadvantages for the investor are that insurance premiums reduce his profits or increase his costs and thus reduce his competitiveness; that most schemes will not cover the full amount of the risk—part must be borne by the investor; that the scheme may not cover the precise circumstance that arises. As against this the investor is assured of recovering a substantial proportion of his investment with comparatively little effort. Nevertheless, insurance does not solve the problem itself and the insurer will be looking to recover on his payments to the insured.

A national may seek the diplomatic protection of his State. This is a cumbersome method beset with major legal and political hurdles. It may be a useful procedure in the case of nationalisation of the investment but may not be available where the dispute arises from other causes. For example, "... the State Department of the United States has a long-standing rule that it will not espouse a claim of one of its nationals based on breach of contract by a state."[46]

If the State is the complainant it may bring informal pressure to bear through the State of the national. This will depend on many political factors. Alternatively, it may take action in its own courts or the courts of the State of the national. The first will involve problems with recognition and enforcement of any favourable judgment that it obtains. The second will raise difficulties in presenting evidence, questions of procedure, etc., and may be tainted by partiality of the tribunal, delays and high costs.

---

[46] T. V. Firth, "The Law Governing Contracts in Arbitration under the World Bank Convention," 1 *New York University Journal of International Law and Politics* (1968), p. 262.

As previously mentioned other arbitral institutions exist apart from the ICSID, *e.g.* the Court of Arbitration of the International Chamber of Commerce; the Permanent Court of Arbitration; the American Arbitration Association; the Japan Commercial Arbitration Association, etc. Of these the first is the only one which is really of significance in the field we are discussing. The Permanent Court of Arbitration is virtually never used although its rules allow for submission of investment disputes involving States and private persons. The other bodies are nationally identifiable and more concerned with strictly private arbitrations.

The ICC Court of Arbitration has a world-wide reputation for the quality of the arbitration it conducts and its efficiency. The record of compliance with awards rendered under the ICC Rules of Procedure is very good. The major problems for settlement of investment disputes are first that it is closely associated with the business world and therefore may be suspect to States; *e.g.* arbitrators, if not appointed by the parties, are selected on the nomination of National Committees of the ICC. Secondly, if default is made in carrying out the award, enforcement may well be difficult. The 1958 New York Convention on the Recognition and Enforcement of Foreign Arbitral Awards has eased this process considerably but there may still be substantial problems, particularly where a State wishes to enforce the award against a recalcitrant national through the courts of the State of that national. For example, the courts may refuse enforcement on grounds that it was contrary to public policy.

IV—CONCLUSIONS

The available alternatives to arbitration under the ICSID suffer from a variety of deficiencies. It is unlikely that these will be satisfied in the short term. There is thus a need in international relations for some such body as the ICSID. Does the ICSID adequately fulfil that need?

From the above analysis the internal factors which bear on the effectiveness of the ICSID do not greatly detract from its value. They do need to be watched by anyone contemplating recourse to the ICSID facilities and procedures. They need not react adversely to the resolution of any investment dispute that comes within the terms of reference.

On the other hand, the external factors discussed are much more significant. The problem with these is that to a great extent the solution of difficulties here rests more with States than with the ICSID itself. This is the age old problem with institutions such as the ICSID. If States want them to be effective then it is the States which have to take action: more ratifications of the Convention, particularly from the developing world, especially South America; greater care in the selection and appointment of arbitrators; increasing level of awareness among the investing community of member States. These are all matters that primarily should be at the door of the States.

Public pronouncements indicate an air of complacency in the progress and activities of the ICSID. This is particularly noticeable in utterances by the representatives of member States at Annual General Meetings of the ICSID; but the ICSID itself is not entirely free of the malady. As the above discussion indicates such complacency is a delusion. It would seem that the progress of the ICSID is slowing down; it has not achieved its potential. Additional facilities are but tinkering with the mechanism.

The cost of maintaining the ICSID is not high compared to its potential benefits. But merely establishing and maintaining the ICSID is not enough. If States are serious in their desire for this body then they must take a more active role.

INTERNATIONAL ARBITRATION
BACK IN FAVOUR?

By

D. H. N. JOHNSON

"IN spite of the steady development of International Law during the sixteenth, seventeenth, and eighteenth centuries, very few cases of arbitration occurred in that period, and it was not until the end of the eighteenth century that it began to constitute a prominent feature in the pacific settlement of international disputes. The period of modern arbitration begins with the Jay Treaty of November 19, 1794, between Great Britain and the United States."[1] "Modern arbitration begins with the Jay Treaty of 1794 between the United States and Great Britain, which provided for adjudication of various legal issues by mixed commissions."[2]

Statements such as these appear in countless textbooks of international law. After referring to the use of international arbitration as a means of settling disputes in ancient Greece, and during the Middle Ages, another work says: "The process fell into disuse, however, until its revival in the nineteenth century by a series of arbitrations between the United States and the United Kingdom arising out of the Jay Treaty (1794) and the Treaty of Ghent (1814)."[3]

That the Jay Treaty was historically important is undeniable. Its significance from the point of view of the development of international arbitration needs, however, to be seen in perspective.[4] What the history of the subject demonstrates beyond doubt is that arbitration, as a means of settling international disputes, suffers from vicissitudes. A major factor is the political climate considered both generally and particularly as it affects the States between whom disputes arise.

Since 1945 the general political climate has not been favourable to international arbitration. The tensions between East and West, and between the "developed" and the "developing" (Third) World, have been too deep and too pervasive to render recourse to arbitration a realistic solution in most cases. Even so, Article 95 of the

---

[1] H. Lauterpacht (ed.), *Oppenheim's International Law*, Vol. 2, 7th ed. (1952), pp. 33–34.

[2] I. Brownlie, *Principles of Public International Law*, 2nd ed. (1973), p. 684.

[3] W. G. Friedmann, O. J. Lissitzyn and R. C. Pugh, *International Law, Cases and Materials* (1969), p. 259.

[4] For a masterly survey of this problem, see G. Schwarzenberger, "Present-Day Relevance of the Jay Treaty Arbitrations," 53 *Notre Dame Lawyer* (1978), p. 715.

Charter of the United Nations provided that "Nothing in the present Charter shall prevent Members of the United Nations from
entrusting the solution of their differences to other tribunals by
virtue of agreements already in existence or which may be concluded in the future."

Article 95 is in Chapter XIV of the Charter, which deals with the
International Court of Justice, so the reference to "other tribunals"
must be to tribunals other than that Court, which is "the principal
judicial organ of the United Nations."[5] An authority on the Charter
has deduced from Article 95 that "clearly, the designation of the
International Court as 'the principal judicial organ of the United
Nations' (Article 92) was not intended to preclude the establishment of other judicial organs under the auspices of the United
Nations or outside the framework of the Organization."[6]

The International Court has itself said of the term "tribunal" that
it suggests a "judicial body,"[7] although that suggestion is not exclusive. In practice, there is little reason to doubt that the tribunals the
draftsmen of Article 95 had principally in mind were arbitral tribunals. "Arbitration" appears next to "judicial settlement" in Article
33 of the Charter, which sets out the various peaceful means by
which "the parties to any dispute, the continuance of which is likely
to endanger the maintenance of international peace and security"
are to seek a solution. Also, historically, arbitration was the pre-
cursor of judicial settlement.

The distinction between "arbitration" and "judicial settlement"
has been much explored.[8] Both are legal means of settling international disputes, as opposed to diplomatic means (*e.g.* negotiation,
good offices, mediation, inquiry, conciliation, resort to regional
agencies). Both presuppose an obligation to accept the Award
(arbitration) or Judgment (judicial settlement). Normally the
Award or Judgment is given on the basis of the present rules of
international law.[9] The main difference lies in the method of establishing the tribunal. Judicial settlement presupposes reference of the

---

[5] UN Charter, Art. 92; Statute of the I.C.J., Art. 1.

[6] L. M. Goodrich, E. Hambro and A. P. Simons, *Charter of the United Nations*, 3rd revised
ed. (1969), p. 559.

[7] *Effects of Awards of Compensation made by the United Nations Administrative Tribunal,
Advisory Opinion,* I.C.J. Reports 1954, pp. 47 and 52.

[8] *Op. cit.* in note 1, above; G. Schwarzenberger and E. D. Brown, *A Manual of Inter-
national Law*, 6th ed. (1976), pp. 194–209; Sir Nevile Bland (ed.), *Satow's Guide to Diplomatic
Practice*, 4th ed. (1957), pp. 437–464; L. B. Sohn, "International Arbitration Today," 108
Hague Recueil (1963–I), pp. 9–109; D. H. N. Johnson, "Arbitration in English Law and in
International Law," 41 *Transactions of the Grotius Society* 91–103.

[9] There are, however, exceptions. Art. 38 (2) of the Statute of the International Court of
Justice empowers the Court "to decide a case *ex aequo et bono*, if the parties agree thereto." In
the case of an arbitration the parties in dispute have power to instruct the arbitrators how to

dispute to a tribunal whose composition is basically fixed, whereas in an arbitration the parties in dispute have freedom to decide who the referees of the dispute shall be.[10]

It is often thought that arbitration is a less expensive method of settling a dispute than judicial settlement. This may be so in national legal systems, but it is not true of international law. The reason is simple. Parties submitting to the International Court of Justice can rely on the fact that "The expenses of the Court shall be borne by the United Nations in such a manner as shall be decided by the General Assembly."[11] Conversely, parties referring a dispute to arbitration must bear the entire costs of the arbitration. These will consist, *inter alia*, of the fees of the arbitrators, payment of secretarial and other staff, and hire of premises, and may be very considerable. Both in

---

decide. An example is provided by Article IV of the ill-fated Arbitration Agreement between the Government of the United Kingdom (acting on behalf of the Ruler of Abu Dhabi and His Highness the Sultan Said bin Taimur) and the Government of Saudi Arabia, concluded at Jedda on July 30, 1954, for arbitration of the dispute as to the location of the common frontier between Saudi Arabia and Abu Dhabi and as to the sovereignty in the Buraimi oasis [Cmd. 9272; Treaty Series Nr. 65 (1954)]. Under this provision the Tribunal was required to have "due regard to all relevant considerations of law, fact and equity brought to its attention by the Parties" and also specifically to such matters as historical facts relating to the rights of the rulers concerned, and their forefathers; "the traditional loyalties of the inhabitants of the area concerned"; "the tribal organisation and the way of life of the tribes inhabiting the area concerned" and various other factors. This arbitration was never concluded as it broke down amid mutual recriminations. See J. B. Kelly, *Eastern Arabian Frontiers* (1964).

[10] Here too the distinction can become blurred. Arts. 26 and 29 of the Statute of the International Court of Justice provide that disputes may be decided by chambers of the Court rather than by the full Court, and Art. 27 states that "A judgment given by any of the chambers provided for in Arts. 26 and 29 shall be considered as rendered by the Court." According to Art. 26 (1) of the Rules of Court adopted on May 6, 1946, as amended on May 10, 1972, "When the Court, acting under Art. 26 (2) of the Statute decides, at the request of the parties, to form a Chamber to deal with a particular case, the President shall consult the agents of the parties regarding the composition of the Chamber, and shall report to the Court accordingly." Explaining the 1972 amendments, Judge Eduardo Jiménez de Aréchaga, later President of the Court, said that their effect was "to accord to the parties a decisive influence in the composition of ad hoc Chambers." Admittedly, the same authority continued, "After the President reports on these consultations, the Court must always proceed to an election of the members of the Chamber by secret ballot, thus retaining ultimate control over the composition of any Chamber. However, from a practical point of view, it is difficult to conceive that in normal circumstances those Members who have been suggested by the parties would not be elected. For that it would be necessary for a majority of the Members of the Court to decide to disregard the expressed wishes of the parties. This would be highly unlikely since it would simply result in compelling the parties to resort to an outside arbitral tribunal or even to abandon their intention to seek a judicial settlement of the dispute." (67 *American Journal of International Law* (1973), pp. 1, 2–3.)

[11] Art. 33 of the Statute of the Court. In practice the expenses of the Court are borne by all members of the United Nations in the same proportion as other expenses of the United Nations, modified slightly by the fact that three countries who are parties to the Statute of the Court, but are not Members of the United Nations (Liechtenstein, San Marino and Switzerland) are available to share the burden.

judicial settlement and in arbitration the parties will have to pay their own costs as well.[12]

If then there is no financial advantage in referring a dispute to arbitration rather than to the International Court of Justice, and if, as is known to be the case, the International Court is not overburdened with work, it may be pertinent to ask why States ever prefer arbitration to judicial settlement. From the point of view of international relations it may matter little which method is used, provided that a peaceful solution is reached. From the point of view of international law, judicial settlement is slightly to be preferred for two reasons. First, every case peacefully settled by this means adds much needed prestige and authority to the International Court of Justice. Secondly, international law as such can be more effectively developed by the Court than by a series of separate arbitral awards. It is true that, as Lord Denning M.R. has said: "International law knows no rule of *stare decisis.*"[13] Nevertheless, as commentators have never ceased to point out,[14] the Court, while not bound by its precedents, pays them considerable respect, and arbitral tribunals do likewise. That is not to say that arbitral awards do not also influence the general evolution of the law, but being handed down, as they usually are, by essentially ad hoc tribunals, which derive their authority solely from the parties who establish them, their awards necessarily carry less weight than judgments of the International Court of Justice.

I—Reasons why Arbitration may be Preferred to Judicial Settlement

There is probably always one basic reason why States, on the assumption that they are prepared to have a dispute settled by legal means—and this may not occur very often—sometimes prefer arbitration to judicial settlement. This reason is that, during the whole

---

[12] Art. 64 of the Statute of the International Court of Justice provides that "Unless otherwise decided by the Court, each party shall bear its own costs." It is highly unlikely that the Court will ever order one party to pay the other party's costs, and it is even more unlikely that States entering into an arbitration agreement would ever provide in the agreement that one party should pay the other party's costs.

[13] *Trendtex Trading Corporation* v. *Central Bank of Nigeria* [1977] Q.B. 529, 554. What the Master of the Rolls meant in this context was that an English court, when deciding a point of international law, is not bound by an earlier decision of an English court of equivalent or superior authority on the same point, whereas—except in the case of the House of Lords—it would be so bound if it were deciding a point of English law. But Lord Denning's words are equally true of international courts. Art. 59 of the Statute of the International Court of Justice provides that "The decision of the Court has no binding force except between the parties and in respect of that particular case."

[14] *E.g.* Rosenne, *The Law and Practice of the International Court,* Vol. 2 (1965), p. 611.

process, the States retain a larger degree of control over the course of events than if they refer the dispute to the International Court of Justice. It is true that, as has been decided in many cases, the jurisdiction of the Court depends on the consent of the parties[15]; that, on certain questions of procedure, the Statute of the Court provides for the agreement of the parties[16]; and that the Rules of Court have spelled out the rights of the parties in this respect.[17] Even so, in the last resort, it is the Court which directs the procedure, according to its Statute, which is annexed to the Charter of the United Nations. In the case of an arbitration, however, the parties draw up the agreement to arbitrate (*compromis*) themselves; and although they normally empower the arbitrators to frame rules of procedure to cover situations they may not have provided for in the agreement to arbitrate (*compromis*); and although normally also they empower the arbitrators to interpret the agreement to arbitrate (*compromis*), in the last resort they reserve to themselves, acting jointly, the right to amend the agreement to arbitrate (*compromis*) or even to terminate the arbitration altogether.

The Model Rules on Arbitral Procedure, prepared by the International Law Commission in 1958,[18] attempted to limit the reserve powers of the disputing States in many respects, particularly as regards establishing—or failing to establish—the tribunal in the first place, frustrating the arbitration by withdrawing arbitrators during the proceedings, and by declaring the ultimate Award to be null and void. This last possibility, which involves invoking the doctrine of "nullification of arbitral awards," is particularly relevant in this respect. As Oppenheim points out: "In this matter arbitral tribunals have been exposed to the possible conflict of two fundamental principles governing their activity. The first is that their jurisdiction is essentially grounded in the will of the parties as expressed in the *compromis* or in the general arbitration treaty, and that an award rendered in excess of the power conferred upon them is null and void as having no legal basis whatsoever. The other principle is that in case of doubt the arbitrator is entitled to interpret the *compromis* or the treaty and thus to determine the scope of his jurisdiction. There seems to exist no provision of a general nature for the solution of controversies arising out of the allegation of a party that an

---

[15] See the cases cited in *op. cit.* in note 14, above, Vol. 1, p. 314.

[16] Art. 39.

[17] Arts. 40, 42, 44, 45, 48, 55, 62.

[18] Report of the International Law Commission covering the work of the Tenth Session, April 28–July 4, 1958; UN General Assembly Official Records: Thirteenth Sess., Supplement Nr. 9(A/3859). The Model Rules were adopted by the General Assembly in Resolution 1262 (XIII) on November 14, 1958, but only on an optional basis, so they are virtually of no effect.

arbitral award has been rendered in excess of the power conferred upon the arbitrator and is therefore null and void."[19]

The doctrine of nullification is therefore the bane of international arbitration. It differs in kind, if not necessarily in effect, from the problem of the enforcement of all international awards or judgments.[20] The latter is a problem affecting the entire international judicial process and cannot be examined within the scope of this article. Nullification, however, asserts that there is not even a valid award to enforce and has its roots in the theory that he who delegates a function has the right to say whether the delegate has exceeded his authority. Nullification has no place in judicial settlement because the International Court of Justice derives its authority, within the terms of its Statute, not from the parties to the litigation in question, but from all the Parties to its Statute.[21] The effects of the doctrine of nullification can be checked, but only in the not very likely circumstance that the party seeking to invoke the doctrine has already bound himself, or can be prevailed upon to bind himself, to accept the jurisdiction of the International Court of Justice to determine whether the Award he purports to nullify is valid or not.[22]

It would be unduly cynical to suppose that the possibility of nullification is the only reason why States prefer arbitration to judicial settlement, when they do so prefer. It would be equally

---

[19] *Op. cit.* in note 1, above, Vol. 2, p. 28.

[20] See E. Hambro, *L'exécution des sentences internationales* (1936); B. Nantwi, *The Enforcement of International Judicial Decisions and Arbitral Awards in Public International Law* (1966); L. M. Reisman, *Nullity and Revision, The Review and Enforcement of International Judgments and Awards* (1971); O. Schachter, "The Enforcement of International Judicial and Arbitral Decisions," 54 A.J.I.L. (1960), p. 1.

[21] Art. 36 (b) of the Statute provides that "In the event of a dispute as to whether the Court has jurisdiction, the matter shall be settled by the decision of the Court." Art. 61 of the Statute gives a discontented litigant a right to apply for revision of a judgment, but it is a very restricted right and lapses altogether after 10 years from the date of the judgment.

[22] See *The Case concerning the Arbitral Award made by the King of Spain on December 23, 1906*, (I.C.J. Reports 1960, p. 192). In this case Nicaragua attempted to argue from 1912 onwards that an Award made by the King of Spain in 1906 in a boundary dispute between itself and Honduras was invalid. Diplomatic pressure was brought upon both countries to refer the dispute to the International Court of Justice in 1957, and the Court ruled that the Award was "valid and binding." Subsequently, with the agreement of the governments of both countries, the Inter-American Peace Committee drafted a Basis of Arrangement, setting up a Honduras-Nicaragua Mixed Commission, which was accepted by both governments and became effective on March 13, 1961. The Commission had a Mexican chairman who was given power to make decisions should the representatives of Honduras and Nicaragua disagree. The Commission's task was to supervise the orderly departure of persons who wished to move to Nicaragua; to aid the two governments in their efforts to guarantee the inhabitants of the territory a choice between the two nationalities; and to supervise the setting of landmarks for the boundary line. The Commission completed its task before the end of 1962, although the impartial chairman was more than once called upon to exercise his power of decision (30 I.L.R. 76).

naïve to suppose that it is never a reason. There are, however, other reasons of a more genuine nature. Amongst these is the rather more flexible character of arbitration. An arbitral tribunal rarely exceeds five persons. Often there are only three arbitrators, and sometimes only one.[23] Inevitably there is more room for informality where proceedings are carried on before such a body as compared with going before a Court which is normally composed of 15 judges, and possibly has 17 judges if ad hoc judges are appointed as well.[24] This factor is likely to be intensified if the parties have chosen as arbitrators persons who are well known to them and in whom they have particular confidence.

Flexibility may be an important consideration where the issue in dispute is not a straightforward issue of law. For example, in the case of a boundary dispute—and many such disputes have been referred to arbitration—it may be necessary for the arbitrators to visit the area (*descente sur les lieux*), or to prepare a map, or to conduct a survey. It is true that all these things can be done by the Court, but experience goes to show that, where delicate questions are involved which require the presence on national territory of international officials, the States concerned prefer, as far as possible, to keep these matters under their own control.[25] Also, for climatic reasons, it may only be feasible to visit the disputed areas at certain seasons. This may render it necessary to alter the timetables for filing written documents and conducting oral hearings more radically than the International Court of Justice would wish to do.

States will certainly prefer arbitration to judicial settlement if they think that the issue in dispute is not exclusively legal but requires the presence on the tribunal of persons with the relevant expert knowledge. For example, in the *Argentine-Chile Frontier Case*,[26] whilst

---

[23] D. H. N. Johnson, "The Constitution of an Arbitral Tribunal," 30 *British Year Book of International Law* (1953), p. 152.

[24] Art. 31 (3) of the Statute provides that "if the Court includes upon the Bench no judge of the nationality of the parties, each of these parties may proceed to choose a judge...."

[25] Art. 50 of the Statute provides that "The Court may, at any time, entrust any individual, body, bureau, commission, or other organisation that it may select, with the task of carrying out an enquiry or giving an expert opinion." This gives the Court wide powers to carry out the tasks mentioned above, and many others, but for the reasons mentioned in the text States tend to prefer arbitration to judicial settlement in such cases. In both the recent Argentine-Chile arbitrations (see below section II (g)) visits were made to the area in dispute. The Permanent Court of International Justice effected a *descente sur les lieux* in the case of the *Diversion of Water from the Meuse* (Series A/B Nr. 70), but it may be doubted if the Court would have readily done so had the canals involved in the dispute not been so close to The Hague. No express authority for such a visit being available, the Court relied on Art. 48, according to which "The Court shall make orders for the conduct of the case." A similar Article appears in the present Statute. (See J. H. Verzijl, *The Jurisprudence of the World Court*, Vol. 1 (1965), p. 460.)

[26] See below, Section II(g)(i).

the President of the Court of Arbitration was a lawyer, the other two members were not, being instead geographical experts. Article 9 (2) of the Geneva Convention on Fishing and Conservation of the Living Resources of the High Seas 1958[27] provides that if the parties fail to agree on the commissioners who are to decide disputes arising under various articles of the Convention, they shall be named "by the Secretary-General of the United Nations . . . in consultation with the States in dispute and with the President of the International Court of Justice and the Director-General of the Food and Agriculture Organization of the United Nations, from amongst well-qualified persons being nationals of States not involved in the dispute and specializing in legal, administrative or scientific questions relating to fisheries, depending upon the nature of the dispute to be settled." In the case of arbitrations under Annex II to the European Fisheries Convention 1964,[28] it is apparently not necessary that any of the arbitrators should be lawyers, although in the case of difficulty in appointing them reference is again made to the President of the International Court of Justice and the Director-General of the Food and Agriculture Organisation. The Statute of the Law of the Sea Tribunal, envisaged in Annex V of the Informal Composite Negotiating Text (ICNT) prepared for the Third United Nations Conference on the Law of the Sea,[29] requires that the members of the Tribunal merely be "elected from among persons enjoying the highest reputation for fairness and integrity and of recognized competence in matters relating to the law of the sea." Annex VI of ICNT dealing with Arbitration simply provides that persons nominated as arbitrators shall be persons "experienced in maritime affairs and enjoying the highest reputation for fairness, competence and integrity." As a result of the protracted negotiations on the law of the sea many persons, such as hydrographers, fishery experts and others, who are not lawyers, have by now acquired a considerable competence "in matters relating to the law of the sea" or "in maritime affairs."

When all is said and done, however, the most probable reason why parties prefer arbitration to judicial settlement is that they have more confidence in an arbitral tribunal, than in the International Court of Justice, the composition of which is largely beyond their control. It is hard to imagine for instance that the readiness of France to sign an arbitration agreement with the United Kingdom over the delimitation of the continental shelf in the English Channel

---

[27] Treaty Series Nr. 39 (1966); 52 A.J.I.L. (1958), p. 851; 559 U.N.T.S. 285.
[28] Cmnd. 2355.
[29] A/Conf. 62/WP.10, July 15, 1977.

and the Western Approaches, referred to subsequently as the *Anglo-French Continental Shelf Case*, on July 10, 1975,[30] rather than to refer that dispute to the International Court of Justice, was unconnected with the fact that France so thoroughly disapproved of the handling by the International Court of Justice of the suits brought against her in the matter of *Nuclear Tests* by Australia[31] and New Zealand[32] on May 9, 1973, that she refused even to appear before the Court in those cases.

II—Principal International Arbitrations Held since 1945

With these considerations in mind, it is now proposed to study the principal international arbitrations that have been held since 1945. The study will be confined to arbitrations of disputes between States. It will therefore not include an examination of arbitrations of disputes between States and foreign individuals or companies; or disputes between private parties of different nationalities; or disputes involving international organisations and their personnel; or disputes of a technical nature between postal administrations. It is worth noting, however, that disputes within these categories frequently are submitted to international arbitration. This study will also not cover disputes having their origin in events during the period of the Second World War (1939–45) or disputes concerned with the interpretation of treaties that concluded those hostilities. Nor will it examine the *Anglo-French Continental Shelf* arbitration, which has been the subject of a separate article in this *Year Book*.[33]

(a) *The Gold Looted by Germany from Rome in 1943*

On April 25, 1951, an Agreement was signed in Washington by the Governments of the United States, the United Kingdom and France[34] for the purpose of settling certain claims with respect to gold looted by the Germans from Rome in 1943. The Agreement first referred to the fact that it had been decided in Part III of the

---

[30] Cmnd. 6280.

[31] In the case brought by Australia, the Court indicated interim measures of protection on June 22, 1973 (I.C.J. Reports p. 99) but found on December 20, 1974, that the claim of Australia no longer had any object so that the Court was therefore not called on to give a decision thereon (I.C.J. Reports 1974, p. 253).

[32] In the case brought by New Zealand, the Court indicated interim measures of protection on June 22, 1973 (I.C.J. Reports 1973, p. 135) but found on December 20, 1974, that the claim of New Zealand no longer had any object so that the Court was therefore not called on to give a decision thereon (I.C.J. Reports 1974, p. 457).

[33] E. D. Brown, "The Anglo-French Continental Shelf Case," in this *Year Book*, Vol. 33 (1979), pp. 304 *et seq.*

[34] 20 I.L.R. (1956), p. 441. See the article by the present writer in 4 I.C.L.Q. (1955), p. 93.

Final Act of the Paris Conference on Reparation that all monetary gold found in Germany by the Allied Forces should be pooled for distribution as restitution among the countries participating in the pool in proportion to their respective losses of gold through looting or by wrongful removal to Germany. It next stated that Germany had looted, or wrongfully removed from Rome to German territory, 2,338·7565 kilograms of gold; that Albania and Italy both claimed this gold as monetary gold within the meaning of the Paris Act; that the Reparation Commission lacked competence to decide these competitive claims; and that accordingly the three Governments requested the President of the International Court of Justice to designate as an arbitrator an eminent and impartial jurist to advise them as to the decision they should adopt with regard to these competitive claims. The three Governments agreed to accept the advice of the arbitrator, and the President of the Court appointed M. George Sauser-Hall, of Swiss nationality, for the purpose of advising them. The arbitrator found on February 20, 1953, that, even though the gold in question was deposited in Rome, it constituted metallic cover for the Albanian note-issue, and was therefore Albanian monetary gold within the meaning of the Paris Act.[35]

This finding brought into play a further section of the Washington Agreement which provided that, if the arbitrator should hold that Albania had established a claim to the gold under Part III of the Paris Act, the three Governments would deliver the gold to the United Kingdom in partial satisfaction of the judgment in the *Corfu Channel Case*[36] unless within 90 days from the date of communication of the arbitrator's opinion to Italy and Albania, either (a) Albania made an application to the International Court of Justice for the determination of the question whether it was proper that the gold should be delivered to the United Kingdom in partial satisfaction of the *Corfu Channel* judgment, or (b) Italy should make an application to the Court for the determination of the question, whether by reason of any right which she claimed to possess as a result of the Albanian law of January 13, 1945, or under the provisions of the Italian Peace Treaty, the gold should be delivered to her rather than to Albania and agreed to accept the jurisdiction of the Court to determine the question whether the claim of the United Kingdom or of Italy to receive the gold should have priority, if that

---

[35] Treaty Series Nr. 39 (1951); TIAS 2252; 2 UST 991.

[36] In this case the International Court of Justice found that Albania was responsible under international law for explosions caused by mines in Albanian waters on October 22, 1946, which caused damage to two ships of the Royal Navy, resulting in many deaths and injuries among officers and men and ordered Albania to pay the United Kingdom compensation amounting to £843,947 sterling (I.C.J. Reports 1949, pp. 4 and 244). Albania's share in the gold pool available for distribution under the Paris Act amounted to about £400,000 sterling.

issue should arise. The three Governments agreed to accept as defendants the jurisdiction of the Court for the purpose of the determination of such applications by Italy or by Albania or by both.

The Washington Agreement represented a skilfully drafted attempt to settle several legal problems in one swoop. These were (i) the problem of enforcing the judgment made by the International Court of Justice in favour of the United Kingdom against Albania, (ii) the dispute between Albania and Italy arising from Albania's law of January 13, 1945, which abrogated the Banking Convention of 1925, an unusual arrangement by which a group of Italian financiers obtained authority to establish the National Bank of Albania and the exclusive privilege of issuing bank-notes which would be legal tender in Albania,[37] and (iii) the problem of priority as between the Italian claim on Albania dating from 1945 and the British claim on Albania which dated from 1946 but which became an actual judgment debt in 1949. The draftsmen of the Washington Agreement, however, overestimated the capacity of the present international legal system to carry such a load, and their ingenious endeavour failed because of the Court's insistence that "where, as in the present case, the vital issue to be settled concerns the international responsibility of a third State, the Court cannot, without the consent of that third State, give a decision on that issue binding upon any State, either the third State, or any of the parties before it."[38]

Despite this failure, it is believed that the strategy of the Washington Agreement was correct: it was to refer a technical point of monetary law to an experienced sole arbitrator, whilst also providing for reference to the International Court of Justice of the broad issues of international legal policy that were involved.

(b) *The Ambatielos Claim*

On February 24, 1955, the Governments of the United Kingdom and Greece referred to a commission composed of five arbitrators the *Ambatielos* claim.[39] It can hardly be said that they did so by

---

[37] By 1943, when the gold was looted, the Italian State had acquired 88·5 per cent. of the share capital of the National Bank of Albania. The Albanian Law of 1945, in addition to abrogating the Banking Convention, confiscated without indemnity the assets of the National Bank of Albania.

[38] I.C.J. Reports 1954, pp. 19 and 33. The proceedings assumed an unusual form. Albania did not file an Application with the Court, but Italy did so within the specified time limit. However, Italy, although the Applicant in the proceedings, also filed a preliminary objection to the jurisdiction of the Court, which the Court unanimously upheld. In a Dissenting Opinion Judge Levi Carneiro held that the Court was not without jurisdiction to decide the issue of priority as between the British and Italian claims.

[39] HMSO Code Nr. 59–126; 23 I.L.R. (1956), p. 306, 12 U.N.R.I.A.A. (1956), p. 83. See the article by the present writer in 9 M.L.R. (1956), p. 510.

choice. Greece had asked the International Court of Justice itself to entertain this claim, regarding arbitration as an alternative solution. The United Kingdom Government maintained that the Court lacked jurisdiction and that in any case the United Kingdom was not obliged to submit to arbitration. After two hearings the Court decided that, while it was without jurisdiction to decide on the merits of the Ambatielos claim, the United Kingdom was under an obligation to submit the claim to arbitration.[40] Eventually the arbitrators decided that the Ambatielos claim was not valid because of the failure of Mr. Ambatielos, on whose behalf the Greek Government was proceeding, to exhaust the local remedies available to him in the English courts.

Although the manner in which this arbitration came to be established was most unusual, the arbitration itself was in the traditional mould in that the issue turned on an allegation of a denial of justice by one State to a national of another State. Insofar as this issue finally turned on the application of the doctrine of non-exhaustion of local remedies, the case bears some resemblance to the *Finnish Vessels Case.*[41]

(c) *The Buraimi Oasis*

On July 30, 1954, an Agreement was signed in Jedda by the Government of the United Kingdom and the Government of Saudi Arabia providing for reference to arbitration of "a dispute as to the location of the common frontier between Saudi Arabia and Abu Dhabi and as to the sovereignty in the Buraimi oasis."[42] It was stated in the preamble "that Abu Dhabi is a State for the conduct of whose foreign relations the Government of the United Kingdom is responsible and that His Highness Sultan Said bin Taimur has appointed the Government of the United Kingdom to conduct all negotiations and proceedings on his behalf for the settlement of the dispute in so far as it relates to territory in the Buraimi oasis claimed by him to belong to Muscat and Oman." The dispute occurred at a time when the United Kingdom was still the predominant Power in the Arabian (Persian) Gulf region and when the rapid expansion of the oil industry in that region, coupled with the fact that desert boundaries are inherently difficult to define and that there were very few internationally agreed boundaries in the region, created a situation that was productive of many such disputes. The attempt to

---

[40] I.C.J. Reports 1952, p. 28; *ibid.* 1953, p. 10.

[41] 3 U.N.R.I.A.A., p. 1479. Judge Bagge (Sweden), the sole arbitrator in the *Finnish Vessels Case*, was a member of the Commission of Arbitration in the *Ambatielos Case*. See also the article by Judge Bagge on the "local remedies" rule in 34 B.Y.B.I.L. (1958), p. 162.

[42] See note 9, above.

arbitrate this dispute proved a total failure because the British member of the tribunal resigned on September 16, 1955, and his resignation was followed by other members of the tribunal, including that of the president. Explaining his decision, the British arbitrator, Sir Reader Bullard, complained that the Saudi arbitrator "is, in fact, in effective control of the conduct of the proceedings on behalf of the Saudi Arabian Government, and is representing that Government on this tribunal rather than acting as an impartial arbitrator," whereas, Sir Reader continued, "I have always regarded my own position as one of complete independence of the British Government, and this I know is the position which the British Government desires me to occupy."[43]

On October 26, 1955, forces of the Ruler of Abu Dhabi and the Sultan of Muscat, supported by the Trucial Oman Levies, moved into the disputed oasis, and on the same day the British Prime Minister, Sir Anthony Eden (as he then was), informed the House of Commons that "Her Majesty's Government have ... felt obliged, in the exercise of their duty to protect the legitimate interests of the Ruler of Abu Dhabi and the Sultan of Muscat, to advise them that the attempt to reach a just compromise by means of arbitration has failed."[44] The basis of the British complaints was that Saudi money was being used to bribe the inhabitants of the oasis and that attempts were even being made to tamper with the impartiality of the tribunal. Naturally, the Saudi Government disputed these allegations and put out a statement complaining that "the sabotaging of the efforts of the international arbitration tribunal was a deliberate step taken by the Government of the United Kingdom to force the Buraimi issue to an armed conflict and not to settle it by peaceful means."[45] It is not the purpose of this paper to take sides on this issue. Suffice it to say that this experience shows that boundary disputes in desert areas frequented by nomadic tribes raise peculiarly difficult questions for international law and that, although arbitration is usually a convenient method of settling boundary disputes, this may not be true of disputes concerned with areas of that type.[46]

---

[43] J. B. Kelly, *Eastern Arabian Frontiers* (1964), p. 203.

[44] *Parliamentary Debates*, 5th Series, House of Commons, Vol. 545, cols. 199–200.

[45] *Op. cit.* in note 43, above, p. 207.

[46] Mention may be made of the Ogaden region in Ethiopia which has been the cause of hostilities between Ethiopia and "liberation forces" supported by the Somali Republic. Nor was the Advisory Opinion rendered by the International Court of Justice in the *Western Sahara Case* (I.C.J. Reports 1975, p. 12) successful in resolving the conflict between Spain, the departing State, and Algeria, Mauritania and Morocco, over the future of the Western Sahara.

(d) *The Lighthouses Case*

This was a complicated case, involving 27 claims by France and 10 counter-claims by Greece, which was peculiarly suitable for arbitration before a small arbitral tribunal rather than for adjudication before the 15-member International Court of Justice.[47] The arbitrators were Professor J. H. W. Verzijl, Netherlands, president; Professor Achille Mestre, appointed by the French Government; and Mr. Georges Charbouris, appointed by the Greek Government.

The dispute had its origin in a concession originally granted to a French company in 1860, though extended on various occasions and terminating in 1949. The concession provided for the construction and operation of lighthouses on various Turkish coasts and islands, together with authority to levy a tax, a given proportion of which was to be handed over to the Turkish treasury. During the duration of the concession there were many wars, peace treaties and political convulsions, notably the replacement of the old Ottoman Empire by the modern Republic of Turkey. As a result of these events, many of the lighthouses came to be situated in areas that were no longer Turkish territory, and in particular some of them came to be in Greek territory.

On July 15, 1931, France and Greece concluded a Special Agreement in which they asked the Permanent Court of International Justice to decide whether the concession contract made in 1913 between the French company "administration générale des phares de l'empire ottoman" and the Ottoman Government was "operative as regards the Greek Government in so far as concerns lighthouses situated in the territories assigned to it after the Balkan wars or subsequently." The Special Agreement further provided that, after the Court had decided that question, outstanding matters between the Greek Government and the French firm should be settled by the parties involved but that, failing agreement within one year, they should be submitted to an international arbitration between the two governments. Under a further Special Agreement, concluded on August 28, 1936, the Court was asked to decide whether the concession was "operative as regards the Greek Government in so far as concerns lighthouses situated in the territories of Crete, including the adjacent islands, and of Samos, which were assigned to that Government after the Balkan wars."

The Permanent Court of International Justice, in two separate Judgments,[48] decided both questions in favour of France. Negotiations for a settlement between the firm and the Greek Government

---

[47] 12 U.N.R.I.A.A., p. 155; 23 I.L.R. (1956), p. 659.
[48] Judgments of March 17, 1934 (Series A/B Nr. 62) and October 8, 1937 (Series A/B, Nr. 71).

having failed, it became necessary to resort to international arbitration. The arbitrators grouped the claims and counter-claims under four heads, namely (a) facts alleged to be attributable to Turkey and dating back before 1924; (b) acts imputed to Crete and dating back before 1913; (c) acts or omissions imputable to Greece as occupying Power or belligerent between 1912 and 1913 and between 1919 and 1924; (d) acts or omissions imputed to Greece as successor State and as grantor by subrogation, during the period 1913 to 1949.

In their Award the arbitrators ordered the Greek Government to pay to the French Government the sum of 23,149,489 French francs. In the course of their Award they examined such important legal issues as the right of the French Government to concern itself in a dispute between a French company and the Greek Government; State succession; the interpretation of peace treaties; the question of prescription; the currency and method of payment; and the question of interest, from what date payable and at what rate.

(e) *The Civil Aviation Cases*

International arbitration has also been found useful in settling two disputes concerning the interpretation of air services agreements. These are the agreements under which States grant each other the right to designate airlines to fly certain routes for civil aviation purposes and may also contain regulations concerning capacity, frequency of flights, the types of passengers who may be carried, questions relating to cargo and so on.[49]

On March 27, 1946, the United States and France signed an Air Transport Services Agreement, under which the parties granted to each other the rights specified in an Annex thereto. One of the rights granted to the United States was a route from the United States *"via* intermediate points over the North Atlantic to Paris and beyond *via* intermediate points in Switzerland, Italy, Greece, Egypt, the Near East, India, Burma and Siam to Hanoi and then to China and beyond...." Article X of the Air Transport Services Agreement, as amended by an Exchange of Notes signed on March 19, 1951, provided that disputes should be "submitted for an advisory report to a tribunal of three arbitrators" and that the parties "will use their best efforts under the powers available to them to put into effect the opinion expressed in any such advisory report." The two governments agreed in an Exchange of Letters of December 8, 1962 to January 9, 1963, to submit this dispute to arbitration and to consider the decision of the tribunal as binding, and on January 22, 1963, they signed an arbitration agreement.

---

[49] See B. Cheng, *The Law of International Air Transport* (1962), pp. 229–487.

Although the dispute was a comparatively minor one, it raised many interesting legal questions, particularly the meaning of the term "Near East," and the use of preparatory work and subsequent practice in the interpretation of treaties. The United States argued that the term "Near East" designated the land-bridge between Europe and Africa to the west and the Indian sub-continent to the east, and thus included Turkey and Iran, whereas according to the French view it designated only the Arab part of the former Ottoman Empire. The tribunal declined to give a general definition of the term, insisting that it must be interpreted in the context of the agreement as a whole.

This led the tribunal, relying mainly on the subsequent practice of the parties, to find that the United States had been granted the rights in question.[50]

In the other dispute the United States and Italy had concluded an Air Transport Services Agreement on February 6, 1948, which granted air transport rights to both parties and also provided for arbitration of disputes.

In 1963 a dispute arose as to whether the rights granted to the United States included the right to operate scheduled flights for cargo only or, as Italy contended, the right only to conduct "combination services" (*i.e.* passengers, mail and cargo). The tribunal, again relying mainly on subsequent practice, found in favour of the United States interpretation, the Italian member, Ricardo Monaco, dissenting.[51]

(f) *The Indo-Pakistan Western Boundary Case*

Having regard to the many hostilities that have marred relations between India and Pakistan following the separation of these two countries when British rule of the Indian subcontinent came to an end in 1947, the submission of this dispute to arbitration[52] must be considered one of the most successful examples of this method of settling international disputes since the end of the Second World War.

The dispute concerned an unusual piece of territory called the *Rann of Kutch*, and indeed the dispute is usually referred to under that name. Although the *Oxford English Dictionary* describes a "rann" as an Irish word, meaning "a verse" or a "strain," the Rann (or Great Rann) in this case was described by the chairman of the

---

[50] 38 I.L.R., p. 182.
[51] 45 I.L.R., p. 393.
[52] 7 I.L.M., p. 633; 50 I.L.R., p. 2. See also J. G. Wetter, "The Rann of Kutch Arbitration," 65 A.J.I.L. (1971), p. 346.

arbitration tribunal[53] as "a unique geographical phenomenon" and by Judge Bebler as "a peculiar surface, most akin to marsh or swamp." Its peculiarity lies in the fact that the Rann is sometimes a desert and is sometimes flooded with water. This led Pakistan to describe it as "a marine feature" whilst India considered it to be land. Pakistan claimed that the boundary should run through the middle of the Rann, while India contended that the entire Rann was Indian territory. The tribunal, in its decision of February 19, 1968, awarded about 90 per cent. of the territory to India and the Award was accepted by both parties.

An unusual feature of the case was the arrangement made for the discovery and inspection of documents. The tribunal adopted a rule of procedure, though on the initiative of the parties, which provided that one party could call on the other party to make available to it for inspection any document that was or was likely to be in the possession or under the control of the other party. Thereupon, that other party was obliged to "provide adequate and expeditious facilities to the party to take inspection and copies of the document" and, on request of such party and at its cost, was obliged to "furnish to it such number of photostat copies as it requires and also produce the document before the tribunal." If the document was not in the possession or under the control of the other party, the latter was to file an affidavit to that effect before the tribunal. This is a useful rule of procedure in the case of territorial disputes involving a long history, and it is understood that in this case visits for the purpose of inspecting and obtaining copies of documents were exchanged between New Delhi and Islamabad.[54] Such disputes, especially if between States formerly under colonial rule, may also raise problems for the former colonial Power involved. In most cases the relevant documents will be in the national archives of the colonial Power and thus available for inspection by anyone. If it were a case, however, of producing the original copy before an arbitration tribunal, or of allowing inspection of documents not yet made available for inspection by the public, it would be desirable for the parties in dispute, and for the tribunal, to come to some arrangement with the third Power providing for access to such documents on equal terms. In the last resort, however, the third Power would not be obliged to permit such access.

Another interesting feature of the case was an argument by

---

[53] Judge Gunnar Lagergren, President of the Court of Appeal for Western Sweden. The other members of the tribunal were Judge Bebler of the Constitutional Court of Yugoslavia appointed by India and Ambassador Nasrollah Entezam of Iran appointed by Pakistan. Judge Bebler entered a dissenting opinion.

[54] Wetter, *op. cit.* in note 52, above.

Pakistan to the effect that the Agreement of June 20, 1965, by which the two Governments agreed to establish the arbitral tribunal "for determination of the border in the light of their respective claims and evidence produced before it," invested the tribunal with power to adjudicate *ex aequo et bono*. India moved that this argument be rejected at a preliminary hearing, whereas Pakistan contended that this issue should not be decided until after the closure of the written proceedings. The tribunal decided to resolve the issue at once, saying on February 23, 1966: "As both Parties have pointed out, equity forms part of International Law; therefore, the Parties are free to present and develop their cases with reliance on principles of equity.

"An international Tribunal will have the wider power to adjudicate a case *ex aequo et bono*, and thus to go outside the bounds of law, only if such power has been conferred on it by mutual agreement between the Parties.

The Tribunal cannot find that the Agreement of June 30, 1965, does authorise it clearly and beyond doubt to adjudicate *ex aequo et bona*.

Therefore, and as the Parties have not by any subsequent agreement consented to confer the power upon the Tribunal to adjudicate *ex aequo et bono*, the Tribunal resolves that it has no such power."

(g) *The Argentine-Chile Arbitrations*

Two disputes between the Argentine Republic and the Republic of Chile have been referred to arbitration in circumstances which must by now be regarded as very unusual, and which are not likely to recur.

(i) *The Argentine-Chile Frontier Case*.[55] On April 17, 1896, these two countries invited Queen Victoria to arbitrate a lengthy section, amounting to 2,900 kilometres, of their common boundary.[56] Queen Victoria accepted this duty but died before she could discharge it. However on November 20, 1902 King Edward VII pronounced an Award[57] which, though it settled most problems, left others unsettled, partly because of inadequate surveys having been conducted and partly because the Award contained ambiguities of a type that, as experience has shown, are all too likely to occur in attempts to define international frontiers with precision. This task is not as easy as it may seem to the layman, and becomes even more difficult when, as happened on this occasion, the arbitrators are

---

[55] (1966) HMSO Code Nr. 59–162.
[56] 88 Br. and For.St.P., p. 553.
[57] 95 Br. and For.St.P., p. 162.

under pressure to produce a result quickly without having been able to conduct a comprehensive survey.

A few months before Edward VII pronounced his Award, the two countries entered into a General Treaty of Arbitration. In this Treaty, which was signed at Santiago on May 28, 1902,[58] the parties bound themselves "to submit to arbitration all controversies between them, of whatsoever nature they may be, or from whatever cause they may have arisen." The only exceptions were disputes affecting the principles of the Constitution of either country or "questions which have already been the subject of definite settlement" (a somewhat ambiguous exception). They nominated as arbiter for this purpose the British Government, but if either party should break off friendly relations with the British Government, then the Government of the Swiss Federation would act. It was further provided that, if the parties could not agree on "the points, questions, or differences involved," then "either of the Parties shall be empowered to invite the intervention of the Arbiter, whose duty it will be to determine the Agreement" as well as various procedural matters. This is an unusual power to give to the arbitrator, although it is a useful one in that, for want of it, some disputes fail to be submitted to arbitration altogether. However, as well as an unusual power, it is a big responsibility to give to the arbitrator who has also to determine an arbitration "agreement" unilaterally for the two disputing parties and who can only do this on the basis of a preliminary hearing, without having had the benefit of the detailed submissions of both parties.

On September 15, 1964, the Government of the Republic of Chile invoked the provisions of the General Treaty of Arbitration and invited the United Kingdom Government to arbitrate a controversy between itself and the Government of the Argentine Republic concerning the location of the boundary line in the sector between Boundary Posts 16 and 17 of the boundary between the two countries as defined in the Award of King Edward VII. As the parties were unable to determine "the points, questions, or differences involved," the British Foreign Secretary, Mr. Michael Stewart, exercised his power to determine the Agreement for Arbitration (*Compromiso*). He did so on April 1, 1965,[59] and in the Agreement he stated that the United Kingdom Government had appointed a Court of Arbitration. The president of the Court was Lord McNair, a former president of the International Court of Justice. The other two members of the Court were geographical experts.

---

[58] 95 Br. and For.St.P., p. 759.
[59] Cmnd. 2682.

The Court of Arbitration, however, did not have power actually to settle the controversy. It was to "reach its conlcusions in accordance with the principles of international law" and to report those conclusions to the United Kingdom Government, in whom the power lay, under the General Treaty of Arbitration, actually to make the Award. In practice, the Award came to be pronounced by Her Majesty Queen Elizabeth II, who, by an inversion of normal constitutional procedure, did so "in the name of Our Government in the United Kingdom."[60] The Award was accepted by both parties.

(ii) *The Beagle Channel Case*.[61] The provisions of the General Treaty of Arbitration of May 28, 1902, were invoked again by Chile on December 11, 1967, this time over a dispute between itself and the Government of the Argentine Republic concerning sovereignty over certain islands situated in the region of the Beagle Channel. This time the two Governments concurred on an agreement for arbitration,[62] so on this occasion it was necessary only for the United Kingdom Government to arbitrate the dispute and not, as before, to determine as well "the points, questions or differences" involved in the controversy. Accordingly, on July 22, 1971, the three Governments signed the Agreement for Arbitration (*Compromiso*)[63] which stated that the United Kingdom Government had appointed a Court of Arbitration, consisting of five members. This time, however, only one of the arbitrators was British, namely Sir Gerald Fitzmaurice. The others were Hardy C. Dillard (United States); André Gros (France); Charles D. Onyeama (Nigeria); and Sture Petrén (Sweden). All five arbitrators were at that time judges of the International Court of Justice so the tribunal was similar in composition, though not in the manner of its composition, to a Chamber of the International Court of Justice as provided for in Article 26 (2) of the Statute of the Court. As provided for in Article 3 of the Agreement for Arbitration, the arbitrators elected Sir Gerald Fitzmaurice as president of the Court of Arbitration.

Just as in the case of the previous arbitration of an Argentine-Chile dispute by the United Kingdom Government, the Court of Arbitration was not empowered actually to settle the dispute. Its duty was to reach its conclusions in accordance with the principles of international law and to transmit its "decision" to the United Kingdom Government. However, it was only if the Court's decision were

---

[60] (1966) HMSO So. Code Nr. 59–162. Under normal British constitutional practice the government acts in the name of the Sovereign, as is indicated by the frequently used title "Her Majesty's Government."

[61] 17 I.L.M., p. 632.

[62] They did so, however, only by the device of each party setting out separately the terms of its request to the Arbiter, and these requests differed.

[63] 10 I.L.M., p. 1182.

ratified by the United Kingdom Government that it would constitute an Award within the meaning of the General Treaty of Arbitration of 1902. Again acting "in the name of Our Government in the
United Kingdom" Her Majesty Queen Elizabeth II pronounced the
Award on April 18, 1977.[64]

This time, however, the Award was not accepted by both parties.
On January 25, 1978, the Ministry of Foreign Affairs of the Argentine Republic delivered to the Chilean ambassador in Buenos Aires
a Note[65] in which it stated that "the Government of the Argentine
Republic, after thoroughly studying the arbitration award of Her
Britannic Majesty on the Beagle Canal (*sic*) controversy, has
decided to declare the award insuperably null and void, in accordance with international law." The Note proceeded to state that
therefore the Argentine Republic did not consider itself obliged to
fulfil the Award and consequently would not recognise the validity
of any title invoked by Chile based on the Award, in order to
arrogate to itself sovereign rights over territory or any maritime
area. The Argentine Government further stated that it was not in
the interest of the two Republics to have the quality of their relationship affected as the result of an Award issued in disagreement with
international law and proposed bilateral negotiations to settle the
dispute.

The reasons why the Argentine Government found the Award
unsatisfactory were contained in a "Declaration of Nullity"
attached to the Note. They included the following: the Court of
Arbitration had distorted the Argentine arguments; the Court had
pronounced its opinion on certain questions not submitted to arbitration and had therefore exceeded its jurisdiction; the Court's
opinion was contradictory in many places and "it is an elementary
principle that something cannot be simultaneously affirmed and
denied of somebody or something"; the Court had misapplied the
principles of international law concerning the interpretation of
treaties; the Court had committed several historical and geographical errors; and there was "imbalance in the evaluation of the
argumentation and evidence submitted by each Party" amounting
to "systematic partiality of the Court in favour of Chile and against
Argentina."

Chile naturally replied to these serious charges with a statement
contained in a Note[66] delivered to the Argentine ambassador in
Santiago on Janurary 26, 1978. The Note stated that the Government of Chile rejected the "Declaration of Invalidity" and asserted

---

[64] 17 I.L.M., p. 632.
[65] *Ibid.* p. 738.
[66] *Ibid.* p. 750.

that it had clear title to sovereignty over the areas in dispute and would continue to exercise its rights. As to the proposed negotiations, Chile was ready "to reach a direct understanding in conformance with international law" as regards the determination of maritime space beyond that settled by the arbitrator. If that could not be achieved, Chile proposed recourse to the provisions of the Treaty signed between the two countries on April 5, 1972.[67] In this instrument, which was entitled "General Agreement on Judicial Solution of Disputes between the Argentine Republic and the Republic of Chile," the two Governments undertook "to submit to the jurisdiction of the International Court of Justice all disputes of any nature which for any motive may arise between same, while they do not affect the provisions of one or the other country (*sic*) and provided they cannot be solved by means of direct negotiations." As in the case of the General Treaty of Arbitration of May 28, 1902, which Argentina denounced on March 11, 1972, it was agreed that "disputes that have been the object of definite agreements between the Parties cannot be renewed"; that "the points, questions or divergencies will be established in a *compromiso* by mutual agreement of both Governments"; and if such mutual agreement could not be achieved, "any of the Parties may submit the matter to the Court by means of a written application addressed to its Secretary (*sic*)."

The Presidents of the Argentine Republic and the Republic of Chile met at Mendoza on January 19, 1978, and again at Port Montt on February 20, 1978, in an attempt to solve the problem that had arisen between the two countries. It was agreed that negotiations should be instituted "that would make possible a direct understanding of the fundamental questions that concern bilateral relations between Argentina and Chile, particularly in those related matters that in the opinion of one or the other Government are pending in the Southern region"; that this understanding "does not pose any modification in the positions sustained by the parties regarding the Award of the Court of Arbitration on the Beagle Channel stipulated in the notes and declarations issued by the respective governments"; and that in the meantime "the Parties will not apply any particular norms that one or the other have dictated on the demarcation, neither will they produce facts that may serve as a basis for or in

---

[67] 11 I.L.M., p. 691. The Argentine Republic's denunciation of the 1902 Treaty became effective on September 22, 1972. It was therefore too late to affect the proceedings initiated by Chile regarding the Beagle Channel controversy on December 11, 1967. The 1972 Treaty was clearly modelled on, and was intended to replace the 1902 Treaty, the principal difference being that it substituted the International Court of Justice for the United Kingdom Government as the body qualified to settle disputes between the two countries.

support of any other future demarcation in the Southern region inasmuch as said norms or facts may cause friction or difficulties with the other Party."[68]

This guarded language indicates that, while neither party was willing to give way, there was a mutual desire to settle the problem peacefully. As of this writing, the negotiations have not led to a harmonious conclusion and the whole episode has regretfully to be accepted as constituting a serious impairment to the arbitral process in an area where hitherto it had been successful. Argentina's attitude amounts also to a serious rebuff to the United Kingdom Government, to Queen Elizabeth II herself and, since the Court of Arbitration was composed of five judges of the International Court of Justice, indirectly to that Court. The practice of two countries entering into long-term arrangements under which they bind themselves to refer their disputes to a third country for solution, as Argentina and Chile did in 1902, is probably also dead, even though ad hoc arrangements along these lines may continue to be made. While it lasted, this practice had certain advantages, particularly in that it made it possible to conduct an arbitration more expeditiously than if arbitrators had to be assembled from different countries. This practice, however, carries with it connotations of hegemony or domination that render it less acceptable today.

III—CONCLUSIONS

It is not proposed to draw any startling conclusion from this survey. The record largely speaks for itself. The record shows: (i) While relatively inactive, the arbitral process in disputes between States is not moribund, let alone dead. (ii) While the political climate since 1945 has not been favourable to the settlement of international disputes by legal means, arbitration seems to have made a slight gain at the expense of judicial settlement. To that extent the draftsmen of Article 95 of the Charter of the United Nations were justified in making continuing provision for international arbitration. (iii) Arbitration is especially suitable for disputes of a technical character and where a certain flexibility of procedure is desirable. For this reason arbitration has often been favoured for boundary disputes. However, the experience of the *Buraimi Oasis* and *Beagle Channel* cases shows that arbitration will not always be successful in resolving such disputes. (iv) Neither arbitration nor judicial settlement will be successful unless there is a modicum of trust between the parties and, above all, a readiness to accept that, once adjudication by a

---

[68] 17 I.L.M., p. 793.

third party is agreed on, there is at least a 50 per cent. chance of an adverse decision. (v) The problem of the enforcement of judicial decisions and arbitral awards is no nearer a solution than it ever was, given the relatively unorganised condition in which international society still subsists. (vi) The special problem of nullification of arbitral awards also has not been solved and, in fact, could only be solved by converting arbitration into some form of judicial settlement, which would deprive arbitration of other features which it has and which render it sometimes a more attractive option to governments than judicial settlement.

PRESENT-DAY RELEVANCE
OF THE HAGUE PEACE SYSTEM
1899–1979

By

GEORG SCHWARZENBERGER

"In Japan, when the Hague is mentioned, it means Peace and Justice"—M. Adatci (1920 Committee of Jurists on the Permanent Court of International Justice).

"Les espoirs formulés en 1920–1922, renouvelés en 1946, n'ont pas été realisés—Judge André Gros (76 R.G.D.I.P.—1972).

AT the lowest, the Hague Peace System[1] has contemporary relevance because of its record performance in surviving, if not preventing, two world wars and its continuing attractiveness to old and new States.

If permanency can be equated with durability, the lifespan of the Hague Peace System has outdistanced, by nearly half a century, those of the League of Nations and United Nations and their judicial organs.

I—An Expanding System

What is more significant than the eightieth anniversary of the Hague Peace System is the worldwide distribution and ideological heterogeneity of the participants. They include the United States of America and the Soviet Union, "committed" and "non-aligned" countries, members of the "old" and "new" Commonwealth, most of the Latin American States and a fair sprinkling of "new" countries in Asia and Africa.

---

[1] The Hague Peace System may be summarised as a compound of optional mediation, inquiry, conciliation and arbitration, with the emphasis in arbitration on optional jurisdiction and ad hoc tribunals, composed of arbitrators of the parties' own choice. See, further, Hague Conventions I for the Pacific Settlement of International Disputes of 1899 and 1907 and the abortive Convention XII of 1907 on the Creation of an International Prize Court.

For background literature, see Schwarzenberger and Brown, *A Manual of International Law*, 6th ed. (1976)—2nd and revised impression), pp. 491 *et seq*. and, for the text of Hague Convention I of 1907, United Kingdom Treaty Series No. 6 (1971)—Cmnd. 4575.

The belated ratification of the Convention in 1970 by the United Kingdom underlines the present-day relevance of the Hague Peace System.

The constitutional basis of the expansion of the Hague Peace System also deserves some attention. The Parties to Hague Convention I of 1907 had undertaken to settle, by a subsequent agreement, the terms on which Powers not invited to the Second Hague Peace Conference were to be permitted to adhere to the Convention. This agreement was never concluded.

Thus, in free analogy to the procedures for the adhesion of 17 Latin American States to Hague Convention I of 1899 and their admission to the 1907 Hague Peace Conference, the Administrative Council of the Permanent Court of Arbitration had to improvise a procedure, consolidated in 1959, to make possible further adhesions to Hague Conventions I of 1899 and 1907. All present and future members of the United Nations (when they became members of the United Nations) which did not yet participate in the Court's work were to be invited by the Netherlands Ministry of Foreign Affairs, as the depositary of the 1899 and 1907 Hague Conventions, to send their acts of adhesion to the Netherlands Foreign Ministry.

This meant that any entity which the United Nations found acceptable as a member became automatically eligible to become a participant in the Hague peace system. Subject to this reservation, the Administrative Council of the Permanent Court of Arbitration committed itself to the goal of heterogeneous universality as the basis of its membership policy.

II—LEGENDS

To understand the functions fulfilled by the Hague Peace System which have ensured its durability, it is necessary to separate the legends that have grown around the system from its realities.

Foremost among these legends are the teleologically-determined descriptions of the Permanent Court of Arbitration as a stepping stone to "truly" permanent and "compulsory" institutions in the field of international adjudication. Others are based on counter-factual assertions regarding the "probability" of an armed confrontation but for the successful use of the Hague Peace System. The treatment in the Doctrine of International Law of cases such as the *Dogger Bank* incident (1905) between Great Britain and Russia and the *Casablanca Deserters* controversy (1909) between France and Germany are to the point.

None of these hypothetical judgments is verifiable and, thus, for purposes of research and understanding they all can be safely ignored. What can be verified are the failures of parties involved in disputes, especially those culminating in the First and Second World Wars, to make effective, if any, use of the Hague Peace System.

Selective use of the material relating to the failure of all concerned in the Summer of 1914 to make any determined effort to use the Hague Peace System has produced a rich crop of war-guilt ideologies. They range from the attribution of responsibility to individual States for the shortcomings of the pre-1914 international system to the allocation of primary or exclusive responsibility for the First World War.

III—REALITIES

A contrast between two pairs of cases may assist in throwing into relief the variety of choices open to participants in the Hague Peace System. At the one end of the spectrum stand the *Dogger Bank* incident (1905)[2] and the case of the *Casablanca Deserters* (1909)[3] and, at the other, the *North Atlantic Coast Fisheries* (1910)[4] and *Palmas* (1928)[5] cases.

The *Dogger Bank* incident between Great Britain and Russia has its bizarre aspects. On the way to the Far East during the Russo-Japanese War, the Russian fleet in the Baltic considered itself to be under attack near the Dogger Bank from Japanese torpedo-boats and fired at them. Actually, the vessels were British fishing boats. Their crews suffered the loss of two lives and personal injuries from the Russian attack, and some of the fishing boats were seriously damaged.

On both sides, national honour could have been invoked as an accepted reservation to any settlement under the Hague Peace System. Yet, both Governments agreed to submit the issue to a commission of inquiry under Hague Convention I of 1899.

The Commission was composed of five admirals (Austrian, British, French, Russian and United States). Over and above its fact-finding task, the Commission was authorised to establish responsibility for the incident and, in this eventuality, the blame attaching to anybody involved. It was left open whether this responsibility was to be determined by legal or moral standards. To this extent, the Commission was entrusted with quasi-judicial functions, albeit of a purely recommendatory character.

The Commission sat in Paris and elected its French member as its president. It found that, at the time of the incident, no Japanese torpedo-boat had been anywhere in the vicinity of the Russian fleet,

---

[2] 1 Scott, *Hague Court Reports*, pp. 404 *et seq.*
[3] 11 R.I.A.A., pp. 124 *et seq.*
[4] *Ibid.* pp. 167 *et seq.*
[5] 2 *ibid.* pp. 829 *et seq.*

and that the opening of fire on the fishing vessels had been unwarranted. Somewhat inconsequentially, the Commission added that these findings did not reflect negatively on the military standing or the humanity (*sur la valeur militaire, ni sur les sentiments d'humanité*) of the Russian admiral or his subordinates.

This rider absolved Russia of moral or legal responsibility for the incident. Great Britain had to content herself with the regret for the loss of life the Czar had expressed at an early stage of the proceedings and the payment of £65,000 offered by the Russian Government to the fishermen and their relatives.

In the case of the *Casablanca Deserters* between France and Germany, the issue was a clash between State organs of the two Parties: French troops had occupied Casablanca, with the presumed consent of the Sultan of Morocco, for the purpose of restoring public order in and around the city. A French officer arrested the six deserters, three of whom had German nationality, on their way to embarkation in a German steamer from Casablanca. The German consul had issued a blank safe-conduct, and the Secretary of the Consulate had included all six deserters in the safe-conduct. When the arrest took place, the party was under escort by a Moroccan soldier attached to the German consulate. In spite of protests by the German consul against the arrest of the three German deserters, the French authorities refused to release any of them.

Again, the Parties ignored the reservation of national honour. In this case, they decided in favour of arbitration under Hague Convention I of 1907. The Tribunal was to sit at The Hague and consist of four arbitrators, two to be chosen by each Party and only one of these two to be a national of that Party. The four arbitrators were to choose the umpire. The Tribunal was constituted as follows: K. Hj. L. de Hammarskjöld (Sweden—Umpire), Sir Edward Fry (Great Britain), G. Fusinato (Italy), H. J. Kriege (Germany) and L. Renault (France).

In its Award, the Tribunal invoked two major rules: the exclusive jurisdiction of any occupying force over its members, which applied also in countries subject to capitulation régimes, and the exclusive jurisdiction, under the capitulation régime then in force in Morocco, of the German consulate over its nationals in Morocco. The Tribunal showed a marginal preference for the first of these rules but balanced it by the statement that, in case of conflict between these rules, this preference had to be determined by the factual circumstances of each individual case.

In the case before the Tribunal, the deserters had remained in the territory under the "immediate, durable and effective" control of the French armed forces. The Tribunal fastened on this as the decisive fact. For the rest, it distributed evenly such blame as attached to either side and held that no further action on its part was required. In other words, it upheld French jurisdiction over all six deserters, including those of German nationality.

In composition, techniques and legal effects, differences exist between the settlement of the *Dogger Bank* incident and that of the *Casablanca Deserters*. Yet, from inter-disciplinary and practical angles, these differences are less significant than the similarity in the functions fulfilled in the two cases by the Commission of Inquiry and the Tribunal. They successfully poured oil on the troubled waters of incensed public opinion. By tactful manipulation of the facts in the *Dogger Bank* case and even distribution of blame in that of the *Casablanca Deserters*, these organs contributed their share to the rational management of crises which, when they occurred, suited neither party.[6]

The only sufferers from these exercises in institutional pragmatism were the organs involved, their members, the Hague Peace System and, in the case of the *Casablanca Deserters*, international law—all of them, in terms of power politics, of marginal relevance and expendable.

Even so, it was advisable not to devalue unduly these devices and to show that, when circumstances permitted, commissions of inquiry could live up to the standards of an "impartial and conscientious investigation" of the relevant facts and "ascertaining the truth," and that parties and tribunals alike were willing to show proper "respect for law."[7] It could be left to the enlightened self-interest of those governments who were more alive than others to the susceptibilities of public opinion occasionally to provide the requisite evidence.

Several reports by commissions of inquiry and (since 1937) conciliation commissions, as well as awards by tribunals under the Hague Peace System, fall into this category. In particular, this applies to the awards in the *North Atlantic Coast Fisheries* and *Palmas* cases. Compared with the best that international adjudication has to offer they may claim to hold their own.

IV—PLUS ÇA CHANGE ...

The optional and ad hoc character of organs other than the Registry in the Hague Peace System permits a variety of choice of organs of mediation, inquiry, conciliation and arbitration. Moreover, parties

---

[6] See, for instance, Z. S. Steiner, *Britain and the Origins of the First World War* (1977), pp. 79 *et seq.* and 264 *et seq.* (comprehensive bibliography), and N. Bar-Yaacov, *The Handling of International Disputes by Means of Inquiry* (1974), pp. 45 *et seq.*

[7] Arts. 9 (1899 and 1907), 19 (1907) and 26 (1907).

remain free to control proceedings at every stage and, by appointing "judges of their own choice,"[8] they are able to make the outcome of awards reasonably predictable. In constituting non-judicial organs or special tribunals, they may even ignore the general list of members of the Permanent Court of Arbitration. It is this exceptional degree of elasticity which has given the Hague Peace System its durable, if subordinate, place in past and present systems of international power politics.

Yet, as is proved by the Andean Arbitrations between Argentina and Chile,[9] the *Rann of Kutsch* Arbitration (1968) between India and Pakistan[10] and the *Continental Shelf* Arbitration (1977; 1978) between France and the United Kingdom,[11] some governments prefer, on occasion, to steer clear of even a peace system as non-demanding as that of the Hague.

V—EXPLORING PASTURES NEW

In the last phase of the inter-war period between 1919 and 1939, when international adjudication was coming to a standstill, the Administrative Council of the Permanent Court of Arbitration authorised the establishment of conciliation commissions, with power to make recommendations to parties in dispute. Yet, then as in the post-1945 period, their efforts met with little response.

The Administrative Council of the Permanent Court of Arbitration also tried to break into the hinterland of quasi-international or transnational law. It authorised the International Bureau to elaborate rules of arbitration and conciliation for the settlement of international disputes between two parties of which only one was a State and to put the Bureau's offices and staff at their disposal.

As with comparable efforts of the International Centre for the Settlement of Investment Disputes in the Bretton Woods nexus, those of the Permanent Court of Arbitration to provide a respectable forum for the settlement of disputes between States and foreign entrepreneurs or investors were only moderately successful, and for similar reasons. They have little to do with the merits or demerits of these or other judicial organs but with the growing impact of politics on international economic relations, the disinclination of States, against which foreign nationals and companies are most likely to

---

[8] Arts. 15 (1899) and 37 (1907).
[9] HMSO (1966 and 1977). See also J. Dutheil de la Rochère, 23 A.F.D.I. (1977), p. 408 *et seq.*, and D. H. N. Johnson, this *Year Book*, Vol. 34 (1980), p. 305 *et seq.*
[10] 50 I.L.R., pp. 2 *et seq.*
[11] *La Documentation Française* (1977), See also E. D. Brown, in this *Year Book*, Vol. 33 (1979), pp. 304 *et seq.*

need protection, to submit disputes regarding services or investments to third-party settlement other than under their own national jurisdiction, and their preference for negotiated settlements.

VI—THE HAGUE AND UN PEACE SYSTEMS

In the context of this paper, the relations between the Hague and United Nations Peace Systems will be examined primarily with emphasis on the Hague Peace System.

Under Article 33 of the United Nations Charter, "the parties to any dispute, the continuation of which is likely to endanger the maintenance of international peace and security, shall, first of all, seek a solution by negotiation, inquiry, mediation, conciliation, arbitration, judicial settlement, resort to regional agencies or arrangements, or other peaceful means of their own choice. The Security Council shall, when it deems necessary, call upon the parties to settle their disputes by such means."

Thus, in a generalised form, the optional machinery of the Hague Peace System is intended to be co-ordinated with that of the United Nations. Yet, when, as for instance in the Helsinki Final Act of 1975, members of the United Nations treat accords reached as "non-registrable" under Article 102 of the United Nations Charter and, thus, as not capable of being invoked before any organ of the United Nations, including the International Court of Justice as the principal judicial organ of the United Nations, the Hague Peace System can be operated as a completely separate system. As participants in the Hague Peace System, parties to the accords incorporated in the Helsinki Final Act remain free to agree with one another to submit issues such as the legal status of non-registrable accords to, for instance, tribunals under Hague Conventions I of 1899 and 1907.[12]

A more than potential connection between the two peace systems exists in another sphere. As in relation to the Permanent Court of International Justice in the era of the League of Nations, so in relation to the International Court of Justice, the Hague Peace System has been made to assist in the proceedings leading to the election of the members of the International Court.

What, for purposes of the Hague Peace System, is merely a general list of names from which parties to disputes may pick members of commissions of inquiry and tribunals of their own choice, has been brought into potentially corporate life under the Statutes of both Courts. The members of the Permanent Court of

---

[12] See, further, the writer's letter to the Editor of *The Times* (London), July 22, 1978.

Arbitration under the head of each participating State have been transformed into national groups.

The function of these national groups is to act as nominating organs for the election of judges of the International Court of Justice by the General Assembly and Security Council of the United Nations. In the case of members of the United Nations not represented in the Permanent Court of Arbitration, candidates are nominated by national groups appointed for this purpose by their governments. The members of these national groups are to be of a standing comparable to those nominated as members of the Permanent Court of Arbitration.

The manner in which some of these national groups are known or suspected to operate is open to criticism. The common denominator of these strictures is the impression that some of these nominations are less inspired by the qualities of judges postulated in the Court's Statute than by extraneous considerations.[13]

Whether nominations are made directly by governments or indirectly by government nominees, the motivations of the selectors, unless disclosed in exceptional cases, are unverifiable. What can be judged is the outcome of such deliberations. If this falls below generally acceptable minimum standards, the time has come to deal more formally with, at least, some of the forms of abuses of the nominating office: for instance, by making incompatible for prolonged periods membership of a nominating organ with candidature for nomination.

In this respect, the Hague Peace System has two lessons to teach. The one is furnished by the transformation, in the case of the *Casablanca Deserters*, of the legal advisers to the Parties into members of the Tribunal deciding the issue. Whatever the pragmatic convenience of letting the two men who had handled the issue on the politico-legal level before submission to the Tribunal carry on afterwards on the arbitral level, this almost instant mutation of advocates into ad hoc judges could hardly increase faith in the judicial standing of the Tribunal or the legal persuasiveness of its award.

The other lesson is provided by the action taken at the Second Hague Peace Conference to avoid repetition of practices that had caused unfavourable comment in relation to the operation of Hague Convention I of 1899. The rebuke to the members of the Permanent

---

[13] See, for instance, Sir Gerald Fitzmaurice, I.D.I., *Livre du Centenaire* (1973), pp. 287–288, and S. Rosenne in L. Gross (ed.), *The Future of the International Court of Justice*, Vol. I (1976), pp. 386–387, and, more generally, on the system of elections to the I.C.J., the report by Judge T. O. Elias in M. Mosler and R. Bernhardt (eds.), *Judicial Settlement of International Disputes* (1974): "a good deal of horse-trading at the best of times" (p. 27).

Court of Arbitration involved was administered in the form of an express prohibition of behaviour considered to fall below the professional minimum standards of the time.[14] In trying to repress some unacceptable forms of free enterprise, the Hague Peace System had stumbled on one means of securing compliance with the more obvious minimum standards of international judicial conduct: the establishment *and* rigorous enforcement of exacting rules of judicial self-denial.[15]

VII—A TRAUMATIC EXPERIENCE

In the Paris Peace Treaties of 1947, provision had been made for the observance of human rights in the three ex-satellite countries of the European Axis: Bulgaria, Hungary and Romania, and for the settlement of disputes between the Parties on the interpretation or execution of the Peace Treaties. In 1949, the United States of America and the United Kingdom became involved in disputes with the Soviet Union and the three East European States over both issues.

It is the settlement-of-disputes Articles in the three Peace Treaties which, in the context of this paper, raise directly relevant issues.

In the absence of procedures specifically provided, any dispute regarding the interpretation or execution of the Peace Treaties was to be referred to the Heads of the Russian, United States and the United Kingdom Missions in the East European country concerned. If, within two months, the dispute was not resolved, and the parties had not agreed on any other means of settlement, the issue was to be "referred, at the request of either party to the dispute, to a Commission, composed of one representative of each party, and a third member, selected by mutual agreement of the two parties from nationals of a third country. Should the two parties fail to agree within a period of one month upon the appointment of the third member, the Secretary-General of the United Nations may be requested by either party to make the appointment." The decision of the "majority of the members of the Commission" was to be the Commission's decision and to be accepted by the parties as "definitive and binding."[16]

In accordance with the settlement-of-disputes Articles of the three Peace Treaties, the United States of America and the United

---

[14] Art. 62 (3), Hague Convention I (1907).
[15] See, further, this *Year Book*, Vol. 27 (1973), pp. 434 *et seq*.
[16] See *e.g.* Art. 40 of the Hungarian Peace Treaty.

Kingdom attempted to bring before the Heads of the Allied Missions in the three East European countries their complaints regarding contraventions of the human rights provisions by each of the three East European States. Yet, the Soviet Union refused to participate in meetings of the Heads of Missions on the subject. When the two Western Powers attempted to activate the Commissions under the Peace Treaties, the three East European countries refused to appoint their national commissioners.

Rather than approach the Secretary-General of the United Nations direct with requests to appoint the third commissioner in each of the Commissions, as provided in the Peace Treaties, the Western Powers thought it preferable to fortify the Secretary-General in taking this step by an appropriate resolution of the General Assembly and an authoritative Advisory Opinion from the International Court of Justice on the interpretation of the relevant Articles of the 1947 Peace Treaties.[17]

In its request for an Advisory Opinion, the General Assembly put four questions to the Court:

(1) *Did the diplomatic exchanges between the governments involved disclose the existence of disputes subject to the settlement-of-disputes Articles of the Peace Treaties?*

In accordance with common sense and an established judicial practice, the Court held, by 11 votes to three, that the mere denial of the existence of a dispute by one of the parties did not prove its non-existence. If the two sides held opposite views on the proper performance of the human rights Articles in the Peace Treaties, a dispute on the issue existed.

(2) *Were the East European States bound to carry out the settlement-of-disputes Articles in the Peace Treaties, including those on the appointment of their own national commissioners?*

Again, by 11 votes to 3, the Court gave an affirmative answer.

(3) *If one of the parties to a dispute failed to appoint its national commissioner, was the Secretary-General of the United Nations authorised under the settlement-of-disputes Articles in the Peace Treaties to appoint the third member at the request of the other party?*

By 11 votes to 2—with the dissenters on Questions 1 and 2 joining the majority, and two members of the majority on Questions 1 and 2 dissenting—the Court decided this question in the negative. It arrived at this conclusion by way of a restrictive interpretation of the

---

[17] I.C.J. Reports 1950, pp. 65 (First Phase) and 221 (Second Phase).

Articles in question, with minimal attention to the duties of good faith in the consensual nexus of *jus aequum*.

(4) *Was a Commission, composed of a representative of one of the parties and a third member appointed by the Secretary-General of the United Nations, a commission competent to make a definitive and binding decision under the Peace Treaties?*

By its negative answer to Question 3, the Court avoided facing up to the verbal difficulties posed by Question 4. In their Dissenting Opinions to both Questions, Judges Read and Azevedo coped convincingly with the hurdles of interpretation from which the Court had shied away.[18]

The differences between the Court and the two dissenting judges on Question 3 in balancing the relevant rules in the *Interpretation of Peace Treaties* case throw light not only on the choices available in the interpretation of treaties and the place of good faith in international law but also on the decline in the standards observed in international arbitration.

These differences can be reduced to three major issues:

(1) In a literal interpretation of the disputes-settlement Articles, the appointment of the third member follows the appointments of the two "representatives" of the parties. Thus, if the first two are not appointed, the appointment of the third member becomes impossible. In the Court's view, this is the "natural and ordinary meaning" of the term "third" member.

Actually, as Judge Read points out, the meaning adopted by the Court is but one of two possible meanings. The other is that "third" is a synonym for a neutral member, as distinct from the two "representatives of the parties."

(2) The Court is content to describe the attitudes taken by the East European States as "negative" and, although involving international responsibility, leading to a "practical impossibility" of creating the Commissions.

In contrast, the dissenting judges emphasise the illegality of any party relying on its own wrong, the estoppels such conduct creates and, in accordance with an established practice of the Permanent Court of International Justice, the Court's right and duty to interpret the Peace Treaties so as to give them full legal effect.

(3) The Court considers that the provisions made in the Peace Treaties for three-member commissions and majority decisions prevent it from substituting for these Commissions potential "two-member" Commissions, and that analogies from the conse-

---

[18] *Ibid.* pp. 226 *et seq.*

quences of subsequent withdrawals or resignations of members in previous international institutions are inappropriate.

The dissenting judges dispose of this reasoning by emphasising that the defaulting States themselves have created this situation, that they are estopped from relying on this objection, and that, at any time, they can remedy it by appointing their representatives. Moreover, in their view, analogies can legitimately be drawn from previous incidents of the withdrawal or resignation of members without replacement from arbitral tribunals. In such eventualities, the withdrawal or resignation does not affect the proper constitution of an arbitral tribunal.

Little doubt exists that the views of the dissenting judges are more in line with the traditions and standards of international arbitration than those of the Court. The reason for the scarcity of provisions covering the points raised by the East European States—especially the duty of parties to treaties providing for disputes-settlement to appoint their own members—is simple enough: Contracting Parties are entitled to the presumption of good faith in their favour and, in relations between civilised States, for any negotiator to suggest treaty provisions on the contingency of the other party's initial bad faith would have amounted to an intolerable display of international discourtesy, if not outright insolence.

It was a measure of the decline in the standards of good faith in the post-1945 period that one of the major Powers involved in the East European Peace Settlements should have encouraged, if not instigated, its junior partners in their acts of demonstrative breach of faith and international law.

A puzzle remains unanswered: Why should the International Court of Justice have exposed itself to Judge Read's strictures on the majority findings on Questions 3 and 4?: "I am bound to take into account the fact that, in the existing circumstances and under existing international law, a defaulting government could not object to the competence of such a tribunal. If it raised the objection before such a Treaty Commission, it would be bound to apply existing international law and refuse to let such a government profit from its own wrong. If it raised the objection in proceedings before this Court, it would be necessary for the International Court of Justice, which is not a law-making organ, to apply existing legal principles and recognise that it was estopped from alleging its own treaty violation in support of its own contentions. It is impossible for me, acting as a judge in advisory procedure, to raise this objection, which the defaulting government itself would be prevented from raising in any proceedings which recognised the principle of justice."[19]

---

[19] *Ibid*. p. 244.

VIII—Reformist Responses

It would be tempting to link the priority place accorded to arbitral procedure on the agenda of the first session of the United Nations International Law Commission in 1949 with the contemptuous treatment the Eastern States had given to the disputes-settlement Articles of the 1947 Peace Treaties. Yet, this was not what actually happened.

Arbitral procedure was the last of nine topics, arranged in systematic order, in a *Survey of International Law in Relation to the Work of Codification of the International Law Commission*. The *Survey* had been commissioned by the Codification Division of the United Nations Office of Legal Affairs, was prepared by Hersch Lauterpacht and, early in 1949, submitted to the International Law Commission as a memorandum in the name of the United Nations Secretary-General.[20]

The wide formulation of the subject and the reasons given in the *Survey* for its inclusion among the nine topics related to codification and development were in line with a strong reformist tradition. It stemmed from the draft regulations, prepared by the Institute of International Law in 1875 and laid before the First Hague Peace Conference of 1899. The abortive Geneva Protocol of 1924, the 1928 and 1949 General Acts for the Pacific Settlement of International Disputes and the 1948 American Treaty on Pacific Settlement (Bogotá Pact) formed more recent inspirations of the reformist thinking then prevalent in and around the International Law Commission.

The issues singled out in the *Survey* for consideration were perennial shortcomings of traditional international ad hoc arbitration: typical grounds advanced to challenge the finality and binding force of awards such as alleged major errors and excess of jurisdiction by the arbitrators, the advisability of granting powers to tribunals of interpretation, rectification and revision of their awards, and a possible remedy for formal and substantive failings of awards: appellate jurisdiction of the International Court of Justice.

On the 1949 agenda of the International Law Commission, arbitral procedure remained the last of a lengthening list of 14 topics. Manley O. Hudson, the Commission's first Chairman, and Georges Scelle, soon to be appointed the Commission's Special Rapporteur on Arbitral Procedure, did not express any sense of urgency in relation to the subject. On the contrary, Scelle commented on the smoothness with which, for over a century, arbitral procedure had worked.

---

[20] A/CN4/1/Rev. 1 (1949) or Hersch Lauterpacht, *Collected Papers*, Vol. 1 (1970), pp. 445 *et seq.*

If, nonetheless, arbitral procedure was included—together with the law of treaties and the régime of the high seas—as one of the three priority subjects, it was because the topic was thought to be relatively uncontroversial, manageable in work-load and prestigious for the Commission during its first three-year term.

The Commission and the Court's Opinion

The International Law Commission took cognisance of the *Interpretation of Peace Treaties* dispute. In his Preliminary Report on March 21, 1950—skilfully used in the oral pleadings by United States and United Kingdom counsel in the case—the Special Rapporteur offered a simple solution for closing the loophole which had emerged in this case. It merely meant incorporating in the Draft Convention Article 23 of the Revised General Act of 1949: if one of the parties to a dispute refused to appoint its arbitrator, as obliged by the governing instrument, the President of the International Court of Justice was authorised to make the appointment.

Two days after the International Court of Justice had rendered its Advisory Opinion in the Second Phase of the *Interpretation of Peace Treaties* case, the Chairman of the International Law Commission expressed his distress on the wider effects of the Court's Opinion: " 'There has been failure to meet an obligation,' said the Court, 'but we can do nothing about it.' Public opinion would wonder what the Court was for." He also complimented the Commission on its foresight in adopting the proposal of the Special Rapporteur.[21]

It took some time for the Commission to realise how much opposition existed in governmental quarters to any tightening up of the good-faith area in the relations between the parties to arbitral agreements. Yet, with minor concessions, the Commission continued on its reformist course. Under the leadership of Hersch Lauterpacht, its newly-appointed General Rapporteur—with the Special Rapporteur temporarily fading into the background[22]—the Commission adopted in 1953 a revised Draft Convention with ten to two votes and one abstention.

As in the *Survey* and preliminary report, the term *arbitral procedure* was interpreted extensively, and the emphasis was put on strengthening the machinery to secure stricter observance of arbitral undertakings.

Ten features of the Draft Convention deserve to be noticed:

(1) *Arbitrability of disputes*. If, before the constitution of a tribunal, parties disagree on the existence of a dispute or the question

---

[21] I.L.C.Y.B. 1950 (I), p. 251.
[22] *Ibid*. 1953 (I). See also the editorial note, *loc. cit*. above, note 20, Vol. 2 (1975), p. 269.

whether the dispute comes within the scope of the obligation to arbitrate, the matter is to be referred—in the absence of agreement between the parties on any other procedure—to the International Court of Justice by application of either party.

(2) *Constitution of tribunal*. In situations such as those which gave rise to the *Interpretation of Peace Treaties* case, the President of the International Court of Justice may make any necessary appointment.

(3) *Compromis*. In case of disagreement between parties after the constitution of the tribunal on the sufficiency of the original agreement to arbitrate, the tribunal is granted power to draw up the *compromis*.

(4) *Self-determination of jurisdiction*. As in other codifications since 1899, the power of the tribunal to be judge of its own competence is reaffirmed.

(5) *Withdrawal or resignation of arbitrators*. In order to ensure the efficient functioning of tribunals, the right of parties to withdraw arbitrators and of arbitrators to resign is severely curtailed.

(6) *Majority decisions*. Again, on the model of earlier codifications since 1899, the tribunal's power to make all decisions by absolute majority is reaffirmed.

(7) *Procedure*. In the absence of any agreement between the parties on questions of procedure, the tribunal is authorised to settle its rules of procedure.

(8) *Subsidiary powers*. The tribunal shall decide incidental or additional claims or counter-claims arising directly out of the substance-matter of the dispute. It may also decree provisional measures for the protection of the interests of the parties, and render its award in the case of non-appearance of one of the parties or failure to defend its case.

(9) *Prohibition of non liquet*. The tribunal may not bring in a finding of *non liquet* on the ground of the silence or obscurity of international law or the *compromis*.

(10) *Finality of award*. Considerable inroads into the finality of awards are made to allow for their rectification, interpretation, revision and annulment, with ultimate reference of unresolved disputes to the International Court of Justice.

Evaluation

The General and Special Rapporteurs and most of the members of the International Law Commission favoured a half-way house of judicial arbitration as the mean between ad hoc arbitration and judicial settlement. To attain this objective, they employed three devices: they tried to close the most obvious loopholes available to parties with an underdeveloped sense of good faith; they stiffened the existing rules of *jus dispositivum* into rules of *jus cogens* and, in order to resolve difficulties insoluble on the level of ad hoc arbitration, they introduced the International Court of Justice as the final arbiter.

The assumption made was one congenial to most law-makers that, at one time or another, States, like other entities, may falter in their law-abidingness. Yet, what the International Law Commission failed to consider or treated as a matter beyond its concern was a closely related issue: why should governments with mental reservations regarding arbitral undertakings or more generally pragmatic attitudes to international relations become parties to conventions which were pointedly designed to curtail typical forms of sharp practice?

Actually, the International Law Commission and its Rapporteurs were sufficiently men of the world to leave open the loophole of loopholes. They discreetly refrained from including in the Draft Convention any final articles and, in this way, avoided the key issue of the admissibility of reservations. It was only the Special Rapporteur who, in the course of the Commission's deliberations remarked that, in his view, "States were entirely free to adopt such a convention with reservations."[23] According to the record, no comment was offered on this shattering observation.

The General Assembly's Verdict

The reaction of the 1953 General Assembly to the Commission's Draft Convention was less than flattering. After an outspoken debate, it adjourned further discussion of the Draft Convention until its 1955 Session. It then referred the Draft Convention back to the Commission, with a terse instruction to report back in 1958 (and not before).

With the General Rapporteur having been elected to the International Court of Justice in 1954, it was left to the Special Rapporteur to pick up the pieces. The Commission resigned itself to eliminate all traces of the mandatory element in the 1953 Draft Convention and, as had been done in Hague Conventions I of 1899 and 1907, reduced the Draft Convention to a set of model rules. Thus, it was left with individual governments to incorporate these rules as they saw fit in future arbitral agreements. The 1958 General Assembly concurred in this form of quietly burying the International Law Commission's exercise on arbitral procedure.

Dispirited reformers had to console themselves with the thought

---

[23] I.L.C.Y.B. 1953 (I), p. 6.

that, in future, "if parties draw up their arbitral agreement or *compromis* in such a way that its object can be frustrated, they will at least do so with open eyes."[24]

The unmistakable message was that the General Assembly had refused to compensate for lack of good faith in cases such as that on the *Interpretation of Peace Treaties* by the creation of organisational devices and the approximation of arbitral to judicial proceedings or the establishment of any links between the two forms of international adjudication.

So, with the 1928 General Act half-forgotten, the 1949 Revised General Act generally ignored, and the International Court of Justice less than fully employed,[25] international adjudication on a universalist level has advanced little beyond what is offered in the Hague Peace System.

IX—CONJECTURAL JURISPRUDENCE TO THE RESCUE

The dismissal by the General Assembly of the International Law Commission's codification and development exercise on arbitral procedure brought again to the fore an unanswered question regarding the *Interpretation of Peace Treaties* case. Why should nine members of the International Court of Justice have preferred to align themselves with the two minority members of Phase One rather than accept the alternative offered by Judges Read and Azevedo?[26]

In his Separate Opinion in the *Admissibility of Hearings of Petitioners* case (1956) and, more fully, in *The Development of International Law by the International Court* (1958), Judge Sir Hersch Lauterpacht presented his answer to the conundrum. He attempted to "accommodate" the Court's Opinion on Questions 3 and 4 "within the framework of legal principle," and he further tried to prove that the Court's Opinion was but an apparent denial of the rule of effective treaty interpretation.[27]

To buttress this hypothesis, Judge Sir Hersch Lauterpacht laid the responsibility for the Court's answers to Questions 3 and 4 squarely on the Contracting Parties, but only in the form of a supposition that the Parties had deliberately left open the loopholes through which, in due course, the Soviet Union and the three East European States made their escape from what they were entitled to treat as merely

---

[24] *Ibid*. 1958 (II), p. 83.
[25] See I.C.J.Y.B. 1977–78, pp. 3–5, 94 and 110, and below, note 33.
[26] See above under VII.
[27] I.C.J. Reports 1956, p. 58, or *loc. cit* above, note 20, Vol. 3 (1977), p. 573, and *loc. cit.* 1958, pp. 284 *et seq*.

apparent treaty obligations. In lieu of proof, he offered a second assumption, as unproven as the first: that a meticulous examination of the preparatory material *might* provide the requisite evidence for his supposition. For good measure, he offered two further assumptions: that the Court, without disclosing that it had done so, might have become aware of the paralegal character of the settlement provisions and, instead of basing its answers to Questions 3 and 4 on the operative reasons, made do with those ostensibly offered in its Advisory Opinion.[28]

Difficulties over dealing with the issue on the suggested level of speculative or conjectural jurisprudence arise on, at least, two grounds:

First, in any academic discipline, hypotheses are permissible in the absence of verifiable (or, more accurately, falsifiable) evidence, but only as the first step towards further search for hard evidence. In this case, a considerable body of hard, and plausible, evidence is available.

From the preparatory material it appears that the United States and United Kingdom Governments had proposed automatic reference to the International Court of Justice of all disputes between Contracting Parties on the interpretation or execution of the Peace Treaties. The Soviet Union wished such disputes to be submitted to a diplomatic body such as the Heads of the three Missions in the East European countries. The compromise reached was the two-tier system embodied in the Peace Treaties.

Similarly, the two major Western Powers had suggested calling the second-tier organs "arbitration commissions." For its part, the Soviet Union preferred to describe them as conciliation commissions, with the clear understanding that, in Russian, the term was fully compatible with the right of such commissions to reach binding decisions. On a United Kingdom suggestion, it was agreed to dispense with any prefix and describe the organs to be created as "Commissions." Yet, it was made clear in the Treaties that the Commissions had the right to decide by majority, and that their decisions were to be definitive and binding.[29]

The material leaves little doubt that there was no vagueness at the drafting stage which could have jeopardised the legal character of the disputes-settlement Articles.

Moreover, in the diplomatic correspondence preceding the advisory proceedings before the International Court of Justice, neither the Soviet Union nor the three East European States

---

[28] *Loc. cit.* 1958, pp. 289 *et seq.*
[29] See *loc. cit.* above note 16.

alluded or referred to any informal understanding reached between the Parties on the supposedly paralegal status of these Articles.[30]

Secondly, before any international judicial organ, the assumption made in the four hypotheses advanced would probably be considered to cast such serious aspersions on the governments concerned and the International Court of Justice as to bring into operation the presumptions in international law in favour of the good faith of the subjects of international law and the international organs they have created. These aspersions would be aggravated in relation to governments which behaved as was assumed, and instructed their representatives in the General Assembly to speak, and in the Court to plead, as those of the Western Governments involved did.

Nonetheless, the conjectures examined have an evidential value of their own. They testify to the difficulties of accommodating "within the framework of legal principle" the Court's Opinion in the Second Phase of the *Interpretation of Peace Treaties* case.[31] They also constitute a deserved if unintended tribute to the courageous and constructive Dissenting Opinions by Judges Read and Azevedo.[32] Finally, they emphasise the need to ponder further—and to have prompted further reflection and inquiry is to Judge Sir Hersch Lauterpacht's credit—on the perplexing question he put, and which, as yet, remains unanswered. If he has proved nothing else, he has proved that whatever the explanation of the mystery may be, it is unlikely to be found on the normative level.

X—THE SINCEREST FORM OF FLATTERY . . .

In faithful compliance with the tenets of *Couéism*, a series of professional conferences expressed their conviction in the post-1945 era of "being deeply conscious of the growing importance of the International Court of Justice" and their primary task to "enhance" this position.

Yet, reality refused to go away. In spite of a spectacular proliferation of sovereign and equal members of the United Nations and, thus, of parties to the Court's Statute, acceptance of the Court's automatic (rather than compulsory) jurisdiction stayed stubbornly below 50, and some of the reservations attached to the declarations under Article 36 of the Court's Statute verged on the derisory.

---

[30] See U.S. Govt. Printing Office, Dep. of State Publ. 2868, *Paris Peace Conference 1946. Selected Documents*, pp. 649, 833A and 1011 *et seq.* and the Documents submitted by the UN Secretary-General to the Court (*Pleadings, Interpretation of Peace Treaties* Case, pp. 23 *et seq.*).

[31] See above, text to note 27.

[32] See above under VII.

Similarly, over the years, the number and significance of bilateral and multilateral treaties with compromissory clauses, establishing the Court's jurisdiction, has sharply declined. Moreover, in the words of a recent U.S. Department of State study, the Court has fallen into a state of "relative disuse."[33]

There is little, if anything, a judicial organ can do about such a phase of adversity. If it tries to take, however delicately and indirectly, the initiative in attracting "potential customers" (to use the terminology of the Court's first Registrar),[34] the results are likely to be counter-productive.

Considering the meagre results attained by the Permanent Court of Arbitration and the International Centre for Investments Disputes in the stony field of disputes between States and foreign contractors and investors, the limitation by the Statute of the contentious jurisdiction of the International Court of Justice to inter-State disputes probably proved a blessing in disguise.

It was in the post-1966 period of the Court's "rehabilitation" after its 1966 Judgment in the *South West Africa Cases*, that the Court fell in with promptings from a variety of well-wishers. They expected much from bringing to life a dormant innovation in the Court's 1945 Statute: the authority granted to the Court to create ad hoc Chambers for particular cases.[35]

The non-use, with a single exception,[36] of Chamber proceedings of any of the various types envisaged in the Statutes of the Permanent Court of International Justice and the International Court of Justice might have counselled caution. It might have suggested a pause before detracting by the Court's own action from its judicial and collegiate character.

Nonetheless, the Court decided to accept what one of its members (and, from 1976 to 1979, its President) described as the majority view of experienced authorities on the work of the Court. They had advised to "concede to the parties some influence in the *composition* of ad hoc Chambers."[37] If this concession was made to the arbitral model, it was hoped, parties would realise that they could have the best of both worlds: judicial adjudication and freedom to select judges of their own choice. Like the judgments of other Chambers,

[33] 16 I.L.M. (1977), p. 187.

On the (always remaining) residual uses of the Court for purposes of games of international one-upmanship, see, for instance, the *Aegean Sea Continental Shelf Case* (Greece v. Turkey), I.C.J. Reports 1978, p. 3 *et seq.*

See also above, note 25, and L. V. Prott, in this *Year Book*, Vol. 33 (1979), pp. 284 *et seq.*

[34] E. Hambro in Gross, *loc. cit.* above, note 13, Vol. I, p. 370.

[35] Art. 26 (2).

[36] *Treaty of Neuilly* Case between Bulgaria and Greece—1924 (A3); 1925 (A4).

[37] E. Jiménez de Aréchaga, 67 A.J.I.L. (1973), p. 1.

those of ad hoc Chambers were judgments of the Court[38] and as such could be enforced—for what it was worth—under Article 94 of the United Nations Charter. Moreover, all the judicial and administrative expenses of proceedings before ad hoc Chambers by parties which were members of the United Nations would automatically be charged to the Court's and, in the end, the United Nations budget.[39]

Up to a point, the draftsmen of the Court's Statute had taken such a demand into account and made two exceptions to the Court's exclusive responsibility for the organisation of Chambers in general and ad hoc Chambers in particular. *First*, to the same extent as in proceedings before the Court's plenum, parties were given the right to choose "national" judges.[40] *Secondly*, in the case of ad hoc Chambers, the Court was authorised to determine the "number" of judges to constitute such Chambers "with the approval of the parties."[41]

Thus, if, with the approval of the parties, the Court decided on the creation of a Chamber consisting of, for instance, three members, and no member of the Court of the nationality of one or both parties was sitting or available, the party or parties were permitted to choose their own judges.[42] Yet, the election of the President of the Chamber remained the Court's responsibility.[43] This, like other elections to any of the Chambers, was to take place, under the Rules of Court,[44] by secret ballot and an absolute majority of votes.

In the revisory work on its Rules, commenced in 1967 and temporarily concluded in 1972,[45] the Court attempted to go further in giving a say to parties in selecting judges of their own choice. It made it mandatory for the President to ascertain the views of parties on the *"composition"* of ad hoc Chambers and report back to the Court "accordingly."[46]

The potential embarrassments of the Court's President having to listen to views of parties on *personalia*, including alleged disqualifications of individual members[47] and, conceivably, compliments on his own eminent suitability as president of the Chamber are surpassed only by those created by his duty to report to the Court

---

[38] Art. 27, Statute, I.C.J.
[39] *Ibid*. Art. 33. See also Art. 64.
[40] *Ibid*. Art. 31.
[41] *Ibid*. Art. 26 (2).
[42] *Ibid*. Art. 31 (2)–(4).
[43] The same applies to judges other than "national" judges in special chambers consisting of more than three members (Art. 26 (2), Statute, I.C.J.).
[44] Art. 24 (2), 1946 Rules of Court. See also Art. 18, 1978 Rules of Court.
[45] See *loc. cit.* above, note 37, p. 1.
[46] Art. 26 (1), 1972 Rules of Court, unchanged in the corresponding Art. 17 (2) of the 1978 Rules of Court.
[47] Under Arts. 16, 17 and 24 of the Statute. See, further, *loc. cit.* above, note 15.

"accordingly." Yet, in equating the words "the *number* of judges" in Article 26 (2) of the Statute with the "*composition* of the Chamber," the Court did more than interpret extensively an exception to the principle of the Court's judicial and collegiate character. It purported to revise its Statute, a task beyond its power.[48] By exceeding its jurisdiction, the Court not only failed to create an effective Rule but also raised further doubts on the manner in which it fulfilled its central function: to apply competently and conscientiously the law, in this case the *jus cogens* of its own Statute, an integral part of the United Nations Charter.[49]

Perhaps some consolation may be derived from the fact that, in the drafting stage, a minority of the Court's members did object to the proposed revision of Article 26 (1) of the 1972 Rules of Court,[50] and from the absence of any need to apply the non-Rule adopted by the Court.[51] Moreover, if imitation is the sincerest form of flattery, the lengths to which the Court went to give parties judges of their own choice is the greatest tribute it could pay to the draftsmen of Hague Conventions I of 1899 and 1907.

---

[48] Arts. 38 and 69–70 of the Court's Statute.

[49] Art. 92, UN Charter.

[50] Art. 17 (2), 1978 Rules of Court. See also E. Hambro in Gross, *loc. cit.* above, note 13, Vol. I, p. 369, and E. Jiménez de Aréchega, *loc. cit.* above, note 37, p. 2.

[51] If, as envisaged under the Agreement of March 29, 1979, on Dispute-Settlement regarding the Gulf of Maine Area between Canada and the U.S.A., the parties were to experiment with an ad hoc Chamber of the Court, the proceedings and any judgment made by the Court in breach of its Statute would be open to challenges on grounds of nullity.

In view of the clear wording of the Statute on the matter, counter-arguments based on a supposed right of the Court's President to indulge in unlimited consultations with parties on the composition of ad hoc Chambers and description of the revision of the Rules as merely a gap-filling exercise appear to be less than persuasive.

Matters are hardly improved by reliance on the consensus Resolution of the U.N. General Assembly (3232 (XXIX), November 12, 1974—U.N.Y.B. 1974, p. 835), acclaiming twice the Court's *de facto* revision of its Statute.

Finally, how, in the *spirit* of a Rule of Court existing since the days of the Permanent Court of International Justice (Article 18 (1) of the 1978 Rules of Court), are secret ballots regarding the composition of an ad hoc Chamber to be conducted in a Court faced by a presidential list agreed between the President and the Court's potential "customers" (see above, note 34).

Pressure on members of the Court is further increased if, as under the above-mentioned Treaty between Canada and the U.S.A., parties provide for the contingency of the Court being unco-operative and, in this eventuality, submission of the issue to an ad hoc Court of Arbitration, composed of members of the parties' own choice, *i.e.*, in all likelihood, those on the Presidential list.

INDEX

351